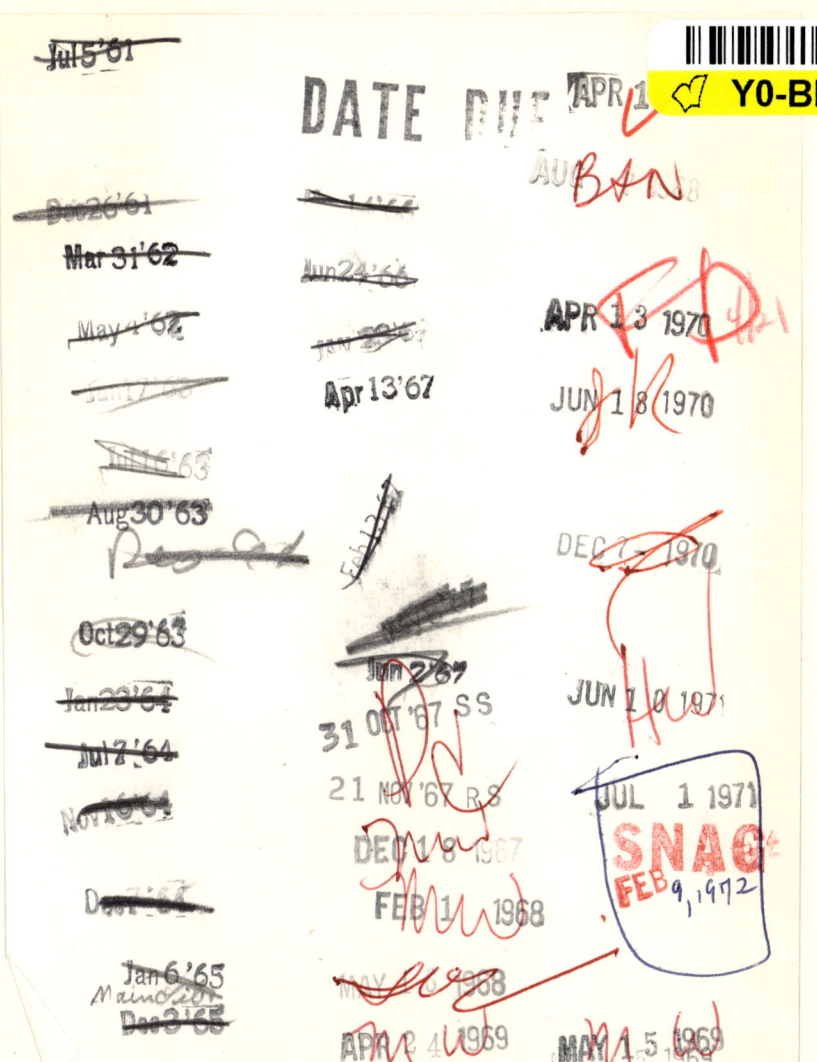

HIGHER EDUCATION
IN THE UNITED STATES

The Economic Problems

Seminar on the Economics of Higher Education, Harvard University, 1958-1959.

HIGHER EDUCATION IN THE UNITED STATES

The Economic Problems

Edited with an Introduction by
SEYMOUR E. HARRIS

With the assistance of
Richard N. Cooper, Reginald H. Green, and Elisabeth Humez

1960
HARVARD UNIVERSITY PRESS
Cambridge, Massachusetts

© Copyright, 1960, by the President and Fellows of Harvard College

All rights reserved

STEERING COMMITTEE OF THE SEMINAR ON THE ECONOMICS OF HIGHER EDUCATION
HARVARD UNIVERSITY

Vernon R. Alden, *Associate Dean of the Faculty of Business Administration*
McGeorge Bundy, *Dean of the Faculty of Arts and Sciences*
Kingman Brewster, Jr., *Professor of Law (now Provost of Yale University)*
David Riesman, *Henry Ford II Professor of Social Sciences*
Cyril G. Sargent, *Professor of Education*
Samuel A. Stouffer, *Professor of Sociology*
Seymour E. Harris, *Lucius N. Littauer Professor of Political Economy, Chairman*

Publication of this volume has been aided by a grant from the Ford Foundation

Library of Congress Catalog Card No. 60–15890

PRINTED IN THE UNITED STATES OF AMERICA

PREFATORY NOTE

THIS volume is based on a Seminar on Higher Education held in the academic year 1958–59, the product of a suggestion of Philip Coombs of the Ford Foundation. Impressed by the failure of economists to study the resource problems in higher education, Mr. Coombs hoped that this seminar would stimulate an interest in these problems.

From the beginning it seemed best not to have too many economists in this seminar. This was made clear in an earlier two-day meeting at Endicott House, when it seemed that economists tended to overwhelm the educators with their jargon and highly abstract economic thought. (Three papers from this earlier meeting are included in our papers.) It is helpful to have non-economists around in meetings of this kind to restrain the economists who might forget that though the limitation of resources is very important, educational values are the major issue. If we cannot exhaust discussion of educational problems without bringing in the problem of limitation of resources, we also must weigh the financial issues against the increments and decrements of educational values.

The classification of members of the seminar and contributors of papers is as follows.

		Number Attending	Number Presenting Papers
1.	College Presidents	18	9
2.	Vice Presidents, Provosts, and Deans	16	6
3.	College Treasurers	17	6
4.	Officers of the Office of Education	4	3
5.	State Commissioners of Education	2	..
6.	Foundation Officers	3	2
7.	Officers of the College Entrance Examination Board	2	2
8.	Economists	11	6
9.	Other Social Scientists	9	6
10.	Undergraduates	1	1
11.	Others: Financial Aid Officers, Private Investment Officers, Humanists, etc.	21	2

The procedure in the eight days of meetings was to invite about six participants to write papers for each session and to distribute them beforehand (not always done), and to allow each contributor to summarize his paper in fifteen minutes. Then there would be an all-day discussion with a stenotypist recording. The contributors then had an opportunity to revise their papers.

I owe much to the Faculty Steering Committee which really steered the Chairman when he tended to over-weight the economics of the issues. My greatest debt, aside from that to Mr. Coombs and the Ford Foundation, is to Richard Cooper, who is mainly responsible for the summaries of the stenotypist recordings, to Reginald Green, who helped with the individual papers, and to Mrs. David E. Humez, who contributed much more than should generally be expected of an editorial assistant. Messrs. Cooper and Green, two of my graduate students, contributed so much that I put their names on the title page — whatever the explanation, the top graduate-school students today seem to be much brighter and more mature than in my generation. Miss Lillian Buller was responsible for the thousands of details in this kind of an enterprise and thus made the whole program workable. Mr. and Mrs. Lawrence Burt, the stenotypists, did an unusually able job. Miss Elizabeth Niebuhr, Radcliffe 1960, also helped. My wife, Ruth B. Harris, read the galleys and page proofs, as did Edward Segel.

The volume includes the following: an introduction by the editor; summaries of the stenotypist recordings; reproduction of most of the papers presented, with some modifications by the authors.

A listing of the parts indicates the scope of the volume:

I. Introduction: Some Broad Issues
II. Pricing and the Student Body
III. Government Aid
IV. Faculty Status
V. Experiment in Higher Education: Educational and Economic Issues
VI. Economics and Educational Values
VII. Investment and Endowment Policies

SEYMOUR E. HARRIS

CONTENTS

I. INTRODUCTION

Introduction: Some Broad Issues 9
   SEYMOUR E. HARRIS, *Littauer Professor of Political Economy*, Harvard University

II. PRICING AND THE STUDENT BODY

Summary of Proceedings 29
   RICHARD N. COOPER

A College Administrator Views the Tuition Problem 40
   BARNABY C. KEENEY, *President*, Brown University

Is the Low-Tuition Principle Outmoded? 44
   ELDON L. JOHNSON, *President*, University of New Hampshire

Higher Fees and the Position of Private Institutions 48
   JOHN F. MORSE, *Vice-President*, Rensselaer Polytechnic Institute

Equalizing Opportunity under Higher Charges 52
   REXFORD G. MOON, JR., *Director*, College Scholarship Service

Some General Observations on the Pricing of Higher Education 55
   CARL KAYSEN, *Professor of Economics*, Harvard University

The Problem of Higher College Tuition 61
   OTTO ECKSTEIN, *Associate Professor of Economics*, Harvard University

Tuition and Costs 73
   W. ROBERT BOKELMAN, *Chief*, Business Administration Section, Division of Higher Education, U. S. Office of Education

III. GOVERNMENT AID

Summary of Proceedings 75
   RICHARD N. COOPER

Some Issues Raised by Recent Legislation 83
   PHILIP H. COOMBS, *Program Director*, The Fund for the Advancement of Education

Federal and State Aid 88
   J. PAUL MATHER, *President*, The American College Testing Program

State Aid for Private Institutions in Pennsylvania 91
   MILLARD E. GLADFELTER, *President*, Temple University

The Tax-Credit Proposal 93
   JOHN F. MECK, *Treasurer*, Dartmouth College

Higher Education and the Federal Budget 96
   RICHARD A. MUSGRAVE, *Professor of Political Economy*, Johns Hopkins University

IV. FACULTY STATUS

Summary of Proceedings 102
   RICHARD N. COOPER

Faculty Problems in the Liberal Arts College 111
   CHARLES W. COLE, *President*, Amherst College

Some Issues of Supply and Productivity 115
   O. MEREDITH WILSON, *President*, University of Minnesota

Non-Economic Aspects of Academic Morale 118
   EVERETT C. HUGHES, *Professor of Sociology*, University of Chicago

Faculty Pay and Institutional Extravagance 122
   THEODORE CAPLOW, *Professor of Sociology*, University of Minnesota

Some Statistical Aspects 125
   ROBERT E. IFFERT, *Specialist for Faculty and Student Services*, Division of Higher Education, U. S. Office of Education

V. EXPERIMENT IN HIGHER EDUCATION: EDUCATIONAL AND ECONOMIC ISSUES

Summary of Proceedings 129
RICHARD N. COOPER AND ELIZABETH NIEBUHR

The Hofstra Experiment for Commuters 136
JOHN CRANFORD ADAMS, *President*, Hofstra College

The New College Plan 140
    I. The Planning Process
       SHANNON MCCUNE, *Provost*, University of Massachusetts
    II. The Plan and its Rationale
       C. L. BARBER, *Professor of English*, Amherst College, Member of Committee on the New College Plan

The Dartmouth Experiment 146
DONALD H. MORRISON, *Provost*, Dartmouth College (deceased)

Theories of Higher Education and the Experimental College 152
NEVITT SANFORD, *Professor of Psychology*, University of California (Berkeley)

Experimentation and the Liberal Arts College 156
BLAIR STEWART, *Dean of the College of Arts and Sciences*, Oberlin College

Some Problems at Amherst 160
WILLARD L. THORP, *Professor of Economics*, Amherst College

The College Plan at Wesleyan 163
DONALD D. O'DOWD, *Dean of Freshmen*, Wesleyan University

VI. ECONOMICS AND EDUCATIONAL VALUES

Summary of Proceedings 166
RICHARD N. COOPER

Some Problems of Assessing (and Improving) the Quality of a College . . 173
DAVID RIESMAN, *Henry Ford II Professor of Social Sciences*, Harvard University

Economies and Educational Values 178
DAEL WOLFLE, *Executive Officer*, American Association for the Advancement of Science

Problems in Estimating the Monetary Value of College Education . . . 180
D. S. BRIDGMAN, *Consultant*, National Science Foundation

Increasing Productivity in Higher Education 185
ALVIN C. EURICH, *Vice-President*, The Fund for the Advancement of Education

Teaching Machines 189
B. F. SKINNER, *Professor of Psychology*, Harvard University

Some Observations on the Allocation of Resources in Higher Education . . 192
KENNETH DEITCH, *Student*, Harvard College

The High Cost of Low-Cost Education 199
FRANK H. BOWLES, *President*, College Entrance Examination Board

VII. INVESTMENT AND ENDOWMENT POLICIES

Summary of Proceedings 203
RICHARD N. COOPER

Difficulties in Determining Investment Policies 214
GEORGE E. BATES, *Professor of Investment Management*, Harvard Graduate School of Business Administration

Objectives of Investment Policies 219
BOARDMAN BUMP, *Treasurer*, Mt. Holyoke College

TABLE OF CONTENTS

Some Examples of Experience with Growth Stocks 222
    GEORGE F. BENNETT, *Deputy Treasurer,* Harvard University

Growth and Income 224
    HULBERT W. TRIPP, *Financial Vice-President,* University of Rochester

Investment Possibilities 229
    JOHN F. MECK, *Treasurer,* Dartmouth College

61 Broadway 232
    LIVINGSTON W. HOUSTON, *Chairman,* Board of Trustees, Rensselaer Polytechnic Institute

Unorthodox Investing 235
    J. PARKER HALL, *Treasurer,* University of Chicago

Should Harvard Borrow? 239
    PAUL C. CABOT, *Treasurer,* Harvard University

Recent Trends in Endowment 242
    J. HARVEY CAIN, *Educational Consultant,* U. S. Office of Education

Special Problems in Public Institutions 245
    ROBERT M. UNDERHILL, *Secretary and Treasurer of the Regents,* University of California (Berkeley)

I. INTRODUCTION: SOME BROAD ISSUES
Seymour E. Harris

Pricing and the Student Body

At the first meeting of the seminar, the writer presented a long working paper on the Economics of Higher Education to serve as a basis for discussion. But since I have already presented some aspects of this paper in a half dozen publications (most recently in *Financing Higher Education*, the McGraw-Hill Fiftieth Anniversary Volume), and since I am to present a much fuller account in a volume to be completed this summer for McGraw-Hill and reflecting the results of a three-year Ford-financed project, I am not including my paper in this volume.

But in order for the reader to understand what follows, it is necessary for me to present a brief summary of my views. Essentially my position is that Institutions of Higher Learning (IHL) need large additional resources, and the additional funds required are not likely to be forthcoming from government and philanthropic sources. Hence it would be necessary to obtain relatively more from tuition.

The point of the argument is that the colleges are worse off than the parents who, unwittingly, have been exploiting the faculty. The case for higher tuition can be supported on grounds of needs, of capacity to pay (tuition accounts for only a small part of total costs of going to college and in the last generation tuition has not at all risen as much as capacity to pay), and on grounds of equity. In fact a rough calculation shows that if costs of capital are included, the total educational expenditures of institutions of higher learning of about $4 billion are all subsidies, for tuition paid roughly equals the cost of capital.

Many contend that it is wrong even to discuss the relation of a college education and the material gains to be had from it, for this results in the wrong kind of emphasis. But though most of us would weigh the nonmaterial gains of higher education above the material, it still seems to many of us that in determining a pricing system we should take account of what the student derives from this investment in future higher income.

I also stressed the point that an abandonment of primitive methods of financing higher education and recourse to massive, long-term loan programs would not only make possible higher tuition and reduced burdens on parents, but also would help democratize higher education. I stressed especially the following gains from long-term financing, aside from its democratizing effects.

(1) Spreading the costs over twenty to sixty years instead of four, through long-term financing, greatly reduces the sacrifices and the concentrated burden on students and parents.

(2) Long-term financing would increase the resources made available to higher education, just as housing and automobile credits have resulted in much larger diversions to these industries.

(3) With per capita income rising both because of inflation and rising productivity, long-term loans would be a mechanism for forcing upon society — that is, the lenders — a greater responsibility for paying for higher education. Repayments would be in dollars of reduced purchasing power and, even more important, each dollar would be available from a greatly increased pool associated with rising productivity.

The general picture of finance in higher education in the 1960's is given in a table below, which I published in the McGraw-Hill volume on *Financing Higher Education, 1960–70*. This is not a prediction but an estimate of funds needed to do a reasonably good job and does not allow for the effects on needs of inflation or capital expansion. That the contribution of tuition is to rise from 25 per cent in 1957–58 to 40 per cent by 1970 and government's share is to decline from 48 to 38 per cent (despite a doubling of their dollar contribution) is to be explained in part by the difficult problems of financing state and local government in the 1950's and 1960's. I say much about that in my book. But it is indeed possible that with strong efforts of alumni, parents, and cooperation of politicians and especially if the economy grows at an even greater rate than I anticipate, the burden on the parent may not rise as much as I assume; and of course the trends will vary from state to state.

TABLE 1. — SOURCES OF FUNDS, INSTITUTIONS OF HIGHER EDUCATION

Source	1957–58 $ million	1957–58 Per cent	1969–70 $ million	1969–70 Per cent
Tuition	904	25	3,800	40
Government	1,752	48	3,700	38
Endowment income and gifts	578	16	1,200	12
Other (scholarship fund from various sources, etc.)	416	11	1,100	11
	3,650	100	9,800	101 [a]

[a] Percentages do not add to 100 because of rounding.
SOURCE: Calculated from Department of Health, Education and Welfare, *Statistics of Higher Education, 1955–56, Faculty, Students and Degrees.*

Not loans alone, but additional scholarship money would help reduce the burden of higher tuition. Stipends for each scholarship holder should rise *pari passu* with the increase of tuition. But in addition as higher tuition puts the marginal (in finance) student out of the running, the *number* of scholarships should increase. Scholarships are not only a means of helping the able and impecunious student; they also make possible much higher tuition income. Without a rise of scholarship funds from $10 to $100 million or more since the 1930's, the increase of tuition income would have been only a fraction of the additional roughly billion dollars of tuition income by 1960 from a level of $100 million.

In reply to my position, President Eldon Johnson of the University of New Hampshire eloquently defended the principle of no or low tuition. The current pricing system in public institutions of higher learning, argued Johnson, produces the millions of college graduates our society needs; our rich society can provide the required resources for a free education for all those who can profit from it; the gains are largely social rather than private. Free tuition to the poor boy of moderate ability provides him (her) with the education, Johnson argues, which the poor but outstanding boy (girl) could get from a private institution through scholarships. My proposal, a program of higher fees for those who could afford them, and use of a large part of the additional income to finance the able and impecunious, for whom low tuition alone was not enough to entice him to go to college, did not appeal to President Johnson.

Mr. Rexford Moon, of the College Entrance Examination Board (C.E.E.B.), one of the most knowledgeable in the field of student capacity to pay, had some interesting comments that are relevant here. According to Moon, 30 per cent of the students in independent colleges had scholarships in a recent year. Of the remaining 70 per cent, about 50 per cent could be financed without unusual sacrifices. But approximately 20 per cent made it only at great costs — much outside work, exercise of unusual thrift, a one-suit wardrobe, improper diets, avoidance of extracurricular activities.

The variations in costs, despite an income differential in favor of students at independent institutions of higher learning, resulted in 70 per cent in the public institutions and 50 per cent in the independent institutions getting by without large sacrifices and burdens.

The income distribution was estimated as follows:

Family incomes	% Public	% Private
>$10,000	25	50
<$ 5,000	30	15

Disturbed especially by the difficulties of those with little income and adequate but not outstanding ability (the 20 per cent in private colleges), Mr. Moon would equalize opportunities for all, not only for the able student. With costs at $2500, and one sibling, he would distribute aid as follows:

Income $10,000 or more	— no aid
8,000	— $ 600
5,000	— $1200

(This is based on the C.E.E.B. estimates of needs at varying incomes.)

Tuition policy has many facets. Obviously administrators of private institutions of higher learning are concerned over low tuition in the public institutions. This concern, as President Keeney points out, is especially great in the West, where the condition of public higher education is strong and fees unusually low. But we would not argue that the public institutions should raise tuition in order to save the private institutions. The latter must offer a differentiated product which has adequate appeal to fill their halls with students of quality.

In this connection some concern was voiced over the possibility that as tuition and costs rose in the independent colleges, they would offer a Cadillac type of education and become the haven of the affluent, and even primarily of those seeking degrees as a cachet. In fact, much concern was expressed over the tendency of the admissions officers of the prestige schools scouting in Pasadena, Westchester, and Shaker Heights and neglecting Revere, Harlem, and Hoboken. In their search for diversity, many of these institutions of higher education were in fact filling their colleges with students of similar background.

One helpful approach suggested was to issue a book giving all information on scholarships everywhere to prospective students. But the College Entrance Examination Board found that lack of cooperation among colleges made the issue of such a bulletin difficult. It would help also if all colleges were apprized of the top 20 per cent in the ninth grade.

Members of the seminar spent much time discussing the relation of price (tuition) and the type of student admitted. John Morse, the able Vice-President and Admissions Officer of Rensselaer Polytechnic Institute, put candidly the problem of an outstanding independent technical college competing either with public institutions of higher learning with low fees, or with the street-car college. First-class engineering schools in the East had to choose, generally, despite the boom for scientists, between depressing their standards or admitting numbers below capacity, with unfortunate financial effects. He could only envisage a viable situation with higher tuition for public universities under pressures from taxpayers, recourse to public scholarship funds with stipends based on need, and help from the federal government for the construction of plant.

What would be the most effective pricing policy? President Keeney urged that costs be estimated on the basis of what was required to do a good job. Then after allowing for possible gifts and endowment income, the private college could then set its tuition.

It is not necessary to set tuition at costs, for some costs are irrelevant, and besides gift (public and private) income is available. In fact when one allows for government appropriations, endowment income, other gifts, and capital plant largely available without capital charges to students, the average student receives subsidies of about $1300, the average for both public and private institutions. (This is subject to a reduction for services not tied to instruction.) It is well to remember that capital costs (except for some dormitories) are not charges to the student. Here a subsidy of several hundreds a year is had without any publicity at all. Silence on this matter is not the best policy even if there is no intention to charge for financing capital.

Obviously discriminatory pricing is to be encouraged in the colleges. To some extent this is current practice. The scholarship student may pay nothing and in fact receive grants in excess of tuition. Others may pay tuition as high as $1500. Charges equal to costs are necessary only when other resources are not available, and excessive emphasis on costs would lead to less than optimum choice of curricula — for example, excessive choice of low cost ones.

Professor Kaysen presents effectively the theory that college authorities should have greater recourse to price discrimination. When the gains to society are large — for example, pure liberal arts, education schools — the charges might be low. When the gains accrue largely to individuals — for example, professional elements in liberal arts, business schools — the charge should be higher.

In higher education we frequently produce joint products — for example, in medical schools, instruction, research, refresher courses, service to patients. What are the costs of instruction? The private businessman charges on the basis of what he can get from different groups. His minimum additional charge is the added cost involved when he can vary the joint product. But in higher education graduate instruction may cost $3000 additional per unit and undergraduate $1000, yet it does not follow that the graduate student would be or should be charged $3000. (In the University of California, a recent survey showed costs per student of $800–$900 in the first two years, $1200 in the upper division, and $2400 to $2500 in graduate schools exclusive of organized research, extension, etc.)

There are attempts, however, to discriminate and charge more to those who can afford to pay. Examples are the recourse to scholarships discussed above or the greater charge for engineering and medicine than for general education, and we tend to demand larger compensation for applied research than for pure research. The degree of discrimination is limited, however, by competition. When alternative sources of supply are available, a college cannot go too far in discriminating — for example, charge the average student $3000 when competitors only charge $2000. The differentiation of product in the minds of the potential student must be clear, despite the important difficulties of measuring the product. Cartel arrangements are required to push discrimination far. But institutions of higher learning could go much further than they do.

Of this we can be certain. Substantial rises of tuition are not likely to be forthcoming without improved methods of finance. Professor Eckstein shows the possibilities of pre- and postfinancing. Under the former I should point out that the saver exploits compound interest, whereas under the latter the advantage is financing out of the rising income of the future. The disadvantage of the latter is that interest is a cost.

Eckstein shows that twenty years of postpayment after a five-year moratorium at 4 per cent interest would cost $425 annually for $4000 of tuition for four years. Twenty years of prepayment at the same rate of interest would cost only $155 a year. At $10,000 of income he finds that postpayment (twenty years at 4 per cent) would cost $200 per year or 2 per cent of income, with payments up to age 67. (Incidentally, I find the costs at 1 per cent, because I put the average income in the period of repayment for current graduates at a substantially higher figure than Professor Eckstein, and I assume loans for only three years. The average enrollment is for three years.)

In summary, the case for higher tuition rests on the need for more resources, and the difficulty of obtaining these resources in adequate amounts through taxation and gifts. The sting of higher tuition can be greatly reduced by improved methods of financing, inclusive of large loan programs, more scholarships, and greater recourse to discriminatory pricing.

But it would be unfair to conclude that there was not much concern expressed in the seminar over the effects of higher tuition on the make-up of the student body. To some the danger of the low tuition in public institutions of higher learning seemed to lie in the pressures put upon independent institutions of higher learning. They were being squeezed by the public colleges, and also by the prestige colleges, which were attracting their best students. With the current rising demand, most colleges could still attract an adequate number of students; but their major difficulties would be in competing for faculty. Even in 1959 the Department of Health, Education, and Welfare found 400,000 vacant places, though when the physical bottlenecks are allowed for the excess was only 200,000.

Government Aid

Obviously more help from government is needed. If government does not greatly increase its contribution, the rise of tuition would have to be great indeed. With government contributions continued at around $2 billion, gifts and endowment income rising to $1 billion, there would still be about $7 billion required from tuition as compared to $1 billion currently. Then tuition per student would have to rise to more than $1000, or about three times current rates. This indeed would be unfortunate. With tuition increasing so much, the effect on enrollment and the structure of the student body would be serious. Resistance to higher tuition would tend to result in moderating the rise of enrollment and, therefore, result in an increase of tuition to a figure below $1000, but also in the exclusion of many capable students.

The case for increased public aid is then strong. But which governments? Most of the state and local governments are in a weak financial position. When incomes are large and growing rapidly, when operations are large enough to assure low unit costs in higher education, when tax systems are not so regressive (heavy relative burdens on the poor) as to suggest large transfers from the poor taxpayers to the rich college students, and when public higher education is strongly entrenched, then the required resources may be forthcoming from state and local governments without any serious rise of tuition.

But conditions vary from state to state. President Mather well brought out the unsatisfactory conditions in Massachusetts. With absurdly low ceilings in salaries, and with enrollment rising by 1,000 a year, the university of a state with great traditions in higher and lower education is stymied by a legislature which is excessively concerned over the exaggerated fears of the taxpayers publicized by tax associations, chambers of commerce, and the like. Here is a state which is forty-eighth in its support of public higher education and which is confronted with a demand for its facilities far beyond what can be met by private institutions. Yet the legislature, even though prodded by a governor genuinely interested in higher education, starves the state university and cuts the governor's request for more than $20 million for a junior college program, previously approved by the legislature, to $1½ million.

In contrast, the legislature in California in 1960 provided for an increase in salaries of 7½ per cent as against an executive request of 5 per cent. A master plan for California for 1970 requires outlays (about two times the whole current budget of Massachusetts) for current needs alone. In this state more than 80 per cent of the students are in public institutions, and it would not be surprising if the figure reached 90 per cent by 1970. But it is also of some interest that despite the strong general support of public higher education, public and private institutions in California have agreed to a rise of fees in public universities for non-instructional services.

Should the burden of higher education increasingly be put on state and local governments with little raising of fees, then by 1970 the likelihood is that public institutions would accommodate at least three-quarters of the students or close to 5 millions. Then, on the assumption that costs rise with the advance of the economy and with the treatment of concealed deficits (low teachers' pay and inadequate plant), the public costs would increase to at least $7.5 billion or at least $5.5 billion above present costs.

Such increases are not likely to be forthcoming, first, because state and local debt and expenditures have increased by more than 300 per cent since the end of the war, second (related), because taxpayers are in rebellion, and third (related), because of the increasing fear of competitive losses to other states from rising responsibilities of state and local governments. Fourth, the factor of rising responsibilities in other areas is especially relevant. The public schools will need $11 billion additional per year by 1970. These are outlays that are not likely to be shifted to the federal government in the next ten years, though in my opinion a much larger contribution by the federal government could be effectively argued.[1] In fact, should state and local government assume the burdens of $11 billion of additional public-school outlays and $5 billion for higher education, the net result would be that all the additional revenue to be expected by these governments would be spent on education. With an economy growing in per capita income and population, and with the problems of urban redevelopment exploding, this outcome is clearly not acceptable.

Recent trends in tuition point to the resistance of taxpayers to assuming an excessive part of the burden of higher education. In the four years ending in 1958–59, tuition rose by 33 per cent in both public and private institutions — $50 and $150 respectively. Hence I would contend that what is likely to happen is increased appropriations by state and local governments — from about $1750 million in 1957–58 to about $3700 million in 1970 — and a reduction of the relative contribution from 48 to 38 per cent. These are, of course, only informed guesses.

Another possibility should not be ruled out. Under this pressure there will be strong demands for economies. These may be forthcoming almost automatically, especially in the middle of the 1960's as enrollment rises rap-

---

[1] See my John Dewey Lecture, *More Resources for Education* (New York, Harpers: 1960).

idly. The tendency in the face of strenuous competition for men and mortar may well be larger classes, an increase in the student–faculty ratio, and improved use of plant. President Kirk of Columbia in the *Saturday Evening Post* in early 1960, in urging a trimester system, presented one of the most effective approaches to economy of plant.

Hence the solution will be in part in increased help by these governments, in part increased income from tuition associated with rising numbers (about one-third of my suggested rise of tuition income at 1970 tuition would be the result of higher enrollment), and in part by economies. But the last may also not be genuine savings resulting from better management, but rather in part a deterioration of product.

In this connection the Pennsylvania experience is of some significance. President Gladfelter discussed the practice of using tax money to support private institutions in his state. With the State University located away from great centers of population, the institutions of higher learning in Philadelphia and Pittsburgh educate large numbers of students who otherwise might have to be supported by the state. The thrust of President Gladfelter's paper is that in providing financial support for the private colleges, taxes are in fact being reduced.

I am not trying to say here that resources are not available from government. Indeed they are, though one must consider the size of the national product, the competing demands on government, and the distribution of spending among different levels of government.

Resources are available. From the fiscal year 1952 to 1959, the spending of the Federal government was reduced from 20 to 14 per cent of gross national product. Had the 1952 rate been maintained there would have been about $25 billion more available for federal spending. But the government proposed to reduce the burdens on the taxpayer both by cutting tax rates and by keeping expenditures down as the gross national product rose.

In addition, the federal government failed to obtain about $13 billion of revenue by 1959 (annual rate) because the gross national product in the years 1952 to 1959 had failed to keep pace with growth during the years 1947 to 1952, following the large deflation of war outlays from 1944 to 1947. Should we add $25 billion and $13 billion (above) and the $35 billion to be expected by the federal government from rising income by 1970, the $73 billion additional might have been available to the federal government annually by 1970. Actually with good management from now on, we should have almost $35 billion more. Out of this sum $10 to $20 billion might easily be made available for welfare services inclusive of education. Then the federal government should contribute at least $4 billion additional to public school expenditures of the $11 billion additional required by 1970, and at least $2 billion additional to higher education.[2] Should disarmament proceed then the government might even go further.

But what form should federal aid take? The most obvious is direct aid for scholarships, fellowships, construction, and even other operating expenditures. The trend seems to be in this direction. Mr. Coombs shows in his essay the breakthrough involved in the 1958 National Defense Education Act, and especially the importance of loans both for the student and the income of the institution. Other members of the seminar suggested a $500 scholarship to each student with a cut-off, say, at $5000 parental income, when there are no other siblings. Scholarships to students in private institutions of higher learning might cut down any waste associated with excessive expansion of public institutions and resultant loss of private investment in education.

So far, however, aside from the National Defense Education Act, federal government has tended to go slow on direct aid. The "G.I. Bills" were, of course, an exception. Fear of excessive movements of students to prestige institutions, stimulated if federal scholarships are available, has dulled the interest in these programs. Yet in view of the attrition of good but impecunious students, a strong case can be made for increased scholarships.

The Administration has shown some enthusiasm for dormitory loans but has opposed loans or grants for academic buildings, as was suggested in 1956 by its Committee on Education Beyond the High School. In fact, the

---

[2] For priorities and further analysis, see my John Dewey Lecture, *op. cit.*

President gave as one reason for not approving a housing bill in 1959 that it included a provision of $50 million for loans for academic buildings.

In the seminar there was a good deal of discussion of tax relief programs, in part because this type of program does not give the government additional responsibilities in influencing spending policies of colleges and universities. Vice-President John Meck was eloquent, both in Washington and in the seminar, in his defense of the Tax Credit Program, which had the endorsement of the American Council on Education. This tax-relief program has some advantages and especially since it gives an equal amount of dollar relief to the poor and the rich and much larger relative relief to the poor — but no relief to those not on the tax rolls. In support of the Meck proposal, President Charles Cole made the interesting point that tax payments to states which finance public universities are deductible from income reported for federal taxes, but if the payment for education is made to a private institution, no tax allowance is to be had.

Against the Meck proposal the following arguments are germane: the erosion of the tax base is increasingly unacceptable, especially when it helps relatively high income groups; a 30 per cent tax credit (for example, $300 against $1000 tuition) would be an inducement for colleges to raise tuition by 43 per cent ($300 = 43 per cent of $700). But I am not sure that a rise of tuition in response to tax credits is necessarily bad. One objective of tax concessions may be to improve the financial condition of the institutions. In fact, the gains of the tax-credit program are likely to be divided among parents and colleges, and each dollar of relief to the parent is likely to be offset by a multiple of relief for the college. The effects are similar to scholarships — from the prewar era to the late 1950's, tuition rose about ten times as much as scholarships. A dollar additional of scholarships enables the college to obtain several additional dollars of tuition income.

We may dismiss another proposed tax-credit program quickly. Under this program, apparently supported by the American Association for the Advancement of Science, all taxpayers would receive equal dollar tax relief for contributions. Thus whereas a middle-income taxpayer gets $200 back from the government for a $1000 gift, a recipient of high income may get back $800 and hence pays net $200. The theory behind the A.A.A.S. scheme is that if those with low income could receive tax relief of, say, 80 per cent, they would increase their gifts. But this in fact virtually gives the taxpayer the choice of paying taxes or spending government money (tax money retained) as he pleases. Moreover, the ratio of contributions to income at different rates of taxes, both at one time and over time, does not suggest any close relation between the percentage of tax relief to contributions. Any such scheme as this one would simply cost the Treasury perhaps $2 billion now received in taxes, and would not provide additional gifts adequate to justify such losses of revenue.

Estimating the likely sums available from other sources, Professor Musgrave concludes that the federal government will have to make a large additional contribution to higher education — not only for scholarships and construction but also for operating expenditures. Higher education comes high in his priorities, and in his view the gains of additional outlays for this purpose greatly exceed those that could be derived from using increased government income made available out of rising income for tax cuts. Musgrave also shows that in part because of our failure to understand that education is a capital investment, we tend to overspend on construction and underspend on personnel.

In summary, public resources are available for higher education, and especially through the federal government. State and local governments can increase their contributions, though how much depends on varying conditions in different states. If tuition is not to rise excessively, state and federal governments will have to increase their subsidies. With the expected rise of the gross national product, the federal government should be able to increase its grants substantially. Tax relief for parents may be helpful also, though the case for tax relief is not without its weaknesses.

Faculty Status

From the discussion in the papers and at the seminar one conclusion clearly emerges: all that is wrong is not merely inadequate faculty pay. Again, I have not reproduced my long working paper. Instead I merely used it as a jumping-off point for the discussion.[3]

Faculty salaries are too low. They are too low primarily because, at current levels, institutions of higher learning cannot attract the men and women of quality required in the next ten years, during which enrollment is to increase by about 75 per cent. This is the most important measure of inadequacy of pay, though the relative decline since the 1930's and the relatively high economic status of professors in the U.S.S.R. vis-à-vis that in the United States are also of some relevance.

The low level of pay results from the inadequacy of resources in higher education and also from the competitive losses of faculty relative to other claimants on college budgets. (It is not easy for even the California Institute of Technology to hold a faculty member when he is offered $750,000 in stock options to join a business firm.) The large needs for capital, the tendency of nonacademic salaries and wages to rise more than academic salaries, the large growth of fringe departments have depressed faculty salaries with the result that they account for a substantially smaller part of the educational dollar than in the 1930's. Messrs. Iffert and Caplow have also commented on the relative losses experienced by faculty. The latter reveals that in two large universities, fringe activities have increased at four times the rate of academic activities.

President Cole and others raised some questions concerning the use of averages in estimating salary trends. In particular, if one is to understand relative salary levels, one should take into account the speed of promotion and the percentage of faculty in different ranks. The good liberal arts college is under pressure to promote early. Amherst has four times as many full professors relatively as one large university (40 and 10 per cent).[4] Should one take into account the average lifetime income (with the early gains increased through compound interest), then one would find that the average pay at a good liberal arts college is relatively higher than is to be inferred from the usual statistics.

Incidentally, one can make a general point here. With the large expansion of enrollment in recent years (and in the future) the average age of the faculty is tending to decline and under pressure of high demand, promotions to accelerate. Hence trends in average salaries for all ranks tend to give an impression of underpayment somewhat greater than justified by the facts. At the same age or the same distribution by ranks, pay has increased somewhat more than is suggested by the usual compilations.

Fringe benefits are an important part of total pay. Dollar for dollar of outlay, they are more effective, if not pushed too far, than current pay. They offer the advantage of insurance as well as tax benefits. Under annuity programs financed by the college, the faculty member gains both because tax rates are much lower in years of retirement (incomes are lower), and the sacrifice of paying taxes in 1990 (say) is much less than in 1960. In my opinion fringe benefits are not pushed far enough. It would be unfortunate indeed if President Cole is correct that once a fringe benefit has been conferred, it is not considered as part of the pay.

This leads me on to the issue of productivity in higher education. In my paper I had raised some questions here. Are we as productive as we might be? Consider the proliferation of courses, the underutilization of plant, the failure to make the most effective use of assistants for the routine tasks — these deficiencies are the responsibility of administrators and especially faculty who are not subject to orders as are executives in a business firm. I am not here discussing the diseconomies related to the size of the college, its location, and so on, for which the faculty can take only limited responsibility. One of the most distinguished university presidents in the last generation told me that if a president had freedom

---

[3] This long essay, now revised and I hope improved, will be part of my book, *The Economics of Higher Education*.

[4] The average per cent over the country is roughly 25, 25, 25, 25 for the four ranks.

to operate he could cut costs by one half and improve the product.

In one respect the college administration, pressed by faculty in many instances, is to be criticized for not making the most effective use of the pay dollar. Administrators tend to devote an excessive proportion of the pay budget in across-the-board, rather than in merit, increases. A case can be made out for adjustments of pay to the rising cost of living. But since faculty pay even by 1960 has barely caught up with the inflation since the 1930's, the result of the application of an "escalator" clause is that increases of pay are largely concentrated on across-the-board increases. A tendency to raise the minimum at each rank has similar effects. Considerations of merit are then largely reflected in promotions in rank.

Assume a 100 per cent increase in the cost of living. Why should not the administrator then use, say, two-thirds for adjustments to the cost of living and one-third for merit increases. Such adjustments would be especially effective in penalizing those with tenure who were proving to be mistakes. I do not agree with President Meredith Wilson that thus reducing the *real* income of tenure members would be an infringement on tenure. In periods of *price stability,* I would like to see say, two-thirds of the funds for increasing the pay budget used for merit increases.

This tendency to underexploit merit increases, and the serious losses of real income suffered by the young faculty members, induced another unfortunate result. The range of salaries tended to narrow. By 1958–59 the range in the nation between instructors' and professors' salaries had been reduced to 2 to 1. This narrowing of the range is especially to be noted in institutions of higher learning with serious financial problems. The effect is unfortunate: with low ceilings, incentives are dulled. There is much to be said for pay ceilings of $30,000 at least for the top 100 institutions and $20,000 for a great many others. But it is to be noted that a doubling of pay by 1970 to an average of about $14,000 and a maximum of at least $30,000 would cost $2 to $3 billion dollars.

In my original paper I had pointed out that educational costs per resident student in dollars of stable purchasing power had risen greatly since early in the century, and despite a rise of enrollment per institution by several times (and to an average size much more economic to run than in the early years of the century), and a trend of enrollment disproportionality towards low-cost operations — for example, undergraduate schools of education and business.

In reply Presidents Cole and Wilson protested that colleges and their staffs were highly productive: witness the scientists, engineers, doctors, and so on, they turn out. Where would we be without the contributions of higher education? Indeed, in this sense they were right. One might also ask, of course, where we would be without our schools, our government, our free-enterprise system, our labor, et cetera.

There is no question that the contribution of universities and colleges is indispensable. We could not survive and we could not have our culture and our high living standards without it. Yet I adhere to the view that we could also be more productive. And more economical: that is, we could get a greater output with our current input of resources. I realize only too well that the relation of faculty, administration, and governing boards is such — and to some extent has to be to preserve and advance our knowledge — as to give the nation less than maximum efficiency.

This does not mean that productivity has not been rising. The explosion of knowledge, the improved training of our faculty, advances in research, the increased contribution of our doctors, engineers, social scientists, humanists — all these point to a rise of productivity. Yet precise measures are not available. Input — for example, the quality of the entering student varies — and the output defy precise measurement. All that we know is that costs per student continue to rise and we infer that the product improves correspondingly.

In the discussions at the seminar, numerous other points were raised concerning productivity. Professor Hughes said teaching in excess of nine hours results in a most inadequate product. But to Professor Caplow, the impressive trend was the steady decline in teaching hours and excessive stress on research and an implication of declining productivity. To several members of the seminar the failure to provide the graduate student with some practice in teaching and the reluctance of senior members of faculties to guide junior members in their early period of teaching — these also are suggestive of a productivity less than optimum. Again President Wilson finds in the tendency to drop as many as 90 per cent of the staff in prestige universities in the first ten years or so of teaching a wasteful use of manpower.

Another sign of low productivity, as Professor Hughes pointed out, is the lack of market organization. Not one market, but many markets prevail. Knowledge is imperfect. Each major university has its own market for personnel, and there is a Methodist, a Presbyterian, a Catholic market, and each major school of education has its own market. It is most unlikely that the best men find their way to the institutions where their talents can be best used. Mr. Caplow's provocative *The Academic Market Place* gives much support to this position. The result is a loss of product.

As chairman of an economics department, I was so struck by the absence of an organized market that I invited the chairmen of the twenty-five universities and colleges turning out the largest number of Ph.D.'s to consider the market problem. The objective was a simple one: to compare notes on available manpower and openings. This was a simple attack on perfecting at least one market, that for Ph.D.'s turned out by leading institutions, as well as to compare notes on openings within these institutions and available scholars who might be moved. Our hope was to improve the chances of tying the right man to the right post.

Faculty pay would be much higher if faculties were more disposed to economize without seriously affecting the educational product. What can be accomplished is suggested by President Hutchins' experience in the Great Depression at Chicago. The faculty dropped 450 courses when the President announced that the one objective was to maintain faculty pay. This the faculty achieved by a drastic reduction in the college offering.

But it must also be clear by now that faculty pay is not by any means the only problem and the only barrier to adequate entrants of quality. Graduate work takes too long with the requirements not too well known. Some universities present an image of excellence which drives away many very able future teachers. In the prestige universities the mass involved in learning is so great that many stay around too long and often under servile conditions. Perhaps, as Professor Hughes said so effectively, what is needed above all is improvements in the colleges to which the young Ph.D.'s go. Often disaffected, they tend increasingly to identify themselves with their disciplines rather than with their colleges. Such innovations as fellowships for young teachers or exchanges of faculty between the major universities and the colleges would improve the situation.

With economic rewards too small, hierarchical considerations have to carry too much weight. Professor Barber well summarized the present situation when he said: "We have undertaken to live like monks, relatively, in an epoch in which there is no ethos to support this kind of life, and we have no cowls to wear to save money on clothes."

Experiments in Higher Education

In the course of a full day the seminar had papers from eight members who discussed new experiments in higher education. For the most part they were interested only in the liberal arts college; but what they had to say often spilled over to the general field of higher education. These eight experts (two representing the New College) discussed the New College (a cooperative program of Amherst, Mt. Holyoke, Smith, and the University of Massachusetts), Amherst, the University of California (Berkeley), Hofstra, Wesleyan, Dartmouth, Oberlin, and Michigan State. For the most part the proposals discussed here stemmed primarily from a desire to improve education, not to increase revenue or reduce costs. Yet the contributors were often aware of the economic issues and did not hesitate to offer economic gains as a reason for pushing experiments. Perhaps the Wesleyan and Berkeley representatives were least concerned with limitations of resources. This might conceivably be explained by the relatively favorable economic position of Wesleyan and the University of California.

In almost every instance, the experiments or studies stemmed from a dissatisfaction with higher education, overly tied to courses, credits, tests, announced or unannounced, unstructured courses — that is, courses for successive years not reflecting increasing rigor, and too many courses and hours in the classroom.

In the views of the speakers and discussants, a large gap existed between what the student might achieve and his actual performance. Much of the trouble arises from departmentalization and excessive sovereignty for departments. This in part explains the proliferation of courses and the fragmentation of knowledge. Hence the sponsors of the New College propose to do away with departments and to treat the course problem by limiting each member of the faculty to one course and two seminars. Courses would be based on the faculty members' interests. To avoid the general departmental type of examination which overweights a student's ability to write in generalities, the sponsors of the New College would intensify study of part of a discipline. Depth as well as breadth would then be required.

Several members of the seminar stressed the point that with an increasing share of the graduates of the liberal arts college going on to graduate schools, it was necessary to reappraise the curriculum of the liberal arts college and rely more heavily on the graduate schools for the narrow professionalism, and on the college for the general education and a training and experience which would make a student run after knowledge and would train him so that he could pursue it.

Above all, students should learn to work independently. They are spoon fed almost as though they were in high school. Thus President Stewart[5] would gradually train the student to work independently. A sudden thrust in this direction would be costly. In the freshman year the independent work should require a large ingredient of faculty time. Much here depends on the quality of the freshmen. (Disturbed by the failure to hold the interest of its best freshmen, Harvard in 1959–60 introduced a program of Freshmen Seminars under the direction of outstanding scholars. The student is required to do a substantial research job which requires "digging" and writing.) With adequate preparation and checking, the faculty ingredient would be gradually reduced in later years. Dependent study could easily become independent.

Several experiments have revealed that experimental groups working independently (for example, eight weeks on their own) performed better than those in the control groups who were supervised.

Most of the contributors stressed the need of much more writing by students, inclusive of a senior thesis which would require a large part of the senior year. Work in small groups (seminars) would be increasingly important. In each course, the student's writing would be subject to scrutiny, and hence there would be no need for courses in writing.

Change requires the support of the faculty. But this is not easily achieved, as is suggested by the partial defeat of the excellent Oberlin plan, and the unwillingness of the faculty to cooperate in broad interdisciplinary courses at Dartmouth. In presenting the New College Plan, Professor Barber urged above all that faculty become both faculty and administrators, thus hoping to break down the conservatism of the faculty. The plan, however, had a built-in flexibility which would help greatly: no departments, courses based on the changing interests of faculty members and society, and no more than one course per member of the faculty. Perhaps even more significant is the danger that the New College might become institutionalized and inflexible.

Professor Sanford presents a novel approach to the experimental college. Here the considerations are couched exclusively in educational terms, the objective being to stimulate the growth of the student. Presumably the financial issues are up to the administration. It is proposed that at Berkeley a two-year liberal arts college for 150 students be set up, with the students in the experimental college selected to match the background, quality,

---

[5] New head of the Midwest College Group.

and so forth, of those in the controlled group. The problem would be to analyze the growth of this group and that of the controlled group over the years. Faculty would not only be in the position of authority and dispenser of information, but also "learner, discussant, disputant, leader or follower of their peers." Students do not grow automatically. They must respond to new situations. Sanford's study of Vassar students showed, for example, that in the early years of college, students become less authoritarian; that by the junior year they have achieved the maximum of independence of thought; and that in their senior year, because they have to respond to a new situation, they tend to worry increasingly. Broadmindedness, independence of thinking, capability for further growth — "these are matters both of the intellect and growth." The experimental college would exploit the increased knowledge of the growth process of the entire personality, inclusive of intellect.

At Hofstra the problem was somewhat different. Here again concern is expressed for the course system, and also for the failure to give the first-year student a helpful experience whether he continues or is one of the 30 per cent who drop out. What especially concerns President Adams is the enslavement of the commuting student to his car: it is his dream, his reason for working, his peer culture, and so on. And unfortunately it interferes with his education. Two per cent of the A students, but 40 per cent of the C students, have cars.

What President Adams proposes is to expose an experimental group of 120 freshmen to an eight-hour day at least four days a week, with a fifth reserved for corrective work and other purposes. In this manner he hopes to force the commuting student — and in Long Island he is a good student, the B+ variety — from his enslavement to his car and excessive tie to his parents. The college also requires a job for the student. Why not make the well-done job an adjunct to his educational experiences?

For eight hours the student would be locked up — more or less — starting with a morning lecture, then discussion, seminars, a course in the afternoon, and library work — and a hope that he would be sufficiently stimulated to work evenings also. One probable result would be acceleration. If properly pursued, this program could put the student into the junior year after one year of this concentrated experience. With this agenda, President Adams hopes, as do the others, to reduce the interest in the extracurricular activities which so seriously impair the educational process.

These are then the educational issues. What of the economics? Savings may be large.

At Oberlin the proposal was that the college be divided into two parts: College A would be in residence two quarters and at work away from Oberlin one quarter, and on vacation one quarter. Similarly with College B. It is at once clear that the physical facilities would provide for twice as many students under this arrangement. For College A and B could be staggered in such a way that students in each would be in residence two of the four quarters, but in different quarters. In addition, since the quarter away would consist largely of independent work, there should be some savings of faculty.[6]

In this manner the college could cut its unit costs substantially, using the proceeds either to reduce tuition or increase salaries. If a college accepts the alternative of not increasing its enrollment, it will face increased competition from those institutions that do expand, and may, therefore, experience serious problems in providing a faculty of desired standards.

In the New College Program its financial problem is that of finding capital to get the enterprise launched. In my view the job could be done with an outlay of about $5 million, of which one half might be borrowed.

The current budget could easily be provided. A good liberal arts college, and especially one with endowment, has to charge at least $1000. At a ratio of 20 to 1 against a national figure substantially lower, that is fewer students per faculty member, the college of 1000 students could easily be financed with a tuition of $1000. With the elimination of the "icing" in colleges — for example, intercollegiate athletics, luxurious dormitories, other extracurricular activities — with savings on adminis-

[6] See President Kirk's able paper in support of a trimester year, mentioned earlier.

tration largely entrusted to the faculty and with a relatively small physical plant, at least 50 per cent of tuition receipts, in my opinion, could be available for faculty salaries.

Hence with one million dollars of tuition income $500,000 would be available for faculty salaries, or an average of $10,000 per faculty member, a figure about 30 per cent above the general average of 1959–60. Since this is likely to be a young faculty, the relative advantage is even greater than here suggested. The New College, in its formulation of deficiencies and their treatment and the presentation of values and financial under-pinnings, promises unusual gains for higher education. It is worthy of the attention of men of affluence who might thus make a large contribution to American higher education.

At Hofstra the college accommodates 8000 students with a capital investment of about $10 million or $1250 per student. In part this small cost is explained by intensive use: that is, 65 per cent occupancy of classrooms, much above the national level. The average investment for the country on roughly similar replacement values is almost $5000, a comparison which suggests one reason for the increased popularity of the commuting college. There are other reasons also for the gains of this type of college. One survey of high-school seniors in an Ohio city showed that they overwhelmingly preferred to commute and have an automobile to residing in a distant college without one.

At Hofstra again, the faculty cost per student for the experimental college would be low. Yet the President hoped to pay six young fellows $10–12,000 for their guidance and instruction of 100 to 120 students. Note again the ratio of fellows to students is from 16 to 20 to one.

At Amherst, similar gains are to be had. The college might expand a few hundred and even from 1000 to 1500 without losing the common experiences which are so important. But the hope is to do so without a rise of faculty. As Professor Thorp points out, the ratio is now 7 to 1, and much to the surprise of the committee, the faculty had grown greatly in the 1950's without any gains of enrollment. The committee was also surprised to learn that there were so many classes of five or less that about a quarter of the teachers' time went to 2 per cent of the student class hours.

At Dartmouth, the Provost found excessive numbers of classes from 25 to 75 where the lecturing is done to small groups, often by young and inexperienced teachers. Why not have more small groups (for example, seminars), and a larger number of lectures where the able teachers who lecture well can be used most effectively? Because Ruml was a Dartmouth alumnus and trustee, the issues of size of classes, number of courses, and the like received much attention at Dartmouth. There the number of hours in class has been reduced from 15 to 12, and the number of courses required reduced from 40 to 32. Reduction of contact hours for students is one of the most effective ways of cutting expenditures without deteriorating the product.

With an enrollment of 2600 and faculty of 200, the student–faculty ratio was 13 to 1. A proposed rise to 3000 could raise the ratio to 15 to 1. It was hoped that the additional tuition of $320,000 ($800 tuition at that time) would be used to increase salaries.

The Dartmouth authorities were concerned that they had too few large lectures (and an excessive number not so booked), and too few small groups. With a 17 to 1 ratio, almost 63 per cent of the work of students could be in seminars, and about 37 per cent in large lecture sections. Each faculty member would teach an average of about 50 students per term and 9 per cent of the teaching hours could be in lectures.

A faculty committee at Dartmouth is also considering the possibilities of a fourth term, a means both of improving conditions of experimentation and also providing for a more effective use of plant.

In summary, outstanding liberal arts colleges are asking questions: how can we realize the potential of our students? The answer seems to be more first-class lectures, more very small groups, emphasis on independent work, on more writing and discussions, on the deflation of courses and departmental sovereignty, on interesting the student so that he (or she) will divert energies from extracurricular activities to education in a more narrow sense. Many of the ideas offered are also relevant for the universities with liberal arts colleges and even to higher education in general.

The economic gains are substantial, though often coincidental. A better product can be had with the same outlay or the same product with a reduced outlay. Faculty salaries especially should benefit from reforms such as those suggested, and the resultant improvement of faculty pay should induce a better product.

Economics and Educational Values

One of the most discussed issues in higher education is the material gains of a college education. Attention to this aspect of higher education is not meant to give the impression that the material rewards are the most important to be had from higher education. Many of us in the academic world fear that parents and students overemphasize the vocational or material gains and understress the other values of higher education. At the same time, in a world where resources are limited, one cannot and should not be silent on the issue of what higher education contributes to the national income or to the income of individuals.

The Census Bureau estimated that in 1949 a college education was worth around $100,000, subject to deductions for the cost of the education. But at the outset, some reservations are necessary. This estimate is based on the average income of college graduates living in 1949 in comparison with the income of high-school graduates. Should we estimate the gains for college graduates living in 1960, the figures would be substantially higher. In his essay, Mr. Bridgman shows that the differential rose from $112,000 in 1949 to $154,000 in 1956. By using a somewhat different approach — that is, by estimating the differential advantage of *college graduates of 1960* (not all living graduates), on the assumption of very small rises of prices and expected per capita gains of income — I find an advantage of $200,000 to $250,000. For the purpose of assessing the material gains of higher education, this seems to me to be the better approach. But this attack is also subject to a reservation, namely, that as the college-graduate population rises — say, from 8 to 20 millions — or more, the relative position of college graduates will deteriorate. In a book published more than a decade ago (*The Market for College Graduates*), I developed the theme that the relative position of the college-trained tends to fall, though absolutely their gains should rise. Note that from 1949 to 1956, per capita disposable personal income rose by 37 per cent, but income differentials for college graduates by less than 30 per cent. In fact there is plenty of evidence of a decline in the relative earnings of the college graduates over a generation.

These are not the only reservations required. First, the gains are not present gains. They are spaced over the working life of the college graduate, and income received in 1980 is worth considerably less than income received in 1960. Second, this differential income is subject to taxes, as is all income. But on the whole this seems to me to be an irrelevant issue. Third, the gains for the college-trained are especially large for the able and not nearly so great for others — as Mr. Bridgman and Dr. Wolfle so clearly show. Fourth, the comparison is not of earnings but of income, and the college-trained tend to receive relatively more of unearned income. Fifth, these comparisons are of the arithmetical mean; the median yields a smaller differential.

One of course should not assume that the higher income of the college graduate is the result exclusively of the college education. He (she) is more able (average I.Q. of 120 for college graduates compared to 100 for the population) and also has better connections. Again, in the past the gain of the college graduate is not related to superior productivity alone; many occupations require a college degree even when in fact the task could be done as well by the high-school graduate.

But all this does not mean that college education does not contribute toward the higher income. We assume that our students learn how to think, to make mature judgments, to communicate, and also acquire needed technical skills. As Dr. Wolfle shows, though income is positively correlated with aptitudes, environmental factors (occupations of parents) and education, the overriding association is with education. A comparison of high-school graduates of *equal ability* (not equal motivation) who went to college with those who did not reveals much larger incomes for the college-trained.

A more general problem relates to the measurement of the whole product of higher education, a problem not easily solved. Crude measures such as percentage of students getting into first-class graduate schools, number of Wilson Fellowships, listing in *American Men of Science* and *Who's Who* are interesting but not conclusive. For output cannot be measured without considering the input, and measures of input such as aptitude scores, high school grades, and the like underweigh such factors as motivation. Professor Riesman underscores some of the weaknesses of these measures and he raises the interesting question: is it possible to have Federal Trade Commission grades for colleges — for example, *not good merchandise?* In this connection, Professor McConnell of the University of California tells me that even high-school counselors, when asked to rank colleges over the country, make the most glaring errors.

The size or quality of the product depends on many variables. Is the small institution preferable to the large? In economic measures, there is much to be said against the many institutions with less than 1000 students. But many college administrators sense important educational values in the very small institution. "Each student knows every other student, and the President knows every student by his first name. All students can have common assemblies." In Professor Riesman's words, there is a critical mass beyond which something is lost through increasing size.

With rising national enrollments each college administrator has to decide the extent to which rising demand will be taken in higher prices (an attractive approach when finances are troublesome) or in higher quality of students. When enrollments are rigidly fixed, the result may well be an excessive proportion of students with high-aptitude and high college grades.

Is the prestige college as good as is generally assumed, and others not so good? Here again, Riesman raises some questions. May there not be a "decompression effect in a high-octane situation"? That is, the student at a high-prestige institution may be harmed in this kind of milieu (for example, he may not be adequately challenged). Whereas the student is fragmented at the high-prestige institution and allows the faculty to dominate, at other colleges the student peer dominates.

In its report the Truman Committee on Higher Education in the late 1940's urged a greater diversification of schools as a means of democratizing and making the most effective use of higher education. We tend to move is this direction as anyone examining, for example, the curriculum of a four-year college (formerly a normal school) in California would readily see. One recent trend in diversification is the spread of the cooperative college where the student works and learns in the same year and thus facilitates financing, extends the years of education, and obtains a different product mix than he otherwise would.

This brings us once more to the general problem of economics: that is, achieving a larger product with the same use of resources or the same product with reduced resources. An example of the possibility of increasing the product without any large expenditure of resources is Professor Skinner's famous teaching machine. Here the student finds a resource which requires him (her) to check the educational results step by step, and the student gets the satisfaction of doing rather than listening. For the teacher the responsibility often is to program thousands of steps using checks which tell him when the pedagogical process is likely to break down — a device not available through the use of only the textbook.

In recent years one of the most eloquent commentators on the need of increased productivity in higher education has been Dr. Eurich. He views higher education as lagging behind the rest of the economy in its flexibility in appropriating the fruits of modern science for the teaching process, and he sees the rise of productivity as the means of raising faculty salaries to a level commensurate with the task to be done.

Two examples from Dr. Eurich's paper will suffice to suggest the possibilities. One university by a re-examination of its maintenance practices saved $1 million in a period of eighteen months. A management firm which specializes in space utilization estimated that from 1957 to 1970, $4.3 billion would be required for new plant if better space programming is carried out in both existing and new facilities, and $12.7 billion if no improvements are forthcoming.

Finally, I come to Kenneth Deitch's paper, written while he was a junior at Harvard. He is a fine example of what can be achieved by a young man capable of original work and sufficiently motivated, working largely on his own.

Deitch's general theme is that it is important to make the most effective use of resources as long as they are limited. It is necessary then to estimate costs of various ways of achieving an educational objective and the benefits to be had. Admittedly benefits are not always easy to measure and there will be disagreement concerning what the educational objective should be. But in a simple example Deitch shows how, if the objective is to widen geographical dispersion of students, one measures costs over the benefits of alternative use of resources — for example, increased scholarship money or additional help in the Admissions Office.

Investment Policies

For the two days of the seminar spent on investment policies, I prepared a long working paper, and again, since I intend to publish a major part of this working paper, revised, in my study of the economics of higher education, I limit myself to a brief summary of the problems I raised in this paper. What the problems are will also be evident from a summary of the two days' discussion as well as from the papers published in this symposium.

At these two meetings we had the help of the current Harvard Treasurer and his associate, and a former Harvard Treasurer, the Treasurers of the University of Chicago, Princeton, California, Dartmouth, Rochester, Mt. Holyoke, and Yale (associate), a few economists, including the Professor of Investments at the Harvard Business School, the head of the biggest investment trust in the country, and other investment authorities.

In brief, I raised the following issues. In the long run, is it not sound policy for institutions to put an even larger proportion of their resources in common stocks? The reasons are first because of persistent inflationary pressures and growth, it is possible to protect college investments better in this manner than through the purchase of investments with fixed yields. Second, because corporations are managed on behalf of the stockholders, not the bondholders, there are certain advantages in purchasing equities. (Professor Bates suggests additional reasons for the practice of shifting of investment to common stocks. He is not, however, as enthusiastic about the trends as others.) I supported my position on the basis of the Cowles study of relative yields of common stocks over a long period. (The reader will find some criticism of this position in Bates' paper.)

One of the most intriguing issues is: how should an institution treat new endowment against old? In view of rising prices of equities — and this is the usual condition — allocation of income on the basis of market values favors the old endowments. For then the relative stake of the old in the endowment income is large because its share is given by the high *market* value of the old endowment (not the *book* value).

Thus assume one old endowment and one new. (I discuss here only restricted endowments. But note Mr. Meck in his paper estimates that wholly unrestricted endowment was only 4, 4, 7, 15, 19, and 23 per cent of total endowment for Princeton, Amherst, Yale, Dartmouth, Wellesley, and Wesleyan respectively.)

(1) Old (gift of 1850):
    original (book) value = $1,000,000
    present value = $5,000,000
(2) New — gift of $1,000,000 = $1,000,000

The issue is the share of the investment income going to (1) as against (2).

Under book value, each gets half.

Under present (market) value, (1) gets ⅚ of the income and (2) ⅙.

In his paper, Mr. Hall of the University of Chicago illustrates the difference made according to the method used; Chicago uses the market — that is, investment trust — method: four $100,000 funds.

(1) 1936 credited in 1959 with $7508

(2) 1947–48 credited in 1959 with $7064

(3) 1952–53 credited in 1959 with $5454

(4) 1957 credited in 1959 with $3383.

I assume pooled funds which facilitate the management of funds and also pool risks. Ex-Chancellor Robert Hutchins of Chicago told about a crisis in Chicago when the chapel had been financed by Ohio oil stocks, at one point not paying income. The issue was: should the chapel be closed? This proved to be a strong and decisive point in favor of pooling investment funds and thus reducing risks for any one fund. (Treasurer John Meck of Dartmouth reveals an interesting episode when a non-pooled fund was used to great advantage for the college.)

My position has been in favor of the book-value approach, largely on the grounds that current gifts should be favored against earlier gifts, since the former are more likely to reflect present values of society than the older gifts. In the vigorous discussion of this issue, the proponents of the market approach (that is, the investment-trust approach when stakes in income are determined by current values) placed special emphasis on the moral issue — that is, the assumed exploiting of past donors who are likely to be deceased. Against this, I argued that the current donors would in later years in turn suffer in favor of the donors (say) of 1990.

Older donors are more likely to favor the book approach, young ones the market approach, for the latter will witness rises in value of their gifts. President Coons of Occidental College tells me they are solving this problem by putting up to the donor the choice of entry at book or market value.

Whatever the merit of the controversy, it is of some interest that, as Dr. Cain shows, about 140 of 200 institutions, accounting for the larger part of endowments, use the book-value approach.

My third major issue related to the problem of heavy investment in growth stocks. I held that an exclusive enthusiasm for growth stocks might well penalize the current generation of students and faculty at the expense of the next generation. I discovered in my visits to colleges that faculty in several institutions were suspicious of their governing boards because they invested heavily in growth stocks. The yield on growth stocks is of course below that on all stocks, and by 1959 well below the yield on bonds. Hence what the current generation gets is capital gains or promises of higher income in the future, not high incomes today. To some extent in 1960, the same argument can be used against investment in equities generally, since the yield is less than on bonds.

The discussion in the seminar revealed to me, whatever the validity of this point for the future — and it may well have more relevance in the future than in the past — that my case was not proved. First, Mr. Tripp showed clearly that, in the 1950's at least, the growth stocks yielded not only capital gains but also higher incomes than nongrowth. That is, though at time of purchase the yield might be (say) only 2 per cent, it was not long before the yield on the original investment was up to (say) 4 per cent. Tripp expressed some doubts about the future, however. And Professor Bates also showed that it all depended upon the kind of growth stocks bought. When future rises were largely discounted, I was more likely to be right in favoring nongrowth stocks than when appreciation in the future had not been discounted.

The Associate Treasurer of Harvard University, Mr. Bennett, describes three investments in growth stocks that yield varying results. In general, the results were good. Gains from appreciation were large as the ratio of purchase price to earnings at time of purchase was greatly reduced in later years.

Perhaps I should point out here that the complaints by faculty against treasurers are not limited to their fear of excessive interest in growth stocks. One well-known economist complained to me of the policy of a major university in overdepreciating its plant, partly, in his view, in order to "play poor" and thus keep salaries down. Other complaints relate to practices of putting aside excessive amounts to income-stabilization funds or reserves and hence not paying out income earned. But then, complaints are the exception rather than the rule. What is more surprising is the lack of interest of faculty and even economist faculty members in the financial transactions of their college or university.

I have a complaint of my own, namely the inexcusably poor presentation in treasurer's reports of the financial condition of a college. Most treasurers make no serious attempt to make their reports interesting and readable. One might expect that since all institutions appeal to the public for help and in this sense all institutions are public institutions, the treasurers would attempt to write reports that would command at least as much interest as those of the better private corporations. But this is the exception rather than the rule. The reader does not get a thoughtful summary of recent developments; in the Harvard Treasurer's Report, for example, expenditures are classified not on the basis of categories (for example, instruction, construction, plant maintenance), but on the basis of purchases (for example, labor, materials). No attempt is made to distinguish between instruction outlays and departmental research expenditures, and so on. Yet this is considered one of the better reports.

But let us return to the issue of growth stocks. One of the major debates in the seminar revolved around an issue related to investment in growth stocks. When the investments are made in equities that appreciate in value, the temptation may be to pay out as income part of the capital appreciation. Should the treasurer rely on capital gains as a substantial part of the income from investments (and capital gains are a large part of earnings paid out), then he may hold that capital gains are in fact income and should be so treated. But some members of the seminar felt that endowment is inviolate and if the original gift is invested and appreciated in value the university is bound to keep the capital intact, original *and* growth, and any disbursement of these sums is a violation of trust. Since capital gains are in fact part of the income, I am not sympathetic with this viewpoint. Perhaps nondisbursements from capital stock given as part of dividends should be large enough, however, to protect the original endowment against possible future declines in value. (This issue is discussed more fully in the summary of the stenotyped report of this session.)

I raised the issue of the place of endowment in the financing of higher education. In the last half-century, the relative contribution of endowment income has steadily declined, though in a recent period of several years as a result of improved techniques and concentrated effort, endowment income increased relatively about as much as general income.

This relative decline of endowment income since 1900 has been the result of inflation (increasingly offset by investment in equities), the reduction of yields (again, recently offset by rising capital values and high profits), the increase of enrollment, and the increased availability of other sources of income and in particular current gifts (soft money, more easily had in periods of high taxes), and public grants. When colleges with endowments have lagged in their rise of enrollment, endowment income remains relatively important. Thus in a recent period of twenty-eight years, the relative decline of the income on endowment of Harvard was surprisingly small, the result in part of an increase in enrollment only about one-sixth that of the nation. Aggressive campaigns for endowment funds and unusual response from alumni are also relevant. In the $82 million campaign of the late 1950's, Harvard alumni contributed almost two thirds, a remarkable record when compared with national figures. With small rises in enrollment, endowment is not spread as thin as it otherwise would be. More than one college administrator takes into account in its enrollment policies the effects of an increase in numbers on the contributions of endowment income. When that income is relatively large, the tendency is greater than otherwise to contain increases in enrollment.

Adam Smith, almost two hundred years ago, raised the question of the desirability of endowment income. His view was that when income was assured, teachers perform badly, for they are inadequately motivated. Oxford at that time was indeed not doing a first-class job. This is one argument against endowment.

Another is that excessive recourse to endowment makes the institution unresponsive to public needs. John D. Rockefeller, Jr., Rosenwald, and Sloan are among the philanthropists who have argued for consumption of capital — and especially under the pressure of insufficient current income.

But despite these arguments, I believe a strong case can be made for endowment. First, to many donors the appeal of a gift yielding permanent income is great. Second, an endowment enables an institution to carry through projects which otherwise might have to be interrupted or abandoned. *Some* independence from outside pressures against an institution is an important ingredient of good performance.

In this connection, one might argue that in some respects, public universities need endowment more than private institutions of higher learning, for they are more subject to the pressures around them than are private institutions of higher learning. But another point is relevant here. The public institutions of higher learning have the tremendous resources of the tax-collector behind them and endowment income is a small counterresource for the private institution. Today endowment income is about 1/10 as large for public as for private institutions of higher learning.

In this connection consider, for example, the $600 millions of endowment of Harvard, the highest in the country and twice the amount available to Yale, the second in this category. Yet the income of this endowment is $21 million at Harvard, or about 1/7 of the total contributed to the University of California (exclusive of organized research) for 1960–61, and many state universities receive more than $20 million from taxes. At Harvard, endowment yields ⅓, gifts ⅓, and the tuition ⅓ (exclusive of organized research). Therefore, Harvard can offer a $3600 education for $1200. But its large subsidies are dependent on restraining rises of enrollment.

On the issues of endowment and investment management, Professor Bates makes a good point. Much depends on the general financial pictures of the institutions of higher learning. If, for example, the institution has large fixed commitments, then it may not be wise to take large risks. In general, Professor Bates seems to lean to the idea that seeking additional gifts is a preferred approach to counting too much on the gains from investment in equities.

My final point relates to the issue of borrowing. Just as the use of credit instills life into our economy and has made possible the large development of such industries as automobiles, housing, and housing appliances, I am impressed by what credit can do to financing both the students and the university. Use of credit enables higher education to arrogate more of the nation's output to itself. I argued that in our inflationary and growing economy, the debtors are relieved of much of the burden of debts, and the longer the period the greater the likelihood of relief. Debt financing is one way of imposing more of the costs of higher education on a reluctant public. When, as one of the discussants contended, an institution can earn 5 per cent on its endowment and borrow at 3 per cent, why should it not borrow? And why cannot all resident students share in the added costs of borrowing, irrespective of whether they are or are not living in dormitories donated in the past? The arguments against a borrowing policy are well put by the able Treasurer of Harvard, Mr. Paul Cabot.

In the discussion of these and other issues one will find a fair amount of agreement among the discussants. In general, as Mr. Bump shows, the first objective is maximum income and assuring high income over long periods. The treasurers generally seem to anticipate long-run gains in capital values in growth stocks. Messrs. Tripp, Bump, and Bennett all reveal the possibilities here on the basis of the records of the past. For example, a $10,000 investment made in five investment trusts in a recent period of ten years would have yielded $8,317, or over 8 per cent, as against 3 per cent on bonds (Bump). Professor Bates, however, does not seem so hopeful as the treasurers and points to the great mistakes of 1929 and 1937 and the failure of the formula systems of investing following these debacles. And Mr. Tripp warns that the 1960's may not be repetitive of the preceding fifteen years.

Both Parker Hall, the able Treasurer of the University of Chicago, and ex-President Houston of the Rensselaer Polytechnic Institute (R.P.I.) reveal the possibilities of unorthodox investments. The University of Chicago has put about 10 per cent of its endowment into these unusual investments and received over a period of ten years an income about 30 per cent above normal from them. Among the investments were the purchase and construction for lease of tankers, lease-backs (that is, purchase of property and then lease back to original owners), lending bank deposits (earnings of 8 per cent on one such transaction, without risk). Then there is the *Britannica*, given as a gift to the University of Chicago and made a very profitable enterprise by the superb management of Senator William Benton. Next to the Rockefeller gifts, this is the second most important philanthropy in the University.

Perhaps even more unorthodox is President Houston's fabulous investment in 1950 in 61 Broadway, New York City, for the Rensselaer Polytechnic Institute. His estimate is that over a twenty-one-year period, R.P.I. will have taken $3.9 million out of the building in ordinary income. And in addition a special cash reserve of $2.5 million is available. Hence the return should be $6.4 million on a $2.2 investment, or 13½ per cent per year. In addition, R.P.I. has increased its equity in the building, through paying off its past mortgages and bank loan, by $7.55 million, and hence the total return has grown to 29.5 per cent per year. Beginning in 1971, the expectation is to obtain $855,000 a year out of the building, or 39 per cent of the original investment per year. This record is even better than what could have been had through an investment in Massachusetts Investment Trust. Nevertheless, had the stock market boom been visible in 1950, President Houston says, this investment might not have been made.

In summary, investment income is not as important as it used to be. But it is still of much significance for many institutions of higher learning. Rises of enrollment, increased availability of other sources of income, and inflation have tended to reduce the importance of investment income. But the shift to equities and especially growth stocks has offset these trends to some extent. Appropriate accounting methods can also contribute to a more effective yield from investments.

So much for the Introduction by the Director of this unique Seminar on Higher Education, and Editor of the resulting volume. Summaries of the discussions and the papers follow.

II. PRICING AND THE STUDENT BODY

Summary of the Discussion to "Pricing of College Services," November 12 and December 11, 1958, meetings of the Seminar on the Economics of Higher Education. Papers were given by Messrs. Stouffer, Morse (November 12), Case, Johnson, Monro, Bokelman, and Moon (December 11).

IN the lively discussion following each of the presentations many sharp differences of opinion and of concern were brought out. Central to much of the debate was the question of low or high tuition rates and the related issue of the attitude of high-school students toward going to college. Several participants felt that keeping tuition fees low in state colleges and universities was vitally important for stimulating interest in college and for the democratic process. Others, agreeing that educational opportunity for all those able to profit from it was of the utmost importance in a democratic system, felt that low tuition rates were neither necessary nor sufficient to provide such an opportunity. The question naturally was raised of what conditions are necessary to make the potential college student aware that it really is both financially and academically feasible for him to go to college.

One of the most important proposals for increasing educational opportunity for students and at the same time easing the financial difficulties of colleges, a loan program on a really vast scale both in coverage and in average size of loan, came under considerable criticism by some members of the seminar and was in turn defended. The possibility of higher tuition, with or without loans, raised old fears regarding undesirable changes in the composition of the student body in colleges and universities. Would private schools with higher tuitions in fact become educational "country clubs"? Would an extensive scholarship or loan program on a national scale result in a migration of the most able students to a few costly schools with high prestige? How would such changes affect recruitment of faculty members? Many observed the "pull-apart" effect which is already taking place among colleges as more families are able to send sons and daughters across the country to college and such programs as the National Merit Scholarships make more students aware of the possibility of acquiring a college education.

Finally, the delicate question of competition among public and private institutions of higher learning was aired thoroughly, and an attempt was made to find that important body of common ground on which both types of institution could base their policies and state their case for higher education to legislators and the public. Too often improvement in the total American system of higher education has been thwarted by unnecessary disagreement among representatives of different types of institution. If improvement in educational opportunity and quality is to be made, most participants agreed that it must be made by joint efforts.

High versus Low Tuition

Tuition policy is relevant for financial well-being and for the composition of student enrollments. A major source of income for the college, the level of tuition also governs to a great extent the economic and social classes from which its students will be drawn. Several members of the seminar felt that President Johnson's eloquent defense of low tuition did not grapple satisfactorily with the problem. There were several important factors which he ignored in his discussion.

In the first place, most educators take considerable pride in the present diversity in the system of higher education in the United States. It is desirable in a pluralistic society to maintain as much of this diversity as possible, so long as the costs of doing so are not prohibitive. In his defense of low tuition, Mr. Johnson did not consider the financial plight of the private schools, which lack access to state revenues and for which tuition is an important source of revenue. Caught between rising costs and fear of losing their students to low-tuition state universities if their own tuitions are raised, many private institutions are put under severe financial pressure. One member cited the case of several church-related colleges in the Midwest which have had to divert funds hitherto used for scholarships into general expenditures, for they had no other source of income. Yet reducing scholarships impairs, rather than increases, educational opportunity for the college-age youth of the country.

Another member posed the problem in this way: "One of two things certainly would happen, if the private institutions all felt obliged to pursue a policy of higher and higher tuition, and if the public institutions succeeded in adhering to a policy of low tuition. One possibility is that many private institutions would be liquidated, thereby contracting the total capacity of higher education. The other possibility is that the stronger institutions would breed a class society rather than a classless one, and I think that some of our so-called stronger institutions today are rapidly moving in this direction of developing a social and economic elite, which is exactly what none of us wants."

In advocating low tuition, then, it is necessary to ask what the consequences will be for our diversified system of education, how it is possible to avoid either the demise of private institutions or their degeneration into a symbol of wealth. Another participant added that he felt no doubt that private institutions could fill their halls in the next few years, due to the tremendous and increasing demand for higher education, at the present levels of tuition. But the crucial pinch will be in terms of faculty; those private institutions which are not exceptionally wealthy or which do not have exceptional reputations will find it increasingly difficult to get first-rate faculty members in competition with high-paying state universities. Salaries are too low today to attract highly qualified academic men to these places. And higher tuition seems the only available source of income for many schools.

A second point which one member felt Mr. Johnson had neglected is that personal incomes have been rising steadily in recent years and have reached a level nothing short of spectacular by all historical standards. Yet college tuition fees have not risen nearly as much. Tuition at the University of Massachusetts, for example, remained at $100 a year from 1933, in the depths of the Depression, until 1959, whereas per capita disposable income grew nearly five-fold during this period. On the average, taking private and public colleges and universities together, tuition has risen only 50 per cent as much as per capita income since 1940. Furthermore, the rise in incomes has been especially large in the low-income groups of the population, among just those people for whom it is desirable to provide educational opportunity. The tradition of low tuition, this member felt, has a long and persuasive history, but it is being outmoded by the rise of incomes and the fact that most college students no longer tend to prepare for low-paying vocations such as teaching and the ministry. Today about one third of all students specialize in business administration alone.

Finally, several participants pointed out that we must not forget that tuition is only a part of the total cost to the student of going to college. And when tuition is low, it is indeed a small part. For this reason it is an illusion to believe that maintenance of low tuition will ensure educational opportunity to able students from low-income families. They might be able to save enough for tuition, but often cannot meet the other expenses associated with going to college. Most important of these are the room and board costs incurred in living away from home, as most students in state-supported universities do. The University of New Hampshire, for instance, is 80 per cent residential. At another state university the tuition was only $100, but annual costs to the student were reckoned at $1300, on the average. In such a case a 100 per cent increase in tuition does not represent a large increase in the total cost of going to college. An exception to this situation is provided by the municipal colleges, such as C.C.-N.Y., to which most students can commute from home.

Because of the high extra-tuition costs of attending college, several members felt that the advocates of low tuition are deluding themselves if they believe that low tuition fees really eliminate the financial barrier to a college education and thus enhance educational opportunity for all. One participant suggested that a much more effective way of achieving this aim would be to *raise* tuition fees considerably and then use a large part of the increased revenue for full-cost scholarships, scholarships which would allow able students from really impoverished families to defray all the attendant costs of going away to college. The families of most students could easily afford the higher tuition, and diverting a large portion of the resulting funds to maintenance scholarships would really increase educational opportunity in the country. The remainder would ease the financial distress of colleges.

In summary, those who opposed the argument for low tuition felt that between the needs of the colleges and the needs of the students, those of the former were greater at the present time. Higher tuition is a major means of meeting the needs of the colleges, and these participants insisted that measures could be found which would ease considerably the resulting burden on students. Higher tuition is certainly not the only way of solving the financial problems of colleges, but it is a feasible one; other possibilities, such as direct public grants to private institutions or various forms of tax exemption, are discussed in Part III. All participants agreed that, even though tuition fees might have to go up, it is not necessary to charge a student what it costs his college to educate him, since public appropriations, endowment income, and gifts cover some of the costs. Full cost pricing is neither necessary nor desirable, since it would bring into question the charitable character of private universities and would unnecessarily burden the student.

Even apart from charging full costs, however, several members had serious doubts about the wisdom of raising tuition substantially. It may be true that incomes are rising rapidly, but the $2600 in tuition and living costs required to attend a major private university still appears a formidable sum to the parents of — say — a high-school senior on the West Coast. With the uncertainty which attends winning a scholarship, and a lack of knowledge about scholarships anyway, such a family often has second thoughts about sending a son to such a school instead of the local city college. A general rise in tuition might raise doubts about whether college is worthwhile at all.

The experience of the University of Vermont is interesting in this connection. Before 1952 it was run partly as a private institution and charged students in arts and sciences $625 a year for tuition. Then it was made entirely into a state university and the tuition to residents of Vermont was lowered to $325. Thereafter there was a sharp increase in the number of Vermont students who attended the university: people who previously had gone into local business, or into nursing school, and so on. One member felt that this was an important illustration — one of the few, since tuition is not often lowered these days — of the psychological impact of tuition low enough to bring college into the array of possible choices facing the high-school senior.

This is certainly one of the most important problems in recruiting able students for college — do they think that going to college is both possible and worthwhile for them? Several members felt that an extremely important variable in determining the answer to this is the "image" of college which is held by these able teen-agers. The existence of educational opportunity is not very fruitful unless people know it is there and are willing to test it. As one participant observed in connection with Professor Stouffer's survey of Harvard freshmen, the relevant question to ask them was not "Could you afford to attend if there were a rise in the cost of going to college?" but "Would you attend?" This is the question which plagues educators: not so much whether people could *afford* to go to college — this can usually be accomplished by working, borrowing, and cutting corners without excessive hardship — but whether they *would* go to college.

Several participants suggested that low tuition may well be an important factor in keeping students aware of educational opportunity. Prospectively, the payment of $100 a year and daily carfare, plus four years of hard work, seems within the realm of possibility to the bright high-school student; $2000 a year is often out of the question. Even when the student is going to school away from home, room and board charges can be rationalized and the money found somehow if only tuition seems within reason. High tuition may destroy the illusion that education can be had cheaply, and thereby remove from the college rolls people who could benefit both themselves and the country by going to school beyond high school.

On the other hand, one member suggested that publicizing educational opportunity may be a one-shot thing; lowering tuition at the University of Vermont heightened interest in college and increased community expectation for going to college, and this is important. It does not follow that raising tuition again would destroy this once the expectations have been created. Whereas previously it was accepted that class valedictorians would enter local business, now it is expected and accepted that they should go to college, and a relatively small rise in the cost of doing so is not likely to change the expectations.

Maintaining Educational Opportunity

Although the question of trying to do too big a job — trying to give a college education to too many people, including those who do not profit from it because of poor motivation or lack of ability — was raised briefly, most vocal participants felt that providing a maximum educational opportunity for a wide range of people remained one of the most important goals of colleges and universities. Providing this opportunity was regarded as an essential part of the democratic process. Stating his own concept of the role of higher education, one representative from a private institution suggested that "the colleges are perhaps the most important part of the democratic process, and if the private universities do not take a significant role in this effort — I do not care how they do it, whether by keeping tuitions low or by organizing a talent-hunting effort and a reassurance effort — we are just separating ourselves from the democratic process, and this is going in a fatal direction. We cannot do it, and we will not do it as long as we maintain our image as a part of the democratic process. This is the heart of our role in society, and if we have a sense of separating ourselves from it, then we really hobble ourselves in trying to arrive at a realistic pricing policy."

While there is a risk in emphasizing the sheer quantitative aspects of higher education, and while one participant's observation that never before in history has a community carried so many of its people so far educationally as in the United States today is perfectly true, there still remains a large number of very able youngsters who never get to college. One estimate has placed the loss at 100,000 a year. Some of these people, of course, would not want to go to college under any circumstances; but with others there are artificial financial or motivational barriers which can be removed with some organized effort — better scholarships, better information about those that exist, better guidance. Several members pointed out that the National Merit Scholarships have done a great deal in alerting the brightest students to the possibilities of college. The losses are not uniformly spread among high-school students. They are much higher among girls than among boys. If a family has several children to educate and cannot afford to educate them all, daughters are usually sacrificed in favor of sons. Some marry upon leaving high school and never enter college. As a rule, those in rural areas are not so well informed about the possibilities and advantages of college as those in towns and cities.

The opportunity to go to college at low tuition has perhaps been very important in the past in getting this group of people interested in college, and some think it is still the most effective way. For the middle range of student, not the brightest, but those in the second echelon, who are not able to win scholarships but are still able to profit a great deal from college, low tuition has been the substitute for scholarship aid. "Many college presidents are not only concerned about the very able, but they are worried about the not-quite-so-able, the great mass of people who must carry the work of the world. These are the people who do not get consideration for scholarships at prestige institutions and these are the people who may not be motivated to go to college. But a large number of these people we have got to get educated, if we are going to do the work of the world in a satisfactory fashion."

Children from wealthy families can go to college anyway, but most private schools do not live up to their own self-image if they concentrate on providing a "Cadillac type of education." It is always possible for the prestige institutions to fill their halls with a homogeneous group of wealthy students, but if they do only that they are failing, in a way in which the land-grant universities are succeeding, to participate in the democratic process. Several members felt that it was most important that private institutions provide something more than a sequestered upper-class education.

These problems are related. Too often recruitment officers from the colleges and universities focus their attention competitively on a relatively few outstanding suburban and urban high schools in the United States, so that this natural medium for spreading information about college and scholarships fails to reach, or reaches only in diluted form, many of the high schools, particularly those in dense urban areas and in rural areas. Some schools are visited from representatives of hundreds of colleges, while others get only a few. Furthermore, a representative of a private college finds himself in an awkward position when he does visit a school attended largely by students from poor families. Inevitably the first question is "How much will it cost?" The answer must be — say — $2600 a year for tuition, board, and room. The long explanation about scholarships, jobs, and loans somehow fails of its purpose after this sum is mentioned; $2600 is $2600, and it may amount to more than half the family's income. It is here that the low tuition fees of state institutions perhaps have their greatest effect, not so much in providing real possibilities, but in shaping expectations.

The danger that these groups of potential students will not be reached will perhaps increase in the future, as the bulge of students reduces the difficulty of filling college halls and the admissions officers may be tempted to sit back and relax for a change. Ironically, the one group of students receiving abundant attention from the colleges, regardless of the high school they attended, are the athletes. A potential football star is fully alerted to the advantages of going to college.

Several members felt that colleges and universities had an important but partly neglected role in advertising their services, and that much could be done if they ceased to compete with one another for the same middle-class, college-oriented suburban students and inaugurated a cooperative program for reaching as many able students as possible. No university is wealthy enough to undertake an extensive program alone, but together the colleges could accomplish much, at little cost to each.

The difficulties with any feasible program are manifest. If the present officials of the colleges were used in a great joint effort, in a vast division of labor to inform adequately the high schools of the country, many of these officials would feel that they could not be trusted to impart a completely impartial picture of the spectrum of colleges, but rather would tend to direct really promising students to their own institutions. Second, it is increasingly evident that reaching deprived groups in the junior or senior year of high school is not sufficient; college aspiration goes back to junior high school, and any program would have to work at that level to have the desired effect. In order to plan their high-school programs accordingly, students must think in terms of college no later than the ninth grade; after that it is difficult to switch into the college-oriented courses.

Several past efforts at cooperation among colleges have foundered on the rocks of competition and misunderstanding. A few years ago the College Scholarship Service tried to compile a comprehensive scholarship handbook, giving a lot of information about the practices of individual institutions, but this was met with resistance at every turn. Colleges felt that too much information was required and that it would result in misinterpretation. They apparently failed to realize that too little information is equally subject to misinterpretation.

A recent effort to arrive at a common statement on ideal scholarship practices, quite general and not representing the actual practices of any institution, was thwarted by minor disagreements among the participating colleges. So cooperation is often easier to talk about than to achieve.

Still another problem in making college availability known is the "positive feedback" — making it generally known that a problem exists will tend only to aggravate the problem, not to eliminate it. For this reason colleges are very reluctant to advertise vacancies, since the very fact that a school has vacancies seems to make the school appear less desirable to prospective students.

One proposal for alerting colleges to the existence of bright students, wherever they happen to be, is the administration by the College Board of a nationwide test to fourteen- and fifteen-year-olds, making the names of the scorers in the top 20 per cent available to all member colleges, so that they would know where to seek these youngsters. The list would be limited, since it is not to be an instrument of acceptance or rejection, but one of identification.

Another program for developing interest in college, one that is actually under way, is an intensive campaign by educators and social workers in some of the deprived high schools, an attempt to motivate students in grades seven to nine and uplift them culturally with close personal guidance, trips to museums, and so on. This approach is a very expensive one, however, and it is still too early to determine how effective it is.

There is a question of how to use the limited resources available to higher education most effectively in widening educational opportunity. Several participants felt that diverting a large portion of government funds which now go to maintaining low tuition at the state universities into extensive scholarship programs, and raising the tuition at these universities, would be much more efficacious than the existing arrangements. And they insisted that allowing private colleges to close because of financial difficulties would serve only to narrow, not to widen, educational opportunity in the country.

An Extensive Loan Scheme

For many members the most attractive proposal for easing the financial difficulties of the colleges and at the same time maintaining and even widening the opportunity for all able students to acquire an education beyond high school was an extensive program of loans to students, for which their education would be the only collateral required. Apart from allowing colleges to raise tuition with a freer conscience, three advantages of loans were cited. In the first place, loans for education increase the number of people for whom higher education is available. Despite the low tuition fees today in many state universities, the costs of attending college are prohibitive to some. Liberal loans will eliminate this financial barrier. Furthermore, loans for education are recognition that an education, however intangible, is an important asset.

Second, in an economy in which credit oils the flow of goods and services, higher education, in the absence of extensive credit, will fail to claim its share of the national output. With so many sectors of the economy offering goods for funds which may be paid in the future, higher education will find itself claiming a smaller portion of the consumer's dollar than it should unless it, too, offers credit terms. How else can college compete effectively with next year's model?

Finally, in an inflationary era, those who buy goods or services on credit gain at the expense of those who defer purchases until enough cash is saved. Loan repayments are made with dollars that have lower purchasing power. Higher education can increase its share of the national output (which all participants agreed was now too low) by borrowing now, repaying later. It is important that the funds loaned to students should not come from the colleges themselves; only in this way can the burden of education be transferred to the real beneficiary: the whole community.

Several suggestions were made for improvements in the new federal program under the National Defense Education Act, discussed in the paper by Mr. Coombs. The government could offer its guarantee to educational loans made with private funds, thus helping to bring in private enterprise to boost higher education, at little cost to the government and great benefit to education. Second, students could be aided still further by making the repayment of principal of educational loans, as well as the interest payment, tax deductible. This would still further reduce the sting of higher tuition since the government would be picking up a portion of the bill. Several participants felt that it was desirable to have no financial-means test, so that loans would be available to any student who wanted them. The Education Act has passed this problem on to the colleges, which must administer the loans, but it was pointed out that the scholarship provisions of the act (partially waiving repayments by teachers) necessitated some sort of means test. So would any loan for which the interest rate was subsidized.

The most notable loan program operated by a university is that at the Massachusetts Institute of Technology. This program has been run since the early 1930's; at present 38 per cent of the undergraduates and 90 per cent of the graduates receive aid of some kind. For every dollar given in scholarships, two dollars are given in loans. The maximum loan to any student is $5000 for a four-year course and $6000 for a five-year course. The terms of the loans are very generous, with 1 per cent interest while the student is still in college and 2 per cent thereafter; repayments are $300 a year. The program has been remarkably successful, with repayments on time amounting to over 99 per cent.

Despite such success at M.I.T., several members felt that there were serious objections to a really vast, nation-wide loan program. One person felt that the American public was not yet prepared to buy through credit such an intangible good as education. He insisted that urban American society rested on a cash-and-carry basis except for durable goods which could be amortized over time, like cars. But what evidence we have suggests that students *are* willing to borrow for an education if the loan program is liberal. The M.I.T. experience bears this out, and so does that of the few other schools which operate large loan programs. In just a few months the New York Higher Education Assistance Corporation loaned $2 million, and at rather unfavorable terms of interest.

A second objection to extensive reliance on loans to undergraduates is that the burden of debt at graduation may inhibit students from going on to graduate school, especially if they have to borrow still more to carry themselves through two or three more years of school. They may be anxious about paying off the debt. In this connection, one participant suggested that this burden of debt may also affect occupational choices, students being attracted into the most lucrative vocations in order to pay off their investment as quickly as possible. In that case the poorly paid vocations, such as teaching and social service, may suffer severely.

Finally, it is not at all certain that liberal loans will in fact provide the educational opportunity which is claimed for them. As one participant put it, "The scholarship device, which is a very ancient device, has not solved this problem of the open door to education half as well as the low-tuition device, and the loan device, which is almost untested anywhere, is a very slender reed to rely on when you are monkeying with a process as important as this. I don't blame the public educators for being angry. They feel that they are guarding an important element in the American democratic society, and I think that we ought to sense that."

Another participant felt that a distinction had to be made between selling a loan program to the country and to parents, and administering individual debts. For the former it is necessary and legitimate to use many "gimmicks," to talk about how important credit is in the economy today, how small a proportion an educational loan will be of one's total life income, and so on. But when it comes to making an individual loan, the self-confidence of the student is very important. If he feels that he will be a successful lawyer and nobody can shake his faith in this, then a loan is not likely to affect his course adversely. If he wants to relieve his family of the burden, the loan will probably not hurt him.

"But it is dangerous to use gimmicks with the student who is frightened, to say to him, 'Well, kid, you are going to borrow $10,000 to buy a house in a few years, and $2000 to buy a car, and why don't you get a little more in debt before you get there?'" said one participant. If discretion is used in administering the loan program, however, credit can contribute in an important way toward solving the financial problems of colleges and students alike, this member thought.

Composition of Student Enrollment

One of the most worrisome problems for some college administrators, touched on above, is maintaining diversity in the student body. Many colleges regard themselves as national institutions, and to support this claim seek a wide geographical distribution of students. In New England, a student from Nevada may be given preference to one from New Jersey. At one time geographical diversity in the student group assured diversity of character, but with the growth of a national suburban culture this is no longer so. The traditional technique for achieving an educational "melting pot" fails to do the job in an era in which the difference in character between Shaker Heights and Pasadena is not nearly so great as the 2500 miles which separates them would suggest. "Farm boys are getting to be at a premium because the number of farmers in the country is decreasing so rapidly. It is going to be desperately difficult to find farm boys twenty years from now, but maybe some farm boys add more to your mixture than boys from Hawaii."

Several members suggested that seeking a distribution among social and economic classes might result in a better composition these days than a geographical distribution does. This gets right back to the problem of recruiting from high schools in slum areas. One participant felt that more diversity was needed with regard to the future of the students rather than their past — diversity in where they will live and what they will do for a living. This would assure the variety of interests among the student body which the colleges seek, and which is such an important part of the educational process at some institutions. But except for premedical students, it is very difficult to predict what a student's future occupational course will be.

Heavy emphasis on standard aptitude examinations may also serve to limit the variety in social background of students. Furthermore, one member felt that these examinations, and high school records for that matter, fail to catch the really creative, imaginative, offbeat individual who in the future will perhaps make real contributions to some field, whether it be art or music, mathematics or law. Unfortunately, examinations for detecting that sort of talent have not yet been perfected.

In terms of expanding the educational horizons of a student through a diversified student body, one participant pointed out that the state universities are the most parochial. Tuition for out-of-state residents is often quite high, comparable to that of some private colleges, and nonresidents are thus discouraged from attending. To the extent that geographical diversity is important, students at these schools are cut off from an important experience. On the other hand, state universities find it difficult enough to justify expenditures of tax revenue for residents of their own state, much less for out-of-state residents. The University of Massachusetts has more applications from within the state than it can accommodate. Still, for an institution like the University of Vermont out-of-state residents may be quite important, since there are not enough Vermonters to make operation of some of the schools economical. Last year the medical school had almost as many students from Massachusetts as from Vermont. One participant suggested that the best thing many state institutions could do would be to swap a thousand students with some other state university across the country. That way the legislators would have less to complain about, and the students would gain.

Several participants agreed that the role of the large urban universities is different from those which attempt to achieve national representation. They provide educational opportunity where it is most needed, in the dense population centers where students can commute from home and thus save on room and board. And in the next ten years, with the great growth in demand for a college education, the role of these schools in the total American system of higher education will become even more important. President Case pointed out, however, that it is no longer accurate to regard urban universities solely as street-car colleges. Thirty-eight per cent of the students at Boston University are in residence, and while applications for admission from the Boston area are increasing at an arithmetical rate, those from outside are increasing geometrically. This seems to be true across the nation. There is no clear interpretation of this trend, but it may mean that families are becoming sufficiently well-off to send their children away to school, and the students are becoming increasingly aware of the horizons that exist away from home. This trend itself diversifies the student body of urban institutions.

In connection with diversification in the student body, the question of size arose. If a college is too large, it is easy to achieve great variety, but the benefits of heterogeneity may not accrue to most students because homogeneous groups among the students are large enough so that students from varied backgrounds do not need to mix. The advantage of a small college is that everyone can know everyone else. On the other hand, small colleges are much less economical to operate than large ones, so one must pay the price of intimacy. Too often, one participant felt, college administrators fail to realize what costs are involved in adhering to some educational policy. The educational values must be weighed against the economic costs. Nevertheless, the small colleges have sent forth a remarkable number of distinguished persons in the past.

Several members raised the question whether most small colleges will continue to attract bright students in competition with the high-pressure campaigning now done by the bigger universities. With countless admissions officers junketing about the country making attractive offers, geographic isolation will no longer work in favor of the small colleges scattered throughout the land. This contributes to the "pull-apart" process which more and more is separating colleges and universities in quality. Certain schools acquire a reputation for quality, and therefore the most able students and faculty members seek to go there, thus justifying the reputation. Several participants thought this a most unfortunate trend; what is needed is more, not fewer, first-rate schools. In many instances applying students seem to judge the institution by the tuition it charges: if the fees are high, the school must be good. It will be very unfortunate if many formerly eminent schools are forced into an intellectual backwash by this process, and are compelled to take a secondary role in the educational world. In effect, the problem of many institutions now trying to improve their quality is to "change leagues" somehow, to develop a reputation for being good. Ironically, higher tuition may be a way of doing this. Regrettably there has thus far been developed no satisfactory method for judging a college's educational quality. Standard accreditation procedures rely on inputs rather than outputs — on the endowment per student, the percentage of the faculty with doctorates, the number of books in the library. Thus it is possible for a really fine educational job to go unnoticed, and in the process of being unnoticed it is likely to become less fine.

Competition Among Institutions of Higher Learning

Underlying many of the financial problems of colleges and universities, and the difficulty of arriving at a satisfactory tuition policy, is the competition — and the differences in position and viewpoint — between private and public institutions. The private colleges fear that tax-supported, low-tuition state institutions may eventually run them into bankruptcy; the public universities are anxious about the ability of private schools to draw the best students with attractive scholarship offerings, leaving to them the obligation of low quality, "mass" education. Put in its strongest form, there is an element of war between the two groups. One participant described his conversation with the president of a midwestern university which was soliciting large endowment funds, pointing out that this made it difficult for the private colleges. "Tell them to quit getting us to raise our tuition, and we will lay off the endowment business," was the reply.

In fact, of course, each college or university is on a spectrum of competition with many others. Boston University competes with the other colleges in Boston for its commuter students, with the University of Massachusetts for some of its resident students, with Dartmouth for some of its wealthier students, and so on. But in many cases it is the close competition with a low-tuition public institution which contributes most to the financial strain. With a low-tuition school in the vicinity, a private college hesitates to raise tuition in order to meet higher costs, since it may thereby lose many of its students. New York University and Columbia compete for some of their students with low-cost C.C.N.Y. Boston University, because there is no public university in the Boston metropolitan area, does not have these problems and is able, along with the other urban schools, to provide a valuable public service in offering a college education to the burgeoning numbers in urban areas.

Many private colleges feel that they *must* raise tuition in order at the same time to provide a high quality education and remain financially solvent. Advocates of higher tuition feel that most people are now able to pay more, and that the public colleges, too, should raise their tuition fees, providing to the really indigent larger scholarships than they now do. But, as the earlier discussion revealed, many educators feel that low tuition is a most important feature of educational opportunity; whether or not people can really afford higher tuition, they may be frightened away by a large dollar figure. Furthermore, many public institutions fear that higher tuition coupled with extensive loans or scholarships will remove the principal advantage which they have over private colleges: the low cost to the student. Both students and faculty members might be attracted to the more prestigious private universities, leaving the public institutions to become second-rate schools. Clearly this would be an undesirable result, both from their viewpoint and that of the entire system of higher education. It was noted that this problem would be more severe in some parts of the country than in others; in some places the public universities are the prestigious ones, and private colleges find difficulty in attracting high-quality faculties.

Another sentiment which governs the view of public educators on raising tuition is that yielding on this issue would aid private colleges and universities without giving them any attendant responsibilities. At present, public institutions have the obligation not only to try to provide education at low cost, which is frequently more a noble aim than a realization, but also to provide space for any qualified applicant who wishes to go to college. They must absorb all those students who are not accepted by the private colleges and universities. There is a strong feeling that private institutions should contribute more than they have been in meeting the national need to provide places for a vastly increased number of students. The same sentiment has been voiced on a smaller scale within individual states: if private institutions are to enjoy exemption from state and local taxes, should they not admit a larger number of students from that state, instead of fishing all over the country for applicants?

Finally, there is still in some quarters an objection to giving public funds in any form to private institutions. This objection is partly related to the fact that, formally, the private schools do not take on public responsibilities, although of course many of them provide valuable public service. Yet in practice this resistance seems to be breaking down. Seventy-five per cent of the scholarship funds appropriated in Massachusetts must go to students attending private colleges; and the scholarship programs in New York, Illinois, and California are all designed to help fill the halls of private colleges. It is a more economical use of public funds to spend $600 on a scholarship to a student in a private college than $1500 on the operating costs and new university facilities required to accommodate that student.

Several participants emphasized that aiding private institutions might in fact be the most effective use of public funds, in terms of providing educational opportunity. Charging those who can afford to pay and providing adequate scholarships for those who cannot is one example of this. Furthermore, considerable plant already exists, and there would be much social waste in expanding public facilities, including the erection of new buildings, while leaving some private colleges half empty. Nonetheless, one participant in favor of higher tuition felt that the preservation of private institutions was not in itself sufficient justification. He insisted that private colleges, if they are to make a real contribution to higher education in the country, must offer a sufficiently differentiated product to attract students despite their higher charges. If these schools offer nothing special, what is the point of going to them?

Summary

At the heart of the financial problems of colleges is the relationship between the level of tuition income and the composition of the student body. From this question too stem many of the differences between representatives of public and private institutions. Higher tuition is certainly one important way of lessening the financial plight of colleges and enabling them to meet the growing demand for college education without a deterioration in quality. Some point out that Americans today can well afford higher tuition, especially if means are devised for spreading the cost over a period of time. Others insist that higher tuition would reduce materially the desire and ability of many able youngsters to attend college, and that the important role which higher education plays in our democratic society would be substantially impaired.

Narrower interests of the parties concerned also play their role in the continuing debate, but it is certainly likely that the nature of higher education in the United States will be materially affected by the outcome.

A COLLEGE ADMINISTRATOR VIEWS THE TUITION PROBLEM

Barnaby C. Keeney

THESE remarks will be based upon considerable thought and study of the problem of financing higher education and, in particular, of increasing the part of the cost of higher education paid by the student. I shall ask questions that are of concern to me and other college and university presidents rather than solve problems in economics, but I devoutly hope that some of these latter problems will be solved by the economists contributing to this symposium.

Several groups of college presidents have given serious attention to a discussion of tuition costs during the past year. There is at present rather general conviction among the presidents of privately supported institutions that massive sums of money must be made available for the continuation and improvement of privately supported education. Generally speaking, they do not feel that philanthropy can provide all this money quickly enough for it to be effective in time. Some, therefore, would turn to the government for subsidy; others, however, feel that it would be more desirable to place a greater part of the cost of education upon the students and simultaneously to redouble efforts to raise current and capital funds.

This conference is largely confined to people from the Northeast,[1] although, of course, many of us are in fairly close touch with the thinking of educators in other parts of the country. The situation here is quite different from that in the Middle West, for example, where the state institutions are considered to be on an equal footing educationally with the best and largest privately supported institutions, and superior to most. The Western presidents and governors of the privately supported institutions are far more nervous about the results of a massive increase in tuition costs than are their colleagues in the East. Furthermore, they are tempted to base their case for increase on an argument that privately supported institutions are inherently better because they are private, but they are deterred from saying so because of fear of retaliation. Easterners are inclined to leave this point unstated, and to base their case on the need for improvement.

The question of increased tuition is now before the public and must be considered from the point of view of public reaction as well as of private analysis.

I feel that we must take these steps. First, establish a formula for calculating the actual present cost of education per student to privately supported colleges and universities and to their public counterparts and the relation between this cost and tuition. Establish the relationship between cost and quality, if there is one. A host of questions arises. First, what shall be included in cost? For example, should the money an institution spends on scholarships be considered in computing the cost of education in that institution or should this be separate? Should the expenditure for research, sponsored or otherwise, be included in calculating cost? Should the operation of athletics be included in cost? If all these things are to be included — and I think perhaps they should be — the justification for their inclusion must be based upon the argument that each is an essential part of education, and the argument will not be easy to construct. Should the cost of buildings and their amortization and maintenance be included in the cost of education or should they be considered as the result of philanthropic contributions?

Second, estimate what the cost would be if the institution were as good as it should be and if its faculty were compensated as it should be. How much of this increased cost must be carried by tuition and how much by income from endowment, current philanthropy, and other sources? The answer to this question is a most important part of our case.

We must then present the case for increasing

---

[1] This was not nearly so true of the 1958–59 seminar as of our meeting earlier in 1958, at which the Keeney, Kaysen, and Eckstein papers were presented (Ed.).

tuition, if we decide to increase it, not as a business move justified by the cost of production and price to the consumer, but as the result of the need for improvement of education in this country and, particularly, the need to compensate faculties at such levels that the most able people will be drawn to the faculties of colleges and universities. If we base our case upon the cost of education, we shall immediately be met by a variety of arguments, some of which will be good and all of which will be embarrassing. Why should a freshman in the liberal arts be charged the same tuition as a graduate student in engineering? Should we not set up differential tuitions for different subjects and levels, as was done in the early nineteenth century? I feel very strongly that we should not, because if we do we shall influence very strongly, and perhaps in a disastrous fashion, the selection of courses of study by students. Other questions will be asked. Why should parents capable of paying subsidize the children of other parents who are not capable of paying? Why should anyone give money to a college or university if it is operating on a cost basis? Will the tax exemption of the institution be affected? Probably not. How can the argument for charging at cost be carried on if every increase in income is used to produce greater expenditure, particularly for salaries, so that the cost rises with every increase in tuition and approximately the same gap between cost and tuition remains at the end of the process as at the beginning? The proper procedure, on the contrary, is to determine what the salary schedule and other expenditures should be ten years from now, determine how much of that amount can be borne by income other than tuition, and proceed to raise tuition to a figure which will enable us to do what we should. This figure will probably lie about halfway between actual present tuition and the projected future cost of education per student.

The reaction of the consumers to the preliminary efforts in this direction has been most encouraging. Most colleges that have fearfully increased tuition during the past two years have expected a spate of angry letters, withdrawals, and cancellations of applications for admission. This has not happened on any large scale, for people seem to understand that the cost of education must increase if we are to have the sort of education they desire. We are, moreover, in a period of dual inflation, in which people expect rising prices and in which the potential student body is being grossly inflated. Now is a favorable time to take action.

We are, however, faced with certain problems. There is a deep conviction that education, including higher education, should be free or nearly free, and on this is based the very low tuition in private colleges and the almost negligible tuition in most publicly supported institutions. It is because of this conviction that faculty salaries are at their present low state, so that the whole profession is endangered. On the other hand, it is the habit of the American people to regard things that cost more as better than things that cost less. This may indeed be one of the reasons that the professor does not carry the prestige in our society to which his learning should entitle him. While Americans sing songs on the theme that the best things in life are free, they aspire to buy mink.

Many feel that it would be easier to produce massive increases in tuition through concerted action. The present practice is for educational institutions to watch each other quite carefully and, after one institution takes a bold step in increasing tuition, the others follow it, sometimes exceeding the increase. Concerted action in this situation, I believe, is essential. It must be concerted to the point at which no participating institution withholds information from the others either through arrogance or diffidence.

We are all concerned with the social effects of an increase in tuition of real magnitude. We fear that the privately supported institutions might become schools in which there would be no economic middle class, for an increase in tuition does not present a serious problem to the very rich or even to the well-off. Under present practices of scholarship aid, the main problem for the poor is the need to search aggressively for aid. If tuition were raised, aid to those now receiving it would be increased in one way or another. The real problem would be the economic middle class, which constitutes a high percentage of the college and university population today. I know of no published study indicating the size of the group that would not be well enough off to pay a tuition of — say — $2000 or badly enough off to be eligible for scholarships under present standards. Where is the point at which this group would decide that a low tuition outweighs the advantages of a high-cost "prestige" college?

Various proposals have been made for prepayment and postpayment of tuition. The proposals for prepayment represent a view of life which, I am afraid, is gone from this country, for people no longer save to pay for things before they buy them; they prefer to go into debt to pay for them after they buy them. "A dollar down will buy more than a dollar saved." Although it is clear that the cost of postpayment will be greater to the individual than the cost of prepayment, I expect there will be more postpayments through loans than prepayments through savings. Any prepayment plan must be handled independently of the colleges and universities, for, if a college accepts prepayment, it also accepts an obligation, real or fancied, to admit the student, even though it denies such an obligation at the start. Any college that accepts postpayment involves itself in the problem of collection, but this, I believe, can be handled.

There is a real need to establish a large corporation to make huge sums of money available for loans to students and their families to be repaid either by the students or their parents in the ten years or more after graduation. This plan might be financed by the government or, on the other hand, by foundations. Colleges and universities must develop within their clientele a frame of mind receptive to loans, for the practice of giving money away to finance education has now reached such a point that it cannot well be increased. Some institutions have already made progress in encouraging payment through loans. Nevertheless, scholarship assistance must be increased for those students who have insufficient financial bases to secure loans. It should be done, however, with the acceptance of a moral obligation on the part of the student to repay the scholarship for the use of others if he rises economically to a position where he can do so.

One of the things that is of great concern to private educators, particularly in the Middle West, is the relationship of the state universities and colleges to this whole problem. They are in deadly fear that a doubled tuition will have the principal result that more students will go to the publicly supported institutions and leave the privately supported institutions without a clientele. This is not considered to be a serious problem in the East, but it may well become so with the rapid improvement of publicly supported institutions. Is this view justified? What will happen if the privately supported institutions double tuition and consequently double salaries? The state institutions will be forced to increase their salaries and will, therefore, need a considerably increased income. It may well be that, when the legislators learn the actual cost of running a first-rate institution, they will balk at paying the bill and the voters may influence them to refuse. It is quite possible that tuition will be increased in the public institutions as a result of the increase in the private institutions. Indeed, this is already the case for out-of-state students.

In any discussion of the cost of education the question inevitably arises, why do not the colleges operate more efficiently? Many proposals have been made to reduce the cost of instruction, some of them very good. For a while there was an enchantment with television. Even more economical than television would be the use of the book and a reduction of time spent with the instructor accompanied by an increase in time spent in study. I do not myself believe that the cost of instruction can be much reduced, although the number of man-hours spent on instruction may be.

I now come to my conclusions. This is essentially a problem in public relations, for the success or failure of any effort to increase the income of the colleges and universities by an increase in tuition will depend on the attitude people take toward it. I believe that we must do the following things and in this order.

Collect and interpret the necessary facts.

Ascertain the present cost of education.

Establish the necessary increase in the cost of education to provide the sort of faculty and education that we ought to have.

Create a conviction in the public mind that,

within their means, privately supported institutions balance the budgets of needy students through one means or another and that, in this respect, they are indeed more democratic than those publicly supported institutions where scholarship and loan funds are scanty.

Encourage a willingness on the part of the public to borrow for the education of their children and a willingness on the part of those children to take over the repayment of the loan when they reach an economic level that justifies it.

The times have never been so favorable for a step of this sort, for the concern with education in this country has reached a level that may never again be attained.

IS THE LOW-TUITION PRINCIPLE OUTMODED?[1]

Eldon L. Johnson

AMERICA has always been full of paradoxes. American education is no exception. Now that we have built a nation, a government, an economy, and a culture on equality of opportunity, some among us yearn to abandon the means by which we arrived.

We are arguing some of the fundamentals of public education all over again, particularly as applied to higher education. While some are trying to bring racial barriers down, others are trying to put economic barriers up. While we attribute Soviet successes to the quantity and quality of freely available education, some of us conclude that education fit for the challenge must be not only hard but hard to get. Hence titles appear like "Education Is Too Cheap," "Low Tuition Is Outmoded," and "Let the Beneficiary Pay."

What sometimes seems to be a full-scale campaign is now aimed at discrediting the conventional means of financing public higher education — low tuition, or indeed no tuition at all, with public appropriations to assure both acceptable quality and accessible opportunity. To those of us in public higher education, these attacks are at worst ill-conceived schemes for making somebody else better by making us worse and at best a serious threat to freely available educational opportunity for all young people regardless of economic means. Much has been said and is being said in a spirit of mutual recrimination, bringing discredit to all education in the public mind. Most of the recriminations flow from the frustrations of inadequate finance felt by all kinds of institutions and from desperate solutions based on a partial approach to the total problem.

To Meet Society's Needs

Every individual has a stake in his own education, but society has a stake in everybody's education. Both interests must be served, partly privately and partly publicly. What is good for one institution, with its special and even exemplary objectives, is not necessarily what is good for general application to all institutions, all youth, and all society. Indeed it might leave out most youth and speak with contempt of "social needs."

It should be made clear to avoid misunderstanding, therefore, that this article is written from the point of view of public higher education. It is solely in defense of a principle essential for such education with its broad, equalitarian obligations imposed by the public. Nothing said here is in derogation of any other kind of education, either its methods of financing or its social contributions. Society gains not only from institutions with fixed public obligations but also from institutions which are selective, which combine high cost with high quality, and which are restrictive in purpose.

The contention here is that in a democratic society with diverse institutions, the generally accepted social ideals will not be fully met without the preservation of low-cost public education. The shocking thing is not that somebody will defend this principle, but that anybody needs to. If anyone wants to see how far we have wandered from the founding philosophy, which James Bryce long ago recorded with some distrust, let him observe expressions when he suggests that instruction should be tuition-free.

The low-tuition principle is not outmoded in the sense of having failed. Its purpose has been that of giving educational opportunity to all according to their talents and in step with the needs of society. Like all ideals, this one has not been fully realized, but its approximation has yielded both opportunities and socially significant results which no other country can equal. The Soviet Union is on its way, with its characteristic taunts about passing us by.

Whoever contends the low-tuition principle is outmoded is taking on a heavy burden of proof if he holds its historical results have been bad, or that it would have been better not to educate so many on such favorable economic terms. Surely no one who looks at the relation

[1] This is the essence of a paper presented at the seminar and published in the *College Board Review*, Spring, 1959. The paper was meant to be a reply to the Editor's views on financing higher education.

between low-tuition opportunities and the rising proportion of youth who became college educated, or at the tremendous contribution of low-tuition education to the nation's supply of scholars and specialists, even through the Ph.D. level, can think the principle has failed. It has failed neither by quantitative nor qualitative standards.

It is true, however, that the low-tuition principle has provided a quantitative as well as a qualitative factor which, for all the criticism, is now envied and emulated abroad wherever the forces of democratization are at work. The less-developed and underdeveloped countries know what we once learned but now tend to forget — that trained manpower at intermediate levels, to say nothing of trained intelligence for citizenship, is indispensable and that attention to the requirements of scholarship does not preclude attention to the needs of society.

Broad Opportunity Ignored

The low-tuition principle is not outmoded by the discovery of any alternative which will widen rather than restrict educational opportunity. The alternatives suggested are more concerned with who pays the bill than with what the bill is for, not whether more or less and not whether public welfare or private gain. The objective is far more likely to be institutional aid than student opportunity. The net effect on the supply of trained intelligence for the nation is almost never explored, but the result can be surmised when one considers that an economic elite will pay the full costs, an intellectual elite will earn scholarships, and the educable masses, seeking loans, will be indentured for many years. How this is to open new educational vistas either for society or for the individual is obscure. The existing low-tuition principle already provides, as President James L. Morrill of the University of Minnesota has pointed out, "the most generous scholarship-assistance program of any nation in the world."

All that can be said for the high-tuition principle for those institutions publicly responsible for broadening and equalizing educational opportunity is that it will raise money. Except as a substitute for support from the public which imposed the social obligation, nothing can be said for high tuition. There is no philosophical defense, whatever the practical economic temptations. If there is virtue in making the student bear part of the cost as one of the beneficiaries, remember the major costs which are left even after tuition is wiped out. If there is some manly recompense which must be preserved by student sacrifice made painfully conscious, then self-support should replace parental subsidy — and for everybody. This is more egalitarian than that which the critics are seeking to escape. Surely no one would contend, despite some current utterances seemingly to the contrary, that what the poor boy learns by hard work the more fortunate boy can learn by the excruciating knowledge that his father paid the bill.

The low-tuition principle is not outmoded by some new means test which allegedly will do more for society. This scheme is indeed splendid for some institutions in a pluralistic democratic society, but it would be much less than that kind of society if all public institutions adopted it too. *Somewhere* in a democracy, education ought to be available to the full extent of talents without artificial barriers of any kind — no more economic barriers than racial or religious barriers. This is the eminently proper place where the rich boy and poor boy should be stripped down to equality, deliberately made evident to both, with no superiority gained by the former in carrying a poor boy on his back and no stigma borne by the latter in having to receive public payment proportioned to his poverty. There are some things money can't buy. Is this tenet of an open society outmoded?

The low-tuition principle is not outmoded by the much-publicized system proposed by Seymour E. Harris, professor of political economy at Harvard University — the system of educational installment buying, "learn now, pay later," with its appalling consequences. Education is treated as a consumer commodity which everybody steps to the counter to buy according to his means. Each gets education for what education gets him! A new kind of indentured service is established in which the poor pay for 20 years (or indeed 40) while the better-off start life debt-free.

Would Bolster Class Lines

The process which acts to distinguish man from the beasts is reduced to the terms of the market place. Whoever can pay the investment in his own future will have a future. Whoever can't will be offered a mortgaged future. Whoever won't, society doesn't care. This is "un-American" in James Bryce's sense of the word. Apparently he used it only once in *The American Commonwealth*: to describe that which preserves and fosters class distinctions. This is the social price we find on the back of the new "bargain" tag.

The low-tuition principle is not outmoded by public inability to bear the burden, although this is usually taken for granted without examination. As implied above, unless such inability can be shown, the case for high tuition is lost because its sole purpose is to raise money. To assume that the richest nation in the world cannot pay its public education bills takes a dim view of public intelligence and public sacrifice as compared with our Communist competitors and also gives education an indefensibly low priority for public support.

One example will suffice. When we consider that the several states put into their land-grant universities an average of more than four dollars for every dollar contributed by students, but that some states put in less than two dollars in comparison, while others put in as high as 20, increased public support in most of our states seems to be neither unbearable nor unprecedented, leaving federal ability entirely out of account for the moment. But more than that, who are we in higher education — or at least some among us — to be going around persuading people that they can put more in highways, bombs, armies, and subsidies, but that *education* is something they can't afford?

Conviction, Not Money, Lacking

Taxes are a very ancient device. They are hardly outmoded. Only by assuming that they are outmoded or that they are inherently regressive can anyone get an emotional charge, as he is supposed to, out of Professor Harris' statement that the poor man is paying for the education of the rich boy. Let the man step forward who wants to explain where the public, in this kind of a world, can better put its money than on education. The problem is not lack of dollars but lack of conviction. Whoever undermines the conviction takes money from all education, and through all sources.

The low-tuition principle is not outmoded by any diminution of the public's stake in public education. Low tuition is predicated on society's gains as well as the individual's. Who would say this dependence is less than before — or outmoded? Is this our answer to Sputnik? To get more specialized manpower, to say nothing of thinking citizens, are we to put turnstiles on the classrooms?

Economic studies show that education does not get priced anywhere by the normal economic laws; charges are not based on costs. Why is this? The "why" tells us something of the special nature of this function. It is in large part social, like national security. There can be no escaping the fact that some significant part of it is in the public domain. How else do high-tuition advocates now justify their usual concession that no student, even if his father could *buy* the college, should pay the full costs of his education? It is tacitly recognized that somebody else must pay because somebody else benefits. Endowment income is accepted as a subsidy, as is *some* public appropriation. The mystery is why an increase in endowment is good but an increase in appropriation bad.

The folly of turning our backs on the public's stake in education for some self-serving, capacity-to-pay principle is shown in current developments in graduate education. Here is surely where the student can pay his way, and ought to if he is ever to do so. But here is also precisely where public subsidies are being heaped on, as in the new National Defense Education Act (and, incidentally, without any outcry from outraged institutional beneficiaries). Why? Because society so desperately needs this kind of manpower. *Society* needs it; society will pay for it. In other words, the ability of a young man to earn $200,000 more by going to college does not prove that he should pay the bill personally; rather it suggests that society cannot remain indifferent to whether his potentiality will be converted into services worth that amount.

In summary, the low-tuition principle is outmoded only for persons who have never been able to embrace the equalitarian ideals and social gains of public higher education. Next to the teacher shortage, the greatest danger to the quality of education in the publicly supported college or university is the effort to combine a democratic devotion to numbers with an economic determination of quality. This meets the standard of "most" but not the standard of "best." The public university can be happy with its two worlds of quantity and quality, but not if it has to take the worst of both worlds. To force on it the obligations of a public institution and the economics of a private institution is to foredoom it to a second-class status.

So unfortunately, a minor but exasperating task for the public educator nowadays is defending his institution against those who would remake it in the image of their own experience. That such a change is in the interest of American youth as a whole has by no means been proved. Would they have *broader* opportunity? Would they have *fewer* obstacles to the development of their talents? Would their accident of parentage and economic status mean *less* rather than more? Would society have *more* trained intelligence and specialized manpower? The answers are disturbingly clear.

Fortunately for the nation, some institutions can meet their responsibilities without low tuition, and some can stick to superb quality *whatever* the tuition. Others, charged with inescapable public obligations under a particular level of public support, must strike a workable balance between the desire to push quality up and to keep tuition down, with ready student access to educational opportunities as the determining factor. Many gradations fall in between. Those educators who are vaguely of the impression that the abandonment of low tuition would somehow solve *their* problem should stop to ask whether it would also solve society's problem.

If we really believe what we keep saying, that America is stronger because of its diversity of collegiate institutions, some publicly supported and some privately endowed, some operated on low tuition and some not, then why not stop trying to make them alike?

HIGHER FEES AND THE POSITION OF PRIVATE INSTITUTIONS

John F. Morse

ALTHOUGH I have agreed with much that has been said here, I have had a feeling that possibly the group participating in this seminar is just a bit too homogeneous to have a thoroughly realistic view of some things that are going on a little to the west.

I do not know of many institutions which I think have made greater strides than my own in the past ten years. It has been through — is in — a dynamic period in its history, with tremendous growth in size coupled with great improvement in the caliber of its student body, despite a very sharp increase in its fees. At the moment, we seem to be in fine shape. Yet, as we look into the future, we are faced with a genuine dilemma.

On the one hand, even this year we are operating on a red budget. So we simply must raise our fees again. At lunch today I was discussing with a dean the faculty promotion schedule at his institution. I asked, "Suppose you had an outstanding young economist — really good, one you knew was going to do important things — and he wasn't due for promotion for some time, and someone else tried to get him away from you. What would you do?"

And the reply was, "Why, I'd say, 'God bless you. Go ahead.'" Now this is possible because at this particular institution the faculty bench is so deep that if they lose one good man, they have two or three others right behind to fill in.

But at most institutions there is no bench at all. The first team may be first-rate. I think there are many men in my own institution who are just that. But we can't afford to lose any of them. Faculty salaries are, therefore, almost more important for us than for other institutions. Since our endowment and gift income cannot possibly rise as fast as our expenses, we have had to be ingenious in many ways. We have stretched small numbers of dollars to do remarkable things. In the end, however, it is largely through fees that we must finance ourselves.

And now we come to the other horn of the dilemma. I have a feeling that we have reached that point when, not gradually, but overnight, we may well drive away the very students we must have if we are to do a job of the quality we have to do. I might go back to my bench simile for a moment. Most colleges represented here have very deep benches in terms of applicants for admission. But I think we and one other engineering school in New York State were the only two able to fill their freshman classes this past fall. One other could have filled its ranks if it had been willing to reduce quality, but it chose to run a hundred short, as it has for some years, rather than do that. This institution is a university, so that its other schools can take up the slack. For us such a shortage of students would mean a terrific financial beating. We could take it for a year or two — in fact we did, back in 1951 and 1952 — rather than reduce the quality of our student body, but if the situation continued, we would have to decide between the quick death of insolvency or the slow death of declining quality.

The problem I am discussing faces, I think, the huge majority of private institutions in this country, and not solely or even chiefly engineering colleges. In fact, it rather amuses me sometimes when groups of institutions which think of themselves as homogeneous because of their antiquity or their common purposes or their relatively equal athletic prowess or their propinquity get together. They give the impression that in this admissions business they are all in the same boat. They all have so many magnificent applicants that they just don't know how to select from among their riches. Yet almost invariably in such groups there are those whose chief claim to selectivity is that the large number of applicants rejected are even poorer college material than the bottom quarter of those admitted. One has only to look at the range of test scores of admitted students as it is published by the College Entrance Examination Board to verify this.

I should say that there are not more than

twenty-five to fifty private institutions in the country which are embarrassed by an oversupply of outstanding candidates. I know I will be told that there are more than that in New England alone. There will be much talk of waiting lists, four applicants for every place, pressures from alumni, and all the rest of the paraphernalia of an admissions shop. All of it will be true, for what will look like an adequate candidate to one institution will be hopelessly unable to make the grade at another. But most admissions officers, if they will be ruthlessly honest with themselves, will admit that a sizable percentage of every freshman class has been accepted largely to meet a quota, and because there were no better candidates available. My contention is that the chief reason for all this is an economic one. Too many good potential candidates will settle — perhaps even must settle — for their second choice, because it is a less expensive institution.

Theoretically, we are in a favored position in New York State because there is no inexpensive state university. We do not have to run into that kind of competition. Nevertheless, in New York State, we really do, because there is no area from which we draw where the student cannot attend college for far less money, first in terms of tuition fees and second in terms of being able to live at home. Furthermore, we draw roughly 50 per cent of our students from states where there are large state universities, and another sizable percentage from areas like the Niagara frontier, which is almost as close to places like Purdue or the University of Michigan as it is to us.

What I fear may happen is that if we raise our tuition, we may put ourselves suddenly, overnight, in the position that many institutions are in right now — an inability to fill our freshman class, or an ability to fill it only by dropping the scholastic requirements of the student we admit. It would be ironical indeed to raise fees in order to hold on to able faculty and at the same time drive away the students that that faculty ought to be teaching. This is the dilemma I have been talking about.

This problem, I think, has not been sufficiently considered in these deliberations. It has been touched once in a while, but never really bitten into. The other participants talk about the percentage of rise in tuition fees and show that it hasn't gone up as fast as the national income. They show that fees at public institutions have gone up faster than those in private institutions. But percentages are misleading. The dollar gap between costs at public and private institutions grows greater every year. And the dollar gap is the really significant figure.

So to tell institutions, good solid institutions, that the solution to most of their problems is to raise their fees, to charge closer to actual costs, and to use long-term loans to finance needy students is to ignore entirely the competitive situation. It is no solution for an institution that is already finding it impossible to fill its freshman class despite the widely acknowledged excellence of the work it is doing. In the long run the other participants may be on the right track, for I think it inevitable that the dollar gap between public and private institutions will close. But for some years the private institutions must find ways to avoid bankruptcy and at the same time hold on to their faculty and students.

I know I shall be asked whether I would advocate raising the fees at public institutions merely to save the private institutions from financial disaster, and the answer is no. Granted, the disappearance of private institutions would place an even greater load on the public. This is not reason enough.

But I believe that fees in public institutions will inevitably rise, and they will rise for two reasons. The first is that the cost of education is mounting so rapidly that I believe that there will be a taxpayers' revolt. It will be a revolt not against our concept of the value of higher education, but against providing higher education heavily subsidized to those who can well afford to pay for it themselves. The evidence of rebellion over the costs of education is already apparent in the defeat of bond issues in many local communities — even in communities that *know* their present facilities are totally inadequate for their *own* children.

The second and more compelling reason I believe fees are bound to rise is that we are not accomplishing with low fees the very objective low fees were designed to achieve. To attend a public institution which charges no tuition (an increasing rarity) now costs between $1000 and $1300 per year, unless the student can live at home and commute. How can a youngster from a submarginal farm in New England hope to go to the university under these conditions? Low fees, or no fees, can no longer assure every student who has the capacity for college a chance to develop his talents. In many ways, because of their highly developed financial aid programs a poor boy has a better chance at a high-cost private institution than he has at the state university.

So the American dream of higher education for all who can profit from it is not being fulfilled, if indeed it ever has been. The likelihood of its being fulfilled seems dim, unless one follows the line this group is taking of stiffly higher fees, large student loans, and lifetime repayment.

But I think there is another answer, and I think the pieces are lying all about us, ready to be put together. As a nation, we are committed to a system of compulsory education which goes roughly through high school. Because it is compulsory and because we are committed to it, I think we are bound to subsidize it fully. With the expanding birth rate the cost of this compulsory system is certain to climb. On the other hand, with the declining death rate we have an ever-greater commitment to social security and welfare. In the middle, between these two demands on the tax dollar, lies the ever-increasing cost of national defense. How, in all this, can we support higher education?

I think we must adopt the attitude suggested this fall by Dr. Pusey at the meeting of the American Council on Education in Chicago, that higher education is for both private good and public welfare. It is reasonable to expect, therefore, that at least to the extent that he is able, the recipient will pay for it.

The advent of reasonably accurate procedures for assessing financial need — or, to put it another way, assessing ability to pay — is one of the pieces of the puzzle we must put together. In fact, to mix a metaphor, I think it is a major milestone. A second one, of equal importance, is acceptance of the legitimacy of granting public funds to students in relation to their financial need. This principle is now both established and accepted in the scholarship program in such states as New York, California, and Illinois, and at the federal level in the gigantic new National Defense Student Loan Program.

By accepting the principle that students should pay within the limits of their ability to pay, and with the corollaries I have just discussed, I believe we are within sight of making higher education truly within the reach of all, with no greater drain on the tax dollar than we are now experiencing.

I am increasingly convinced that the solution lies within a dual program for students — state or federal scholarships plus a greatly expanded federal loan program. The scholarships should be elastic according to need, but pegged to only one variable: the financial strength of the family. The two-variable approach (the other variable being the cost of the institution to which the scholar goes) gives too great advantage to the strong, expensive, private institutions.

The scholarships should have sufficient range — say $0 (honorary) to $1200 — to cover full cost at some institutions, but to leave a gap at high-cost institutions. This gap would be filled by summer work, term-time work, and loans. Since, however, the scholarships would vary according to need, the gap would remain fairly stable for all, and the *least* and *most* needy would tend to graduate with about the same amount of debt. I can advocate such a dual approach; I cannot advocate a full credit program, which would place the largest debt on the neediest student.

I have been opposed to federal scholarship programs so far suggested, largely because they seemed to me so small as to promise more harm than good. I believe 10,000 federal scholarships might have driven out 20,000 state and private scholarships. In fact, the mere talk about federal scholarships effectively killed the New York Department of Education's proposal to increase New York State Scholarships by 5,000 last year. So a federal government program would have to be massive if it were to accomplish anything.

I am inclined to favor state programs largely because I feel it would be easier to handle measurement of need at the state than at the national level. Rigorous evaluation of need at a state level might require less courage. The only difficulty is that the neediest states (Vermont? Mississippi?) might fare least well in a state scholarship arrangement.

This formula of state scholarships and federal loans requires, as has been pointed out in this seminar, very little of the federal government, other than subsidization through low interest. I would suggest that the other appropriate federal participation might be a matching or even outright grant for physical facilities.

It is on these three rocks that I would build my program. They would enable public institutions to raise, as I am convinced they will have to raise, their over-all fees without denying education to even the neediest. They would enable the private institutions to raise their fees and increase their facilities without increasing the dollar gap between public and private institutions that is already causing trouble. They would place a part of the burden of paying for an education where *part* of it surely belongs — on the recipient — without increasing student indebtedness to the enormous extent that a credit or loan program alone would do. This direct three-point attack seems to me in every way preferable to such devices as various tax-credit plans that are makeshift, inadequate, and basically artificial.

EQUALIZING OPPORTUNITY UNDER HIGHER CHARGES
Rexford G. Moon, Jr.

PREVIOUS writers have concluded that the educational charges of institutions of higher learning should be increased. I am in sympathy with this idea. My reasons are similar to theirs, but my belief that public as well as private means should be used to meet these increased charges may not be in complete accord with their reasoning. Higher education benefits the individual as well as society in general. Both must share the burden. The effect of increased educational charges on the student (and his family) is going to depend a great deal on who must pay the bill. If it is the student alone, then the effect will be most devastating upon both the individual and the economy. If it is a sharing proposition, which I feel it should and must be, the greatest benefits will accrue with the least deleterious effect on either party.

I shall discuss the effect of higher charges on students, but I cannot, with a clear conscience, do so until I point out that increased charges affect actual as well as potential students. The "potential" student does not go to college because of high charges or other factors. The "actual" student does go and is affected, though differently, by them. High charges can deter potential students completely from college attendance, or can cause a shift in student populations, unless the colleges and the country as a whole respond adequately to help people meet these increased charges. The loss of "potential" students because of high charges is a major problem, but beyond the scope of this paper. Suffice it to say that "actual" students could become "potential" students unless they are handled with care.

There are two groups of actual college students between which we must first distinguish, in order to gain understanding of the student's problem. The first consists of those who do not now pay all the stated charges for their education. These are the financial-aid holders, representing about 30 per cent of the enrollments of our independent colleges. Few, if any, of the families of these students have incomes in excess of $10,000 per year. The other group is made up of those who are paying their own way under existing charges.

Among the paying customers (70 per cent of the students), a further distinction is necessary. Some of these students come from families where the economic status is no better than that of financial-aid holders. In some instances, it may be worse. Because of high motivation, small family size, extra effort by the student, and pride, and at considerable family sacrifice, these students are going through college without even partial institutional financial support. I estimate that this group constitutes at least 20 per cent of the enrollment of our more expensive institutions. The balance of the paying-customer group, roughly 50 per cent of the total student body, has sufficient family financial strength to meet current charges without institutional help and with only a modest effect on the family's standard of living.

Though these three groups are present in all types of institution, the percentages of enrollment which they represent vary considerably between independent institutions and are of marked difference between institutions of public and private support. For example, private women's colleges, in contrast with their male counterparts, will have a greater percentage of paying customers and, of this group, only a very small number will be from the lower income group. In the public institutions we find, *first*, a much higher percentage of students actually paying the charges without partial institutional support, and, *second*, a greater relative financial ability to do so without the excessive financial sacrifice that characterizes part of the paying-customer group in the independent colleges. My guess is that about 70 per cent of the students in public institutions, in contrast to 50 per cent in the private ones, can meet existing charges without great sacrifice. Probably fewer than 10 per cent in these institutions, in contrast to the 20 per cent in private ones, are making what might be termed excessive financial sacrifice under existing pricing. One further comment: though the public institutions contain a much greater proportion of students who are able to meet, without sacrifice, existing charges, this balance could be very quickly upset if public education were priced at a higher level. In public institutions, 75 per cent of student family incomes fall below $10,000 per year in contrast to 50 per cent in the private ones. Thirty per cent fall below $5,000 in the public ones, while only about 15 per cent fall below this point in the private ones. Any increase in the price of public education would have a deleterious effect on a very high percentage of their enrollment. A group, numbering over 50 per cent of existing enrollment, which would be unable to meet higher public charges without great sacrifice, would be produced if only a modest increase were effected.

The effect of increased charges on two of the three student groups I noted need not concern greatly the independent institution. These are the present recipients of aid and the group whose families are meeting existing charges without great personal sacrifices. In dismissing these I recognize that greater effort may be necessary for both, but, on the one hand, scholastic ability gives one group assurance that their help will increase with new pricing, while the other has assurance that their financial flexibility will be adequate to meet higher charges for the product which their current living standard dictates they must have.

The third group, which is already severely strained, should be our greatest concern. These students have the economic qualifications for financial assistance, but few, if any, of the academic ones. They are good students, admissible to the finest institutions, but because of limited funds, the institution has not given them aid. These students work during the term and holidays, and extra hard during the summer; they have only one suit apiece; they stay on the campus on week ends; they take little part in athletics or extracurricular activities of the college; they send their laundry home. Their families make considerable sacrifice, too; vacations stop; the already old car gets older; the house goes unpainted; Mother does Dad's shirts and may even go to work; the younger brothers and sisters feel the pinch, too. The mortgage is increased, the little insurance that does exist is borrowed on, and those War Bonds are finally unloaded. The original image which this group had of college has considerably blurred under the strain.

As charges increase, more and more of this group will move away from private education, not out of dissatisfaction with the product, but because of inability to carry on longer under the strain. This would be a great loss, for these are the people who give our private institutions what little socio-economic heterogeneity they have.

How can these already overtaxed people be saved from disillusionment and retained during this period of spiraling cost for the immense good they contribute? The only way to do it is to make our financial aid programs truly equalizers of educational opportunity, which they are not at the present time. They are currently opportunity equalizers for only the most able student.

The best way to achieve this equalization for the inflation ahead is to use our current pricing and its related effect on our three student groupings as a bench mark while liberalizing our attitudes towards the use of noncontingent aid (tuition reductions, jobs, scholarships) with all admissible students.

I can best illustrate what I have in mind by hypothesizing a situation where, under new pricing, tuition is at $2,000 per year, bringing for students at most institutions a total-expense budget of $3,200 per year.

My proposal is this: scholarships, grants-in-aid, college employment, and such other forms of aid that, concurrent with attendance, reduce the student's financial burden, should be used to increase the purchasing power of all students who are admissible to an institution but who do not now have such financial strength. Funds of this kind should be awarded to any admissible student up to a point where they give that individual the same financial flexibility as a family which, under current pricing, can meet without excessive strain the college's present charges. The income figure representing this flexibility will vary, but for purposes of illustration we will say this is a minimum of $10,000 per year at an institution where existing total charges are $2,500. Experience indicates that the family with an income equal or greater is now paying about $2,500 per year for a child's education at many of our colleges. If a family has only $8,000 income, it would need, according to my figuring, $600 in gift aid and/or student employment to give it the same educational purchasing power as a $10,000 family. Similarly, a family with an income of $5,000 per year would need about $1,200 to have this same flexibility. These need figures are based on the expectancy tables of the College Scholarship Service.

If our over-all charges are now $3,200 instead of $2,500, even the family with just $10,000, which previously could, with only modest effort, meet our charges, will be hard pressed. For them a loan is appropriate, as it is for each other group whose income falls below this point, but only after we have helped them with noncontingent aid up to this point of equalization. Families whose incomes fall between $10,000 and $15,000 per year will probably also need to borrow. Under the arrangement I have suggested, credit would be used to support the increased charges, but from an equalized base rather than, as some are now doing or suggesting, from an unequal one. (Some colleges make the most impecunious student do the most borrowing.)

My income figures are only suggestive. They should be adjusted to meet local conditions. For example, with the various figures I have used, the maximum loan that a student would need might be only $600 per year. If the institution's attitude toward credit was more liberal than this, the "income equalization case" could be lowered. If an institution felt it proper for a student to borrow $1,000 per year, the income equalization base would be $8,000, not $10,000. This means that fewer scholarships or remissions, but more credit, would be necessary. In the time remaining, further elaboration is not possible. Suffice it to say that substantial income increases would result from this approach; at the same time equal treatment of all students whose current purchasing power is in doubt would be assured.

In conclusion, then, I should like to note several points.

(1) I support the need for increased charges.

(2) I believe, even though my remarks have implied that private means can carry these increased charges, that public means should and will be forthcoming to assist with them, particularly for those with low purchasing power.

(3) There are three groups of students to be affected differently by increased charges. Only one, the already overtaxed group, need concern us greatly.

(4) The effect of substantially increased charges on students in public institutions would be considerably greater than in private institutions because of the marked differences in family financial strength represented here.

(5) More liberal attitudes toward giving gift aid must be achieved if the "overtaxed" group, which adds so much to heterogeneity, is to be continued in our independent institutions.

(6) Noncontingent financial assistance (scholarships, grants, remissions, jobs) must be used to equalize opportunity for all admissible students.

(7) Any institution which substantially increases its charges must establish an "income equalization base," below which noncontingent aid is given and above which *only* contingent aid (credit) is extended.

(8) The availability of financial assistance under liberal terms can serve as an important motivator to able but underprivileged students who might otherwise turn away from education and be only "potential" students, the so-called "lost talent."

(9) The most successful approach to motivating this "lost talent" is to begin in the early school years to awaken the student to cultural opportunities beyond his limited background. This does not eliminate the necessity of providing financial support for his higher education or negate the importance of such assistance as a motivating factor in itself.

SOME GENERAL OBSERVATIONS ON THE PRICING OF HIGHER EDUCATION

Carl Kaysen

AN economist asked to discuss a pricing problem for an audience of practical men — and in this connection even college presidents and foundation executives become practical men — does well to begin by reminding himself and them of the economic functions of prices in broad terms. As the economist sees it, the most important function of prices is to serve as signals to both producers and users that will guide them in deciding how society's resources are divided among the production and consumption of various goods and services. Ideally, the signals should be such that prices indicate to both what goods and services are worth and what they cost. A well-functioning price system operating under ideal circumstances leads to the happy result that each kind of good or service is produced and consumed in such quantity that, at the margin, what it is worth to the consumers who pay for it is just equal to what it costs the producers who supply it — and in turn, just what it costs society, in terms of foregone alternative uses of productive resources. Or, in the economists' traditional terms, the price system is functioning well when the price of any particular good or service is equal to the long-run marginal cost of producing it in the quantity actually consumed. This is, I repeat, a general ideal. In order to decide to what extent it provides a useful guide for our particular problem of pricing educational services we must examine two further questions. First, what is the character of the relevant long-run cost function? Second, do or can money costs and prices adequately represent the respective costs and benefits to society of the services in question, as well as the costs to the colleges and universities and the benefits to the students?

The first question is important because it is only under conditions of fairly constant long-run costs per unit of service that marginal cost pricing is a trouble-free prescription. If average cost per student falls as the number of students educated rises, then marginal cost pricing will not cover total costs, and subsidies may be necessary even under "cost-pricing." If, as is more likely, average costs per student rise with increasing numbers of students — assuming that we are counting all costs including capital costs, not merely allowing for more intense utilization of a fixed stock of plant — then marginal-cost pricing will give rise to surpluses — in this case, profits — and questions may arise as to their propriety and their disposition. This, to be sure, seems a remote contingency indeed, but it is worth mentioning to indicate that one important problem requiring attention and effort is that of getting some usable accounting records on the basis of which the shape of the average cost curve might be established, and some conclusion reached as to our present position on costs. For the purposes of further discussion, I shall ignore this problem, and assume that long-run marginal costs and long-run average costs are the same.

The second question is the more important of the two. Not every good or service is of such a character that the rules of an ideal pricing system are applicable to it. For most goods and services, it is the case that the benefit of their production, or most of it, is received by their specific consumers, and any particular consumer may consume them in such quantity as he wishes and can pay for without directly affecting others. But for many important goods and services this is not the case. National defense, for example, cannot be consumed by different households in differing quantities, according to their individual tastes; all of us must have the same amount of it and consume it collectively, in that it cannot be provided for one without also being provided for all. An example still closer to our present purpose is that of vaccination: it does benefit the direct consumer, but it also conveys an important benefit to everyone else by reducing the chance of epidemic, and the more widely used it is, the greater the indirect benefit. It would clearly not make sense for us to charge "cost" for vaccination and let individuals buy it or not as they chose. We long ago made a social decision that primary and secondary education are goods which benefit the community as much or more than they do the children receiving them, and therefore we offer them on a collective basis without direct charges, rather than on a cost-price basis. Is the same true of higher education? Is the whole idea of "cost-pricing" inapplicable to it?

To answer this question, we must examine the "output" of colleges and universities carefully, for what we have been calling "higher education" is a complex bundle of products rather than a single one. The great universities typically produce at least four sets of outputs of rather different sorts: liberal education, preprofessional and professional education, applied research in both the natural and social sciences, and fundamental research and the preservation of knowledge and, more broadly, culture. These outputs have complex interrelations in both production and use: typically, production of one involves production of another as well, and frequently the consumers desire some mixture of the separate products. Thus, graduate education, fundamental research, and applied research in the physical sciences are joint products; similarly, medical education and medical research are joint products, or preprofessional and liberal education are generally consumed together in a single combination. Smaller universities and liberal-arts colleges may have simpler output mixture, but they rarely supply only the single good, "liberal education." Usually, at least some preprofessional training and some activity in research and the preservation of culture is also involved.

Not all these products are consumed by the same class of consumers, nor do they have the same pattern of benefits to direct users and the rest of society. Liberal education alone, stripped of elements of specific preprofessional training, is both an important individual consumer good and a social good as well. Many of the arguments that justify public provision of primary and secondary education can easily be extended to training in arts and sciences at the college level. And even the pure liberal A.B. is not a simple commodity. On the one hand is the substantive education itself, on the other is the degree. Ideally, the latter functions as a warranty which testifies to the quality of the former. In practice, it has important independent significance as a symbol of social status, and the relative content of education and status-symbol in educational output varies widely not only among institutions but within them. The proposition that a liberal education creates benefits to the community which are large enough in relation to benefits to the graduate to justify charging him something less than the full average cost may be sustained if we focus on the substantive content of education; it becomes much more dubious if we talk only of the degree as a caste-mark.

Professional and preprofessional training presents a quite different situation. In medicine, law, business management (which some are willing to call a profession), engineering, dentistry, veterinary medicine, and so on, we in general allow the price of professional services to be set in the market place and their supply to depend on the career choices of individuals, subject, in medicine, to some fairly effective guild restrictions enforced chiefly through the admission policies of medical schools. With some relatively small exceptions, we view these services as individual goods, to be paid for by their users on a market-price basis. As long as we do so, it is logical to view professional and any strictly preprofessional training in these fields on the same basis, as being the purchase by the student of a species of (intangible) capital which will make it possible for him to sell certain products in the market. Accordingly, the universities should charge for this training its full average costs.

Applied research in the natural and social sciences is also a product which could be viewed as salable to its consumers — industry and the government — at a price which at least covers full average costs. To a substantial extent it is so viewed today; but methods of cost accounting continue to raise problems. It is likely that prices for these outputs are now more frequently too low than too high.

On the other hand, basic scientific research

and the preservation of knowledge and culture are not products of the same sort: no particular group of users short of society as a whole can be said to get the benefits of these activities, and therefore society as a whole should support them. In the past, they have been supported chiefly through the gifts of wealthy men. The volume cost of these activities has grown greatly relative to the stream of private gifts, and some other basis of support must be found. Graduate training for the Ph.D. degree is intimately bound up with these activities, and, to the extent that the bulk of Doctors of Philosophy go into the academic profession, can be viewed as part of the same product. To be sure there are fields such as chemistry in which the majority of Ph.D.'s go into industry, and in which their graduate training should, in principle, be viewed in the same way as training in law or medicine.

Our problem is made even more complex by the fact that several classes of products with different markets are in common supply. Many kinds of applied research are better done in an institution in which some fundamental research is also carried on. The teaching of medicine is produced jointly with the provision of hospital services and also with medical research. The liberal-arts colleges attached to great universities offer a kind of liberal education different from that of the non-university colleges because the faculties of the former are engaged in advanced teaching and research. Many of us think university education is superior for that reason. It is impossible to train graduate students without doing research; for many kinds of research, a supply of graduate students as assistants is essential. In this situation the question arises, how much of the cost of the total product combination can or should be charged to users of some part of it? What proportion of the cost of research and graduate training is part of the costs of liberal education in the university college? How much of the cost of running teaching hospitals is part of the cost of medical education?

Where several products of the same activity are in joint supply in the strict sense — always yielded in fixed proportions (such as cotton and cottonseed, in the standard textbook example) — the usual answer to the pricing problem is that prices will be determined by demand: those of the joint products for which demand is intense will have high prices; those for which it is weak will have low prices. But for any particular one of these combined commodities, the price will have to be high enough to cover any extra costs required by its production, above the joint costs of producing the whole bundle. Application of joint-cost pricing principles to the array of products described above might suggest that applied research and professional education be charged for at high prices, while liberal education and, still more, graduate education in the arts and sciences be charged for at low ones. At present, this principle is not being followed to any great extent.

The outputs of the smaller university and the liberal-arts college are less varied than those of the great university, but even among these institutions pure single-purpose operation is rare. The usual liberal-arts college offers a significant amount of preprofessional training in business, medicine, and engineering, and often in other fields as well, and in most liberal-arts colleges faculties engage in some scholarly activity outside that strictly necessary for their teaching, if indeed such a line can be drawn. Any university, of course, is by definition engaged in multiple activities in the terms discussed above.

While the model of joint supply is a helpful starting point in discussing the pricing of higher education, in fact the multiple products of the university are not strictly in joint supply. The proportions of liberal education, professional education, applied research, and fundamental research and the preservation of knowledge are variable. These proportions can be varied within any given institution, and — more important from the overall viewpoint — they can be varied in higher education as a whole by varying the numbers of institutions of different types ranging from junior colleges to institutes for advanced study, and the distribution of resources among them. Though the model of strict joint pricing is not applicable, the lesson it teaches is: prices can vary according to demand. Here we have one species of what the economist calls price discrimination, in which the proportion of the total costs of a bundle of multiple outputs assigned to any particular one is dependent on the strength of the demand for it. The successful practice of discrimination of this kind requires either an absence of alternative sources of supply for the higher-priced outputs, or the concerted action of all possible suppliers. One university can charge industry or the government "high" prices for applied research only if there is no other university which can do this research, or if all possible alternative performers charge similarly "high" prices. This point is of particular relevance to the problems of tuition in the private institutions, and the limits to private-college tuition placed by the existence of state-supported institutions with lower charges. Any scheme of differential charges — say, higher for professional education and lower for liberal arts training and graduate training in the arts and sciences — can succeed only to the extent that it is uniformly adopted, or to the extent that the private institutions are sheltered from competition.

I can summarize this part of my paper in three propositions.

(1) Since institutions of higher education produce multiple products with partly overlapping and partly different users, it is important for them to learn what their product mix is, who in fact are the beneficiaries of particular products, and, so far as possible, what are the separable costs of producing each class of output.

(2) Some beneficiaries should and may be expected to pay the "full costs" of the particular outputs they use, and, in fact, prices to them may appropriately be higher in relation to directly assignable costs than for others. Some types of output benefit the community as a whole so much, and particular individuals so little, as to make it both inappropriate and infeasible to expect to charge for them on a cost basis. Thus a combination of interproduct price discrimination and a flow of receipts not contingent on the "sale" of particular sorts of output is indicated.

(3) Actual and potential competition sets limits to price discrimination; therefore some kinds of pricing schemes will require joint action by all private institutions and even coordination with state institutions as well.

Let us turn now from the costs and pricing of all the varied items in the bundle of university outputs to the narrower question of tuition charges. Universities and colleges already typically engage in some price discrimination between parents of different income statuses by their scholarship and loan-fund programs. This is discrimination somewhat different from the kind suggested above, but of course it rests on the same fundamental economic principles, that those with stronger demands — in this case as determined by higher incomes — can be charged higher prices for the same output. In general, colleges and universities do not practice this kind of discrimination as much as they could. Nominal tuition rates could be raised substantially, and a broad "scholarship" program, based on family income, family size, and some minimum standard of scholastic competence, could be used as an instrument of a more thoroughgoing program of differentiation of actual tuition charges. The price structure might be further varied by making tuition depend on grade standards for all students, not only "scholarship" students, with higher prices for less able students. The rationale of such a scheme is the argument that the less able students, in general, are more interested in the cachet than the substance of education, and the contribution that their education makes to the rest of society in relation to the contribution it makes to them is small; the converse is true for the excellent students.

The high costs of education are concentrated within a very short space of time in the family life-span; much more could and should be done than now toward spreading them over a longer period of time. Pre- and postpayment plans — insurance policies and loan funds — are both possible and useful; they differ in that the former do not in themselves make it possible for children of low-income families to go to college, while the latter conceivably might. For any prepayment plan to be of greatest usefulness it must be organized in such a way as to permit the family to accumulate funds at a variable rate, and to draw them down at the appropriate time as needed. It would be clearly advantageous to have a few large Higher Education Finance Corporations (HEFC) to do the job, rather than have the universities and colleges try to do it themselves. While commercial insurance companies could do it, there are reasons against reliance on them, which will be indicated below.

The same institutions could also function as "banks" to lend money for education to those who cannot prepay the costs. The savings of the prepayers could form a substantial part of the capital needed for loan purposes, although it would be undesirable to limit the loan operations to the scope which these savings would permit. Such an HEFC, organized as a nonprofit corporation, might serve as a vehicle for federal assistance to the finance of higher education and be a sort which would carry with it no threat of interference or control. First, the federal government might provide it with some of the initial capital. Second, the government might subsidize the interest rate which borrowers were charged, so that between parents of different income statuses loans might be carried at a rate of, say, 2½ per cent, instead of the, say, 5 per cent any commercial institution would charge. The federal government has subsidized interest rates on power-dam construction and rural electrification; higher education is at least as justifiable a cause. The value to society of an additional college graduate (beyond the social benefits he himself enjoys) is justification for the difference. Third, the government might act as guarantor of the loans, assuming perhaps 80 per cent of any default loss. These three devices together would make a significant reduction in the burden of repayment on the individual. These devices would also facilitate the charging of higher fees for professional education and to students of lesser ability.

If loans (rather than prepayments or tax-supported free tuition) were nearly universally used, we would imagine a device which would create something like a market for higher education and which would place a market value on it. Suppose the HEFC made it a condition of a loan that each graduate offer himself for employment only on condition that his employers pay the service and principal repayment charges on his loan contract during the duration of his employment. Employers not selling products or services in the market and not possessed of the taxing power — that is, universities, colleges, private schools, churches — might be exempted from the requirement, and the costs thereof charged to the general government subsidy to HEFC. Others would then be faced with the question of whether the additional advantage of hiring a college graduate or professionally trained person would be worth the additional costs involved in meeting his HEFC loan costs. Thus some market value for training of various kinds might be established, and some indication registered of whether or not more is now being supplied than is really worth while. This scheme is relevant in principle only to that part of education which is viewed as "professional" rather than "liberal." Practically, of course, there are serious obstacles to applying it: the graduates of tuition-free or low-tuition state universities would drive those of high-tuition private institutions out of the market; college girls would come to their husbands with negative dowries; enforcement of the obligation would be difficult, if not legally impossible. But nonetheless the notion has some value in making clear what we mean when we talk about making those who benefit from higher education pay for it. And while it might not be at all practical on any universal basis, it might well work for a limited number of large corporate employers in relation to a selected group of employees. Indeed, they could well make it part of their competitive offer in the market to assume all or some part of the burden of the loan contract.

All the pricing schemes I have discussed so far involve one or another form of discrimination in price. In general, economists view price discrimination with some disfavor and prefer uniform prices for all buyers, unless a case can be made out for discrimination on the ground that it makes possible the provision of a good or service desired by the community which could not otherwise be paid for. In this situation, we can say that discrimination provides an alternative to tax-support, and it may be viewed as a kind of private taxation of consumers on the basis of their willingness to pay for the particular good in question, as opposed to the public taxation on a variety of bases, including ability to pay in general. Can the discrimination I have proposed above be so justified? It is at present difficult to tell. While it is clear that present pricing schemes fall far short of covering present costs of operating higher education, and that future prospects for filling the gap by increased endowment, gifts, and taxes are bleak, it is not clear to what degree discrimination would be justified if an attempt were made to price the separate outputs at their appropriate costs, so far as possible, and to provide some non-sales income to cover the costs of those activities which in any case cannot be "sold," in any meaningful sense, to particular buyers.

So far, I have not discussed directly the question of how much of each kind of product should be provided. To the extent that we consider a particular output marketable, in the sense that professional training and applied research have been so described, the answer is given by that quantity which is demanded at the price set, at least full average cost, and possibly, as was argued above, more. But for the partly marketable and unmarketable yields, there is no simple answer. As far as pure science and the preservation of knowledge go, I can say little as an economist. In the past, the magnitude of these activities has depended largely on the chances that make men rich and the whims that move them in spending their wealth. Universities and foundations have tended to rationalize somewhat the process of allocating the total resources available for these activities among various specific uses from biophysics to hieroglyphics, but they have themselves hardly determined the totals. We need to make some social decision on this matter; in my view, it should be at least in part a collective and public one, in which a total budget for science and scholarship is determined on some fairly broad basis: perhaps $2500 per year per member of the faculty of arts and sciences (or its equivalent) of permanent rank with the Ph.D. or equivalent foreign degree, for every university and liberal arts college, with the internal allocation left to the institution. Again, the question of how much liberal education should be provided is not one which can be answered on an economic basis. The subsidized-loan scheme would determine the answer in part by the size of the subsidy, but admission and expansion policies of existing institutions would also be an important determinant. We, especially those of us who are college presidents, sometimes say that we wish to see a situation in which no one is denied a college education for financial reasons. In one sense, this is an admirable sentiment; in another, however, its wisdom is questionable. College education is expensive in resource terms; before we decide in principle that enough should be spent to provide it to everyone who wants it at whatever cost, some second thoughts on what these costs are and what are the benefits are certainly in order.

Finally, we need not accept as given the present range of outputs. Perhaps more attention to institutions of less scope and lower pretensions than the four-year liberal-arts college would not be out of order. Perhaps the state universities, already committed to admitting all high-school graduates in the state who apply, might be the appropriate institutions to lead the way in this respect, providing a two-year general college education universally and without charge, but reserving the four-year college and graduate training for those the cost of whose education society has some reason to be willing to meet, if the students cannot meet it themselves.

THE PROBLEM OF HIGHER COLLEGE TUITION

Otto Eckstein

THIS paper [1] will deal with two aspects of the problem of college tuition. First, it will discuss the pros and cons of raising tuition fees. Second, assuming that tuition charges will continue to rise, it will explore some of the ways in which the burden on the student and his family might be lightened. Most of our attention will be devoted to the pricing of private undergraduate education.

Costs and Student Fees

In 1953–54, student fees covered only 52 per cent of those educational and general expenses of private colleges and universities which might properly be attributed to students. This is the figure which leads to the common argument that every student enjoys a large scholarship from his college. Table 1 gives the relevant figures for several years. It is clear that the average price of higher education is far below average cost.

TABLE 1. — COSTS AND STUDENT FEES IN PRIVATE COLLEGES AND UNIVERSITIES, SELECTED YEARS

Year	Costs [a] (thousands of dollars)	Student fees (thousands of dollars)	Ratio of fees to cost (per cent)
1939–40	239,579	144,133	60.6
1949–50	681,816	289,629	42.5
1953–54	686,881	358,100	52.1

SOURCE: U.S. Office of Education, *Biennial Survey of Education*, 1939–40, 1949–50, 1953–54.
[a] Costs include general and administrative expense, departmental instruction and research, library operating costs, operation and maintenance of plant and equipment, and activities related to instructional departments. They exclude organized research, auxiliary activities, extension and public-service activities, and scholarships and fellowships. Figures include junior colleges, except for some in 1939–40 which did not award degrees.

These figures do not distinguish among levels in college or among fields. Evidence on relative costs is scanty, but the Commission on Financing Higher Education has presented some examples. Table 2 shows the instructional expenditure per full-time student in various fields and at different levels at one university. It can be seen that there are tremendous varia-

[1] This paper was prepared in the spring of 1958, and no attempt has been made to incorporate subsequent developments, such as the experience with the new federal loan program.

tions among fields and also that costs rise very sharply, particularly in the arts and sciences, in later years of study.

TABLE 2. — INSTRUCTIONAL EXPENDITURES PER FULL-TIME STUDENT EQUIVALENT AT UNIVERSITY C, BY FIELD AND LEVEL OF STUDY, 1950

Field	Lower division	Upper division	Graduate classes	Graduate research
Arts and sciences	$134.10	$353.87	$873.53	$3,248.17
Business	89.91	152.26	380.65	1,312.00
Dentistry	...	416.77	1,496.81	...
Education	333.32	661.22	538.38	1,827.99
Law	...	...	287.55	...
Medicine	...	...	1,723.83	...
Music	489.65	440.26	611.41	...
Agriculture	291.34	317.55	411.04	451.26
Engineering	434.35	383.53	618.60	2,850.38

SOURCE: J. D. Millett, *Financing Higher Education in the United States*. The Staff Report of the Commission on Financing Higher Education (New York, 1952), 146.

Table 3 shows the ratio of student fees to instructional costs in major divisions of five universities. In three of the schools, fees exceeded instructional costs in most fields, with the margin particularly wide in business schools, but also quite substantial in the arts and sciences, law, and education. The other two schools are heavily endowed.

TABLE 3. — RATIO OF STUDENT FEES COLLECTED TO INSTRUCTIONAL EXPENDITURES AT THREE PRIVATE UNIVERSITIES, BY INSTRUCTIONAL UNIT, 1949

Program	University D	University E	University F	University G	University H
Arts and Sciences	1.6	1.8	1.7	0.7	0.6
Architecture	1.6	..	..	0.6	0.3
Commerce and Business	4.3	3.0	2.0	1.1	0.6
Dentistry	1.4	0.6	..	..	0.2
Education	1.9	2.0	..	..	..
Engineering	1.4	1.6	0.8	0.5	0.4
Journalism	...	..	..	0.3	..
Law	1.9	1.8	1.3	0.9	0.8
Library Science	0.8	..	..	0.5	..
Medicine	0.5	0.7	..	0.2	0.2
Music	...	..	1.0	..	..
Pharmacy	1.7	..	..	..	..
Public Health	...	..	..	..	0.1
Religion	0.4	..	0.4	..	..
Social Work	0.8	..	..	..	..
University College (adult education)	3.5	1.0	1.4	..	..

SOURCE: Millett, pp. 147, 148.

In these cases student fees did not match instructional costs in arts and sciences, nor in most other fields, but the relative pattern of the ratios of fees to costs is quite similar.

For one of the heavily endowed schools, figures for departments within the field of arts and sciences are available. Table 4 shows very wide variations.

TABLE 4. — RATIO OF STUDENT FEES COLLECTED TO INSTRUCTIONAL EXPENDITURES, BY DEPARTMENT, UNIVERSITY G, 1949

Department	Ratio
Humanities	
Chinese and Japanese	0.2
English and Comparative Literature	1.3
Fine Arts and Archeology	0.4
Comparative Linguistics	0.7
Germanic Languages	0.6
Greek and Latin	0.5
Music	0.2
Philosophy	1.2
Religion	0.1
Romance Languages	0.6
Semitic Languages	0.4
Slavic Languages and Literature	0.4
Social sciences	
Anthropology	0.7
Economics	0.8
History	1.0
Government	1.1
Psychology	0.5
Sociology	0.8
Natural sciences	
Astronomy	0.9
Botany	0.2
Chemistry	0.4
Geology	0.3
Mathematics	1.0
Physics	0.7
Zoology	0.3

SOURCE: Millett, p. 149. English, economics, history, government, and sociology, the fields with the largest undergraduate enrollments in most universities, had very high ratios, greater than one or close to it; the same was true for mathematics, philosophy, and astronomy, but these figures will vary considerably among schools.

Instructional costs are only a fraction of the total cost of educating undergraduates. Table 5 gives the percentage breakdown of student-related costs for institutions of several types. The cost of departmental instruction and research, the closest concept to pure instruction cost, is approximately 50 per cent of relevant cost in private institutions, slightly more in public liberal-arts colleges and universities, and 66 per cent for public junior colleges. Thus the overhead per dollar of departmental expense is almost 100 per cent; and even this figure does not include any allowance for investment in plant. When one adds overhead to the ratios of student fees to instructional costs, it becomes clear that even the student in the large department pays for his education considerably less than its cost.

Joint Costs, Average Costs, and Marginal Costs

The figures cited above represent average costs, including a certain number of arbitrarily allocated joint costs. But the cost figures which are relevant to decision-making are rather the marginal (or incremental) costs: that is, the extra costs of expanding the total teaching load in each specific field, in groups of fields, and finally in the institution as a whole. Similarly for the pricing of college tuition fees, it is the marginal costs that should be considered; for if we are to apply market economics reasoning to the problem, the economically efficient solution requires that each student be faced with a charge equal to the actual costs that he causes to the institution, which, of course, are the marginal costs, not some average figures. We also need to know, to solve the pricing problem, the nature of the reaction of the demand for higher education at the institution to higher prices.

In the absence of more appropriate figures, we must pass some judgment on the degree of error which is introduced by the use of average cost figures. I offer the hypothesis that average costs are an adequate measure for broad purposes of policy in the present situation. When we consider first the deviations between average and marginal costs, there is reason to believe that if they are not the same, marginal costs will be the larger of the two. Policies that would raise tuition fees toward average costs would therefore also bring them closer to marginal costs. Physical plants will need to be expanded, at high construction costs. Additional faculty may need to be hired, at rising faculty salaries, although greater growth of staff implies a younger average age of teachers and more teachers of junior rank. On the other hand, the good financial experience of schools during the "G.I. Bill" period, plus the plight of a number of small private liberal-arts colleges, suggests that there remains some underutilized capacity of plant and staff in higher education, which, at least in some places, would keep average costs above marginal costs.

TABLE 5. — PERCENTAGE BREAKDOWN OF STUDENT-RELATED COSTS, BY TYPE OF INSTITUTION, 1953–54

Costs	All institutions	Private universities	Private liberal-arts colleges	Private junior colleges	Public universities	Public liberal-arts colleges	Public junior colleges
Administration and general	16.15	16.94	24.95	26.31	11.73	14.16	13.86
Departmental instruction and research	53.75	51.84	51.10	48.35	54.53	58.50	65.90
Libraries	4.08	4.52	4.56	2.90	4.19	4.44	2.62
Plant operation and maintenance	15.57	13.07	17.72	21.73	14.49	17.64	16.73
Organized activities related to instructional departments (e.g., hospitals and farms)	10.45	13.63	1.67	0.71	15.06	5.26	0.89

SOURCE: U.S. Office of Education, *Biennial Survey of Education, 1953–54, Statistics of Higher Education: Receipts, Expenditures and Property, 1953–54*.

The extent to which the cited average cost figures overstate marginal costs of individual output depends on the level to which the concept is applied. Figures for individual activities, or for a specific year in college, contain a large element of arbitrarily allocated costs. But if we are dealing with policy about undergraduate tuition which is uniform among fields and levels in college, the marginal costs of all undergraduate education, including four years of courses, admission, administration, health services, and so on, become the relevant dimension. The allocated element in this big bundle is relatively small. There remains the joint aspect of the several products of colleges and universities discussed by Professor Kaysen: education, research, and preservation of knowledge. There is no reason why all the salaries of staff members should be allocated to education when much of faculty time is spent in the other pursuits. However, in institutions where emphasis on research and scholarship is strong, tuition is a particularly small fraction of total costs: that is to say, much of the joint expense in these schools is borne by other sources. Nevertheless, this is an important point, which would preclude setting tuitions mechanically equal to cost even if marginal cost pricing were the governing principle in setting tuitions.

Market Imperfections in the Demand for Higher Education

In order for marginal cost pricing to be applicable, the demand for the product must be efficient. Demand for a consumer good must reflect consumer preferences. Higher education is peculiar insofar as the purchaser is not the consumer; it is in large part the willingness of parents to educate their children which determines the demand. But perhaps the family unit should be considered the consumer: after all, parents make lots of other consumption choices for their children, and our culture is noted for the goods it lavishes on its youth. There is also the question of perfect foresight — can one foresee the beneficial effects of education over a lifetime? Yet insofar as higher education is a consumer good, there is no evidence to suggest that there is a systematic bias against it as compared to other goods; thus it cannot be argued that it should be priced below marginal cost to offset such a bias.

Higher education is also an investment, of course, and in order for this aspect of the demand to be considered efficient or rational, the rate of return on marginal investment in education should equal the return on other marginal investments. The average college graduate earns an income considerably higher than the typical high-school graduate, and, if we are willing to attribute the difference wholly to education, the rate of return proves to be very high. Of course, there are other characteristics of the college group that tend to raise their incomes: they have better natural talents, are more highly motivated, come from families that can assist their careers, and may receive property incomes. Nevertheless, at least for certain kinds of higher education, the rate of return is higher than the rate in other fields of investment in our economy.

But the underpricing of tuition is much too broad an instrument of policy to bring about this needed improvement in the allocation of the nation's capital. Loan and scholarship programs attack the problem more directly, making the capital available where it is needed. Also, while low tuition improves the demand for investment in education, it limits the supply and makes the quality deteriorate.

To summarize this section: if tuition policy is to be based on rather narrowly defined concepts of economic efficiency, an increase of tuition toward closer correspondence with costs is called for.

Strengthening the Academic Institutions

To my mind, much the strongest argument for raising tuition fees is the need to strengthen our universities and colleges. I take it as a postulate that the functions these institutions perform to the society are important; they do most of the basic research in the natural and social sciences, are centers of creative and of critical thinking, and affect the values by which at least some portion of the American people live. Higher tuition is not the ideal means of solving their financial problems; but no alternative appears in view.

The impending flood of students lends immediacy to the problem. Already the increased number of teachers being hired is driving down personnel standards; among the men and women entering full-time college teaching in the last 4 years, the proportion of those holding Ph.D. degrees has diminished by 25 per cent.[1] The need for staff will be met in terms of numbers; it is the quality which will deteriorate. Active teacher recruitment and the awarding of fellowships will ameliorate the situation, but higher faculty salaries are also necessary to bring more good candidates into teaching.

Other Sources of Revenue

Voluntary giving has been rising in recent years as Table 6 shows. The table includes the unrepeated gift of $200 million of the Ford Foundation for faculty salaries; but even without this sum, total gifts rose 54 per cent in two years. Corporate giving is a particularly promising source for further increases; the General Electric plan of corporate matching of alumni-employee gifts has already been adopted by 38 corporations. A large potential remains in this area; the recent increase brought corporate gifts to a level of 0.2 per cent of corporate profits, with their total philanthropy well below 1 per cent. The income tax authorities allow 5 per cent of profits to be deducted for gifts. And surely the continued subsidized supply of college-trained manpower adds more than 0.2 per cent to corporate profits.

The advantage of these sources of finance is large. Voluntary giving is a noble act, presumably giving some satisfaction to the donor, and tying him to the academic institution he is supporting. More important, at least from the teacher's point of view, the attitude of the student is healthier if he knows he is subsidized by the university and its alumni than if he feels he is paying the full price of services received. A thoroughly business-like attitude about the transaction of purchasing higher education from its purveyors is really undesirable. Excessive preoccupation with receiving full value will affect the student-teacher relationship, will lead to student coddling and an ever-higher personal-service level on the part of the faculty. Perhaps college teachers should be more concerned with the quality of their service; but there are better ways of achieving that aim.

Despite these advantages, voluntary giving cannot be considered a substitute for higher tuition charges. The amount of money that could be raised is not sufficient to meet financial needs, which will mount into the billions in the next decade.[2] Nor is it wise to make institutions dependent on gifts for routine recurring expenses. Endowment income is suited for sustaining going operations, but new gifts must be set aside for new purposes. They are the funds which permit colleges and universities to keep up with changing times, to enter new fields. With the total funds that can be raised from this source limited, an increased diversion of funds into routine educational

---

[1] National Education Association, reported in the "Rockefeller Report" on Education, *The Pursuit of Excellence, Education and the Future of America*, Special Studies Project Report V (Rockefeller Brothers Fund, 1958), p. 23.

[2] See Seymour E. Harris, "College Salaries, Financing of Higher Education and Management of Institutions of Higher Learning," *Bulletin of the American Association of University Professors*, September, 1958, pp. 589–595, for estimates of the magnitude of the problem.

TABLE 6. — SOURCES OF COLLEGE GIFTS

Rank in 1956–57	Source	1956–57 Amount contributed	1956–57 Percentage of grand total	1954–55 Amount contributed	1954–55 Percentage of grand total
1.	General welfare foundations	$319,085,152	39.04	$50,247,322	15.0
2.	Religious denominations	78,100,606	9.55	42,853,747	12.8
3.	Business corporations	76,897,762	9.41	39,432,625	11.7
4.	Bequests	74,274,211	9.09	35,699,311	10.6
5.	Alumni	62,654,683	7.66	52,100,093	15.5
6.	Governments	53,691,505	6.57	29,855,030	8.9
7.	Other individuals and/or families	52,507,574	6.42	90,938,033	9.2
8.	Non-alumni, non-church groups	37,497,821	4.59	18,681,890	5.5
9.	Governing board	29,400,237	3.60	9,651,036	2.9
10.	Other sources	17,199,691	2.10	15,271,058	4.5
11.	Trusts, annuities, life contracts	16,068,775	1.97	11,299,954	3.4
	Totals	$817,378,017	100%	$336,030,099	100%

SOURCE: Council on Financial Aid to Education, reported in *New York Times*, April 30, 1958, p. 1. Figures for 1954–55 are for 728 institutions, for 1956–57 for 904 institutions. Some gifts to public institutions are included.

costs means a withdrawal of resources from the growth fields of higher learning. Thus, while some of the income of past gifts can continue to help defray instructional expense, eliminating the need to have tuition match full cost, the new money from this source should not be used merely to widen the gap between costs and charges.

A Possible Side Effect: Changes in the Composition of the Student Body

The most serious hazard of higher tuition charges in private universities lies in the potential narrowing of the social and economic base from which applicants for admission are drawn. Higher education has been a traditional route of occupational mobility in America, one of the main safety valves in our social system, and a strong factor serving to prevent the calcification of our social structure. With a considerable number of scholarships available, all our universities have been open to the most talented high-school graduates, and, with tuition fees at fairly low levels, students of relatively modest means have been able to go to private colleges, as well as the public institutions, even if not eligible for scholarships.

In principle, the scholarship group might be unaffected by higher tuition charges, since a sufficient fraction of the extra revenues can be poured back into larger scholarships, to leave the net cost to the student unchanged. However, in fact, there are imperfections in this process. Knowledge of the higher tuition charges will discourage applicants, particularly since considerable time will elapse before it is widely known that larger scholarships are available. This will be particularly true of students in the fringe areas of application, geographically remote, or in public high schools that send few students to private universities. Some effect on applicants in this group is inevitable — and it is an important group of applicants, providing an intellectual influence on the whole student body, and containing a large number of future scientists and scholars. An intensive public-relations campaign can much reduce this effect, but cannot offset it, since the usual university channels of communication are weak in reaching this group.

The second group, applicants from families with fairly limited means and with talents closer to the student average, will be affected more widely. Scholarships will not act as a mitigating factor, and the higher tuition fees will impose some financial strain. If tuition fees everywhere were to increase by similar amounts, applications to private colleges would be affected in a fairly modest way. But in many sections of the country, public universities provide a strong alternative, and even where the state and municipal educational systems are weak, nothing would more surely generate legislative willingness to spend large amounts of money on higher education than the closing of private universities to lower-middle-income families through prohibitive tuition charges.

Apart from switching applicants to the low-cost public colleges, the impact of higher tuition fees on applications can be expected to remain small. Evidence from the several studies of college attendance indicates that the strict economic factor is of some influence, to be sure, but that there are several other variables of at least equal weight. Not necessarily in order of importance, intelligence, sex, father's occupation, geography, and the quality of the high-school system attended appear to be other important factors.[3] Among superior students (defined as those within the top quarter of their high-school class), it has been estimated that one third of those who fail to go to college do so for financial reasons. But as Professor Harris has pointed out, the change in tuition will increase the total cost of college by a small percentage. Below the top quartile in high school, the fraction of college-bound students who have only modest means diminishes, though the value of the higher education to the student may also diminish. The data for a really firm estimate of the effect of higher tuition on college attendance have never been collected; but what evidence there is suggests that the number of people on the margin is not very large.

[3] For a survey of the evidence see C. C. Cole, Jr., *Encouraging Scientific Talent* (New York, 1956), 57–85.

While the number of lost applicants may be moderate, their importance is high. From the point of view of the country, there is need for a fuller development of the potential talents of the population. Given the many-dimensioned East-West competition, we can ill afford to have any increase in the attrition rate between high school and college. For the colleges, any narrowing of the base from which applicants are drawn will be a serious matter. The influence will be slow and subtle; but over a number of years, attitudes toward intellectual activity in college, which already are unsatisfactory, will deteriorate, as social and extracurricular activities and even a sort of inactivity are emphasized.

To minimize the side effects of higher tuition charges, means must be found to make the new burdens easier to bear. Several schools have already taken steps to spread the payments more evenly through the school year; loan funds have been increased and eligibility requirements for loans and scholarships have been eased.[4] But much more can be done to spread payments over time. In the following section we shall explore some of the possibilities.

[4] For some examples see *New York Times*, April 20, 1958, p. 82.

II. SOME PAYMENT ARRANGEMENTS FOR HIGHER EDUCATION

Prepayment and Postpayment

Our economy has evolved credit institutions for financing most of the major investments of consumers. Virtually all houses are financed through mortgages; two thirds of all cars and about half of all consumer durables are purchased on the installment plan. Yet higher education, a very sizable investment for middle- and lower-income families, is usually paid for on a strict cash basis.

Installment payment schemes can be of two forms, prepayment and postpayment. Table 7-A shows how large annual payments would have to be under various prepayment arrangements. The figures given are the annual payment which must be made for each $1000 of tuition, where tuition is to be paid for four years. For example, if tuition is $1000 a year for four years, if payments are to be made for ten years, including the four college years, and if the interest earned on the accumulated funds is at the rate of 3 per cent, then the annual payment will be $365. Were tuition fees to reach $2000 a year, the annual payment would double. Of course the greater the number of years over which payments are spaced, the smaller the annual cost will be; and the higher the interest earned, the lower need be the payments. Figures are also shown which include a term life insurance policy on the parent, assuring availability of funds for tuition in the event of his death.

TABLE 7-A. — ANNUAL PAYMENT PER THOUSAND DOLLARS OF ANNUAL TUITION FOR FOUR YEARS [a] UNDER DIFFERENT PREPAYMENT ARRANGEMENTS

Prepayment over T years, including the years in which the student is in college. For example, T = 10 involves payments for six years before college entry, plus four years in college.

Number of years [b] interest rate	Without life insurance [c] on parent	With life insurance on parent [d]
10 years		
3%	365	383
4%	354	372
5%	342	359
15 years		
3%	225	242
4%	212	228
5%	199	214
20 years		
3%	156	171
4%	143	157
5%	130	143

[a] The table assumes that tuition is paid in midyear in each of four years and that interest is collected until the money is paid. Many students, particularly with limited financial means, graduate in less than four years, thus effecting some saving in living expenses and perhaps of tuition as well.
[b] Our cost figures assume one annual payment. Monthly premium payments might involve an increase in total cost of 7 per cent, following private practice.
[c] The figures in this column are also a good approximation for the cost, including life insurance on the parent, provided the policy has no value in the event of the death of the intended student.
[d] This figure will vary slightly with the age of the parent. The table assumes the parent to be fifty years old when the student graduates.
The insurance consists of a term policy for the unpaid balance.

The size of the payments is not unreasonable.[5] For example, fifteen years of payment — which requires that payments start when the child is seven years old — at an interest rate of 4 per cent, and with insurance, implies an annual cost of $228. This should be contrasted with annual mortgage payments of $1,600 on a $20,000 house,[6] or the average an-

[5] My figures are based directly on annuity tables and the standard mortality statistics. They make no allowance for the loading charge, which would cover underwriting costs, payment collection, or administrative overhead. These costs would raise the charges somewhat, but as long as the system is not burdened by large selling expenses, the extra cost will be relatively small.
As a check, we can compare our computed charges with the actual rates offered by the Government Employees Insurance Company, a private insurance company that does not employ agents. It offers policies that correspond quite closely to our table, although not precisely. Its rates for twenty-year educational endowment policies correspond to our annual payments if computed at an interest rate of 3.7 per cent; for fifteen-year policies, an interest rate of 1.7 per cent is implicit; for ten years a rate of 1.4 per cent. The last case would correspond to an annual payment of $384, versus $365 in our table.
[6] This assumes it is paid off in twenty years with interest at 5 per cent.

nual payments of $1,050 on new automobiles purchased on the installment plan,[7] or to the cost of $400 for a $20,000 life insurance policy. If advance provision is also to be made for resident living expenses, a larger sum will be required of course. Assuming tuition plus living expenses to reach $3000, and assuming the student to earn $1000 each summer and during the school year, $2000 a year would be required. This calls for an annual payment of $456 under the above assumptions.

The interest rate to be applied, it seems to me, could be on the order of 4 per cent. This rate is somewhat below the rate earned on college endowments, and assumes that part of the funds is invested in common stocks. Were a private insurance company to administer a program of this sort, it would allow a rate of 3 per cent, and would also include a loading charge.

Table 7-B shows the annual payments under a genuine installment plan, with payments made after graduation. The figures again represent the annual cost per thousand dollars of tuition for four years. If the plan is one of postpayment, life insurance should presumably be included; as the period of repayment is lengthened, annual costs fall less than proportionately, because of the rising insurance cost. Table 7-C gives figures for postpayment after a moratorium of five years, allowing the student to complete a graduate education.

The annual cost of postpayment is considerably higher than prepayment. For example, twenty years of postpayment, after a five-year moratorium, at an interest rate of 4 per cent, requires an annual charge of $425 per $1,000 of annual tuition paid for four years; twenty years of prepayment would cost only $155. The period of repayment would also have to be rather long. For example, a ten-year period of repayment after the five-year moratorium at an interest rate of 4 per cent would require annual payments of $638. Thus, instead of paying $1,000 a year for four years while in college, the alumnus would have to pay $638 a year for ten years. Or, to cite another comparison, prepayment of $228 for fifteen years would correspond to postpayment of the same

[7] This is the actual average figure paid in 1957 (*New York Times*, April 4, 1958).

TABLE 7-B. — POSTPAYMENT OVER T YEARS, PAYMENTS TO BEGIN THE YEAR AFTER GRADUATION

Number of years Interest rate	Annual payment without life insurance	Annual payment including life insurance [a]
10 years		
3%	491	521
4%	524	556
5%	559	593
15 years		
3%	351	381
4%	382	414
5%	416	451
20 years		
3%	281	311
4%	312	346
5%	346	384
25 years		
3%	241	273
4%	272	309
5%	306	348
30 years		
3%	214	248
4%	241	280
5%	281	325
35 years		
3%	195	231
4%	228	268
5%	264	312
40 years		
3%	181	219
4%	214	260
5%	251	305
45 years		
3%	171	212
4%	204	253
5%	243	302

[a] The insurance consists of a term policy for the unpaid balance, starting in the freshman year. The insurance cost is only an estimate, using average American mortality figures, assuming an age at graduation of twenty-two years, and making no allowance for loading charges or underwriting costs.

TABLE 7-C. — POSTPAYMENT OVER T YEARS, PAYMENTS TO BEGIN AFTER A FIVE-YEAR MORATORIUM

Number of years Interest rate	Annual payment without life insurance	Annual payment including life insurance [a]
10 years		
3%	570	618
4%	638	692
5%	713	773
15 years		
3%	407	451
4%	465	515
5%	531	589
20 years		
3%	326	370
4%	380	432
5%	442	502
25 years		
3%	279	323
4%	331	384
5%	391	453
30 years		
3%	248	293
4%	299	354
5%	358	423
35 years		
3%	226	274
4%	277	337
5%	337	409
40 years		
3%	210	261
4%	261	324
5%	321	399

[a] The insurance consists of a term policy for the unpaid balance, starting in the freshman year. The insurance cost is only an estimate, using average American mortality figures, assuming an age at graduation of twenty-two years, and making no allowance for loading charges or underwriting costs.

amount for forty years. These are the actual costs, including the interest cost, which cannot be overlooked in any rational computation. Thus, if the scheme is to be on an actuarial self-financing basis, prepayment should be urged, rather than postpayment, though the latter alternative should be offered for students from lower-income families, from families with many educable youngsters, or for students preparing themselves for particularly lucrative careers.

There are some administrative difficulties in prepayment, however. Since no school will guarantee admission to a student, some centralized organization would be required. To be sure, not even this agency could guarantee admission to any of its participating institutions, but it could, if necessary, return the cash value of the policy.

A Federal Credit Program?

The federal government has traditionally supplemented the supply of capital to purposes that are unable to command a proper share of the country's investible funds. Credit for farmers, for small business, and for residential housing has long been aided by federal credit institutions. There can be little doubt that the supply of capital for investment in the education of children of low- and middle-income families is inadequate, and it is therefore reasonable to consider the possibility of having the federal government enter this field. Certainly from the point of view of economic efficiency, the availability of better credit for investment in intellectual resources would be a thoroughly justifiable policy measure.

In addition, a federal credit program would serve some other useful purposes. It could become a center for bringing educational opportunities to the attention of that alarmingly sizable group of high-school students who have the talent for higher education but come from an environment which does not provide them with the requisite motivation. The program might also serve to lighten the interest burden of educational loans, by giving the student the full advantage of the credit standing of the government.

There are also other advantages of a federal credit program. First, it would make the higher tuition charges much more attractive, and would thereby go a long way toward solving the financial problems of the colleges and universities.

Second, it could be an administratively desirable form of federal aid to higher education. It would involve no control over the policies of the institutions, since there is no direct grant of funds from the government to which strings could be attached. The only possible source of control would be an accreditation procedure which would specify which institutions were considered suitable for the students utilizing the credit; under the "G.I. Bill," this power was given to the state governments.

Third, the credit program could be set up as an independent agency, given a certain amount of capital, and thereby be divorced from the annual uncertainties of the federal budgeting process. This is an important consideration, for one of the hazards of federal aid is its great variability. Surely we cannot let our colleges take on the feast-or-famine characteristics of the defense and other industries whose output is purchased by the government.

There are, of course, also some important factors to be listed on the negative side. First, it would have to be shown that the agency is really necessary. After all, our consumer credit facilities are very highly developed, and there may be ways to draw existing private institutions more deeply into the education credit field.[8] And the creation of any new government agency involves a set of headaches which should not be incurred lightly. It would be my view that unless the federal credit program is tied to some form of subsidy, it cannot be justified.

If the credit program is to include a subsidy, the question must be raised whether it will be an appropriate one. Will it accrue to families on whom higher education is really a severe financial strain? Or will it simply be a windfall to all parents of college students, a group which, after all, includes most families in the upper-income groups and excludes most lower-income families? Certainly the recent proposals for making college tuitions deductible from taxable income would have produced another typical instance of erosion of the tax base.

A federal credit program might concentrate on guaranteeing the repayment of loans made by private lenders. The extraordinary success of the mortgage-guarantee programs of the FHA and VA suggests that government guarantees would make much more capital available and reduce the interest cost successfully, while costing the government virtually nothing. There is no assurance that the delinquency rates on student loans would be equally low, and of course an education cannot be foreclosed or repossessed. On the other hand, the absence of collateral makes the unguaranteed loan extremely risky, a fact which may be the reason for the dearth of private loans of this sort. While the delinquency rate may be somewhat higher, the reduction in risk which would be accomplished by government guarantee would be great. And the residual risk of the program which would fall on the government would certainly not be prohibitively large. Administration of the program by the student's college would serve to reduce delinquencies, if we may judge by the good experience of college loan funds.

Some Policy Issues of a Federal Program

Several policy issues are raised by such a program. First, should the program arrange for prepayment, postpayment, or both? In the case of prepayment, it is not clear that there is any advantage to the federal aegis, nor is there any ready way in which prepayment might

---

[8] Notice the acquisition of Tuition Plan, Inc., by C.I.T., one of the largest consumer credit corporations.

incorporate a federal subsidy. A postpayment plan seems better suited to a public undertaking. For one thing, postpayment is open to everyone, where prepayment would be confined to middle-income and top-income groups. Also, it could easily incorporate subsidy schemes. These could be of at least two forms: first, interest could be set very low, or waived altogether. A revolving fund could be set up, which would be replenished by repayment, but would collect no interest. The absence of interest charges would make a tremendous difference in cost. For example, the annual cost of repayment of the four years of tuition of $1,000 over twenty years after a five-year moratorium at 4 per cent interest without life insurance is $380; it would drop to $200 if interest were not charged. Failure to charge interest is of course a subsidy, one which has been employed for irrigation projects over the last fifty years. In the latter field, it has led to unfortunate results; great political pressures for projects of dubious merit have been generated, leading to a considerable waste of the taxpayers' money. Perhaps the results would be better in the field of education, though it seems to me that it would be essential to confine the availability of interest-free loans to families that have few interest-earning assets and low incomes. Otherwise these loans simply become another windfall at the taxpayers' expense.

Another form of subsidy would be to waive, or at least to reduce, the amount due, provided the beneficiary pursues some particularly worthy career. For example, teachers, scientists willing to serve the interests of national defense, doctors agreeing to spend some time in military service or in particular hospitals, perhaps ministers, might be allowed to benefit from such a provision. This type of waiver could be combined in several ways with the waiving of interest: interest might be waived only for these special cases, which would keep the subsidy to a modest level; or interest might be waived for all eligible candidates, with some fraction of repayment waived in addition for the special cases.[9]

The eligibility requirements are another set of issues. Loans could be limited to students who score high on a competitive examination, either on a nationwide or state-by-state basis, or perhaps by Congressional districts. But it seems to me that a scholarship program is the proper way to encourage particularly talented youngsters to develop their potential. A loan program should use a wider sieve; its main purpose is to facilitate the education of qualified students who are prevented from attending college by economic circumstances.

What about a means test? If there is little subsidy, there is no reason to limit eligibility to low-income families; but the bigger the subsidy that is incorporated, the more stringent must the means test be made.

Should loans be made to cover only tuition? Certainly while it is part of our democratic creed that all able youngsters have some right to develop their academic potential, the right does not extend to attendance at a residential college. However, many students may not live within commuting distance of an appropriate school. Also, loans for residential expense would bring students attending state universities into the program, an outcome which may be desirable.

The availability of federal funds may also be subjected to some regional constraints; that is to say, the law may require that the total funds be made available in some fixed geographic pattern. Clearly there are disadvantages to restrictions of this sort, since they prevent the selection of the most deserving applicants in the country. But the absence of some such requirement has a rather odd and undesirable side-effect: the federal money would go to those states that are most backward in providing public higher education, i.e., where education is most expensive.

Other Forms of Tuition Pricing

So far, we have assumed that the total in-

---

[9] The recently enacted education program, under the National Defense Education Act, calls for a loan fund of $40 million the first year, $60 million in each of the three succeeding years, or a total of $220 million. The maximum loan would be $1,000, with no interest until one year after graduation, and 3 per cent thereafter, with a maximum repayment period of ten years after graduation. Also, up to 50 per cent of the loan is written off if the student enters the teaching profession, with forgiveness at the rate of 10 per cent per year of teaching. This program is a very substantial step toward meeting the financial problem, though the period of repayment is too short.

crease of income from student charges is to be brought about by a flat increase in tuitions, partly offset by more and larger scholarships, and ameliorated by improving the availability of credit. As an alternative to a flat increase in rates, different systems of tuition charges could be instituted. Most of these would involve some form of differential pricing, probably of a discriminatory sort.

One possibility would be to gear tuition to the costs of the field of study or even of the course. Data in Table 4 suggest that costs, including, presumably, marginal costs, differ significantly among fields, and so an efficient system of prices should vary from field to field or from course to course. There are many reasons for not adopting such a system of charges. First, students take a mixture of courses from many fields, though this factor alone would not eliminate differences in costs among students. Second, differential charges might influence course selection, a result which would probably be undesirable. Third, the charges might be high in the sciences, although this is the field into which students should be attracted as a matter of national policy. What is more, the average family income of students electing science is probably lower than for those in the social sciences, and is certainly lower than that of students in the humanities.

A more attractive scheme of differential pricing would be discrimination according to ability to pay. High tuition fees, plus a more extensive system of scholarships of different magnitudes, really is tantamount to this form of discrimination, except that the desirability of the student to the college because of intelligence or special ability also affects the size of the payment.

In the past, ability to pay has usually meant that of the parents. This is, however, not the only relevant financial dimension. After all, the future income of the graduate might be considered an equally significant indicator. And even though schools may claim more credit than they deserve for the success of their graduates, the quality of the education is presumably of some influence in this success.

Discrimination on the basis of lifetime income after graduation would require innovation in the payment system. Perhaps a student could be made to sign a repayment contract,[10] specific not in terms of a fixed annual charge, but as a percentage of income. The income considered taxable by the federal government could serve as a basis for computation, imperfect though it may be,[11] with perhaps some adjustment in the treatment of capital gains and a few other key provisions.

The size of this tithe for education cannot be estimated precisely, because such an estimate requires information on the lifetime income distributions of the alumni bodies of different schools. With an interest rate of 4 per cent and payments up to age 67, the average annual payment for the entire alumni body would be about $200 per $1,000 of annual tuition for four years, without insurance, $250 with an allowance for those who die before that age. If the average income of college graduates is $10,000, a number that is not unrealistic if one allows for the continued rise in per capita incomes, then the assessment would be 2 per cent of income. This is comparable with personal income tax payments equal to 11 per cent of income for families earning $6,000, and 20 per cent at the $20,000 level.

Such a financial outlay is quite a considerable burden, and some objection may be anticipated. For example, students of vast inherited wealth may feel that the cost is completely beyond reason. There is also some legal question whether a commitment of a fraction of one's lifetime income does not constitute a kind of slavery. Finally, the scheme is, of course, unworkable for the majority of girls who do not pursue extended careers.

The form of this payment also makes it particularly competitive with voluntary giving. To some extent it would be a substitute, particularly for the annual gift campaigns. Whether this adverse effect should be weighed heavily depends upon the degree of universality of giving. Does the broad mass of alumni give some reasonable percentage of its income; or

[10] See the paper by Professor Kaysen, pp. 55–60.

[11] Treasury estimates of understatement of federal tax liability have been on the order of 10 per cent, with understatement for business and professional income perhaps twice that figure. See Marius Farioletti, "The 1948 Audit Control Program for Federal Income Tax Returns," *National Tax Journal* (June, 1949), 142–50; also *National Tax Journal* (March, 1952), 65–78.

is the voluntary burden carried by a small minority?

These are some of the more superficial difficulties of discrimination by lifetime income. However, this form of discrimination is a very attractive one. Perhaps some new ideas on voluntary annual giving might produce a result which was not dissimilar, yet would avoid the drawbacks. Class insurance with a premium which is a percentage of income rather than a constant dollar amount might be one device.

Conclusion

This paper presents no settled conclusions. In Part I the case for higher student charges has been examined, and while on the whole my arguments suggest that charges probably should be raised, I find myself with some concern for the consequences. I think the strengthening of our institutions of higher learning must be the dominant objective, especially in view of the East-West competition for world leadership, and if this goal requires higher tuition fees, that in itself is sufficient argument. In Part II some of the alternative methods of extracting an increased amount of revenue without undue hardship were considered.

As for questions for further study, I suggest these priorities:

(1) Could the technology of higher education be improved to reduce costs without deteriorating the product?

(2) Should the product itself be changed?

(3) How could more money from private nonstudent sources be obtained?

(4) How could federal money be properly channeled into higher education? Finally, to the extent that we fail on the first four issues,

(5) how could more money be raised from students?

TUITION AND COSTS
W. Robert Bokelman

MY concern with the pricing of college services is not centered either on the institutional or individual financial aspects but on some less immediate but perhaps more important effects. I will mention later some of the studies that the Office of Education is undertaking and others that have been completed which might be of interest to the reader.

On a trip from an airport to a hotel, my cab driver mentioned that he drives a cab only in the evenings and that, during the day, his regular job is driving a truck. He explained that it takes a lot of hustling to keep a family of four children going.

His need to hustle reminded me of the situation that is apparent over the country. There are many faculty and administrative people in second jobs, or if not, other members of the family are in second jobs. To enjoy the luxury of teaching, they have to have some other source of income.

Some figures that might be of interest appear in the 1955–56 biennial survey of higher education income and expense. In 1955–56, tuition and fee income provided 31.8 per cent of the total current funds expended for education and general purposes less sponsored research. Income for sponsored research was omitted, since it tends to be a purchase of services. For public institutions alone, the percentage was 15.3; for private ones, 54.5. Expenditures for instruction, administration, library and operation, and maintenance of the plant were included in the total.

Scholarship expenses are included in student aid. Tuition is reported gross. Expenses did not include costs of student aid, additions to plant, or auxiliary enterprises. Total education and general expenditures in 1955–56, as identified above, amounted to $2,789 million. In addition to this $2,789 million, expenditures for auxiliary enterprises amounted to $640 million, student aid to $96 million, and plant additions to $648 million.

We recognize that this total cost, which amounted to approximately four and a quarter billion dollars for higher education in 1955–56, did not represent the true actual cost. An additional cost was the subsidy contributed by faculty members through low salaries. Another deferred cost was inadequate maintenance, the continued use of substandard and obsolete facilities without adequate repairs or replacement. Also, there is no estimate of the amount saved through tax exemptions.

In addition to the problems faced in attempting to finance adequately the current operations of higher education, we should not overlook the problems of providing needed buildings and equipment for the instructional program. While there has been a tendency for income-producing properties to be financed on a self-supporting basis, this financing technique is not possible for instructional, research, and general buildings under our present concept of financing.

In the Office of Education, we have completed some studies and have others going on which, we hope, will supply information for more adequate analyses in some of these problem areas. These include a study of costs of attending college, student retention and withdrawal, institutional financial-aid programs, and higher-education planning and management data. The last study includes information on salaries, tuition rates, and room-and-board rates.

At the present time, and particularly in the years ahead, I think a principal feature of higher education is going to be cooperation, using our total facilities as best we can, rather than competition. In the past, and perhaps in some areas now, there is quite a bit of competition. I gather that there tends to be some difference of opinion between low-tuition institutions and high-tuition institutions.

We need to recognize common interest and to advance through cooperative efforts as much as we can. The concept of long-term individual educational financing which Professor Harris has suggested serves a useful purpose in that it forces people to think about the problem. There will be compromises along the way, but at least it identifies an issue for people to discuss and act upon.

In regard to the increase of tuition between public and private schools, we found that the public institutions had increased their tuition rates 9.2 per cent in one year, while the private institutions had increased their tuition rates 7.3 per cent. Because of the difference in the original base figures, the difference in amounts were $36 in private institutions, and $13 in public ones. In percentages, public institutions increased their rates faster than private ones, from 1956–57 to 1957–58.[1]

From the letters received by the Office of Education, we realize that tuition is still a competitive thing. Recently a university in the Rocky Mountains asked whether we had current tuition-rate data. Their legislature wants more facts on what other institutions are charging. It appears that not only salaries but also tuition rates are set on a competitive basis. In practice, administrators want to know how much they can raise tuition rates without getting out of line with similar institutions in their general area.

Another observation is that many of the universities are increasing their enrollments in the upper levels and graduate schools, while their freshmen and sophomore enrollments are beginning to fall off. It is too early to speculate whether this will be a pattern that will continue, and that eventually many four-year colleges will become feeder institutions. The trend is particularly noticeable in the state institutions. There were many universities whose underclass enrollment actually decreased absolutely as well as in percentage terms. A recent estimate that 50 per cent of all high-school graduates now began some post-high-school degree-oriented program would not seem far out of line if the over-all ratio of enrollment to college-age population is between 30 and 32 per cent nationally. We found in our retention and withdrawal study that, of the students who enter college, eventually 60 per cent graduate. Forty per cent graduate in a four-year sequence.

Despite all the troubles with our present pricing policies in both public and private institutions, it is remarkable that some 50 per cent of those who finish secondary schools — and, of course, they don't all finish — are continuing their education beyond high school. That 50 per cent is not a random distribution on the basis of ability. Other studies have indicated that a very high percentage of the top 10 per cent in ability go to college. While we obviously want to do better than we are doing in encouraging those with high ability to continue their education, we are doing remarkably well now compared even to five years ago.

Across the country, as was indicated earlier, there is still much extra unused instructional space. The problem is to get the students to go where spaces are available. A scholarship program, presumably, could help.

When we made the first part of our facility survey in 1956, we asked for the number of full-time students in attendance, the additional number of full-time students that could be accommodated in existing instructional facilities without jeopardizing present standards of operation, and the net number that could be accommodated after considering availability of housing either on campus or in the community. The additional numbers that could have been accommodated in instructional facilities was slightly more than 25 per cent of enrollment in the spring of 1956.

These are preliminary figures from a study in process. On the basis of the institutions' own estimates and not jeopardizing their present standards of operation, they could have taken care of about one-fourth more full-time students. Then, when they took into consideration the limits of housing, the total would be reduced by 200,000, making the net figure 400,000. This includes law schools and the other graduate schools. Thus we have a problem of utilizing our higher-education capacity more effectively, as well as expanding that capacity.

To sum up, our information on higher education in the United States — on the real costs to society of running the system, on the financial and other pressures on students, on the effective utilization of our present colleges and universities — is inadequate, although improving. We know that actual outlays do not represent the total costs of higher education due to underpayment of staff and undermaintenance of plant.

---

[1] In four recent years (ending 1958–59), the percentage rise was 33 per cent each for public and private institutions, but $50 and $150 respectively (Ed.).

III. GOVERNMENT AID

Summary of the Discussions of the January 15, 1959, meeting of the Seminar on the Economics of Higher Education. "Federal and State Aid" was the topic considered. Papers were given by Messrs. Mather, Meck, Gladfelter, and Musgrave.

Government Aid and Competition of Public and Private Institutions

Earlier discussion had established the impending financial distress in which colleges will find themselves in the absence of large additional revenues. The question of higher tuition, perhaps accompanied by an extensive loan program, was considered in Parts I and II. An alternative source of funds is direct government aid to colleges and universities. Of course, public universities already receive sizable appropriations from state and municipal governments. One of the questions facing these institutions is how much they can expect such appropriations to rise with the coming bulge in enrollment. State governments are pressed financially from other quarters as well, particularly from the primary and secondary schools.

Extensive federal aid is another possibility. Any program of federal aid gives rise to difficult problems such as the distribution between public and private schools and the degree of control which the government is to exercise over the schools in exchange for this aid. Many private colleges fear that aid given to public universities alone will enable them to retain their present low tuition fees, whereas private colleges will have to raise fees in order to pay increasing costs. This tuition differential may result in a significant shift in applications from private to public colleges, and the country may find itself in the anomalous position of trying desperately to construct buildings for public universities in order to satisfy the enormous demand, while many private colleges have excess space. In a period in which demand for college education threatens to exceed the nation's capacity to satisfy that demand, it is clearly in the interest of society to prevent private colleges from closing their doors.

On the other hand, any program which tends to equalize the cost to the student of private and public colleges, such as higher tuition in public colleges or a vast federal scholarship plan like the first "G.I. Bill," may result in a migration of the brightest students to prestige institutions, leaving "mass" education to the remaining schools. New faculty members would perhaps be separated in the same way. This would create an even greater divergence in quality among the country's institutions of higher learning than there is today, and it is not to be expected that schools with less prestige will accept this down-grading with equanimity. While we usually think of certain private colleges and universities as being the prestige institutions of the country, it is not clear that private colleges would gain the most from an equalizing program. Particularly in the Midwest and the Far West, the prestige institutions tend to be public rather than private schools. But it is likely that some of the most promising students of all regions, in the absence of financial impediment, would be attracted to national universities like Harvard, Massachusetts Institute of Technology, and Amherst. And the schools which lose these students will resent being thought of as "quantity" rather than "quality" institutions.

This controversy provides the background to specific proposals for government aid to education. This is quite apart from the difficulties pointed out by Professor Musgrave in finding government finance. It was felt, however, that his estimates for federal revenue and expenditures in the coming years were too pessimistic. In the next ten years or so, the Gross National Product can be expected to rise $100 to $200 billion, of which roughly $55 billion will be taken in taxes, $30 billion by the federal government. In the absence of war, $10 to $15 billion of this sum might be available each year for additional civil expenditures. It is this sum for which higher education will have to compete with other nonmilitary needs. One discussant felt that the federal government might be able to provide $2 billion a year to higher education ten years from now.

[75]

Tax Credits or Direct Aid

Some members were critical of the tax credit proposal presented by Mr. Meck and sponsored by the American Council on Education. First, allowing a tax credit on tuition payments does not help the institutions. They receive only the tuition, as before, while the families with children in college recoup directly in the form of lower taxes part of these tuition payments. Only if college tuition fees rise because of the tax credit will the proposal alleviate the financial difficulties of the colleges. It is true that many institutions might feel less hesitant about raising tuition if they could be sure that a substantial part of the burden of the higher cost would fall on the government rather than on families, who might not send their children to college because of the expense. But for this reason alone, advocates of low tuition as a principle are not likely to support a proposal which can only benefit colleges by facilitating a rise in tuition rates.

Some members of the seminar pointed out that even without a rise in tuition the tax-credit proposal would help colleges if it permitted a reduction in scholarships which are paid from the general revenues of the school. This effect is likely to be small, however; the reduction in taxes would generally comprise only a small proportion of the family income which is used to compute how generous a scholarship is needed.

Furthermore, the proposal benefits only those who do pay taxes, and thus misses completely the one-fourth of all families who pay no federal taxes at all, yet may have children who would profit from a college education. This proposal would have to be supplemented by another to meet the needs of very poor families who want to send children to college.

Another objection is that this proposal would be a windfall to all those families who now send children to college and are able to pay the tuition. The net effect of the plan might be to increase "luxury" expenditures rather than expenditures on higher education, since the family would be free to use its tax rebate as it chose. This assumes that tuition fees are not all automatically raised 43 per cent as a result of the 30 per cent tax credit. In that case the colleges will be better off, but families will find it no easier to send their children to college, and families paying no taxes will even find it more difficult to do so.

A final objection to the scheme, particularly important in the eyes of tax experts, is that it results in still further erosion of the tax base. The Congress is most critical of such proposals.

The tax-credit proposal represents one of a group of suggestions for aiding higher education through the back door. Several members felt that a positive appeal for direct aid should be made on the grounds of the fundamental importance of higher education to society, rather than for indirect aid through relief to taxpayers. As one participant put it, "There are many different groups in the country which can put up cases for special concessions in the income tax laws, and I think that this proposal tends to make the higher education institutions look like a rather selfish, self-interest lobby. The case for tax money going to higher education is a tremendously strong one and it ought to be based right squarely on its own merits, rather than through this back-door approach."

While conceding this in principle, others pointed out that certain practical considerations had to be taken into account. In the first place, the tax-credit proposal was first made at a time when there was not the tremendous public concern for education which seems to exist now. The political prospects for direct aid are now immeasurably better than they were a few years ago. Furthermore, the fact that the tax credit is a form of tax reduction instead of a new expenditure is likely to recommend it to election-conscious Congressmen even today. In addition, the tax-credit proposal involves no expensive administration, as any form of direct aid would; only one more line on the income tax form is required.

A final consideration which favors the "back-door" approach (through a tax-credit or similar plan) is the absence of possible government controls or interference in the affairs of the institutions which receive the aid. Students are not required to sign loyalty oaths, and universities are not required to offer special programs, and so on. These "strings" need not accompany direct aid either, of course, but legislation without them would be much more unlikely. Even apart from special conditions, direct aid must be allocated among different uses, and it is not clear that the federal government always knows the best allocation; indirect methods of aid allow for some degree of individual and institutional choice.

Scholarships to the Poor?

One participant suggested an alternative form of aid which would retain some of the advantages of the tax-credit proposal and meet some of the objections to it: a flat federal scholarship of $500 a year to college students from families with low income. Need could be determined on the basis of income and the number of children in the family. For example, the only child of any family with income below $4,000 a year would be entitled to the scholarship. If there were two children, $5,000 might be the cut-off point, with $6,000 for three children. Any young person from such a family gaining admission to a college would get the scholarship; there would be no evaluation of need or aptitude beyond that. Hence the cost of administering such a program would be small, though not negligible. Such a scholarship would go to the individual, and he could choose any school to which he was admitted. This program would increase the opportunity for the children of very poor families to go to college, and would aid colleges insofar as it saved their own scholarship resources. Here again, though, there would be little improvement of the financial position of colleges unless tuition fees were raised, and if this were done the children of poor families would be no more able to attend college than they would have been before receiving such a scholarship. The main purpose of this sort of scholarship program might be to increase educational opportunity; in that case, other measures would have to be adopted to preserve the financial solvency of many colleges and universities.

Any program involving a cut-off point runs into problems around the margin. A family with three children, earning $6,100 a year, would not benefit from this program, even though perhaps it should. Some families would be tempted to adjust their recorded incomes downward in order to be entitled to the scholarship, but the power of perjury behind the income tax return could be relied on to prevent gross abuses. An additional program of loans could help children of families with incomes of $6,000 to $15,000.

A minor problem is that of students whose expenses are actually less than $500 scholarship — those living at home and going to a municipal college with low or free tuition. Many complaints have been made about the scholarship students in the New York City colleges on this score. Adjusting the stipend to actual expenses would require some administrative machinery which the program in its simplest form is successful in avoiding. But this is not a serious flaw; furthermore, children from families with very low incomes probably need money for incidental expenses like clothing and books.

A few members felt that this proposal did not meet the main problem facing higher education: namely, the growing tuition differential between public and private institutions. As private colleges continually raise tuitions as the only source of revenue in the face of rising expenses, and public universities lack this compulsion because of their access to public funds, all but the most prestigious private institutions will "price themselves out of the market." Others insisted that this was *not* the major problem of higher education; providing adequate educational opportunity for the whole population remains the greatest task. In any case, they said, the scholarship program would help the small private colleges maintain enrollment in spite of rising tuition. Experience after the Korean War under the "G.I. Bill," in which veterans were given fixed sums, cast some doubt on the second proposition, however. These veterans tended to go to institutions where the tuition was low and the stipend could be stretched as far as possible.

Other Public Aids

Still other proposals for federal aid were mentioned. A modest one is to make tax deductible the repayment of principal on an educational loan. Interest payments are already deductible from income for tax purposes, and outstanding debts can be deducted from an estate before the estate tax is applied. If a sizable loan program were developed, this could be an important federal contribution to higher education. Such a benefit can probably be had today if loan repayment is made a moral rather than a contractual obligation, since then the "loan" repayment can be deducted as a charitable contribution to education.

Alternative forms of aid which were mentioned briefly are (1) the tax-exempt privilege of educational institutions, (2) government guarantee of educational loans, (3) government grants to colleges for buildings, (4) additional tax exemption for students at college, and (5) equalizing the individual contributor's proportion of charitable gifts. The last proposal arises from the effect of a progressive income tax on tax-deductible contributions. For a person with a very high income, a dollar given to education may really cost him only 20 cents, since his tax obligation is reduced by 80 cents. In contrast, a person with a low income may have to contribute as much as 80 cents, since his tax is reduced by only 20 cents for the dollar given away. The proposal would raise the tax share of contributions by those with low incomes to the 80 cents, say, which high-income givers save on taxes.

Competition of Public and Private Institutions for Aid

All these proposals involve a contribution by the federal government. But state and municipal governments already play a very important role in higher education, and several members suggested that this role should be expanded sufficiently to meet the needs of the future. State appropriations should be large enough to maintain and even extend the existing educational opportunity provided to all by the low tuition fees of public institutions. If private institutions could not compete with these low-tuition universities, that is only sufficient evidence that they no longer offer a product distinctive enough to offset the high tuition, one participant suggested.

Furthermore, the actual waste involved in expanding some colleges while others are closing can be exaggerated. That 200,000 vacant spaces exist in colleges in the United States is not in itself sufficient grounds for believing that there is much waste and that some more effective plan could eliminate it. In the first place, some vacancies will always exist due to incomplete fluidity — students dropping out of school when they were expected to return, transfer of students, and so on. Second, many of these vacancies represent "products" which are no longer in such high demand. Often they are in small, church-related colleges, and the churches do not now play the important role in guiding higher education which they did in the last century.

As one member put it, "You will never convince the son of a mechanic in Lowell that he should go to a small college out in Missouri, just because there is an empty spot out there, even if you gave him a full scholarship and put him on the train and sent him on his way. He thinks the Indians are still out there. . . His folks just wouldn't let him go out there in the wilds and he isn't going to let some college tell him that he has to go to church every morning and he has to drink milk."

All participants agreed on the importance of having colleges in the communities in which there is a demand for college education. Moreover, the presence of such colleges close to home stimulates an interest in going to college. That these colleges should be state-supported at low tuition fees was not so obvious, however, and was the source of considerable argument. One member noted that state appropriations for this purpose are not in fact permanent subsidies as had been suggested, since incomes are higher than average for those with college educations, and a large part of the cost will be returned to the state in the form of higher tax payments later in the life of the graduate. Thus low-tuition schools can be regarded as providing a kind of postpayment scheme; the graduate pays back years later in the form of higher taxes the difference between the costs of educating him and the tuition he paid.

It was pointed out, however, that there is a private gain as well as a social gain — while *part* of the increased income which could be tied to the college education returned to the state in the form of taxes, an even larger part did not. Since college students on the average come from families with higher than average incomes, and since state tax structures tend to be regressive — that is, they bear more heavily on the poor than on the wealthy — low-tuition state-supported schools in fact often involve a subsidy of the rich by the poor. On equity grounds, then, one could argue for raising tuition fees in state institutions and lowering state taxes.

One member added that the argument above logically applies to any form of investment, not just to education. If a new firm moves into the area, sets up a factory, and is profitable, it increases the community's income and hence its taxes. Perhaps, then, the state should provide investment funds for such firms, hoping to recoup them later in higher taxes. Where is one to draw the line?

But why should there be a differentiation between public and private colleges in the use of state funds? One participant described the Massachusetts scholarship programs. Under a 1957 law, $100,000 is provided annually for scholarships to Massachusetts residents through the Board of Educational Assistance. The law stipulates that no more than 25 per cent of the funds can go to students in public institutions, but up to 90 per cent can be used in private colleges, including scholarships to Massachusetts residents going to colleges out of the state. The average stipend under this program is about $250.

A second program, the Massachusetts Scholarship Foundation, also operated in the last academic year with $100,000, although the funds are private, resulting from a governor's appeal, rather than publicly appropriated. These scholarships can go to any graduate of a Massachusetts high school who is attending college in Massachusetts, and stipends vary from $200 to $800. Both New York and California have more extensive programs than these, the latter state providing about a million dollars a year in scholarships for students in both public and private colleges.

One member suggested that this was perhaps the solution to the conflict between low-tuition state-supported institutions and private institutions which must raise tuition fees in order to remain financially solvent. The states could provide some students with scholarships which would enable them to attend colleges with high tuition fees. The taxpayer must consider what is the best investment for his money: expanding public institutions, providing funds for poor students to go to private institutions, or some combination.

In this connection, all the participants of the seminar were impressed by the remarkable success of state aid to private colleges in Pennsylvania. Here there is direct aid through state appropriations. Several members raised the question of the apparently arbitrary allotment of state aid to three out of the sixty-three private institutions in Pennsylvania. This was largely for historical reasons, although Temple University is not as old as some other schools in the state. All three private institutions which receive state aid can be regarded as especially important appendages to the state system for higher education, however. They are all in concentrated areas of population, where the demand for higher education can be expected to grow most rapidly. In spite of their relatively high tuition fees, they have been absorbing much of this new demand, which Pennsylvania State University is not well located to satisfy. The low tuition there is partly offset for most people by having to live and eat away from home and by the added travel costs.

A similar situation exists in Massachusetts. With three million of Massachusetts' five million people concentrated in the Boston area, the University of Massachusetts, located in Amherst in the western part of the state, is not in a position to provide a maximum educational opportunity, even with its relatively low tuition of $200. The costs of travel, dormitory living, and eating out are high enough to deter many would-be college students. Within the Boston area, however, Tufts College, Northeastern University, Boston University, and Boston College are serving a large part of the need for which a state-supported system would otherwise have to provide.

Temple, for example, with only 600 out of a total enrollment of over 16,000 living in dormitories, largely serves the educational needs of the Philadelphia area, and saves the state legislature $15 million a year, which it collects in tuition. With tuition at $730 and most of we do about tuition fees or scholarships or loans, or any other proposal, they must see this possibility."

Motivation versus Aid

Several examples of the importance of creating favorable motivation were given. One town in Massachusetts had available much scholarship money for high-school graduates, but very few were interested, despite many competent students; there was a failure somewhere in the school guidance program. A similar situation existed in Corning, New York. Bright high-school graduates followed the pattern of their parents: job, car on credit, wife, children. The Corning Foundation then established an annual "College Day," on which eloquent college presidents were brought in to talk to the students about the advantages of a college education, and to explain the process of application. Since then the college-going aspirations of the town's students have increased many times. It was not a question of money, but of proper motivation.

The study of medicine in Vermont was another interesting case. A much higher proportion of the students in Vermont aspire to become doctors and more of them go on to do so than in the neighboring states. The existence of a medical school with very low tuition at the University of Vermont, it is thought, places the study of medicine within the realm of possibility for the high-school freshman. He does not rule it out from the beginning, as he might if he thought the cost of medical school was, say, $1,500 a year.

Others added that even high tuition fees would not be a psychological deterrent if high-school students received proper counseling on the availability of scholarships and loans and the high lifetime income of college graduates. One member proposed a rise of $100 in college tuition, the extra revenue to be used in an extensive high-school counseling and guidance program. This, several felt, would do much more to increase educational opportunity than merely maintaining low tuition and not disseminating information broadly about what the actual possibilities were. But there was no general agreement on this point.

In any case, it is clear from the illustrations above and from others that arousing a college-oriented motivation, as well as removing financial impediments, is important. Providing money is not enough.

Title 5 of the National Defense Education Act of 1958 provides for strengthening the counseling and guidance services of the high schools. Several members pointed out the important role which can be played by liberal arts colleges in implementing Title 5, since these are entitled to offer their own programs for guidance training, and qualify for aid under the Act. It need not be left only to colleges with formal programs in education. A more effective guidance program on a national scale could do much to get capable students into college.

One participant observed, however, that a genuine, well-publicized national scholarship program like the "G.I. Bill" might reduce considerably the need for extensive college guidance services. An increasing awareness of the existence of colleges and the possibility of going to college without large financial strain would result in larger participation of the able but poor.

Finally, even in the absence of an extensive guidance program in the high schools, whether financed by the federal government or the state educational authorities, the colleges themselves can do much in stimulating an interest in attending college. It is too big a job for one institution or even ten, however wealthy, but by working together 200 to 300 public and private institutions could do much at little cost to each, by hunting for talent in areas now rarely reached in the regular rounds of college admissions officers: the Chicago slums, small towns, the South, and so on. In this way much "lost" ability could be located and developed even without an elaborate program of government aid. Fifty thousand dollars a year might be enough to inaugurate such a program, and then increasingly other colleges would be expected to join and make small contributions.

* * * *

In summary, government aid to higher education, although highly desirable in principle, raises a number of difficult choices which must be faced in working it out in detail. Should the aid be from the federal government, with its vast fiscal resources but correspondingly large claims on them, or from state governments, poorer but closer to the scene? Should it be through the back door, in the form of tax concessions to individuals, or through the front door as direct grants to institutions? Should direct grants be for specific construction, or for general operating costs, including faculty salaries? Each proposal has its proponents and, even more, its opponents. The danger is that in failure to agree on the form which the aid should take, none will be given.

SOME ISSUES RAISED BY RECENT LEGISLATION

Philip H. Coombs

IT is too early to tell how the various titles of the National Defense Education Act are going to be administered. It might be worth bearing in mind, however, that what is happening on the federal front in education is going to influence considerably the whole context within which educational decisions by individual institutions or even by state governments are going to be made. We have not yet learned to give enough weight to the effect of federal activities on education.

In the early fall of 1958, soon after the new Education Act was passed in August, I spent considerable time in Washington trying to learn about the provisions of the legislation and to assess its possible impact upon education generally. In this process, I talked with numerous people on Capitol Hill, in the administrative agencies, and in the volunteer educational agencies. For me it was quite an education. I had spent some years in Washington on other matters, but I had much to learn about the politics of education.

Several observations can be made about the new role of the federal government in higher education. First, the National Defense Education Act is, by all odds, the most important educational action taken by the federal government — at least since Lincoln signed the Morrill Act. It may turn out to be even more important in terms of what it will lead to in the way of further action.

Furthermore, even though many people are still engaged in the great semantic battle over the federal role in education, the passage of this Act marks the end of much of that battle. In passing the Act, Congress made a decision to put the federal government deeply into education, financially and in other ways.

The manner in which Congress acted was anything but neutral with respect to some of the great issues that are currently controversial in education. It was not as if they passed a big lump-sum grant for school construction. Instead, Congress took relatively careful aim, as if with a rifle rather than a shotgun, at several selected problems that are currently critical in American education, at both the secondary-school and college levels. In passing the Act, Congress implicitly took a stand on such important issues as the education of gifted children, the relative importance of different subjects in the curriculum, and the need for innovations in teaching methods.

A careful reading of the Act and consideration of its legislative history make it obvious that Congress knowingly took positions on these issues which the educators themselves are still debating. Congress in effect took a stand in favor of differential programming for abler students in the schools and colleges. It took a stand on some debatable curriculum questions by giving special attention to foreign languages, science, and mathematics, even though the total effect of the Act is to cut across the whole curriculum. And it also took the stand, with which many educators do not yet agree, that modern media of communications such as films and television should be given a much larger role in the learning process.

Some of these specific measures are going to affect virtually all colleges and universities whether they like it or not. For example, the federal student loan program will inevitably affect tuition decisions. It will tend to encourage private colleges to raise tuition faster than they otherwise would. (In all candor, the chief interest of college administrators in loan programs, which has mounted greatly in the last two years, has been, so it seems to me, mainly a matter of taking the sting out of tuition increases, even though there is much talk about helping needy students.) Loans are a counterbalance to tuition increases.

In more and more states, the loan program will probably also work in the direction of increasing state-university tuition fees. The availability of student loans on liberal terms will greatly weaken the long-standing argument for low tuition: to insure equality of educational opportunity. The administrators of state universities may not agree, but it does weaken their case, and it gives the economy

[83]

bloc in the state legislature a new argument.

The loan program of this Act is not its only feature which will affect higher education in the United States. The guidance program has great potentialities for good or harm, depending on how it is handled. In either case, it is going to affect the quality of the job colleges are able to do, for it affects the work done in identifying the right youngsters below the college level and giving them the right kind of advice on their academic programs and choice of college.

Here is one point where the colleges should show more interest than they have to date in the administration of this Act. To my knowledge, thus far the only people who have taken part in any serious discussions in Washington about the guidance title are the professional guidance counselors. While they undoubtedly have much to offer, it seems evident that college admissions officers and others who are familiar with the problems of young people and with the precollege training their institutions need in order to do a good job also have much to offer. In some respects, perhaps, they should be preferred in the administration of the guidance title because they are not the captives of a professional folklore.

Another important point of interest for college administrators is the fellowship title. It aims, although not exclusively, to produce more college teachers, and it is one more big step by the federal government which will affect graduate education throughout the country. Now, I feel sure that nobody in Washington has a calculated scheme to affect all graduate education. As a matter of fact, I could find no individual or agency in Washington, including the Bureau of the Budget, that could provide even a simple list of all the fellowship and student-grant programs operated by various federal agencies which impinge on education above the undergraduate level. An educational planner, whether with good motives or bad, would certainly have such a list and would try to assess the probable impact of all the federal government measures combined.

Nobody seems to have thought seriously about this. Yet the federal agencies are today running many separate programs, most of them with specific delimitations which very decidedly and directly affect the graduate schools. Far from being a carefully designed pattern, the situation more recently resembles a national tug-of-war for talent, with the National Health Agency, the National Science Foundation, the military services, the Atomic Energy Commission, and now the Office of Education, all holding out rather substantial bait — much better bait than most universities could offer — to attract scarce talent into particular fields. The new Office of Education fellowship program is the only one I know of that is not limited in subject matter; it cuts across all major subject fields. But the net effect of these federal fellowships and research grants may be to pull people out of teaching and to pull them from one field to another. No one knows, and no one has tried to find out. Yet the federal government, more or less unwittingly, has become a major force in shaping the future of graduate education in this country. I think it is high time that somebody sat down and tried to see what it all adds up to.

The new program is definitely calculated to expand the distribution of graduate capacity, both geographically and by types of institutions. One aim is to increase the number of universities offering the Ph.D. degree, and that is partly why that title is constructed the way it is. The very fact that the money is made available to the university and not to the student is indicative of the effort to encourage Ph.D. programs at universities which do not now offer them. It is significant, for example, that the graduate dean of Harvard went down to Washington to administer this title, and neither he nor anyone else felt that there would be any conflict of interest, because Harvard obviously was not intended to receive any of these fellowships.

Some observers interpret the Act as not only making possible but requiring that the Commissioner of Education take over coordination of all graduate fellowship programs operated by the federal government. However, that is not quite accurate. There *is* a provision under Title 10 (I haven't found anyone in the Office of Education who knows how it got there; apparently it was added during Congressional committee work) which directs the Commissioner of Education to inform himself about the various educational activities of the whole federal government, particularly as they relate to such matters as fellowships and college teaching, and to work for their coordination. The title is very fuzzy. It clearly does not empower the Commissioner to take over "coordination" or to dictate to any other federal agency on how it shall conduct itself. The word "coordination" is there, but the hope seems to be that the availability of the facts will in itself encourage coordination.

But there is still *nobody* in the federal government, unless it be the President, who can exercise directive power over all agencies, each of which at present has its own hoard of fellowship or research funds and each of which seems anxious to avoid coordination by anybody.

No Cabinet officer, particularly the Secretary of Health, Education, and Welfare, who is the junior secretary, is in the right position of power in the federal government to direct or control his colleagues in the Cabinet.

Moreover, there is some question about how responsibility should be divided between the Commissioner of Education and the Secretary of Health, Education, and Welfare. Many hold that the Commissioner is independent of the Secretary. Indeed, the Act refers largely to the Commissioner and gives him the power. Obviously, however, a man without even Cabinet rank is not going to have much influence on all those other independent agencies.[1]

In the comments above, I do not mean to sound unsympathetic either to the Act or to the individuals administering it; I am describing the situation rather than the people.

Now, with the great power of the federal government having been turned loose on education in an almost laissez-faire manner, and with everybody expecting something to happen, it becomes important to ask how well equipped the federal government is to exercise this power wisely and fairly toward the betterment of education.

As far as the Office of Education is concerned, requiring it suddenly to administer the new act is rather like taking the operator of a small corner grocery store and suddenly giving him a new shopping center to operate. It is no criticism of the old hands in the Office of Education to say that they have been given a job that is 'way over their heads, in terms both of the amount of time and energy they have and also in terms of their experience and general competence to do some of these things.

The Office, at least for many years, has been oriented toward primary and secondary schools, not toward higher education, and most of the people in the Office came up through the school tradition. Many of them, for instance, have been principals, school superintendents, or state commissioners. They come out of that particular tradition which at times has been at war with the other tradition of higher education. The small higher-education staff has worked manfully over the years to try to shed a little light on what higher education looks like in this country, through the collection and dissemination of data, but they have never had operational responsibility for a program. Now, suddenly, they have it.

This means, then, that the Office of Education, faced with these enormous new administrative responsibilities, needs a few of the ablest people in the whole United States to help launch the new program under the various titles of the Act.

Yet — and this is a problem for our political scientists to worry about — the federal government has managed, over the years, to tie its hands almost completely in terms of its ability to attract and hold scholarly talent. The Office of Education simply does not have enough top salaries to pay, and under the conflict-of-interest laws (designed for a very different purpose) no private university or philanthropic foundation can help remedy the situation.

[1] Many people are wary of more centralized authority in the field of education. If authority is given to the Commissioner of Education, many fear that there will be extensive direct influence of the federal government all over the country. If authority were given to the Secretary of Health, Education, and Welfare, many would object that this is really the function of the Commissioner of Education. He is appointed independently by the President, and is therefore not fully subordinate to the Secretary. Diffuse control in the hands of the Secretary would arouse the disapproval of professional educators; authority in the hands of the Commissioner would arouse the fear of excessive federal domination of education. This dilemma is partly responsible for the delay in coordinating — or even examining systematically — federal activities in higher education.

It is illegal to contribute to the compensation of any person for rendering services to the federal government. These conflict-of-interest laws were originally written to keep the businessmen from raiding the Treasury, but now they stand in the way of the education program, the science program, the health program, and other important government activities that require rare ability. This is a major problem that someone ought to try to solve.

This whole problem also descends to the states and their Departments of Education at a later time. Some portions of the Act provide for much more traffic through the federal-state channel of funds that presumably will be handled through the offices of the state Commissioners of Education. This raises the question of how well these state offices are prepared to cope with these problems. The people in these offices are school-oriented. In most cases, they know practically nothing about higher education, and many of the functions they will be required to perform will be entirely new and foreign to them. In some respects, the state Offices of Education are even less well prepared than the federal Office of Education.

What this suggests is that, in terms of our mechanisms for decision-making and for administration in the realm of education, there are serious deficiencies. The deficiency is not limited to the executive branch. Congress is even more deficient in proper staffing and mechanisms for making decisions in education. The committees on Capitol Hill that consider education are primarily labor committees. They have staff members who know much about labor problems, but they do not pretend to know much about educational problems. They are subjected to all the pressures of organized educational groups as well as anti-education groups. They do not dare take them too literally. Yet they do not know where to turn for objective advice. There is nothing like the Council of Economic Advisors in the education field. The President could not today write the equivalent of the Economic Report in the field of education. The facts are not there; the analysis is not there.

Thus, the whole federal government, having stepped heavily into the education picture, is really quite ill-equipped to perform effectively there, and the state governments are no better off.

The problem is a difficult one, and the White House position has been that while the need for some kind of coordination of facts, if not of policies, is recognized, there is a fear that it might be construed that the administration was tooling up to control education. But the federal government is already well on its way toward affecting the situation in a variety of ways, and the most irresponsible way for the federal government to act is to shoot off in all directions without stopping to ask what it is doing. It is interfering with education blindly.

One other comment on the weaknesses of our present mechanisms should be made. We know that in our system of government voluntary organizations play a very important role in hammering out policy. They provide the countervailing forces which are indispensable to democratic action. There are great contrasts among the educational organizations in their degree of sophistication in playing a role in public policy-making and in the administration of public policy. The school-oriented people are comparatively old hands at this. They know their way around Congress, around the Office of Education, and elsewhere, and they have been at the trough before. They know how to get bills written and how to make their views known and implemented.

But the organizations in Washington representing higher education, perhaps with the exception of the land-grant-college organization, which has had practical political experience before, strike me as being ill-equipped to perform their roles in this new era. Educational institutions, especially colleges and universities, tend to behave very autonomously, and, although they will go to conventions together, they have never learned how to pull together in formulating a common policy for the good of education. They argue among themselves and rarely reach agreement on major issues that really count. Yet one of the high functions of an educational organization at this point in history ought to be to help its constituents formulate sensible policy positions that will at least not hurt education and might help it. When this test is applied to the existing organizations in higher education, they fail it pretty badly. Therefore, here is another area about which we ought to be concerned.

One final point which affects our considerations is illustrated by an old saying, allegedly based on a research study by Paul Mort at Columbia Teachers' College. He found the average time-lag between the innovation of a sound idea in education and the time when it is fairly generally applied to be about fifty years. This is not a joke. It is a fact.

The new environmental conditions in this country, however, are such that educational change is going to occur at a far more rapid rate in the future. Both the need for and the acceptance of change and experimentation have shifted dramatically in the last five years, especially in the last year or two.

The attitudes of Congress have changed radically. Many of these educational problems are going to find themselves in a quite different context a year or five years from now — a context conducive to rapid change. Thus, in any consideration of matters of tuition, finance, curriculum, or whatever, we must take heavy account of the direction and speed of this change.

FEDERAL AND STATE AID

J. Paul Mather

I WOULD say, in the first place, that as far as my own professional and personal philosophy is concerned, I would endorse without any reservation everything that Dr. Eldon Johnson says in his paper. Beyond that, in terms of the position of the University of Massachusetts and the recent rise in tuition, part of the policy is localized by the peculiar Massachusetts statutory and legislative position of the University vis-à-vis the position of other land-grant and state universities. I regard the increase in tuition which the board of trustees voted early in 1959, and in which I acquiesced reluctantly after four years of fighting any increase whatsoever, as basically a compromise with expediency, political and otherwise, and not a fundamental expression of what those of us who are still defending low tuition really believe. In the long run, the members of my board who were reluctant about the move — which doubled the tuition at the University of Massachusetts from the $100 rate established in 1933 — believe, as I do, in a long-range philosophy of *no tuition*.

It might be of some interest to point out that the most ardent supporter of this thesis is a graduate of Dartmouth and Harvard on the Board, a Boston lawyer who, according to his background, would be assumed to be on the other side — that is, a defender of high tuition and of private education. However, he fundamentally believes in the philosophy of public education, as I do. Public higher education, as Mr. Johnson has pointed out, is not often very well defended in the northeastern section of this country.

The University of Massachusetts is trying to expand its annual budget to meet mushrooming demands for public education in the next few years. Massachusetts is the largest of the New England states in terms of population and fiscal resources, but it stands at the bottom of the national totem pole in public education. It is impossible to contradict the fact that Massachusetts ranks fiftieth in per-capita expenditure on public higher education and in the percentage of its state budget spent on operating funds for public higher education each year. In that atmosphere, we face greater than average difficulty in translating fiscal attitudes at the legislative level into financial support for the expansion which the University has undertaken in the past five years and, indeed, since World War II, particularly with the Commonwealth's own fiscal situation in a critical position. This entire situation creates an atmosphere of financial expediency rather than one based on public need.

The University in an expansion program, however, is faced with a need which is not merely financially expedient, for raising faculty salaries or increasing operating funds. I imagine that everyone else in the country is striking for increased faculty salaries. In Massachusetts, however, legislative restrictions have (even after the winning of our "freedom-bill" legislation in 1956)[1] kept us in a strait jacket of minimum and maximum classified pay schedules (established by legislation) that leave us with maxima, particularly for our professional administrative staff, and, most important, for our associate and full professors, too low to compete. By "too low," I mean they are below all of our sister land-grant institutions in New England and far below the midwestern and western institutions. When the University of Rhode Island has higher maxima by $2,000 for a post than the University of Massachusetts, then in terms of comparable economic resources or any other fiscal policy, the University is in bad shape.

This means that we inevitably lose able faculty members, especially when we have distinguished professors whom we are trying to retain against "raiding," which is now reaching dangerous proportions. Some people try to cover this up with a kind of maudlin altruism, saying that the private colleges and the public colleges all love each other, and somehow we are all going to share our faculties and resources. This is nonsense. In my opinion, we

---

[1] Legislation which, for example, freed the University from committing itself too early for tenure appointments (Ed.).

are engaged in the greatest degree of buying piracy restricted only by our budgets, public or private, and we ought to recognize it now, long before the period of acute shortage in the supply of professional people confronting us in the next ten years.

What happens is simply that we cannot retain our outstanding associate and full professors. In the instructor and assistant professor ranks the University finds its salaries more competitive. The University of Massachusetts has recruited some, even from Harvard, an act for which I have no apologies.

In terms of publicly expressed policy, I have no sympathy at all with the assumption that the private-college people are going to do a quality job from here on out, and somehow or other, we in public institutions are going to take their left-over professors to work with the mass education problem. At present, however, we cannot retain our best associate and full professors with our low maxima, let alone recruit new ones, when we are expanding this fall to accept another 900 students, with enrollment rising from 5,100 to 6,000. The Massachusetts Legislature and the state administration have provided us with facilities through appropriations of some $28 million in a five-year period, primarily for the arts and sciences. Unless this plant is going to become big skating rinks, empty of either students or faculty, we need to recruit faculty members, and the Legislature still assumes a 15 to 1 ratio of students to faculty, 45 per cent in the two upper ranks and 55 per cent in the two lower ranks.

Recruiting that new faculty is going to be impossible in the coming market and, to make our problem even more critical, we plan to enroll about 1,000 students more each year, reaching a total of 10,000, admittedly a rapidly accelerating program. Please note that this is in terms of new admissions, to create a college the size of Amherst College every year. We know that we are not going to be able to recruit faculty for such a program without higher salaries.

How far behind we are in Massachusetts is indicated by the fact that we didn't — we couldn't — admit any freshman last year who didn't stand in the upper 15 per cent of his high-school class for four years, plus having a Scholastic Aptitude score of 550 or better. Those are our minimum admission standards. Much of this discussion, I think, is not a discussion of economics. It is a discussion of how to use the admission standards for the two types of institutions to interpret your philosophy of economics, either private or public. My philosophy of economics is that already expressed by Mr. Johnson — that of low-tuition, first-rate public institutions able to accept as many qualified students as seek admission. On our side of the fence, a public obligation for lower and middle-income-class families exists. I don't believe you will ever be able to translate this concept into mortgage loans, the proposal now widely discussed as a means of financing higher tuition.

In the Commonwealth of Massachusetts, we face the problem that we are among the very few state land-grant universities in the nation, all of whose revenues, *tuition and other*, are returned to the General Fund. For this reason, a rise in tuition does not commit the Legislature to return the tuition by appropriation for faculty salaries. This is particularly true when they are assembled in an atmosphere of bankruptcy predicated by the administration and by comments of legislators. As long as this is so, inadequate faculty salaries cannot provide the rationale for a rise in tuition. I think what the board of trustees at the University did in raising the tuition was merely to make a gesture of recognition of the depreciation of the dollar between 1933 and 1958. They said that the best justification for doubling the tuition was a current 50 cent dollar value.

And, by such an increase, they maintain that in the New England region where Maine, New Hampshire, Vermont, and Rhode Island all charge higher tuition than Massachusetts (Connecticut was the only one with the same tuition and fee rate before our change was made), we come to the Legislature with the implicit agreement that we have covered the cost of an improved salary structure essential for the preservation of the quality of the program. We hope that the state administration and all those concerned will be able to translate to the Legislature the dire need of linking to the salary increases this tuition increase, as it comes both from present enrollments and from increased increments from students in the future.[2]

The philosophy of public education, in which I firmly believe, is one which we have inherited and expressed in the state universities as nominal tuition rates from an agrarian, almost anti-intellectual society. Those nominal tuition rates, when they were first assessed, in my opinion, were compromises of expediency in which the people said that they would not apply to higher education the concept of free education which they have progressively applied to secondary and to elementary schools. It is my own view that, by 1975, when the population of this country has risen to 230 million, we will have persuaded the American public that public and private higher education are worth investing in as a prime recoverable allocation of material resources. I hope that in 1975, moves of the kind that my board made will be judged, as I feel they are today, expedient and wrong. By that time, I hope that the American public will have regarded the bachelor's degree as they publicly regarded the high-school diploma in the period from 1900 to 1958 — it should be available without payment of fees and it is the responsibility of the public to make this possible.

We, at the University, are *against*, on philosophical as well as long-range *social-progress* grounds, any increase in tuition beyond a nominal amount. We regard a $500 tuition rate, which would give us the highest in state tuition in the country, as ridiculous.

I sometimes feel as I read the press that the land-grant colleges west of the New York line are fortunate in having a body of alumni so much greater than it is in the northeastern part of the country. Legislators, with whom I am becoming more and more familiar by the year, are certainly of a constituency or class that doesn't quite resemble the gray-flannel-suit or Ivy League graduate. I think they will defend in the long run the same thesis that I am defending here.

As far as federal aid is concerned, out of a $10,300,000 operating budget last year we received $1,200,000 from the federal government, a major portion of that being for federal agricultural extension and experiment-station programs. I have a growing apprehension over the justification of expending the amount of federal funds that we spend on extension and experiment-station agricultural programs in New England. I have difficulty defending them either against the faculty outside agriculture at the University or to the state and others. They greatly doubt that this expenditure is justified, even though it is allocated on a farm-unit formula. Productive agriculture in the Commonwealth represents less than 1 per cent of the gross product for the state, and I believe that many of these programs are so weak as not to justify their outlays in relation to overall higher education budgets in terms of contributions to the economy of New England or of Massachusetts.

We are beginning to receive increasing amounts from the federal government in grants, such as the Atomic Energy Commission grants for equipment and medical or biologically related allocations for capital expenditure. We received some $500,000 last year on two new buildings that are under way in these fields.

I was one of the heretics at the land-grant meetings in December 1958 who voted against the concept that federal funds for capital outlay in higher education should go only to public institutions. I voted that if they were to increase, they should go to both public and private institutions.

---

[2] President Mather courageously fought for the increase of University of Massachusetts faculty salaries. In protest against the hostility, anti-intellectualism, and *excessive* concern for the taxpayer of the State Legislature, he announced his resignation as President of the University of Massachusetts, effective at the end of the 1959–60 academic year. The impact of this action undoubtedly contributed to some later concessions by the legislators (Ed.).

STATE AID FOR PRIVATE INSTITUTIONS IN PENNSYLVANIA

Millard E. Gladfelter

SOME of the problems which will need to be solved by higher education during the next decade have been set before us by statisticians and researchers. Nearly every metropolitan community and most of the official bodies responsible for education in the fifty states have appointed committees or commissions for an appraisal of the projected needs of higher education. Most of the resulting reports have been published, and the statistics and figures presented therein confront us with irrefutable facts. Among them are these:

(1) We will not only have more available youth for college, but also a larger percentage of the available youth will seek post-high-school education.

(2) Those responsible for programs of higher education are confronted with the task of re-examining our offerings with the intention of adapting them to the needs of the increased college population.

(3) We can anticipate a change in the present pattern of financial support for higher education.

Of course, there are many other problems that will make demands upon our energy and resources during this period, such as the need for expanded physical facilities, the shortage of teachers, and the need for a revision of programs with respect to graduate education. It is my purpose here to make brief statements about the first three problems mentioned.

The inevitability of a rapidly growing college-age population is, of course, not a matter of dispute. Likewise, it is rather certain that the proportion of our youth of college age who will continue their education beyond high school will also increase greatly. This number will vary among the states and indeed among localities within each state.

Pennsylvania, like some other areas of our country, has a smaller percentage of its youth of college age attending college than has the nation as a whole. This is difficult to understand, in view of the fact that Pennsylvania is among the states with the largest number of chartered institutions of higher education. One can readily see, therefore, that states like Pennsylvania, which have high industrial and agricultural activity and are rich in natural resources, are likely to increase greatly over the present rate the percentage of youth attending college. As a result, there will be a greater opportunity and need for the development of institutions that concentrate on programs that do not now exist and for which need will arise.[1]

The areas in which we are accustomed to group our activity in higher education are (a) two and three-year programs, (b) baccalaureate programs, (c) graduate and professional education. Past practices for each of these will be subjected to change because of the stress that will be brought upon them by the enlarged number of applicants and the limitations of physical facilities and staff.

The Pennsylvania State University and Temple University have extended their services to the Commonwealth through junior colleges and community college centers. These are established in populous areas that do not now have opportunities for appropriate college programs within commuting distance. The programs include technical as well as liberal arts courses. The program in general education is planned for transfer purposes. Financial support for these units is derived chiefly from tuition income and in some instances the units have been established in facilities provided by local communities. Although enrollments now number less than 5,000 students in units of this kind, one can safely predict, on the basis of experience elsewhere in the country, that these units will continue to grow rapidly. For a heavily populated state like Pennsylvania, this is the most practical and economical way to extend educational opportunity. To establish residence facilities at distant points for

---

[1] The argument here is, if I understand this passage, that Pennsylvania's enrollment in institutions of higher learning is low for a state with such high incomes and economic potential. Relatively large increases in enrollment are therefore to be expected (Ed.).

the large college-going population from urban areas would be very costly, but, by maintaining the urban university in the large cities and providing two-year programs for students in the less populous areas, residence costs for the individual would be reduced, and the likelihood of attendance by many able young men and women who do not now go on to college would be increased.

The need for graduate programs for teachers has accelerated greatly during recent years. It is impossible for all in the Commonwealth to share easily in the opportunities for graduate study when the institutions offering graduate programs are located at great distances from them. Accordingly, at the invitation of five liberal arts colleges in southeastern Pennsylvania, Temple University offers graduate programs on their campuses. These colleges are Albright, Franklin and Marshall, Lebanon Valley, Muhlenberg, and Ursinus. This program involves not only the use of physical facilities, but also the sharing of staff and library resources. This type of cooperation extends educational opportunities with the least expense to the institutions and the taxpayer. There are many valid objections to off-campus graduate centers, and yet institutions must be prepared to distribute and diversify their resources as the demands for them increase, or else less desirable means for attaining the ends will be employed.

This program of interinstitutional cooperation was made possible by a subvention from the Fund for the Advancement of Education. Aside from the specific procedures in teacher education that were the main objects of study, other benefits came to the faculty members and the institutions that participated. The faculty members pooled their experiences and talents into a "circuit-riding" staff that brought about a unity of purpose in an educational venture and developed an appreciation of the value of interinstitutional cooperation. It emphasized the importance of the teacher, the procedure used in the classroom, and the place of books, reports, and discussions in the educational process as against the assumed influence of the architecture of massive and sometimes hideous buildings or the possibility of some intellectual pollen falling and fertilizing the mind of one walking across a college campus.

Finally, we are already witnessing a change in the pattern of financial support of higher education. Tuition fees are rising, publicly supported institutions are increasing their fees, and in many instances annual contributions are now used for capital rather than endowment purposes. Many of the reports of state and metropolitan committees and commissions recommend that when new institutions are established, support for them should come from several sources. The Pennsylvania Commission recommended that for new quasipublic institutions, these sources should be tuition, contributions from the local community, and appropriations from the General Assembly. It would appear, therefore, that the plan which has been in effect in Pennsylvania for supporting private universities which are dedicated to meet the needs of the people of the Commonwealth in undergraduate, graduate, and professional programs is in growing favor. An extreme burden would be placed upon the Commonwealth by any program which would provide higher education for all people in the state at public expense.

The plan which has developed whereby the General Assembly supports the state institutions and grants financial aid to the three state-aided universities — the University of Pennsylvania, University of Pittsburgh, and Temple University — not only extends educational opportunity but also enables the state to spread its resources more widely. The tuition income and private support which also come to the state-aided universities relieve the Commonwealth of much of the cost for current operation.

It is becoming increasingly clear that it will be more desirable to meet tomorrow's needs through institutions that now exist rather than to establish many new ones. If this is to be done, we must be prepared to change our present patterns of operation if we are to meet the public demand.

THE TAX-CREDIT PROPOSAL

John F. Meck

THE tax-credit bill started several years ago when tax relief was in the air. There was, and still is, a feeling on the part of many Congressmen that they wished to provide some relief to taxpayers in the college education of their children and, at the same time, to alleviate institutional financial problems.

The tax-credit plan did not originate with me. I merely became the spokesman for it before the House Ways and Means Committee in 1958 in my capacity as chairman of the Committee on Taxation of the American Council on Education. Simply stated, the tax-credit plan is one way of using the tax laws to aid education. There is probably more agreement on this proposal than on any other that has been advanced.

There is nothing unusual about seeking Congressional aid for colleges and universities through the tax laws. I feel that this means of aid is sometimes dismissed too lightly. An example of this sort of aid was the increase in 1954 from 20 to 30 per cent in the permissible deduction for charity from income reported for taxes — a change which was achieved with relatively little effort. On the other hand, some educators worked very hard on the 1954 Internal Revenue Code Revision to obtain certain additional tax deductions for parents of college students. Aid is also given to colleges through the subsidized interest rate on loans through the Federal Housing Program for the construction of dormitories and other buildings. Both public and private institutions, incidentally, have benefited from this.

The tax-credit plan started about five years ago, and it is essentially quite simple. The word "credit" has special significance, in that it is a credit against the tax, not a deduction from taxable income. In other words, a taxpayer computes his tax and then deducts the amount of the credit directly from his tax bill. The approach for which I testified was a credit of 30 per cent of the amount paid for tuition and related fees to an institution of higher education. There was a maximum credit of $450. Thus, if tuition were $1400, the credit would be $420; if it were $600, the credit would be $180; if it were $100, the credit would be $30. The taxpayer would reduce his tax liability by 30 per cent of tuition, up to the limit of $450. Generally, this gives a much more substantial benefit to the taxpayer than would a deduction from income prior to the computation of tax.

There is a precedent in the Internal Revenue Code for tax credits in the provision for dividends credit. Anyone who receives dividends and has filled out his forms and taken the 4 per cent credit knows exactly how the tax-credit plan works. The existence of this provision has helped considerably in the presentation of the tax-credit plan to the Ways and Means Committee and other professional men in Congress.

The purpose of the credit approach, of course, is to equalize the benefit between the taxpayer in the high tax brackets and the taxpayer in the lower brackets. Take the example of an institution charging a tuition fee of $1000. The taxpayer in the 20 per cent bracket gets a credit of $300 against his tax, and the taxpayer in the 80 per cent bracket will also get a $300 credit against tax.

That, compared to other possible approaches, is an advantage. The ordinary way of providing relief would be to allow a deduction from the gross income subject to tax. However, a deduction greatly favors those in the high tax brackets and is rather unfair to those in the lower brackets. Under the tax-credit plan, any taxpayer with a child in college would benefit from this to some extent, except where an institution charged no tuition whatever.

It would, of course, help only the individual who is paying some income tax. It would not help the taxpayer who receives a large part of his income from tax-exempt bonds, nor the individual whose exemptions are large enough to cover his entire income.

Some have objected that the benefit would be wasted on students with well-to-do parents, in that these individuals do not need tax relief to send their children to college, and the government would lose the revenue. This loss could be limited by placing a ceiling on the credit. Anyone who has examined the medical deduction under the present Internal Revenue Code will realize that the tax relief is, in practice, limited to those in low income brackets. Once an individual's income reaches, say $10,000 a year, he would have to have had several appendicitis operations and much other grief in the family all in one year to be able to take advantage of the medical deduction. There could be a similar limitation put in the tax-credit plan which would, in part, meet this objection.

In the bill as presented, the credit is available to whoever pays the tuition, whether it is Uncle Joe or Father or the student himself. Perhaps it could even go to someone subsidizing a star halfback, if it were permissible within the athletic rules of the particular college.

Hence the plan is simple. It has much support in and out of Congress. Two test surveys, one among private colleges in Pennsylvania and the other covering about 75 private colleges, including none of the so-called "prestige" institutions, were made. In general, the plan has appeal, especially to a college president who feels an emotional strain every time he raises the tuition.

There were a number of objections to the plan. Professor Harris has emphasized the erosion of the tax base, but the present Internal Revenue Code has many other erosions in it. Why should educational institutions be treated less favorably than other, perhaps less socially useful, special interest groups?

The biggest practical objection to the tax-credit plan is the opposition of the Treasury Department to loss of revenue. The loss has been estimated by one economist at $150 million, but the Treasury Department estimated that about $500 million in taxes would be lost. Professor Harris estimates that the loss would be around $300 million.

One of the practical problems in Washington was that the Treasury Department under Secretary Humphrey really dominated all fiscal thinking. But our past experience indicates that Administration opposition is not necessarily fatal. The tax-deduction limit on gifts was raised from 20 to 30 per cent over Treasury objection. That was in an omnibus bill. Sometimes it is easier to secure passage of a measure in an omnibus bill; sometimes a single bill meets less resistance. Of course, we have not had affirmative support on the tax-credit plan from the land-grant institutions or the state universities. They are opposed to higher costs to students; they view the tax-credit program as a device for raising the tuition.

The tax-credit plan has been presented as a measure of tax relief; it has been absolutely essential, from the standpoint of the American Council, to present it this way. I think there is no doubt but that it would provide a considerable measure of relief.

Some of the less thoughtful criticism has been that the "prestige" institutions would simply use this plan as a device to raise their own tuition fees in an amount equal to the tax benefit conferred. But the answer to that is that tuition fees have been rising anyway. They are going to continue to rise whether this proposal passes or not. Certainly, any tuition increase will be dictated by other considerations. There is no doubt that if this measure were enacted, the tax-credit plan would make it somewhat easier for less well-known private liberal-arts colleges to raise their tuition. But that is not the main point. I feel there is no doubt that the bill would benefit the colleges. If it were enacted, I doubt that Harvard would immediately raise its tuition by 43 per cent, nor would Dartmouth. But, undoubtedly, next time the colleges felt the need for more income, the effect of the bill would be one of the factors taken into account in determining the size of any tuition increases to be made.

President Cole's remark about the wealthy taxpayer who gets a deduction for his state taxes paid to support public education but no deduction for tuition paid private institutions, is another argument supporting the tax-credit plan. In this regard I am intrigued by a description of the public image of education made by David Riesman:

Education serves as a consumer's good competing in the market with other consumer's goods, such as recreation.

As indicated, people should be free to choose how they will spend their money and their leisure, whether they will spend them for schooling or for other goods and services. As citizens, people should not be compelled to buy education for themselves or be taxed to buy it for others nor should they be forbidden free access to education, even where their only use of it is for personal development and enjoyment beyond the publicly enforced minimum.

I think that is one of the problems and is a partial answer to the argument that the tax-credit plan is wasteful. Let us bring the argument down from the "well-to-do" to the people in the marginal groups — say, the people earning $8,000 to $16,000 a year. They are the ones, certainly in the private colleges, that we worry about; it is very hard to ascertain the need in this income range. Certainly, in that group, a bill like this would be real, positive relief.

Although the consumers are in the habit of going out and buying automobiles, refrigerators, or anything else on credit, they have thought of education as being different. They always think of it as something for which they have to pay as they go. It is quite a shock to them suddenly to be presented with a bill for $2,000 in any year. It seems to me that there are some signs that that concept is changing.

Parents don't have to send their children to college. They don't have to take this tax benefit if they don't want it.

In the preparation of my testimony, I considered bringing in some of Professor Harris' material on the earning power of graduates and the fact that the government would recover its tax credits later on from the additional taxpayers in the higher income brackets. I was talked out of presenting this idea by the other people helping to prepare the testimony, but this point does demonstrate the plausibility of the argument that this is not necessarily a costly program in terms of long-run loss of revenue.

I think this bill is still very much alive, although the current budgetary outlook doesn't make the chances very good right now. The direct approach is favored by some. Most of the educational organizations would favor the federal scholarship program as against the tax-credit plan. But the tax-credit plan still has a strong appeal to Congressmen.

HIGHER EDUCATION AND THE FEDERAL BUDGET

Richard A. Musgrave

FEDERAL expenditures to date have played a minor role in the financing of higher education, but their importance is bound to increase in the future. Such will be the case because the other sources of finance cannot keep step with rising requirements and because it is becoming increasingly apparent that adequate provision for educational services is of the prime importance to the nation's safety and welfare.

Present State of Federal Contribution

Let us begin with a brief look at the present state of the federal contribution to higher education. One way of looking at the matter is to examine the relative importance of federal payments as a source of income to institutions of higher learning. For this purpose, let us consider the breakdown of current income for 1955–56, the last year for which the complete data are available.

TABLE 1. — ANNUAL INCOME OF INSTITUTIONS OF HIGHER LEARNING (*in millions of dollars*)

Source	1955–56 [a]	1957–58 [b]	1969–70 1957–58 pattern	1969–70 Adjusted pattern
Student fees	726	904	2,500	3,500
Federal Government				
For veterans' education	16		—	—
For research	356	535	1,500	500
For other purposes	123			2,200
State governments	892	1,086	3,000	1,900
Local governments	107	131	400	200
Endowment earnings	145	167	450	300
Private gifts and grants	246	411	1,150	900
Sales and services	192	346	1,000	500
Other	81			
Total	2,881	3,580	10,000	10,000

[a] See U. S. Department of Health, Education, and Welfare, *Statistics of Higher Education, 1955–56*, chap. 4, p. 29.
[b] From S. E. Harris, "Financing of Higher Education: Broad Issues," in *Financing Higher Education, 1960–70* (New York, 1959), p. 72.

As shown in Column 1 of Table 1, federal payments amounted to about 15 per cent of total income, as against 35 per cent from state and local governments, 25 per cent from tuition, and 40 per cent from other private sources. Also, note that about three quarters of the federal contribution took the form of payments for research. As such, it was largely a payment for services rendered and only in part constituted an aid to education.

TABLE 2. — FEDERAL SUPPORT FOR HIGHER EDUCATION (*in millions of dollars*)

Allocation	1955–56 [a]	1959–60 [b]	1960–61 [b]
Department of Health, Education and Welfare			
Surplus property	184	[c]	[c]
Other	13	15 [d]	15 [d]
Defense education program	—	134	170
Veterans' Administration			
Veterans' education and training	781	445	316
Other	33	35 [d]	35 [d]
National Science Foundation, science education	8	54	70
Other	13	15 [d]	15 [d]
Total	1,032	698	621
National Science Foundation, basic research	—	71	101
College Housing Loan Program	—	185	148
Total	1,032	954	870

[a] From U.S. Department of Health, Education and Welfare, *Biennial Survey of Education in the United States, 1955–56*, 1959, chap. 1, p. 20.
[b] From *Budget Message of the President* and *Summary Budget Statements*, 1961, pp. M56, M66, 270.
[c] Not available.
[d] My estimate.

This view of the matter does, however, understate the extent of federal support since it excludes payments made to students rather than to institutions. A more general view of the federal contribution is taken in Table 2, listing what is officially referred to as Support for Higher Education.[1] As shown in Column 1 of that table, total federal programs in support of higher education amounted to somewhat above $1 billion. Of this, nearly 80 per cent originated in the Veterans' Administration, consisting largely of payments to veterans under Public Law 550. Another 20 per cent originated in the Department of Health, Education and Welfare, with nine-tenths of this amount taking the form of donation of surplus property.

[1] A precise reconciliation between the 1955–56 total of $495 million in Table 1 and the total of $1,032 million in Table 2 is not available. However, a large part of this difference is explained by the fact that Table 1 excludes the bulk of outlays on veterans' education and training, which appear in Table 2, while Table 2 excludes the bulk of research expenditures included in Table 1.

The remaining minor amounts originated in the Department of Defense and other sources, including a small beginning under the National Science Foundation. As a whole, outlays in "support" of higher education amounted to 1.5 per cent of total budget expenditures, and the very special nature of the programs (for example, veterans' payments, surplus property, and defense) suggests that hardly a beginning had been made toward a significant program of federal aid to higher education. The picture is much the same if the sources of addition to plant funds are considered.[2]

Since then such a start has been made, emerging under the pressure of rising college population, inadequacy of the traditional revenue sources, and the challenges of the sputnik age. It is important, therefore, to compare the picture for 1955–56 with that of the current scene. Since adequate data are not available, this can be done in sketchy form only, as shown by the last two columns of Table 2. While the total amount has declined substantially, the structure of the outlays has changed and the beginnings of a stronger program have emerged. Under the National Defense Education Program of 1958 funds are provided for student loans adequate to cover a substantial part of a student's college education, and some four thousand three-year fellowships are to be offered. The program for science education, administered by the National Science Foundation, was expanded considerably, and a program was established in the Housing and Home Finance Agency to provide homes for college housing. Also, educational institutions have benefited from the expanded research activities of the federal government, which, in all, now amount to $690 million. (They are not, however, fully compensated for costs.) These amounts are still far short of needs, but development of the last few years show that an increased federal contribution to higher education is well on its way. This is evidenced also by the variety of proposals now under consideration by Congress. Some of these are modest in scope, such as the Administration's plan to replace loans for college housing with a federal guarantee of bonds issued to finance college construction and of some federal contribution to their retirement. Other proposals provide for more ambitious assistance to construction as well as scholarship programs and other forms of aid. While the prospects are not for a massive flow of federal funds in the next few years, chances are that there will be a considerable extension of aid in particular areas.[3]

Future Requirements

Let us now look at the level of future requirements and the extent to which they would have to be met from federal funds. In 1957–58 the total current income of institutions of higher education amounted to $3.6 billion,[4] as against the $2.8 billion for 1955–56 as shown in Table 1. According to estimates of the Office of Education, enrollment will rise to about 6.4 million students by 1969–70.[5] Holding the cost per student constant, this would give us a total of $7.2 billion. Such, however, is clearly insufficient. If we assume faculty salaries to rise by 50 per cent over the ten-year period, we arrive at a 1969–70 total of $8.5 billion.[6] Certainly one cannot assume a lesser increase and probably should assume a substantially larger increase, if the quality of instruction is at all to be maintained. Changes in other costs may involve various balancing items, but some increase must be allowed for as well. A 1969–70 total of $10 billion is thus a reasonable estimate. The question is how this total can be financed.

[2] For 1955–56 these sources were distributed as follows:

	$ million
Federal government	13.3
State & local government	240.1
Private gifts	142.0
Other sources	40.6
Total	436.0

See U. S. Department of Health, Education and Welfare, *Statistics of Higher Education, 1955–56*, 1959, chap. 4, p. 120.

[3] See C. W. Radcliffe, "Higher Education in the 86th Congress," *Higher Education* (November, 1959).

[4] See S. E. Harris, "Financing of Higher Education: Broad Issues," in *Financing Higher Education* (New York, 1959), p. 73.

[5] See Harris, p. 74.

[6] We assume that the total for 1957–58 included $1.6 billion for salaries and $2.1 billion for other costs. This uses the same ratio for salary to other costs as in 1957–58. (See Harris, p. 73.) Raising the former item by 50 per cent, we arrive at an adjusted total of $4.5 billion for 1957–58. Allowing now for the increase in enrollment from 3.4 to 6.4 million, we obtain the total of $8.5 billion.

In Column 3 of Table 1 we show the breakdown of receipts in 1969–70, based on the assumption that the pattern for 1957–58 was maintained. Closer inspection shows that this is an unrealistic picture. Receipts from student fees may be expected to provide a larger share, allowing for a substantial increase in tuition. Not only will rising family incomes be available to pay for tuition, but a growing awareness of the profit of higher education may be expected to increase the parents' willingness to contribute. Assuming a doubling of tuition on the average and allowing for the indicated increase in enrollment, we arrive at a total tuition income of about $3.5 billion. Whether this will be feasible remains to be seen, and its desirability will depend also on expansion of available loan and scholarship programs. However this may be, the assumed total of $3.5 billion is probably on the optimistic side.

The gain in receipts from state and local governments, on the other hand, will surely be less than would be required to maintain their current share. The same revenue sources which in 1957–58 financed a contribution of $1.2 billion may be expected to yield $1.7 billion by 1969–70, reflecting the growth of the economy and resulting increase in tax base. However, maintenance of the 1957–58 share would require a total of $3.4 billion, thus calling for a significant increase in revenue sources. Given the heavy demands on state and local finances for other purposes, education at lower levels in particular, it seems most unlikely that this total will be forthcoming. A total of $2 billion would seem to be the maximum allowable in a realistic estimate.

Endowment earnings for obvious reasons will not rise at the rate required to maintain their present share. The future level of private gifts and grants will depend upon the extent of tax subsidy which is permitted under the law, but again it is unlikely that this source of income will maintain its present share. The amounts entered in Column 4 for endowment and gifts are both liberal estimates.

Adding up these various sources of income, we arrive at a total of $7.1 billion, which would call for a residual federal contribution of $2.7 billion. In other words, the federal share would have to rise because the gain in the tuition share alone will not suffice to match the declining share contributed by the other sources. If our reasoning is correct the increased federal contribution will have to be very largely, and indeed almost entirely, in forms which contribute directly to the cost of instruction, and not in outlays for contract research. Such outlays are primarily purchase payments, and while they have beneficial side effects for the institutions concerned, they contribute only in relatively small part to meet the increased costs of instruction and teaching operations.[7] If federal expenditures on research increase beyond the amount allowed for here — and they surely will — our calculations suggest that a correspondingly larger contribution from the federal government would be required.

The reader may object to our determining the federal contribution as a residual amount. In some respects this involves circular reasoning, since the contributions available from other sources may depend to a significant degree upon what the federal government does. Thus the desirability of raising tuition or the students' ability to pay it will depend upon the availability of federal funds for fellowships and other aid. The ability of state governments to sustain increased budgets for higher education will depend on the level and structure of federal taxation, and the extent of federal aid to education at lower levels. The support available from gifts and endowments will depend upon provisions under the federal income tax, and so forth. Moreover, there is not a perfect substitutability among private, state and local, and federal sources of finance, even if all were available in adequate amounts. The structure of higher education, as it will emerge over the next decade, will not be independent of the sources of finance. Thus the problem is not only one of fiscal but also of educational policy.

[7] Compare the similar estimate by Harris, p. 72, who arrives at a required level of federal contribution of $1.3 billion. Of the difference between this and our figure of $2.7 billion, an amount of $800 million is allowed for by our larger total and $300 million by our lower figure on tuition fees. Note, however, that Harris divides his federal total into $1.3 billion on research and $500 million for "other" purposes. Our calculations seem to suggest that this would be altogether insufficient and that the latter item must be very much larger in order to meet the increased cost per student on which the calculation is based.

Ability of Federal Budget to Support Higher Education

Finally, the problem of federal aid to higher education must be looked at as well from the point of view of the federal budget itself, taking into account both the capacity of the federal budget to render this service and the relative importance which should be attached to this particular function.

TABLE 3. — ESTIMATED UNITED STATES FEDERAL BUDGET EXPENDITURES FOR 1960–61

Use	Billions of dollars	Percentage
Major national security	45.6	57.1
International affairs	2.2	2.8
Commerce and housing	2.7	3.4
Agriculture and agricultural resources	5.6	7.0
Natural resources	1.9	2.4
Labor and welfare	4.6	5.7
Veterans' services and benefits	5.5	6.9
Interest	9.6	12.0
General government	1.9	2.4
Total	79.8	100.0

SOURCE: *The Budget of the U. S. Government for the Fiscal Year Ending June 30, 1961,* p. M14.

The most significant fact about the federal fiscal picture is the extent to which the budget is dominated by the requirements of national defense. In the proposed budget for 1960–61, major national security programs account for 57 per cent of total expenditures. If we add international affairs, veterans' payments, and interest on national debt, which has largely been accumulated in time of war, nearly 80 per cent of the total is accounted for. "Purely civilian" programs are only a minor part of the total picture, and federal aid to education, even at the substantial magnitude here arrived at, would only be a very small fraction (2.3 per cent) of the 1969–70 budget total.

This much is clear, but the question cannot be settled quite that simply. The same claim might be made for other relatively "small" items, which in combination might assume sizeable weight. A problem of priority remains to be considered. At the same time, the basic fact is that the future of the federal budget, the level of federal taxation, and hence the federal capacity to render other services, will depend to an overwhelming degree on the outlook for defense spending. This outlook, therefore, is an important part of our problem.

In line with an optimistic view of the federal budget outlook, it has been argued that continued growth of our economy will take care of all fiscal problems. Let us suppose that the gross national product will rise from its present level of close to $500 billion to, say, $700 billion by 1970. This will increase taxable income profits and sales accordingly, so that federal tax receipts obtained from present rates of tax may be expected to climb from their present level of $80 billion to a 1970 level of, say, $110 billion. Thus we may look forward to an automatic gain in tax yield of about $30 billion. If major national security expenditures remain constant, this additional amount will became available for expanding civilian programs and/or for tax reduction. The leeway left will be so substantial that it will be possible to take care of the major needs, including those of higher education, and to have some reduction in tax rate at the same time.

There is nothing wrong with that part of the argument which suggests that an automatic gain of yield in this order of magnitude will take place. The fly in the ointment is in the assumption that expenditures for national security will remain constant. The silver lining disappears as one makes the alternative and perhaps more realistic assumption that such outlays (be they direct defense or other substitute items, such as space exploration) will rise at the same rate as the gross national product. We are then back to the problem of having to forego alternative expenditures or of having to find the additional finance to meet this particular need.

The events of recent years have shown that the maintenance and strengthening of educational standards is of greatest importance for the future of our country. These educational services are needed not only as a means toward obtaining a fuller life, but as a condition of national survival. For one thing, the revolution of weapons technology over the last decades has rendered scientific advance and training a crucial, perhaps the most crucial, element in national defense. For another, our leadership in the Western world requires that our economy continue to grow at an adequate rate so as to maintain our position of relative economic strength in the world. Investment in human capital through education is a most important and direct way of accomplishing these objectives. Moreover, among all policies to stimulate growth, that of advancing education is most in line with the social objectives and ideals of our society. For these reasons it is evident that aid to education demands highest priority in determining the alternative uses of federal funds. This priority would seem to be much above that which attaches to other programs — such as a nationwide system of superhighways — for which funds are more readily forthcoming. The question of how federal aid to education should be divided between higher education and education at lower levels is more difficult to decide, and one on which I myself am in considerable doubt. Certainly all levels of education must be allowed for in arriving at a proper evaluation of the federal contribution, but this cannot be done in the context of the present paper.

There remains the question of whether federal aid to education is to be preferred to tax reduction or whether it is worth the price of increased taxation if needed. Thinking in terms of a program of, say, $3 billion, the tax reduction foregone might be in the form of a 3 percentage point reduction of the first bracket rate of the personal income tax, a $100 increase in the personal exemption, or a 5 percentage point reduction in the corporation profits tax. These costs are significant, but the immediate gain (in releasing purchasing power for other uses) to be derived from such reductions appears slight as compared to the resulting loss in national security and in reduced economic growth. Similar considerations remain applicable if we consider the larger amounts needed (running up to, say, $10 billion) to provide for adequate assistance to all levels of education.

It is important not to confuse the point here at issue with the current debate as to whether "public consumption" in the United States is too small relative to "private consumption." Whether more should be spent on public parks for visiting and less on private cars by which to visit, is a proper matter of political controversy, but hardly of crucial national concern. But this is not the case with assurance of proper support for education. Here the issue is one of investment in our national strength and future, not one of alternative forms in which to enjoy luxury consumption. This being the case, the priority of adequate support for education clearly outranks that of tax reduction.

Special Problems of Federal Support for Higher Education

Considering the strength of the general case for federal support to education, it is startling to find that government has done so little to provide for an adequate program. The reason lies in the fact that federal aid to education involves collateral issues of a highly controversial sort. These include concern over infringements of centralized direction on educational freedom and with it the states' rights issue. There is a fear that federal aid be made contingent on compliance with policies for racial integration, thus involving another area of intense controversy. People are aware that publicly financed education will be supported by more or less progressive taxes if the finance is federal, and by more or less regressive taxes if the finance is state and local. Hence, questions of income distribution are involved. Also, there is a further aspect of redistribution between high- and low-income states. And last but not least, there is a question of how federal aid will affect the relative positions of public and private institutions. For these and other reasons, constructive action has been difficult and will remain so for some time to come.

Leaving aside these broader matters of policy, a few points might be noted which are of particular concern to the economist. Most important is the need to keep in mind that outlays on education are investment, basically investment in human resources, and that this quality of capital formation is present whether the expenditures are on buildings, books, teachers' salaries, or stipends. The tendency to apply the concept of capital to buildings only leads to a bias toward *con*struction as against *in*struction programs, it being held (if mistakenly) that capital programs may prudently be loan financed while current programs must be tax financed. Thus arrangements may be made whereby aid to construction does not show up in the budget deficit while aid to teaching operations does. This reinforces the bias for construction and against human investment, which results because the fear of political influence is attached to the latter. This confusion must be resolved if a sound program is to be planned. The question whether federal outlays should be tax or loan financed must not be made to depend on the distinction between aid to construction and aid to instruction, nor should this distinction be permitted to determine whether the aid is to be given in the form of grants or loans. Above all, safeguards are needed to assure that the substance of the aid program is not determined by the political objectives of window dressing the impact of the program on the apparent (if misleading) level of budget surplus or deficit.

Next, we should be most hesitant to accept a program in which the aid is provided through tax relief. Such a program would accomplish less and be less equitable than a system whereby the aid is given directly and financed through the general budget. This applies in particular to proposals for tax exemptions or credit under the personal income tax. If aid to higher education is to take the form of aid to students, the scarce resources will be used to best advantage if conditions of scholarship are attached thereto, with or without supplementary consideration of need. Moreover, the cost of the program should be distributed equitably as part of the general tax burden, and its financing should not take the form of opening yet another series of loopholes in an already riddled income tax.

Next, it would seem that federal aid to education — be it at the higher or the lower level — should allow for the high differentials in fiscal needs and capacities which exist between the various states. The need for assuring a minimum level of performance — especially at lower levels of education — is one of the main reasons and, apart from considerations of national defense, *the* main reason why federal action in this area is called for. Therefore, a sound federal program in education is inherently one which involves some degree of redistribution from high- to low-income regions.

Undoubtedly federal aid to higher education will be developed in a variety of forms involving aid to construction, fellowship, student loans, and expanded research contracts. All these will be helpful and important, but the most crucial issue will not be met until the problem of direct assistance to the operating costs of institutions of higher education comes to be faced. This involves the setting up of a mechanism which excludes political influence while assuring efficient use of funds. Beyond this, and more difficult, it must be determined just how this assistance is to be distributed between public and private institutions, and among institutions of various types in each group. This is a problem which to date has received rather little discussion but which must be solved efficiently if the assistance is to do most good.

IV. FACULTY STATUS

Summary of the Discussion at the February 5, 1959, meeting of the Seminar on the Economics of Higher Education. "Faculty Status" was the topic considered, and papers were given by Messrs. Cole, Bundy, Wilson, Hughes, Caplow, and Iffert.

Faculty Rewards, Economic and Noneconomic

The question which aroused most interest among the participants in the seminar was how to attract alert minds into college teaching and keep them vigorous throughout a life of college work. This was touched upon by all the papers. The crucial period — or at least the one in which improvement over the present situation seems most desirable — spans the later years of graduate study and the very first years of teaching. Here seem to lie most of the obstacles, both those inhibiting students from going into teaching and those producing early demoralization of young faculty members. Later in the seminar, when several discussants challenged Mr. Caplow's suggestion that there was much economic waste in university administration, the group turned to a rather different issue.

Picking up Professor Hughes' contention that the average graduate student, taught to believe in extremely high standards of creative excellence, is severely disillusioned when he leaves his university to teach in some small college, one member pointed out that this is more likely to occur just a few steps down the academic ladder than much further down. It is in the middle range of colleges, depositories of the almost-successful, where the "smell of expectation" exists, that the problem of an uncreative and demoralized faculty is most acute. Faculty morale in colleges still less known is often very high. These colleges are alive with faith in their own survival and their ability to achieve their goals.

This post-degree slump seems to vary among fields as well as among colleges. As a striking illustration, one member cited the difference in morale between anthropologists and sociologists teaching at places of lower prestige than the universities at which they received their degrees. The anthropologist is in the field; he may be working in an Indian community. He has a sense of working with the natives. In contrast, the sociologist always wants to know what Merton is doing or what Parsons is doing, and is not happy unless he is within five minutes of the news. By examining more closely the different disciplines, perhaps it would be possible to discover the essential elements of novelty in them, and to emphasize these rather than mere fashion or prestige. If this could be done effectively in the graduate schools, students would be less dissatisfied at having to leave the places in which they have done their graduate work.

Another member approved of the current trend among students and teachers of identifying themselves more and more with their disciplines, and less with the colleges or universities which they attend. Such a trend, of course, could go too far; but the ability to identify with a discipline, and the opportunity to achieve some stature within it regardless of the academic prestige of the institution with which a faculty member is associated, provides an offset to the decline in creative activity which so often occurs in the first few years after leaving graduate school. Moreover, the incentive thus provided may make it possible to establish more than the dozen or so existing first-rate graduate centers — one of the most urgent current needs of higher education in America.

While not disagreeing with the views expressed above, a third participant felt that they did not emphasize the purely financial considerations sufficiently. He surmised that the economic loss of caste of the academic profession as a whole, as academic salaries fell relative to other incomes in the community, has put tremendous pressure on prestige as a reward, and has resulted in a psychology of hierarchy rather than a psychology of self-respecting individual enterprise. The academician's inability to enjoy the satisfactions which are dominant in the community and to keep at least not too far behind his neighbors economically has resulted in a real distortion of his attitudes. "We have undertaken to live like monks, relatively, in an epoch in which there is no ethos to support this kind of life; and we have no cowls to wear to save money on clothes."

If this is so, then a considerable movement toward restoring a self-respecting image among young college teachers could be achieved by raising academic salaries substantially. And if it is true that attending a prestige university contributes toward advancement in the business or political world, this is a privilege for which these universities could charge appropriately, and with the increased proceeds reward their own teaching staffs adequately.

Others agreed with this statement of the problem, and added that certainly one of the necessary conditions for achieving an adequate image of what an institution of higher learning is and can be is a financial pattern in which the sense of grinding need, excessive sacrifice, and insecurity is removed as far as possible. But several members took issue with Mr. Caplow's suggestion that a maximum salary of $80,000 a year was necessary to do this — or even whether such a high salary was conducive to the avowed scholarly commitments of the academic profession. Everyone agrees that faculty salaries should go up, indeed that it is necessary for them to go up if teachers of high quality in sufficient numbers are to be attracted into college teaching, but no one knows how much the rise should be. Doubling the present level is often mentioned. One participant suggested that the average salary of full professors in the leading universities should be between $20,000 and $25,000 a year, with perhaps $30,000 as a maximum. These amounts would rise with the general productivity of the economy.

Preparation for Faculty

Another member felt that this increase in financial security should be taken right back to the graduate student, many of whom are married and at present are harried by numerous and irrelevant financial pressures. He suggested that the scholarships for these students should be at least $4,000 a year, and that the consequences of such a level should be carried up through the academic salary scale, with young instructors starting at $6,000, and so on. Since colleges are now near the end of their financial resources, he felt that such a goal could be accomplished only with federal aid on a vast scale.

Second, however, this member felt that present graduate-school techniques are gravely at fault in respect to the lack of psychological and technical preparation with which graduate students now go out to their first teaching jobs. Students may be well trained in the material of their fields of study, but they are not well-trained in the use of this material. Even in those cases where some teaching is done in the graduate school, it is a kind of drill work and the entire joy of teaching is taken out of it. Furthermore, this teaching is not related to the graduate study itself. Graduate students have yet to learn how important teaching is as a mode of learning. Experiments could be tried in which the graduate student is sent to a small college for a year or so, as an integral part of his graduate training, to teach a course in his field, and then is returned to his graduate school to complete his work there. This would serve both to interest the student in teaching as a career and to add vitality to his approach to his discipline.

Finally, the professor should be brought much closer to the student. Today the only thing they have in common is the subject matter. Learning needs to be made a much more vital process in which both the student and the teacher participate, right from the freshman year on through the graduate school. Not only would the student develop a greater momentum in scholarship, but, this member felt, many of the status factors now so prominent in faculty life would disappear. Teaching young scholars the things which one cares about would take on a missionary quality, and morale would certainly improve.

Such a call for radical revision of the approach to teaching would require an important change in attitude by many people now in the profession. A more practical suggestion for change, another participant thought, is to reduce the Ph.D. program to a three-year course, much as a law school does. The seemingly endless process required for earning a Ph.D. was seen as a major obstacle to the recruitment of new college teachers. Alert students learn that it takes four, five, six, or seven years to finish, and this tends to put them off. Shortening the program to three years, or to four with some teaching experience, would not require a serious reorganization of the graduate schools. Even now, students encouraged to finish can complete the Ph.D. with less than three years of graduate work. To make this a normal occurrence would be quite practicable.

Another obstacle in the path of advanced education is the chaos created by the Selective Service program. This produces an important and unnecessary diversion of people. No male knows when he will be drafted, or whether he is going to be drafted. In the uncertainty created by this situation, a student cannot now plan intelligently either for a three- or a seven-year Ph.D. program. He does not know where he stands, and he has no way of finding out, unless he is clearly 4-F. As a result many anticipate the draft by joining one of the services, and by the time they finish the endless Ph.D. program looks as though it will carry them into middle age, so they turn to something else.

A third deterrent to considering teaching as a career, or even to entering graduate school at all, is the excessive standard of excellence which prevails in many schools. Several instances of this were cited. A physics student with a high I.Q. received B's in two advanced physics courses, decided he could not become a good physicist, and went into business instead. His record may have prevented him from getting into the very top institutions, but he was certainly capable of receiving a Ph.D. degree from a good university. One Greek professor, a wonderful scholar, put off more potential instructors in Greek by failing seven out of a beginning class of thirteen and giving five D's. His standards were too high. There is a growing legend in physics that those who do well at theory become theoreticians; those who do not become experimentalists. This sort of prejudice can do great mischief. Another myth is that college teaching is only for members of Phi Beta Kappa. This achievement can be blocked for a perfectly capable individual by a poor grade in the freshman year or something equally irrelevant to his ability to teach well. Faculties have to learn that not everyone can be in the top 1 per cent in excellence.

One participant added that he has often felt tempted to advise students: "Don't go to the best graduate schools because there your standards of excellence will be so high that you will never write your thesis because of what will be expected of you. Go to a slightly less than good graduate school. You will finish in three years."

Another member pointed out that in fact these "standards of excellence" may be only standards of uniqueness. He cited a proposed cooperative research project in a large university which never got started because no group of faculty members would participate as a control group. They were not willing to have their teaching under surveillance. The professors perhaps felt that they have a unique standard which could not necessarily be identified with excellence, at least of the measurable sort.

In addition, there is an inherent difficulty involved in this question. On the one hand, excessive standards of excellence may prolong the educational process indefinitely and thus discourage students and divert them into shorter routes to a career. Yet one of the major objectives of a graduate school is to hold out to its students an image of the highest kind of excellence. Many teachers in graduate schools do not succeed in doing this, of course, but if the graduate schools have any ideal, it is that here one can learn about the very frontiers of knowledge, even if one's life is not spent on them. But currently graduate schools are not always successful in promulgating the idea that these frontiers are not limited geographically to Berkeley, Cambridge, Morningside Heights, and so on, that the pursuit of new knowledge can be carried on at any longitude.

An Improved Ph.D. Program

Several proposals for increasing the number of new college teachers and for preventing the period of intellectual decline which so often occurs for those who do become teachers emerged from the discussion. These included a standardization of the Ph.D. program, the addition of some of the elements of teaching to graduate-school work, and a periodic return of college teachers to one or another of the important graduate schools for the purpose of re-establishing direct contact and becoming psychologically involved once more with the frontiers of their subjects.

On the question of streamlining the Ph.D. program, however, there was serious disagreement on the practicality of any specific proposals which would achieve the desired end. A complete change in thinking would be required of many professors in graduate schools. A scholar in Eastern European history, for example, may feel that every graduate student in that field must learn Greek, German, French, and Russian before he is fully qualified for a doctorate. Topics dealing with the Far East present even greater difficulties. Three years is too short a time for the average, capable graduate student to master this field and produce a serious piece of research.

Furthermore, standardizing the program would require the department to state more carefully exactly what the Ph.D. degree is. As it is now, "the graduate schools insist on making the mystery of the academic Ph.D. degree so ethereal, so beyond analysis by the strong light of science, that they insist upon the time in order not to have to define what they are doing." As a result, the students prolong the process unnecessarily by permitting interruptions, such as going off to teach for a year, because they are not quite sure how to define a thesis topic.

One study at Columbia revealed that since the war the lowest median time from registration to completion of the Ph.D. requirements was 5.3 years, in chemistry; the highest median time was 12.5 years, in Germanic languages. Such periods look formidable indeed to a student eager to get on in some occupation. Several members of the seminar pointed out, however, that Columbia was not a typical case, due to the very large number of part-time students there. Often Columbia accepted students who could not get into other graduate schools because of their full-time residence requirements. At other graduate schools the median times for completion of a Ph.D. are undoubtedly less, but still unnecessarily long.

Other members felt that it was a mistake to take the professions like medicine and law as a model in this matter. It is an illusion to think it possible to make a good doctor in four years or a lawyer in three. Furthermore, the mentality of students in a professional school is rather different from that of graduate students; there is much more concern by the former for sheer mastery of the subject, without the creative thought necessary for extending it.

Another problem in standardizing the Ph.D. requirements is that liberal-arts colleges may find their departments trying to transform them into pregraduate schools. One president observed that this was already being done.

The basic issue is what one signifies by "a Doctor of Philosophy." If it is supposed to mean a finished scholar, then it is difficult to deny that three years is not enough time in many cases. If it means only three years spent in working toward some form of serious scholarship, that is a different matter. As one member put it, "The purpose of a Ph.D., in my thinking, is not to make a sociologist, but to teach a man how to think like a sociologist. Once he knows how to do this, he can make one by himself. Three years is normally adequate to teach a man how to think like a sociologist or a historian or an economist."

Another member suggested that it might be more appropriate to tamper with the A.M. degree than with the Ph.D. The graduate school must serve two functions. It must train people for scholarly research, and it must provide a recruiting ground for college teachers. The conclusion that graduate schools must provide more teachers in the coming years is not the same as a conclusion that they must award their most advanced degrees more liberally. By asking the right questions about the qualities required of an effective college teacher just as law schools ask about the qualities required of an effective lawyer, it might be possible to devise a solid A.M. program which would contribute much toward alleviating the coming shortage of college teachers.

A second major proposal for change, already mentioned, is the addition to the graduate curriculum of some sort of instruction in teaching — *not* formal education courses such as are given now for public-school teaching, but some training in coverage of the subject matter. This could be combined with some actual teaching experience, well integrated into the program of the graduate student. As things are now, they "are put through a course of frustration in doing a piece of major research under Laputan conditions... Having dragged out this process and convinced many students by this sincere experience of frustration that research is something they ought never to try again, we then proceed to set up a set of assumptions in the profession that bars them from further instruction." In many fields, a serious piece of research requires financial support of an amount simply not available to graduate students. Once a student has obtained his degree, it becomes a loss of professional dignity under existing norms to work under the supervision of someone else. Many universities will not exempt even their own faculty members from tuition when it is obviously to the school's advantage to have them continue studying. And there is often no way at all for them to gain any instruction in teaching.

Some participants felt that this statement exaggerated the weaknesses of the system, but added that some teaching experience would certainly be desirable. Someone suggested that universities should establish a rule of not hiring their own recent Doctors of Philosophy until after — say — five years. This would serve both to alleviate the personnel problems of some of the smaller colleges and to reduce the demoralization which occurs when a new Ph.D. must leave his graduate school while a few of his contemporaries have been asked to stay on as teachers there. Moreover, to begin a teaching career at a high-powered institution is often too great a task for a novice; failure is too catastrophic.

Refresher Treatment

The Ph.D. program is an integral part of the process of training successors and colleagues, a matter of the utmost personal importance to faculty members. Every department, even though it may acknowledge the need for more Ph.D.'s, will insist that it must keep up its standards. The essentially ritualistic character of the program is seen in the fact that *any* change is regarded as a lowering of standards. But resistance to change reaches back even into the undergraduate program, where less of professional ritual is at stake. More emphasis in the graduate schools on the teaching aspects of study for an advanced degree will not help the man who has been away from the centers of research activity for too long.

A third suggestion was provision for postgraduate fellowships which would bring teachers in small colleges back to graduate schools, their own or some other, every five or seven years. The teacher could recharge his intellectual batteries, so to speak. Such a program could be run by the departments in the colleges, by the universities, or even by some autonomous organization which could process the applications. Several hundred college teachers returning to graduate school each year and re-establishing their connections with some parts of the profession could have a considerable effect on faculty morale. It was pointed out that the Ford Foundation did sponsor such a program for teachers in the small law schools, which are mostly oriented toward teaching legal skills. These men were given considerable intellectual motivation by being brought to several of the major law schools.

Another member added that much gain might be had, at very little cost, by a simple yearly exchange of professors between the small colleges and the large universities. One man would go in to the university for a year, and a counterpart would replace him at his college.

Faculty Resistance to Improvements

Any of these proposals, except perhaps the last one, would encounter stiff resistance from the only people in a position to institute them: the faculty members of the colleges and universities concerned. One member suggested that departments and faculty committees are reactionary in the precise sense of the word. Changes are threats. One of the basic problems is that any suggestion for a change emanating from outside the faculty itself, particularly those coming from the administration in the university, is regarded as interference, a suspicious encroachment on the prerogative of the faculty, and frequently is never examined on its own merits. As long as this attitude prevails, and as long as faculties remain conservative in their outlook regarding their own affairs, little is likely to be achieved. One member thought that only by a *force majeure* exercised by leadership in the departments were significant changes likely to be effected. Any such attempt from another group, however, would meet unanimous resistance from a jealous faculty, and, if it succeeded, would certainly undermine faculty morale.

One faculty member of the seminar suggested that beyond a point there is an inverse ratio between the amount of teaching a man does and the number of hours he spends in the classroom. "If you would go through the classrooms of this country where people are teaching more than nine or ten hours a week, if you just went up the halls and listened at the keyholes, you would hear some of the most awful droning that has ever been heard by man; and if you increase their pay, they will talk more slowly, so they will get even more per word." We know that students who are listening to lectures for fifteen hours a week cannot be studying during those fifteen hours in the week. If the number of classes were cut in half at most institutions, this professor suggested, the quality of education might improve greatly. But both students and faculty would be terrified with so much time on their hands. They do not know what to do if they are not going to classes. Too many teachers are "hiding behind their agenda," and it would be a great gain to America's education if this prop were removed. And students would benefit if the assurance that they would get a degree in some fixed length of time were removed.

One member suggested, in conclusion, that an important step in achieving reforms in higher education was a much more thorough understanding of the decision-making processes of faculty groups, the internal political system of higher education. Many of the changes suggested involve a considerable violation, not of the objectives of universities, but of the rituals and procedures and folklore of higher learning. Until this whole milieu is much more completely understood, and the necessary changes in this internal governmental system have been made, there is likely to be much more resistance to change than compulsion to change.

Waste?

Turning to a rather different topic, several members of the seminar took issue with Mr. Caplow's contention that there was an extraordinary amount of economic waste in the large universities. The large existing expenditures almost always reflect the desires of faculty members or friends of higher education, and usually they could be justified in terms of the background of the particular institution. One of the most troublesome questions, discussed only in part by Mr. Caplow, is that of replacing faculty members. One participant pointed out that the failure to replace a retiring faculty member would raise the student-faculty ratio. Most educators would regard this as a bad thing. But if the ratio is not to be raised, a new appointment will have to be made somewhere in the university each time a faculty member retires. The really difficult decision is to determine how that new member is to be deployed. It would take a very bold administrator to suggest, say, that a retiring history teacher should be replaced by a new teacher in sociology. Only when the student-faculty ratios in individual departments become highly distorted is it politic to step in with that sort of suggestion.

Furthermore, it is often possible to blur the departmental lines in order to achieve, in practice, a more efficient use of teaching staff. A common problem for the older schools is a heavy endowment in the field of the classics. Rather than abandon these chairs, some colleges have had great success with classicists teaching history or English or general education courses in the humanities. Where specific shortages exist, people from outside that department can fill in. Mathematicians and chemists can teach elementary physics, often to the great benefit both of themselves and their students. Thus redeployment can take place in an informal way as well as formally — with a much better effect on morale.

Another member pointed out that these changes often take place during the process of growth. With a growing faculty, the department which does not grow is really contracting, but without the ill effects of actually removing a man. Making departmental shifts in a university is a very delicate process, and any measure which can make the changes as subtle as possible is desirable. Conflicts appear even within departments. One university had the problem in a department of shifting the emphasis from one historical period to another. This was done by resisting all nominations by the older group, on grounds that the funds were not available, and by yielding to appeals for funds by those favoring the more recent period. In fact, of course, this device did not fool anyone, but the change was carried out in a much less offensive way than if it had been made with one blow, so to speak. The things faculty members usually care about were not directly challenged. Several participants felt that this sort of method would not always work, however. But it certainly would be possible to establish a clear-cut rule that no person can nominate his successor, and that no succession is automatic.

A second issue was raised by Mr. Caplow's striking example of eleven secretaries doing a job where one part-time secretary would have been enough. This sort of criticism was thought to apply particularly to extracurricular activities. Even there, however, several members felt that the organizations concerned were aware of the important balance of operating costs in relation to income, and that in the case of alumni offices, for example, the exceptional growth of such a service not related to the educational objectives of universities was probably justified in terms of the revenue which flowed to the institutions as a direct result of these activities.

Another member felt that an increased use of secretaries and other help in the academic departments, far from being a wasteful excrescence, would be highly desirable. Professors spend far too much of their time these days doing essentially routine tasks: grading papers, typing reading lists, filing letters, and so on. They are more efficient in more academic pursuits, and their value for the institution would probably rise if they could be relieved of some of their nonacademic tasks. This would be so even if the department had to cut down on faculty members in order to provide salaries for the secretaries and assistants.

As for other noninstructional expenditures, someone added that it was important to remember that buildings and grounds accounted for only 15 per cent of the total budget. Thus the waste involved in hiring too many men to cut the grass, if this is done, amounts to a very small sum. A university could stop paying for all these services except heat and electricity, and it would save only a small percentage of the total budget.

Thus the issue of waste was unresolved. If one includes the psychic income — or loss of it — the elimination of some of the apparent sources of waste would be very costly indeed. But for other discussants, that was exactly the point: the entire attitude of the faculty regarding the efficient operation of a university should be changed. One member cited several cases in which departments actually initiated fund-saving reforms, because of the promise that the gains would remain within the department, and thus could be used for higher salaries or other amenities. Part of the problem is that in many universities, changes proposed *to* the faculty are not couched in economic terms, and changes proposed *by* the faculty are not weighed against their economic costs. Another member felt that even this would not help until there was a radical change in the faculty attitudes toward suggestions from outside the faculty.

Merit versus Across-the-Board Salary Increases

A final issue, relating to a paper by Professor Harris not published in this volume,[1] was raised. This concerned the relative merits of across-the-board raises in faculty salaries as against merit increases on an individual basis. Universities so far have inclined toward across-the-board raises for the entire faculty as the

[1] See S. E. Harris, *Economics of Higher Education* (to be published by McGraw-Hill).

cost of living and the standard of living in the nation rise. But the problem will become more acute as colleges find themselves caught between a shortage of funds and a need for new teachers which exceeds the numbers of those entering the field. Already colleges have yielded to market forces in a number of ways: the man who receives an outside offer is given an increase in salary or is promoted, while the man who does not receive such an offer remains at his former salary.

There is also a delicate question of morale involved. Should the permanent appointee who turns out to be a disappointment receive increases right along with the most productive and most useful members of the faculty? If he does, his colleagues are likely to feel very sour about it; if he does not, he will perhaps be of even less use to his university and his students. Professor Harris had suggested that the difficulty could be mitigated as the standard of living continued to rise and general inflation persisted. Inflation erodes the real purchasing power of fixed incomes. In a period in which prices rose 100 per cent, instead of having an across-the-board rise of salaries of the same amount, the university might increase pay only 50 per cent to some, and as much as 150 per cent to others. Those who were failures would thus be penalized with a lower real standard of living, and those most successful would be rewarded in proportion to their merit, yet everyone would get a raise of some sort.

Such a system, it was pointed out, would remove some of the security of the tenure system, and conceivably the ability of the administration or of faculty committees to award differential increases in salary in a period of rising prices would result in undesirable control over traditional academic freedoms. At the same time, however, such leverage would not be complete; the tenure system would assure — say — 75 per cent security; but this plan would prevent tenure appointments from becoming sinecures.

Several members observed that the recommendations of the A.A.U.P. Committee on Accreditation favored across-the-board increases rather than increases based upon merit. Their emphasis was on minimum salaries in each rank, rather than average salaries, so that those institutions which raised their minimum salaries would receive a higher rating than those which raised their average salaries through merit increases but left the minima at the old levels. If one man were passed over in a general rise, even though this was the proper thing to do, the A.A.U.P. accreditation rating would remain unchanged — or even drop, as the ratings were brought into line with a new cost of living. At the same time, as one member added, an appointee "mistake" is often even more irksome to his colleagues than to the administration. With both an effective tenure system and across-the-board salary increments, there is no way of rectifying an error in hiring.

The present system, one participant felt, lost some of the advantages of each of two extreme systems. A civil-service type of system provides complete security and respect for seniority. Everyone knows exactly where he stands. Alternatively there is a market system, in which salaries are determined completely by market forces. The present system, which allows adjustments of seniority based on the market, loses the complete security of the civil-service system and the assurance that one's rights will be respected, but it lacks also the vigorous selection of a market system. This member felt that institutions should move closer to one or to the other of these systems, rather than remaining suspended between them.

One serious difficulty with the market model was raised. It is a difficulty which colleges will have to face increasingly as the market for college teachers becomes tighter. There is no way of equating the market value of a man with his merit. "The very things that may make a man extraordinarily important to the life of the college and the faculty in terms of his internal contribution may make him substantially invisible within a range of ten or fifteen miles." An administration cannot maintain a healthy faculty and a happy university community without taking account of such people. One member cited a college at which no attention was paid to outside offers or market forces; salaries were based solely on the contribution of a teacher to the school in terms of teaching, and it happened that six or eight of these "invisibles" were the highest-paid faculty members there.

On the other hand, the civil-service type of system is not without its own disadvantages. An extreme form of it is illustrated by the imperial universities in Japan, where tenure is absolute, professors are able to appoint their successors down the line, and faculty control is complete. Pay is low, but all increases, one participant thought, are across-the-board, with regard only to rank. The stultification there is severe. A counter-example, however, is provided by the system in Holland.

Whatever the virtues of each system, a definite stand between them is gradually being forced upon schools as the competition for qualified college teachers becomes more intense; here is one of the most important issues affecting faculty morale.

FACULTY PROBLEMS IN THE LIBERAL ARTS COLLEGE
Charles W. Cole

IN one sense the assignment to discuss the faculty problems in a first-class liberal arts college is a difficult one. Faculty problems at liberal arts colleges are not very different from those at many other places. Nonetheless, there are a few important differences which might be worth mentioning.

Before going into those, however, I would like to comment briefly on some aspects of Professor Harris' position which I feel are relevant. First, I do not yield to him in my enthusiasm for raising faculty salaries; I think that he has done Trojan work for that cause and I would back him in it.

There is, however, one feature of the problem which I feel he has neglected. The general rise in wages which he talks about is a function of productivity. This is unarguable from the economic point of view, whether we are talking about farmers or about automobile mechanics. As I understand Professor Harris' position, he feels that professors have not participated in this rise in productivity. He has pointed out that when productivity is rising in some parts of the economy faster than others, and wage rises reflect these differences, people will shift from the positions of low to those of high productivity. He has argued that neither the college professors nor the colleges themselves are highly efficient or highly productive, and that as long as this continues to be so professional people will be inclined to go into more productive lines. If doctors get very high pay and college professors do not, then fewer capable people tend to enter college teaching.

But this is rather unfair to college teachers. Although it is difficult to do, I think that the case can be made that the productivity of professors has been rising. Of course, the productivity of the physician has increased greatly in the last few years, too, in terms of the number of people he cares for and in the quality of medical treatment. The case of college professors is less obvious, but I think one can demonstrate an increase in their productivity in a rather roundabout way. The products that they are producing, the trained people of the country, are the ones producing the general rise in productivity. Their training presumably has a good deal to do with their ability to enhance productivity, and the training is received to a large extent in the colleges and universities. Hence, in an indirect way, much of the general rise in productivity can be attributed to the college professors. This is a case which Professor Harris fails to make.

I also think that his comparison with other professions is perhaps misleading in that the real wages of all white-collar professions, even in the case of the doctors, have declined relative to those of the mechanical and industrial workers. There has been a relative rise in the remuneration for labor of a skilled and semi-skilled sort. We as teachers are merely sharing in this general situation.

There is another factor, emotional and historical, that we cannot ignore: namely, that teaching has long been thought of as one of the service professions — like the civil service, like the ministry, like medicine. It does have attributes like tenure, which we could argue about indefinitely. But there is in teaching a sense of service to the community which is real and important, and I think we ought not to lose sight of it. It is a feature we do not want to lose.

The doctors have been in a wonderful situation. They have both had their cake and eaten it. They have exploited the shortage of doctors, which they created by limiting the output of the medical schools. On the other hand, they have kept their status as a service profession in two ways. First, through the remarkable progress of medicine, for which they are partly responsible, they do cure many more people much faster than they used to, and the public is aware of this fact. Second, even the highest-paid doctors quite openly and with considerable publicity give a great deal of free service in clinics and elsewhere. Since this is well known, it keeps people thinking of doctors as a service profession when they are really exploiting the public more successfully than any other profession. Professors cannot do so well, because they cannot both exploit the coming shortage and maintain quite the same public feeling about their calling.

Let me say that I do agree that the salaries of college professors should rise greatly. It is rather futile to say whether they should go up 50 per cent or 150 per cent, since there are no over-all criteria on the basis of which the appropriate increase can be judged. It is my honest opinion that the competitive forces in the next decade will take care of it.

We are living now in the beginning of the competitive situation. Those of us who are college presidents are living more closely with it than some of the rest. But it is already taking hold and, by the mid-sixties, it is going to be so severe that state universities, reaching in the taxpayer's pocket, are going to pay high salaries with which the other institutions will have to compete if they wish to retain competent faculties. These competitive forces are going to be so intense that, without our trying to set a goal, a fairly reasonable salary situation will be attained. This is not a laissez-faire policy, but a prediction. This is what is going to happen, almost inevitably. But it does, nonetheless, seem to me to be worthwhile to keep on through the years, exploring the whole process, so that we are conscious of what is happening.

Now, let me tackle the question of the liberal arts college. The liberal arts college typically has one difference (I am now thinking of the separate college that is not part of a university) from a university, in that it is not in a position to use "slave labor." The typical university has a vast number of teaching fellows, part-time assistants, graduate students, part-time instructors. I have interviewed literally scores of them in the last ten years. I have found none of them receiving a decent wage. Though many of them are supposedly teaching half-time, or two-thirds time, actually many are teaching as much as or more than the faculty members who have tenure and status. They are getting paid, to use current examples of people supposedly teaching half-time in great and distinguished universities, $1,800 to $3,000 a year. The great and distinguished university, therefore, is able to support a relatively high faculty salary structure because a major part of its instruction (sometimes as much as half of the actual classroom instruction and work with the students) is carried by this slave labor of the subfaculty.

The great university is thus able to support a salary structure which is going to make recruitment very difficult for the liberal arts college which does not have the opportunity to employ graduate students as a subfaculty. This is a problem that is going to put the liberal arts college in a very difficult position, because it is not going to be able to show as high a salary scale as that of the university. On the other hand, the university never publicizes what it is paying the slave laborers or how many of them it employs. I have never seen a university that told how many assistants it had, how many teaching fellows, how many part-time instructors, or how much it paid them. I would be very interested in seeing the figures from any one of our great universities, public or private, for I think it would give rise to a better understanding of the salary picture.

Nor, may I say, do the universities tell their prospective undergraduate students that a great deal of the instruction is going to come from the subfaculty. This lack of an accurate public picture of the university college is another competitive disadvantage for the liberal arts colleges.

Some of them will be able to face the difficulties, but I am very worried about the marginal ones. They are going to have a hard time in the mid-sixties in their effort to maintain competent faculties. My guess is that they will have to recruit teachers from the local high schools, and that this step will produce a dilution of faculty quality that will be serious.

Another point about the liberal arts college that distinguishes its faculty problems from those of the university and which, unfortunately, is not visible in figures for average salaries, is this: the typical, independent liberal arts college has quite a different faculty rank structure from the college in the university. Amherst is not atypical. About 40 per cent of our faculty are full professors. I know of a big urban university where there are only 10 per cent of the faculty who are full professors. Many of the great universities have full professors in the proportion of 10 to 25 per cent. Some liberal arts colleges have as many as 50 per cent full professors.

This fact means that in such a college there are not only many more full professors and perhaps also more associate professors than instructors, it means also than many liberal arts colleges have a policy of relatively rapid promotion. They have found that, if they wish to retain their best teachers, they must promote more rapidly than the university does, and they tend to do so.

I tried to trace this problem back in Amherst's history and I find that the policy as far back as I can go, back into the nineties, was one of fairly rapid promotion.

What does such a policy mean in the long run? It means that, at a lower salary scale, the lifetime earnings of a man at a liberal arts college with a policy of rapid promotion may be much higher than his lifetime earnings would have been at a university with a considerably higher scale. These earnings would be reflected in fringe benefits like the Teachers Insurance Annuity Association. I have tried to make some rough calculations on this, and I am sure the statement is true. Rapid promotion can mean as much over a man's life as a considerably higher salary scale. But Professor Harris' figures will not take this point into account. Perhaps we should work out an index for comparisons between institutions by taking the average salary of a full professor and dividing by the average age.

The youngest full professorial appointee I recall at Amherst was in his twenties. Promotion to the rank of full professor rarely occurs deep in the forties, and I would say that the average period is probably in the range of thirty-five to forty. If you allow for compound interest on the higher salary, since some of the money is received at an earlier date, the case is still stronger. It is a real point, and for T.I.A.A. some of the money is actually at compound interest.

My point is that the structure of the faculty and the promotion policy of the institution are factors in compensation just as real as the salary scale and yet very hard to analyze.

There is another feature, too. This the liberal arts colleges share with the universities much more clearly than the other problems I am talking about. I have been trying to make what Dean Bundy would call some models. It has been suggested that the most immediate need at Amherst is to raise instructors' and assistant professors' salaries by 40 or 50 per cent. I think this could be argued, but it would mean in effect we would tend to give a man tenure when we appointed him. If our salary scale were very far out of line it would be difficult or impossible for young teachers to move to other institutions, for it is very hard to go downhill.

If we had today an average salary for instructors of, say, $7,500, we would find it desperately hard to move anybody along, though we do have a firm policy of not keeping a man more than five years at either the instructor or assistant-professor rank unless we think, pretty clearly, that he is going to be a permanent member of the faculty. No one college can get too far out of line as to salaries at the lower ranks, if mobility is to be maintained.

Another interesting fact about the independent liberal arts colleges is that the fringe benefits tend to be higher than at the universities. This fact again is not usually obvious. At Amherst, for example, we provide some 80 housing units. The average subsidy on each unit is $50 a month — a substantial fringe benefit.

Last year we tried to calculate what the average full professor's fringe benefits totaled, and they came to over $2,000. But such benefits are not very visible. The A.A.U.P. deals rather left-handedly with fringe benefits, but, in so far as they are income-tax-free, I think they constitute a very important addition to salary. Much of the $2,000 is before tax; on some other portions of it, the tax is irrelevant.

Let me note another factor which has surprised me. I had originally thought that tax-free fringe benefits were better, dollar for dollar, than salary increases, but in terms of morale, I am now convinced that such is not the case. I think that the faculty members welcome a fringe benefit when they get it. They treasure it while they have it, but they forget about it rather quickly. A fringe benefit conferred three years ago is just part of the atmosphere. It is not a fringe benefit any more. What the faculty member thinks of most often is the dollar figure of his salary. Economically, it is better to give fringe benefits, but, for morale, it is better to give salary increases.

We have experimented at Amherst — I know that other colleges have, too — with salary increases and have arrived at a system which we think has much to recommend it and which meets Professor Harris' criteria. We alternate, as far as we can, across-the-board increases with merit increases. The first type is to meet inflation, the second to recognize merit. When we give merit increases, we always give everybody something, so even such increases have an across-the-board element in them.

In allocating merit increases, we have evolved an effective system. We have an executive committee of the faculty, elected by the faculty, called the Committee of Six. When considering merit increases for the full professors (others are based on departmental recommendations), each member of the Committee of Six, the President, and the Dean make a list of the ten full professors whom he considers to be most valuable to the college. It is stressed that this list should include the less conspicuous professors, Dean Bundy's "invisible people," as well as the ones who are visible to the outer world. Then we take all the lists, tabulate the votes, and also make some slight adjustments for teachers who, for one reason or another, were overlooked. This system has been eminently satisfactory. We have used it twice and I think it works remarkable justice, rewarding both the man who is making a conspicuous contribution to his field and the man who is making a contribution to the college which is not conspicuous to the outside world.

One other problem is weighing on my mind now, one which is related not just to the liberal arts college but to salary comparisons in general. Amherst has some objectives for salaries for 1960–61 in terms of averages. Influenced, perhaps by leading economists (like Professor Seymour Harris) writing on the subject, we have come to think in terms of averages. This procedure presents real difficulties because, if we make too many promotions in the next two years, we impair the chance of meeting our objectives. The point is that when we take the top man out of the instructor rank and put him at the bottom of the assistant-professorial category, we have lowered the average salary of both the assistant professors and the instructors. We have even lowered it very seriously. Last month I had estimated that we were going to achieve our salary objectives in terms of averages. But now it appears that there will be enough promotions this year, particularly from instructor to assistant professor, to make it very doubtful whether we will achieve our goal in averages. Everybody is going to be better off. Everybody is going to be happier. The faculty is going to be getting more money, but we are not going to make the averages in Professor Harris' terms. This situation leads me to doubt whether the averages are always the right criteria for us to use.

Let me say in general that the liberal arts colleges are going to have both another area of difficulty quite related to this salary question and another countervailing advantage. Typically, the independent liberal arts college is in a rural or quasirural environment. This is not always the case, but it is very generally true. For obtaining certain faculty members, salary is never the only criterion. The professor moving from an urban to a rural environment loses something. He is further from a great library. He sacrifices some of the urban cultural and scholarly advantages.

On the other hand, the rural setting is in other ways so much more attractive than living, say, in New York City that it weighs heavily with the faculty member. My guess is that, as the parking problem gets more and more acute (last time I came to Cambridge, it took me thirty-five minutes to park) the liberal arts college is not going to be as disadvantaged as it has been by its location. The advantages of the rural environment, less expensive housing together with rapid communication, are beginning to outweigh the disadvantages of remoteness from the cultural facilities that are represented in the urban environment. Such advantages and disadvantages now seem to be more nearly balanced than in the past.

SOME ISSUES OF SUPPLY AND PRODUCTIVITY

O. Meredith Wilson

I AM very hesitant to undertake the discussion of teacher supply at all in an atmosphere dominated by the statement, "Teachers are not productive," because it suggests that I urge people into a profession which is only an adornment to our society. The assertion that "the teacher is not productive" is nonsense. The phrase is an unfortunate consequence of a special vocabulary and rests upon a perfunctory rather than a fundamental analysis of forces in our economy. It is a very superficial view of our society, which teachers themselves ought not to be guilty of sponsoring before nonteachers or in society at large. It is altogether too easy for the business or professional man to be persuaded that teachers are not productive when he looks at classroom workloads, which at Harvard may be as low as four hours a week.

The medical doctors who are defended as suddenly having become more productive were produced by teachers. Each of the other professions is produced by teachers. Almost anything that operates successfully in our society operates because teachers produced it.

I am more willing to discuss how teachers may become more productive if how much they already produce is first acknowledged. This polemic in defense of the idea that the teacher is productive is incomplete. It suggests only the direction I would like to take to defend my talking about why the supply of teachers ought to be increased.

The statistics I employ are those with which most readers are familiar. Their familiarity is the only justification I have for using them. You remember Josiah Stamp's remark, "The government are very fond of statistics. They add them and they multiply them and they extract the square root and they make very beautiful charts about them. But you must always remember that, in the first instance, they are dependent on items put down by the village watchman who just puts down what he damn pleases."

In a sense, these statistics were composed because I put down what I pleased, but there are reasons why I put them down.

I begin with the number of students who will be in institutions of higher education by 1970: 6,500,000, as estimated in an inter-office memo for one of our national offices of education.[1] This is an imperfect figure, because no one tells whether it will include graduate students, for example. In the course of my argument, I am going to press for the increase in college teaching preparation which might add at least 70,000 to the people in graduate schools and, therefore, add to the burden of the teaching.

Six and a half million, the figure used for 1970, is roughly 100 per cent more than enrolled last fall. In order to take care of the attrition in teaching ranks, and to take care of the increase in registered students, 440,000 new teachers will have to be appointed between now and 1970. The same national office estimates the total teaching staff required for 1970 as 553,000, implying a student-teacher ratio of roughly 11.7 to 1, a ratio only slightly more unfavorable than today.

It was the estimate of the American graduate schools in 1954 that there would be 235,000 doctors of philosophy produced between then and 1970. The national manpower studies of that time estimated that there would be only 135,000 produced in the same period. It is my judgment that, between now and 1970, there will be somewhat more than 220,000 produced, which is higher than either of the above figures, since the first estimate includes four additional years.

Present experience indicates that only 50 per cent of these Ph.D.'s will go into college teaching. Therefore, we can have only 1 in 4 of the total number of teachers whom we will recruit for college classrooms between now and 1970 prepared with Ph.D. degrees. Forty per cent of the present college teaching force hold doctoral degrees. The above figures indicate that this average must drop to roughly 25 per cent.

When I first looked at these figures, I had the impression that we had reached the rock bottom

---
[1] Graduate students are included (Ed.).

now, since the last year of Ray Maul's study [2] indicated that only 25 per cent of all the new teachers employed in the last year of his index had Ph.D.'s. At the other end of the spectrum, roughly 23 per cent had education below the degree of A.M.

We are not at the bottom of the trough yet, however. According to Ray Maul's studies, of the Ph.D. candidates now working for degrees or presently to receive them, roughly 45 per cent will enter the classroom; 12 per cent will go into administration, but most faculty members will not count us administrators as productive. Of the 45 per cent that actually engage in teaching, according to my calculations, 46 per cent were already teaching. In other words, 46 per cent of the Ph.D.'s produced in 1956 who are counted as going into teaching were already in teaching and were just upgrading themselves. Fifty-four per cent of that 45 per cent were available as new recruits for college teaching.

By using Ray Maul's figures regarding new teachers and where they come from, you discover that the 110,000 Ph.D.'s going into teaching now will dwindle to roughly 60,000. Instead of being able to have 1 Ph.D. out of 4 of the new teachers appointed, there may be only 1 Ph.D. in 12 or 13.

The natural consequences of looking at these figures is either complete depression or the presumption that something heroic must be done.

Part of my reason for choosing a larger figure than the American graduate schools chose as the number of Ph.D.'s to be produced between now and 1970 has to do with the state of the market, and the respect that the young man in undergraduate school now has for teaching as a potential career. I think the Woodrow Wilson National Fellowship program has had some effect. I suspect that more teachers are less sour about their economic status than they were, despite Dean Bundy's statement that we shall not make as heroic changes in salaries as inflation or future productivity might justify. I think we are already making startling changes that we did not believe to be possible five years ago.

[2] *Teacher Supply and Demand in Colleges and Universities* (Ed.).

This is an addendum, but I think it useful. I have been President of the University of Oregon for five years.[3] The first year, we tried to persuade a board to request a 7 per cent faculty increase, but were told that it was an intolerably large figure. Our request was reduced to 5 per cent. The second time we asked for 25 per cent and got 24. And, if the measure has any success in the 1959–60 legislature, in a five-year period the University of Oregon's salary schedule will have increased 40 per cent.[4] In 1954, nobody would have accepted such an increase as politically possible even if he approved it as socially desirable. And I think our experience is not unusual. I would hesitate to predict limits to the number of times we will multiply salaries, if national income continues to grow.

The already apparent increase in income has affected the disposition of people to go to graduate schools. By spot-checking, I would judge that there was a marked increase in registrations in graduate schools this year, and that graduate enrollments are probably going to increase geometrically for the next five years. The estimate of 220,000 Ph.D.'s may be substantially lower than will actually be prepared by 1970.

Graduate schools in the United States will have done an irreparable disservice to the country if they treat this increased enrollment as though it were more of the same "business as usual." There is a major need for clarification of what should happen to a student in graduate school, if the output of Ph.D.'s is to be 300,000, say, or even 220,000, in the next twelve years. If these men are treated cavalierly, and allowed to move as slowly or with as little precision through the graduate process as is the present custom, tremendous social damage will be done to education and to the individuals involved.

The promise of an increased number in graduate schools needs to be recognized as an additional burden on the men and women now teaching. There is something self-limiting about the speed at which graduate schools can

[3] President Wilson has since accepted the presidency of the University of Minnesota, effective in the fall of 1960.
[4] The requested increase was provided by act of the Oregon State Legislature in the spring of 1959.

expand in their present form, since, with very few exceptions, the graduate faculty is also part of the undergraduate faculty, and the undergraduate faculty is in desperately short supply. The shortage is more acute, in my judgment, than it was in the secondary schools five years ago. That means we must not accept programs for deploying faculty of the sort that seemed to be applauded by Professor Harris when he was writing about Professor Hutchinson's proposed five-to-one ratio. A five-to-one student-faculty ratio, either at the undergraduate level or in the graduate school, ought to be challenged as nonsense, in the light of the crises we are facing.[5]

We have to be more careful about the uses of potential teachers than is implied by a program which proposes that 50 per cent of all the people employed in a given institution will have to leave at the end of four years, that an additional 40 per cent will have to leave at the end of another six years, so that 10 per cent are left in the institution after ten years of service. I know that Mr. Hutchinson was trying to make an economic case for a given institution. He was not driving for a prototype. But American education certainly cannot afford to drive out 90 per cent of the teachers. Everyone in collegiate education must discover that it is worthwhile, indeed essential, that our undergraduate colleges make good teachers out of the first employed men, rather than force them to struggle for survival, sloughing off all who fail from lack of help. As a matter of fact, if 50 per cent of teachers in their first employment must be sold down the river to something less desirable at the end of four years, and another 40 per cent sold down the river to a less desirable place (at least in the intellectual judgment of the president) in another six years, so that 90 per cent have been told that they are wanting at the end of ten years, we have done very little to build confidence in the profession. Such a program is an indictment of the institution, not the men. By implication, it admits that the institution has done nothing to help make a recent student a successful teacher.

We are in a position where teachers are in short supply. Many places are hiring masters of arts because doctors of philosophy are not available for the classrooms. In these conditions our personnel program cannot be one of hiring and firing; we must cherish the manpower that is available.

I think that major reform in graduate education is required, reform not only of the way a Ph.D. is produced, but also in our view of the master's degree. But, in my judgment, you cannot reform a master's degree program by dealing only with the master's degree, for it allows you only one year in which to work. Moreover, there is great difference in the admissions standards among graduate schools, and the range of quality of bachelor's programs is tremendous.

My guess is that graduate schools and liberal arts colleges will have to break through the caste system and talk to high schools. The speed-up which will make it possible for a man to emerge with a master's degree in time to help do the world's teaching will depend in some part upon an understanding of the total academic community. We require a situation in which a teacher in college has confidence in what happens in high school. Now a college professor meets his freshman class with the attitude: "My first obligation will be to unteach whatever you have learned, so that you will start clearly with what is true about American history." This cannot be allowed to continue on the undergraduate level, nor can parallel situations be tolerated at the first-year-graduate stage. A reform in a one-year master's degree offers little hope, but by revising our expectations, in seventeen years (from grade one through the master's degree) we shall have time to produce excellence for the college classroom.

[5] The editor is fearful that he was misunderstood. He has favored increases in the student-faculty ratios (Ed.).

NON-ECONOMIC ASPECTS OF ACADEMIC MORALE

Everett C. Hughes

GOOD morale does not mean that professors are contented cows, but that they are in a mood to keep up a good pace of work themselves and to set up a good pace and standard of work among their students. A great many of the academic people in this country are teaching in places where there is no morale in this sense. There are hundreds of institutions in this country where no education on a high level is going on and where the teachers hardly touch at all the orbits where such work is done, institutions where the question, "Who are my colleagues?" could not be answered with any satisfaction.

Part of the problem of morale is that of bringing about a degree of creative tension in some of these colleges and making it possible for the people who teach in them to have some of the satisfaction of having good students and good colleagues. It seems to me that this affects institutions of the quality represented in this symposium in a number of ways.

There has been talk here of the way faculty structure is affected by the fact that elite institutions require so many more teachers than they can give tenure. A great many young teachers who start in such institutions must leave after a few years. If they continue to teach, they must do it in universities which they regard, rightly or not, as less desirable. Such people can, in this country, always find some place to teach. Indeed, there is somewhere in this country one institution or another in which almost any moderately literate person could find a post. Once in the academic profession in this country, a person can stay in it. He may have to go to an institution he doesn't like or even respect, and he may have to accept hard terms, financially and professionally. But he can stay in.

Part of the problem of academic morale in this country arises from the fact that young men must leave stimulating colleges and graduate schools to teach in less stimulating places, and from their fear that, once out there, they will not be able to swing back into the quality orbit. Of course, many of the "outlying" places are better than people think; many are also worse than anyone who has not seen them could believe.

Sometimes the exiles form little mutual-admiration societies, which serve also as mutual-complaint societies. They sometimes gather around a visitor to tell him how much better they are than their stupid "home-guard" colleagues. We have all had this experience. It is not a sign of good morale.

Involved in all this is the immense size of our total academic market, and its relation to the size of the quality market. So far as I know, the relations of total to quality market have not been worked out in their economic and academic consequences.

Before I go further let me impress upon you just how great can be the shock of going out from a good graduate school to an institution which has not yet achieved high standards. A young man who likes to teach and may develop into a research man is asked to a college or a university by a department head who says, "Now, we older men here have never had much time to do research. We are going to create a special position for you, so that you can help us build up the department. You will have some advanced courses from the start, and will have time for a seminar and a little research."

When he gets there he is met with this: "We're sorry. The enrollments are a bit bigger than expected, so you will have to teach more sections of the introductory course. Besides, the dean didn't quite understand the situation. But next year, you can get along with the original plan. Hope you don't mind. We have all had to take our turn at these chores." By about the third year, when he presses things a bit, he is told, "Well, who the hell do you think you are to think you should have privileges the rest of us never got?" There are many varieties of this sophomoric initiation. If the young man organizes his courses in his own way, using a syllabus, the dean may call him in to say, "Now isn't it fine that you want to outline a course in your own way. But are you sure you have it well organized? The students complain that they never know what tomorrow's assignment is. Maybe you should use a textbook until you have had a little more experience." Or suppose the young man, a sociologist, thinks it might be interesting to study, let us say, the artists of the region. The older colleagues say, "Oh, yes, so-and-so who was here before you tried something like that." There is no need to tell you these are devices used on eager newcomers in industry, the army, and reform schools.

We should not underestimate the morale-busting power of men who, after a few disappointing years, are jolly well going to see to it that smart young newcomers shall not enjoy privileges and opportunities they did not enjoy and set standards of excellence which they themselves did not set. It is amazing how quickly academic people can lose their identity with the world of excellence and join with the home guards to prevent change.

Why is this of interest to people in leading colleges and universities? For this reason. We cannot, I imagine, change the proportions of non-tenure, middle-level, and tenure positions in the great universities very much. More people than can be kept on and promoted will start their careers in such institutions and in the host of affiliated enterprises which gather around them. Many will have to move out to other institutions. Unless we can raise all our academic institutions to the same level, or drop them all simultaneously to the lowest level, the moving will often have to be from places of more to places of less prestige.

This, I think, is being somewhat offset at the present time by what one might call the overflow of the East. The East, incidentally, is no longer a geographic concept. In studying a medical school in Kansas, we took careful note of what schools people named as "eastern" medical schools. There are only four or five "eastern" medical schools in the East, and the easternmost state, I believe, that has a medical school has among its medical schools only one "eastern" medical school. Stanford is sometimes mentioned as an "eastern" medical school, a fact that shows that "eastern" is a concept and not a place.

There is a great extension of the East in this sense. It is overflowing very strongly into Ohio, as far as small colleges are concerned, because there are quite a number of small colleges there which are old enough to have some old red-brick buildings and to have celebrated their centennials quite a few years ago.

The demand for quality education is going to expand greatly. Many colleges can and will take advantage of it to upgrade themselves (not by changing their names, as agricultural colleges and normal schools do, but by flaunting their age and trying to act it). But that will not take care of all of the increased demand. The state universities have always filled part of that demand, in the liberal arts as well as in the sciences and in practical fields. Some of them are making great strides toward quality now. Their part in quality education in the future will increase both absolutely and in proportion.

This brings me to the problem of self-image. A self-image has a number of facets. It includes one's notion of who one's true colleagues are, the league one's institution plays in, one's notion of one's students. The latter can be defined according to who their fathers are and how good they are, and these concepts can be considered in various ways. Some teachers are disappointed at the small number of their students who follow them into graduate school; this is the preprofessional definition, as opposed to the "general-education" attitude of prizing the freshness and intelligence of the immediate responses of the students. The struggle between these two — the preprofessional and the general-education view — is reaching far down into the early years of college now. What balance between the two leads to high morale is itself an important question. The college of the future, if it is to get good teachers, will have to gain a reputation as a place where one will have both good students and good colleagues. It is hard to separate the two. An occasional lone star may attract good students to an otherwise unexciting place; such tours de force are not common, and generally do not last longer than it takes some better college to hear of the attraction. Students and colleagues of quality are likely to be found in each other's company.

Now a large university is a bundle of varied enterprises and no doubt can have a number of self-images which members of its component parts manage to present to their particular constituencies. But a small liberal arts college has to have one consistent self-image and live up to it, although many a good college president has been able to present slightly different views of the college to alumni, members of the church, students, foundations, and private donors. In general, however, a small college cannot cultivate many images at once. But images can be changed. And there is quite a repertory of them available to smaller colleges who want to go in for quality education. We need to learn more about how a small college can change its self-image and its public image and make the reality correspond to the ideal.

The larger universities and the state universities probably cannot get along with one self-image. They might have one global one, such as, "This is a place that does many good things and does well by its staff"; but I think that any larger and varied institution has the possibility of creating several self-images inside it, several smaller groups of colleagues, and several publics. I have an idea that, if I were in a state university, I would be doing what certain of them are doing — namely, undertaking with a good deal of force and imagination to create quality nuclei in the center of their institutions. This would do a lot for the morale of the staff.

This brings up another point. We seem to need many teachers, and some of these teachers are much better than others. This situation is going to exist for a long time.

The American demand for schools — not especially for higher education, but for schools in which the young person will spend more years of his life — is certainly going to increase. Of course, youngsters are also making money with twilight jobs. But the general demand that they go to school longer will increase. Automation will, on the whole, further increase this demand. So that quality education, which means quality teaching, too, will be done in a situation in which, let us say, not-very-good education is increasing. If our number of youngsters going to college increases, the number of poor ones going to college will also increase.

So there is no way that I see of getting around the problem of educating or sending to school many who want very little from school. They do not want high-quality teaching, and they will, in effect, not stand for high-quality teaching or demands for great effort. We have to face this fact. There are thousands of bright youngsters in this country who don't know any better than to go to fifth-rate colleges, and there is no way to tell them this or to make the distinction among poor, fair, and good.

Our problem is not to increase everybody's morale by direct means, although that is a good enough objective. Our real problem is to increase the number of places where faculty can have good morale. I think this can be done, but it will take much ingenuity. I think that it will mean, in putting out little quality nuclei here and yonder all over the country, that some institutions will be able to change their whole self-image and get a new class of staff and students.

Why is that of interest here? It is because the better these places are, the more nuclei of high academic morale in my sense there are in the country, the better is going to be the morale of all the youngsters who can't stay on at Harvard. More than any other institution in the country, the Ph.D.'s from there have that secret yearning, "If only they would ask me back." We have it to a lesser extent in Chicago. There are people who won't leave town. They get their Ph.D. degrees and they pick up a little research job here and there, or three or four research jobs at once. They just ask to be hired as slaves, so they won't have to leave town. The big problem in morale for the country as a whole, as I see it, is to increase the market for quality teachers, the number of places where they can go with some sense of not being let down.

This raises another pair of questions that I will only mention in a few words. One of them is the orbits of circulation. I don't think we realize fully that we have at least ten or twenty or maybe more academic markets in this country. We have the Catholic, the Methodist, the Southern Baptist, and other denominational markets. We have regional markets around each state university. Every state school of education has its state as an almost monopoly market. The graduate departments have their orbits and markets, and so on.

A large part of a person's self-image is his conception of the orbit he is in and the one that he would like to circulate in. If we can expand the orbit of quality places, we will take part of the pressure off a few places and also do a great service to quality education in the rest of the country.

Another issue I would like to discuss briefly is career faults. I will give you an example. In Germany, the number of full professors has remained practically fixed for fifty or sixty years. The number of people teaching in the universities and the number of students have multiplied many times. The crucial thing that a man has to begin to decide at an early age is whether he will try for one of the few positions as Ordinarius or pick some alternative. In German language, literature, and history, or in other languages, the only alternative to the university career is teaching in the excellent secondary-school system. But to go up the seniority ladder in the secondary-school system, one has to enter it before he is thirty-three. The average age at which one can be sure one is on the academic ladder in the universities is thirty-nine. This is what I mean by a career fault. A man must make his decision one way six years before he has security the other way.

I could point out a dozen or fifteen career faults of this kind in this country. This is another morale problem not only because the expansion of the quality market will influence morale in the best places and perhaps the flow of teachers besides, but also because the alternative careers to the academic are a factor in morale, and a great many people do move out. The archeologist has few alternatives; he can stay in the university, go to a museum, or marry a rich wife who will put her fortune into archeology. In physics the alternatives are many. The alternatives in the social sciences are expanding greatly. The quality of the alternative careers, the way they enter into a man's self-image, the extent to which he thinks he is giving up his academic commitment by moving over into them, and the quality of the work he does there and the ability to move back: all these can cause good or poor morale.

The general disposition of the faculties, incidentally, is never to let anybody come back to the academic world if he has been out and has had a taste of some other kind of life. He is a traitor just as, if he deserts his department, he is a traitor; this creates another kind of career fault.

Part of the problem of morale is to smooth out these career faults, and to understand the relations among the many academic orbits a man may move in. The best way is to increase quality in as many institutions as possible, so that the alternatives to the best places will be good.

FACULTY PAY AND INSTITUTIONAL EXTRAVAGANCE

Theodore Caplow

IT has been said several times that the market will take care of our natural desire to see professors better paid. I think this is unquestionably true. Not only the market but all sorts of committees and foundations and propagandists are busy at work on the problem.

It seems to me that perhaps the major problem is not how to raise faculty pay, but how to improve the academic institution, that perhaps we are not sufficiently aware of the need for fundamental reform.

We do propose to do something extraordinary and odd in doubling the size of higher education as an institution (having already doubled it recently), and yet making no real changes in the way the thing is put together. Nobody would double the size of a foundry or a Boy Scout troop in this fashion, and I have some doubts as to whether you can do it to a university.

To some extent, at least, universities are wasteful, and to some extent, at least, professors are unproductive. If we are moving into an era of vastly increased costs, it may not be amiss to ask, how could we make universities less wasteful and how could we make professors more productive?

If we concede that there is a margin for improvement, there is the interesting question of how the fruits of improvement might be distributed. What is an optimum distribution of the increased faculty salaries we see on the horizon, and what is the optimum distribution of internal savings as they are made?

Take the first question, the ability of the institution to pay and its relation to the waste of resources that does go on in universities. We know from a recent study that in two state universities the average increase of fringe facilities has been something like four times the average increase in the budgets of academic departments. In one of these institutions, there is not a single superfluous function — by "superfluous" I mean police, buildings and grounds, alumni relations, student services of the more peripheral type — that has not increased more in the past ten years and in the past fifteen years and in the past twenty years — I take them all separately — than any academic department in the institution. An enormous proportion of the increased revenue of the university is being funneled into these channels.

Furthermore, the rates of increase of remuneration have been higher in the nonacademic positions, and where outright sinecures can be detected, they fall mainly here. In another state institution, I know a man who has eleven secretaries to do a job in connection with an alumni function which could adequately be done by one girl working half-time.

While there are some disciplinary controls on the increase in, say, the department of economics, there are no disciplinary controls on the increase of the campus police force. Campus police forces commonly use two patrolmen on beats as dangerous as a nursery school.

This means a fundamental dispersion of resources, a kind of breach in the dyke that can hardly ever be checked without reorganization.

There is the phenomenon which Professor Harris has mentioned, the departmental insistence on replacing individuals, making the entire faculty payroll a fixed charge before any increases and innovations can be considered. Not only are people replaced who do not need to be replaced, but they are often replaced at levels which are inappropriate, because a full professor retires and it seems appropriate to the department — no, it is conceived as a vital interest of the department — to get back the full professorship and not lose any of its share in the general budget.

There is further — and this we academics have been reticent about, with proper professional self-regard — the real decline of the teaching workload. It has been mentioned occasionally as a possible trend. I submit that it is a conspicuous and salient fact. I know of no major university at which the teaching load approaches what it was ten years ago or at which, ten years ago, it approached what it was thirty years ago. People teach less and less, in general, and on a less continuous calendar.

The Minnesota study to which you referred [1] showed a decline of about an hour and a half per week per year in the total work load — not merely teaching, but the total commitment of time to academic purposes. If we were to compare hourly wages over the years, we might find that we have surreptitiously retrieved some of our own back from the cost-of-living index.

There is the further fact that tuition is both low and unrealistic so that the increasing cost of instruction is not passed on either to the clientele or to the general public. Even in tax-supported institutions, this is a debatable policy. In private institutions, it can be suicidal.

There is the reluctance to supervise which leaves the inefficient junior teacher without the benefit of the experience or even the oversight of his seniors, so that no possibility of improvement is held out to him, except for the influence of colleagues who never have an opportunity to view his work.

There is, of course, the general conflict of research and teaching, a tendency to reward people who neglect teaching in favor of research, and the inequitable distribution of research opportunities.

All of this is terribly expensive. It is expensive in detail and it is expensive in general.

The productivity of the professor is the other side of this coin. We allow, unlike any other institution in our economy, highly skilled personnel to do work for which the going rate is a dollar an hour — typing, grading papers, sweeping out the office. One of my students, on taking his Ph.D., went to a college which had a most promising prospectus. It promised a pure liberal-arts program, but used the faculty to park cars at football games.

This is shocking in terms of status, but it is no more wasteful than the practice of having the faculty type out class cards and do similar clerical chores.

There is, throughout the academic system, inadequate assistance to professional jobs. The professor who by means of foundation grants has stolen himself enough assistance to do his job properly, just a minimum that any junior executive would require, is regarded with awe by his colleagues and regards himself as a little unscrupulous in having made the system produce what is not counted among his normal perquisites.

There is the career decline, which introduces a peculiar difficulty in the whole concept of merit in the academic market place. Excluding a few eminent men, it is sadly true that around the midpoint of an academic man's career, his market value begins to fall catastrophically — catastrophically, if he intends to make use of it — and sometimes with a concomitant withdrawal of industry and zeal.

In European systems, where this is not the case, professors continue in the leadership of major projects somewhat beyond the age at which their American colleagues are in full retirement.

All of us know men in their fifties and sixties who did good work at one time but who ceased to work long ago. It is difficult not to connect this with the fact that the profession and the institution have ceased to offer them rewards beyond the mere continuation of a paycheck, and also threaten them with a kind of progressive loss of esteem, as younger colleagues parlay their merits into higher salaries.

I confess to the gravest reservations about this whole matter of salary and merit because, if you look at Professor Harris' means and medians,[2] you get some notion of how narrow the dispersion is. The amount of solid economic reward involved in differential salaries among full professors is actually rather small. What we have is a system of invidious comparison and it is difficult to demonstrate that invidious comparison is the best basis for motivating good work.

We have a rank system among professors of which we make almost no use. We water it down in the first place by salary differentials and then we limit the possibilities of hierarchy until we have merely labels of esteem — professor, associate professor, assistant professor. We disregard the possibility of effective supervision or guidance from one rank down to an-

[1] Ruth E. Eckert and Robert J. Keller, *A University Looks at Its Program*, Minneapolis, University of Minnesota Press, 1954.

[2] To be published in S. E. Harris, *Economics of Higher Education* (Ed.).

other, except as it may develop informally.

The whole theory upon which most systems of occupational rank are founded, that older and more experienced men can bring younger men up to their own degree of competence, is essentially abandoned in our system, and I do not know any compelling reason for this loss, unless it be the assumption that academic work is too sacred a calling to be supervised. But, along with this, we take the unfortunate position, unique among the professions, that we do not train men to minimum competence. Our whole system for appraising junior professors is based on the assumption that most of them are not properly trained; that, at any rate, you cannot hire a man who has a good degree and trust him to do the job of work for which he was trained; that, instead, you must watch him through his entire early career to see if he is one of the minority who is professionally competent. You must, in other words, watch for incompetence, but you may not provide the supervision which might transfom it into competence.

All this strikes at the self-regard of the individual and at the claim of the profession to be a corps of specifically qualified men.

SOME STATISTICAL ASPECTS

Robert E. Iffert

I MUST make the standard disclaimer that people from Washington always make, and that is that any views expressed are not necessarily those of the sponsor. Those who have been around Washington know, of course, that there are very few items which are discussed in Washington on which there is unanimity of opinion, anyway.

Table 1 is a summary of some salary data for the current year prepared in the College and University Branch of the Office of Education. I think that these tabulations will be of interest. These go beyond faculty salaries; salary data on management personnel are also included. Some educators have mentioned the seeming facility with which staff members who are concerned with physical facilities manage to get higher salaries than faculty members. This is a genuine problem to many of us in the Office of Education. It is so much easier to get consideration in Congress for measures to increase the facilities on the college campus than it is to get consideration of measures to improve the faculty.[1]

Another area in which there may be some interest is the study, also prepared in the College and University Administration Branch, which analyzes the functions of governing boards of publicly controlled institutions of higher education. The following facts are included. In the United States there are 45 coordinating and operating boards, of which 39 have responsibility for the professional faculty. Seven boards are coordinating only, and none of the 7 has responsibility for the special staff. There are 129 boards that are governing only; of the 129, 120 by regulation or law have responsibility for the faculty. There are also 21 other boards, of which 7 have responsibility for the faculty. It should be pointed out that the large number of governing boards is due to the fact that states have established individual governing boards for teachers' colleges and other special-purpose institutions.

Another area of study which concerns the Division of Higher Education relates to predictions of staff needs. Table 2 is a summary

TABLE 1. — 1958–59 MEAN SALARIES OF FACULTY MEMBERS BY RANK AND ALL RANKS COMBINED IN UNDERGRADUATE COLLEGES OF FOUR-YEAR INSTITUTIONS

Rank	Public and private		Public		Private	
	Number	Mean salary	Number	Mean salary	Number	Mean salary
Professors	15,868	$8,840	9,776	$9,040	6,092	$8,510
Associate professors	15,321	6,920	10,179	7,150	5,142	6,470
Assistant professors	20,665	5,860	14,047	6,060	6,618	5,430
Instructors	13,047	4,840	8,644	4,980	4,403	4,580
All ranks combined	64,901	$6,630	42,646	$6,780	21,255	$6,350

SOURCE: *Higher Education Planning and Management Data, 1958–59*. U.S. DHEW, Office of Education.

These salary data from the Office of Education study are all on tabulating cards and can be assembled and listed at a very small cost. If an individual has a justifiable request for comparative analyses involving specific types of institutions, this request will be honored within the limits of available funds and personnel. Only an individual's own institution will be identified on an otherwise anonymous list.

[1] For details, see especially *Higher Education Planning and Management Data, 1958–59,* U.S. Department of Health, Education, and Welfare, Office of Education, esp. Table IV.

of the actual and estimated total annual enrollments in higher educational institutions and full-time equivalent staff for higher education in the continental United States. It shows separate projections for institutions under public and private control.

The figure for the 1965 enrollment of 4,677,000 is slightly different from the figure that had been reported in an earlier prediction of the Office of Education. The difference is due largely to a slightly different definition. We have counted here only students who are degree-

TABLE 2. — ACTUAL AND ESTIMATED ENROLLMENTS AND PROFESSIONAL STAFFS IN INSTITUTIONS OF HIGHER EDUCATION IN THE CONTINENTAL UNITED STATES UNDER PUBLIC AND PRIVATE CONTROL, 1945–1965.
(Figures given in Thousands)

Fall of	Total Enrollment [a]	Total Faculty	Publicly Controlled Enrollment	Publicly Controlled Faculty	Privately Controlled Enrollment	Privately Controlled Faculty
1945	1,074	136	502	69	572	67
1947	2,338	196	1,153	99	1,185	97
1949	2,457	210	1,219	106	1,238	104
1951	2,116	198	1,052	106	1,064	92
1953	2,251	209	1,204	113	1,047	96
1955	2,721	252	1,531	146	1,190	106
1957	3,104	287	1,738	161	1,366	126
1959	3,402	311	2,003	176	1,399	135
1961	3,790	351	2,274	211	1,516	140
1963	4,189	388	2,597	240	1,592	148
1965	4,677	433	2,946	273	1,731	160

[a] Projections published by Research and Statistical Services Branch of the Office of Education in March 1956.

candidate students — students who are in degree programs, eliminating the others. Also, the earlier figure was for the total United States. We have restricted this to the continental United States, which yields a slightly lower figure.

The projections show a lower rate of increase in the number of staff members required at privately controlled institutions compared to publicly controlled institutions. That is based on an assumption which seems to have some basis in fact: namely, that the sources of support for privately controlled institutions will not keep pace with the public resources. There is also the assumption that a greater proportion of the undergraduate or lower-division instruction will take place in public junior colleges, with the growth of that type of institution.

There are several other observations that might be made with reference to the projection of staff needs. The over-all ratio of staff to students remains fairly constant. It rises considerably above the present level for privately controlled institutions, because these institutions will tend to become more uniform in character and have, in general, fewer reasons for maintaining small classes. Currently we have one full-time equivalent staff member per 10.8 full-time equivalent students. In 1965 we estimate, largely because of the higher ratio in the privately controlled institutions, that the total ratio will remain 1 to 10.8, with 1 to 10.8 in publicly controlled institutions and 1 to 10.8 in privately controlled institutions instead of the present ratio of 1 to 10.4. If that seems to be a rather optimistic prognostication, it is simply extrapolation on the basis of certain assumptions which I have stated.

The report on the degrees granted in the year 1957–58 [2] supports the observation that President Wilson made with reference to the production of earned doctorates. It is interesting that, in the twelve-year period from 1926 to 1937, there were 25,871 doctorates granted. In the next ten years, there were 25,381. In the eight-year period from 1948 to 1955 doctorates awarded totaled 56,347. For the last three years the number granted was 26,601, a total in excess of that for the twelve years from 1926 to 1937, or the ten-year period from 1938 to 1947. There is certainly evidence of a rapidly increasing number of earned doctorates.

There is also evidence from studies in our office and those of the National Science Foundation and other places indicating that the share of the holders of the doctor's degree that the colleges are able to hire is going down. This tends to dampen some of the optimism associated with the increase in the number of degrees granted.

In November, 1958, the Secretary of the Department of Health, Education, and Welfare called in representatives of a large number of organizations and a few institutions so that they could brief him and the department on what were desirable goals for the Office of Education. I have selected from the suggestions, which are about six pages in length, a

[2] *Earned Degrees conferred by Institutions of Higher Education, 1957–58*, Circular No. 570, U. S. Department of Health, Education, and Welfare, Office of Education.

few that refer particularly to higher education and to the problem of faculty supply.

(1) It was unwise for the National Defense Education Act to exclude college teachers from the "forgiveness" feature of the student loan program.

(2) College teachers who do not have a Ph.D. degree should be given fellowships to continue their work in summer sessions.

(3) It is common experience, particularly in the sciences, when recommending someone with a Ph.D. degree for a college teaching position, to find that he held a fellowship for a number of years but has had no teaching experience whatsoever. Perhaps all fellowship students should be required to spend at least one year in teaching without pay under supervision in the department in which they are enrolled.

(4) The Ph.D. degree needs very much to be overhauled and improved, and it is hoped that a great many graduate schools will revise their requirements. Provisions should be made so that the recipient of a fellowship can be given a part-time teaching position, possibly with pay, while doing his graduate work, so that he can have the opportunity to gain appreciation of college teaching. This seems to be the best way we can interest our graduate engineers in teaching.

(5) Much of the staffing problem in higher education could be solved if qualified women were given teaching positions. Perhaps the federal government should examine what facilities are available for reporting staff vacancies and needs rapidly and accurately.

(6) The Office of Education should call attention to the caliber of teachers our colleges and universities are getting in the humanities.

I do not want to be provincial in my remarks, so I refer to some other activities in Washington. The National Education Association's Department of Higher Education is currently working on a study of conditions of work for college faculty and administrators. The purpose of the study is to identify the key factors which affect working conditions for faculty. This study promises to add a great deal of information to the areas discussed earlier.

The American Council on Education is now interested in taking up one of the suggestions made at the Secretary's conference by studying placement services in higher education. The purposes of this study are twofold: (1) to obtain factual information upon which appropriate educational organizations may consider the possible need for some form of centralized services or other cooperative action, and (2) to make widely available to those seeking faculty members in higher education a report on existing placement services. I know that the American Council is seeking financial support, through foundations, to carry on this study.

I hesitate to get into a discussion of the features of the National Defense Education Act bearing on higher education, because its operation is in its infancy. We have had many complaints. The American Association of University Professors and other educational organizations are concerned about the disclaimer clause in the law. It was not put there through any action on the part of educators as a body, I am sure. Efforts will be continued, I understand, to determine what risks and political realities are involved in attempting to have that phase of the Act modified.

There is considerable interest in providing for the forgiveness feature for people preparing to teach in college. Beyond that I would not be able to say what revisions are most urgently needed. Those of you who have seen the figures showing allocations for loans will have reason to be perplexed, to say the least. But, without alibi-ing or taking a defensive position, I call your attention to the fact that what happened was due to more "counting by watchmen." Under the terms of the law, the allocations must be in terms of need, and the interpretation of "need" is the amount requested. Some institutions went overboard in their requests, so that the total amounts by states were considerably (that is an understatement) in excess of available funds. No one received as much as he requested, and the reductions, accordingly, resulted in some rather foolish allocations, but since the first allotments, they have improved and can be expected to continue to do so.

I might comment on one or two points in connection with tenure. We find, in trying to recruit personnel in Washington, that the only way we can get men like Dean Peter Elder of Harvard to come there is to assure them that there is no tenure. The phenomenon that we observe in trying to procure personnel on a permanent basis is that the individuals who have the capacities and know-how are already receiving salaries higher than the federal government can pay, or have reached a stage in their careers at which they could not possibly put enough years of service in the government to benefit appreciably under the Civil Service Retirement System. So educational institutions are not the only ones with recruitment and tenure problems.

V. EXPERIMENT IN HIGHER EDUCATION; EDUCATIONAL AND ECONOMIC ISSUES

Summary of the Discussion to papers on "Experiment in Higher Education" given to the Seminar on the Economics of Higher Education, March 12, 1959. Papers were given by Messrs. Morrison, Adams, McCune and Barber, Stewart, Thorpe, O'Dowd, and Varner.

NEW colleges offer a concrete opportunity to re-examine the tenets and rigidities on which our system of higher education is based. If the re-examination is fruitful, new colleges usually become "experimental" colleges, since they involve in some degree breaking away from the conventional and accepted modes of college organization, curriculum, and student-faculty relationships. They involve the introduction of novelties which tend either to move the new college closer to the immediate needs of society or closer to the educational ideals of academicians and educators.

Discussion of these papers on "experiments" which actually have reached the advanced stages of planning focused on four important issues: (1) the merits of a nonresidential, eight-hour-day college; (2) the evaluation of any changed method of educating — how do we know whether an "experiment" has succeeded? (3) the position of two- and four-year liberal arts colleges in an era in which a larger and larger proportion of students are going on to graduate schools, and (4) the possibility and advantage of eliminating academic rank and tenure.

The Eight-Hour Day for Nonresidential Colleges

The first question raised in the discussion concerned the degree to which educators and "Higher Education" should make concessions to the culture from which the students come. The plan described by Mr. Adams for a branch of Hofstra College was used as an excellent example of an educational endeavor which adjusted to current culture without abandoning certain standards and requirements of the academic disciplines. The principal "concession" was, as Mr. Adams pointed out in his paper, the organization of the college day according to the demands of commuters, and the principal means of offsetting this concession was to schedule the college day in such a way as to require of the student eight full hours of hard work within the college walls.

The eight-hour day for college students, generally speaking, was felt to have both merits and disadvantages. Several members felt that an eight-hour day would be infinitely more effective than an intensive extracurricular or co-curricular program, no matter how well organized, in offsetting and undermining the temptations of car, television, and beer. Extracurricular programs, it was noted, had not proved strikingly effective in the past: "They do not work as well as they should. I am afraid that the car being what it is and the family group being what it is, intensive extracurricular programs are going to be a rather disappointing route in solving the problem of keeping students in a college environment for most of the day."

Most participants, therefore, considered the eight-hour day one of the best ways of arranging both academic and nonacademic activities in a nonresidential college, provided that the students are made to realize that it is possible to continue beyond five o'clock their work in fields that interest them. Moreover, in a college where one can assume that the majority of the students will be adhering to a similar schedule for the rest of their working lives, it might prove extremely exciting to provide, during the usual work day, provocative and essentially "unbusinesslike" academic materials.

Several participants observed that the eight-hour college day gives the students more leisure time than is usual for students and professors, but that this is desirable if they are stimulated enough to use their leisure time productively or to provide needed and justified relaxation. The idea of "making the whole day work," it was agreed, has considerable potential educational value. One participant pointed out that many students, particularly freshmen, suffer from their inability to utilize their time effectively;

they might be helped enormously if they know what is expected of them and are held to a certain time schedule. A further advantage of the Hofstra Plan is that it allows a student to go to college for less than $1,000 a year.

In considering the relative merits of residential and commuters' colleges, the real problem seems to be how to persuade the students of the intensity and seriousness of academic work without the added persuasions of the "residential experience." As one participant said, if students have had a good but perhaps not very serious education in high school, "How can you persuade them that college is different, if you don't keep them overnight?" The answer suggested by one member is to present the students with a radically different curriculum from the one to which they have become accustomed, "to reverse everything they have been doing in method and technique . . . and shock them into a new procedure."

Furthermore, "if students are going to be moved along academically in a radical way, they need some extra-academic base of emotional security. This can be achieved in many ways. Going steady is one. A job is another, the home yet another; even a car can be one." The emotional security of home or car is not broken in a commuter college, as it sometimes is when students leave for a residential college. The problem is to achieve the correct balance of interests and involvements in the daily cycle of the life of the student.

Several participants raised the question of integrating these experimental branches into the four-year college. While the arguments above support the eight-hour-day commuter college, this pattern may be broken when students transfer to another school for upper-division work. And there is the repeated problem of getting the work done at an unusual college — particularly one which tries to condense two academic years into one calendar year — accepted by more conventional colleges. Mr. Adams envisioned ultimately a system of several branches which would feed into Hofstra College, enabling the latter to specialize in advanced courses and graduate courses.

Another objection to the principle of "locking the students in" during an eight-hour day is that it yields to the prejudice that students cannot work unless they are being evaluated all the time, unless they are locked in and continually examined, tested, and ordered about. This problem of "giving in to" — or is it "coming to terms with"? — the accepted standards of academic work to which the students are accustomed is another aspect of the greater issue of how a college "comes to terms with a culture, or how it tries to influence it." Although many teachers and administrators — not to mention the students themselves — are convinced that constant evaluation and testing are necessary to produce good work, it is dangerous and unnecessary to proceed exclusively upon such an assumption; in any case, there are certainly good examples of college programs which have demonstrated that college undergraduates can do good work without being threatened and coerced.

Independent Study

"Independent study" is an issue which plagues most educators, for many feel that only through such study — independent inquiry by the student into the nature and diversity of things — can a person become really educated. But effective self-study requires a more efficient use of time than the average student can manage; most American schools have not prepared the student to work on his own. "The student comes to college not expecting an independent program, and, therefore, if you impose it upon him, you give him something that he is not yet ready for. You have to get him ready for it, and that takes time."

One member mentioned an experiment at Antioch College in which the faculty, after four weeks of the term had passed, announced that there would be no more classes, handed out reading lists and syllabuses, and told the students to do their own preparation for the final examination. "There was terrific student reaction against this. They were outraged. They said, 'What are we paying our money for?' But there is no evidence that they didn't buckle down and do the work. The student performance was neither better nor worse than usual as a result." It was agreed that it would be harmful to make too great demands on the students, but the chances are good that they do better independent work than either their teachers or they themselves suspect.

Another point must be considered when discussing student reaction to independent work. Various experiments and tests have demonstrated that independent study programs produce academic work of as high caliber as that done in formal courses with close instructional supervision, despite the protests by the students that they were "missing out on something." But perhaps the student is right; several participants suggested that perhaps he has really missed "something," something which cannot be measured, when he has not been "exposed" to an instructor. This raised the issue of the effectiveness of tests and experiments in evaluating education.

Large versus Small Classes

One of the most controversial questions in higher education today is whether or not the educational value of small classes exceeds the extra cost entailed in ignoring the economies of the large lecture. And because the conclusion seems to turn on an empirical issue — do students gain more from small classes than from large ones? — the debate has been extended to the methodological questions concerned with testing and evaluating the results of experiments involving people.

Several members pointed out that tests and experiments run at various colleges demonstrated fairly convincingly that the amount of knowledge acquired and perhaps even the degree of interest created in the student for the material did not vary significantly with the size of the class in which the material was presented. Some suggested that since small classes are also considerably more expensive to run, they should be abandoned in favor of large lectures, perhaps supplemented by intimate seminar groups.

Why, then, do small classes persist, particularly in view of the financial difficulties of many colleges? In the first place, one participant pointed out that quite apart from ideology there are many institutional obstacles to eliminating small classes. It is often impossible to control the proliferation of departmental course offerings, a mushrooming growth which results in many small classes not wanted by the administration. It was agreed that colleges should make every effort to prevent this, but it is not always possible to do. Growing difficulties in recruiting qualified faculty members reduce the leverage of the administration over the curriculum. Young faculty members — instructors or lecturers — increasingly wish to teach courses of their own after only a few years of teaching, and will leave for another institution if they are not permitted to do so. In order to keep them, the college must allow them courses of their own. This often results in undue course proliferation and small classes. The New College plan intelligently avoids this problem by constructing the curriculum in such a way that each professor will teach only one course at a time.

Second, as another discussant pointed out, small classes are not always intentionally small; often a course will be offered that is expected to draw a large number of students, but which in fact draws only a small enrollment. A college will not always wish to discard it, if the material is worthwhile and if those students who took it profited from it.

But in addition to these "accidental" reasons for small classes, there are many who favor small classes in their own right. In reply to the battery of statistical results thrust at them, proponents of small classes question the validity of the tests attempting to measure academic performance. Some participants felt that testing and measuring the results of learning and teaching processes was admirable in principle, but that most tests fail to control and to isolate adequately the various aspects of the situations under examination. In testing any educational variable, such as class size, the greatest difficulty is controlling the other variables; different teachers in the experimental groups and control groups may invalidate the results. Indeed, one participant pointed out that the same man may be a different person in a large lecture hall from the one he is before a small discussion class. This is true of students as well. Others felt that successful testing of teaching methods, no matter what care is taken, is simply impossible.

One member observed that the usual evaluation of what the student has learned depends upon his demonstrating how much he has remembered immediately after finishing a course, whereupon, if he performs satisfactorily, he gets "credit" for the course and is counted as having "had" the subject. The whole American edifice of education is constructed with these building blocks of credits. Yet memory retention declines very rapidly after exposure, and we know very little about the ultimate effects of the student's educational experience — what a certain course left with him ten years later, for example. Some experiments are now being run to ascertain some of the results of education more imponderable than the accumulation of factual knowledge. At Oberlin College a series of tests of students' reactions to art and music are being administered throughout their four years there. There are tentative plans for following these through the postgraduate years.

A strong intuitive point in favor of small classes is that the students can enjoy in them exciting and stimulating contact with their instructors which they would conceivably miss if their schedules included only large lecture courses. Some felt that this contact was essential to the academic well-being of the student, but others thought it was more an ideal than a reality. The real issue regarding the connection between the size of the class and the quality of the education, according to some, is the kind of relationship established between the students and the instructors. The same applies to the entire college community. As one member put it, "If you have a faculty of six and a student body of a hundred, the students do not think 'We' and 'They.' But get it up to a certain size and you get a student culture versus a faculty culture, because you cannot differentiate that many people. The ratio does not change, but the image changes on both sides. After a certain point the faculty begins to speak of the students as 'They,' and the students begin to think of the faculty as 'They.'"

Evaluation of the effectiveness of small or large classes depends upon this sort of indeterminate and intangible but perhaps highly valuable characteristic of the college community. For others, however, these were sweet but unsubstantiated words. The validity of experiments which have been done may be questioned, but at least they suggest that the burden of proof should be shifted to the proponents of small classes.

Opinion also varied on a related issue. Some members felt that it was important to test and evaluate carefully new curricula and new pedagogical techniques before becoming irretrievably committed to them. "Just being enthusiastic about television, and adopting it (or any program) because we get excited about it, does not seem to me to be an appropriate approach." All agreed that a faculty should not blindly and extravagantly undertake an expensive and unknown procedure just for the excitement of it. But one member thought it would be a very good thing "if faculties said, 'Let us do this,' not because it can be tested out, but because it is an act of creating a change." Another added, "I cannot help feeling that our real problem in all of these things is not to get tests and measure results, but to make acts of faith about a kind of process that relates to a social situation and social aspirations. The fixed image of the American college eduation is getting in our way."

Aims of the Liberal Arts College

The preceding remark reintroduced the question which all experimenters in college education must face: what *does* the American college provide; what *is* a liberal arts education? One of the innovators said that in discussing this question his group came up with the answer: "We want an end product which, in essence, is a man who will run in the pursuit of knowledge. We start him off as a crawling person, and we hope to teach him how to start walking and then let him walk with some of his peers, and we hope that by the time he graduates he is off and running. This is quite different from the kind of educational program which we often hear about in the normal type of college. They simply give the student the degree, his diploma, and say to him, 'You are out now,' and he slows down to an absolute walk or sits in front of a television screen."

But the role of the liberal arts college is gradually changing. As one participant observed, the good undergraduate schools no longer provide the last and fullest body of academic work which their students will face — they no longer have to worry about putting on the "finishing touches" — for now a large majority of their students go on to graduate schools. Administrators and faculties must consider this new fact in planning their curricula, but the colleges do not want to become merely "pregraduate" schools, catering solely to the desires of the graduate schools. One member argued that if a college kept up its standards and stuck to its guns, it could persuade the graduate schools that what they were getting was what they wanted.

This dilemma of the liberal arts–pregraduate college is most acute in designing the curriculum. It can be argued that since most students going on to graduate school will be subjected to rigorous and detailed studies in "depth," the college must provide the best kind of general education: a broad understanding of the philosophical "shape" of the student's chosen academic field, a knowledge of its methodology, its materials, and its wider applications. Accompanying this should be a sufficient excursion into other disciplines to provide some perspective and also to create other interests. "Depth" can come later on.

One participant suggested that there are two kinds of "depth" which must be distinguished. The first is the one too often emphasized in pregraduate schools today: "It comes down pretty much to a mass of facts. It is technological education." But then there is "a kind of depth which is not so much the prerogative of most of our graduate schools. It is philosophical depth. I would argue that it is this second kind of depth which really belongs in the liberal arts curriculum."

Junior Colleges

Another curricular problem is raised by the role of junior colleges in the changing character of American higher education. These will be handling an increasing part of the undergraduate population in the near future. How is it possible to fit their program into the more conventional four-year course leading to a bachelor's degree? Dr. Conant has suggested that junior colleges should assume that a large proportion of their students will go on to the state universities, and that the latter should in effect determine the curricula of the junior colleges for those intending to go on, even though this may cramp their curricular freedom considerably. This is now done in California, with its extensive system of junior colleges, the graduates of which transfer to Berkeley or U.C.L.A. in large numbers.

Outside a well-developed system such as that in California, transfer students, whether or not from junior colleges, have an especially difficult time. Colleges like to develop their students from the cradle, so to speak. An unwritten rule prevents transfer students from receiving scholarships from the schools to which they change. There is already fierce competition among colleges in attracting the most promising students as freshmen; to induce them away from other schools as juniors would arouse much resentment. And the good teacher at a poor school is castigated as a traitor if he urges a bright student to transfer to a better institution. For all these reasons transfer students do not receive the attention they deserve, and the junior colleges suffer from it. Unless they are to be an educational dead end, the junior colleges must be able to get their students into advanced standing at four-year institutions.

In regard to staffing junior colleges, a participant suggested that there be no formal requirements beyond the A.B. degree for faculty members. To require more would result in turning away many excellent and perfectly competent teachers. Inaugurating such a policy would involve some difficulties in becoming accredited under present procedures, however.

Faculty Recruitment and Tenure

Recruitment of competent academic staffs is also a problem for four-year colleges. Such colleges often do not enjoy the advantage of a reservoir of graduate students from which to draw part-time teachers; they must hire on a full-time basis young teachers who are not, perhaps, ready to take on all the teaching responsibilities which go with professorial rank. Several participants inquired about the possibility of eliminating the uncertainties for a young teacher associated with a system of tenure and the invidious comparisons implicit in academic rank. Apart from a brief trial period, there is no compelling reason to differentiate among professors by labeling them "assistant" or "associate." Salary gradations, whether for merit or service, are a different matter, but they need not be accompanied by formal titles.

Similarly, tenure was felt to be an unnecessary vestige of academic tradition. As one participant put it, "Tenure represents the leftism of the thirties, still held on to by faculties who don't need it any more, partly because they are too safe, but partly because they have a free market. So I would say that only bad faculties need tenure. Good faculties can do without it." It would be a painful if not impossible process to eliminate the system where it already exists, but creation of a new college provides an opportunity to expurgate time-worn remnants from the past.

A dean suggested that a tenure system is appropriate, even necessary, for a large research-oriented university with many graduate students, but undesirable for the liberal arts college. He proposed that when a college hires a man with some experience, the new teacher should be told he may stay permanently if the first year works out. In the tradition of the English common room, he may never get a raise, but he can stay. Since twenty years without promotion can sour a man, a concomitant of this policy must be elimination of academic rank. Then no one else would know that the disappointing appointee had never received a raise.

But at a large university it is more difficult to do away with the tenure system and the "six-year neurosis" which precedes tenure appointment. Here permanent teachers will be instructing graduate students and doing research, and it takes longer than a year to ascertain whether or not a man will make a first-rate sociologist, say, as distinguished from a competent teacher of sociology.

Some felt that the tenure system induced stagnation and unnecessary conservatism. Others thought that resistance to change was not necessarily related to tenure; whether or not there is a tenure system, there will be "the bird who has been around for twenty-five years, and who has soured on life." Keeping such a man in the mainstream of the intellectual and cultural life of the college so that he will not go sour depends only partly on tenure and salary.

Issues for the New Colleges

In any case, the new experimental colleges offer fledgling teachers new career lines which could be free from the encumbrances of the tenure system, the usual courses, and curricula which have become institutionalized and inflexible in established schools. On the other hand, one participant added that experimental colleges, once they have settled in, are often the worst offenders in sticking to over-conservative practices which cease to have the greatest educational value. It is not so much the policies of the college itself as the ingrained attitudes of faculty members which prevent radical new experiments which would enliven the college curricula. (It was noted that most participants in the seminar were administrators, not faculty members.) As an illustration, one member stated that he could see no reason why professors adhere religiously to the plan of thirty-five or forty lectures per semester. Frequently as much value could be gained from only five or six special lectures a term.

The plan for a New College in the Connecticut valley tries to end the faculty-administration conflict over educational policy by building in a mechanism for encouraging change. Faculty members in administrative positions will, it is hoped, come to view some of the problems of the college in a different light, and will act from their dual faculty-administrative role in implementing desirable improvements. Several participants expressed reservations about this arrangement, however; one suggested that a necessary condition for progress within a college is a good deal of tension between faculty and administration.

The problem of financing new and experimental colleges was not discussed at any length, although for private institutions, at least, it is certainly one of the most formidable obstacles to starting operations. Acquiring the physical plant is especially difficult, with capital costs for dormitories alone averaging around $4,000 a student, and total capital costs running in the neighborhood of $15,000 a student, according to one estimate. By using less conventional building methods — for example, lift slab construction and electric heating instead of steam — capital costs can be reduced by as much as one third for dormitories and somewhat less for other buildings. But the job is still very expensive. Much waste is inherent in a classroom building, where 50 per cent utilization is regarded as good. Classes are not always full, classrooms cannot always be scheduled for use all the time, athletics and other extracurricular activities conflict with late-afternoon use, and so on.

On the other hand, while a new college may be expensive to start, it need not be more expensive to operate, and indeed may be considerably cheaper than established schools. Several of the proposals involved a more efficient use of faculty, a higher student-faculty ratio than the national average of 14 to 1. The resulting economy may be absorbed, however, in paying higher-than-average faculty salaries, a much needed reform and an additional inducement to faculty members at these new colleges. As one participant put it, "The primary objective is to improve the educational program of the college. We feel that one way of doing this is to pay our professors better salaries, and get better people into the college."

THE HOFSTRA EXPERIMENT FOR COMMUTERS

John Cranford Adams

AT Hofstra College, located in suburban Nassau County twenty miles from Manhattan, we are confronted with a segment of higher education probably unknown to anybody in the major colleges. I am speaking not of the elite that readily goes to college and by and large is successful there. I am speaking of the segment of the "good-average" student — the B, B-plus, A-minus student, who is present in such vast numbers in America's new educational bulge. Hofstra College in the last five years has tried to study the problems of this "good-average" commuting student to see if the college can devise a more effective and rewarding educational experience for him. What I shall say has to do wholly with that particular point of view.

I begin with a résumé of the facts we all have read in recent months. Already, the majority of American college students commute to college; they are not residential students. Their average age is close to twenty-five. More than half the classes in American institutions today are under ten in size, and consequently two-thirds of all colleges operate in the red. Academic salaries in this wealthy country are shockingly low; the current average professorial pay is said to be $6,325.

One or two additional headings will help define my position. Our standard practice has been to emphasize verbal skills at the expense of most other things — College Board Examinations are set up primarily on verbal skills — course testing procedures, and so on. But if you are dealing, as I am, with students of second- or third-generation Americans, those verbal skills are not highly developed. In our earlier experiments, we found that if we let a youngster with a Spanish background write his papers in Spanish, he might get an A. But if we required him to write in English, he would get a D.

I am one who believes that we are living with an outmoded course structure. We are all wrapped up in the red tape of the semester system, the four- or five-course program, the "prerequisite" — all these various details, to such a degree that I think that both faculty and students are wasting much time. What about the youngster who drops out at the end of the freshman year? Two hundred eighty-three per thousand drop out at the end of the first year, and the average curriculum has not had much meaning for those youngsters. They merely failed at what we offered them.

If the drop-out figure is going to persist, let us see if we can devise within the four-year framework a curriculum that is meaningful for that one-year experience.

Hofstra is a place which has had to learn how to make efficient use of its plant. We cannot go out and, in two years, raise $85 million on top of what we have. Our college began with an endowment of about $500,000 and about $500,000 in plant. It was believed that Hofstra could grow to a college of about 500. Some 300 were enrolled when I went there fifteen years ago. We now enroll 8,000.

We have been able to build up a campus worth about $10 million by operating with at least 65 per cent occupancy of classrooms and laboratories in an eighty-nine-hour week, when the national average is less than 40 per cent occupancy in a forty-four-hour week. Of course, Hofstra operates around the year. Now, we do not have the intelligence to adopt a three- or a four-term system. We still have two normal winter semesters. But we do also have two summer sessions of six weeks each.

This means that Hofstra draws 3,000 or 4,000 students during each of these summer terms; the plant is in full yearly operation and the faculty has as much opportunity to work (they may not teach in both summer sessions) as they would like.

It has already been mentioned in the brilliant review of the Dartmouth plan by Provost Morrison[1] that we are all concerned with a much more efficient use of faculty — to get the teacher and the student together most of the time and to minimize all those other things that keep them apart.

Statistically, I think it is quite clear that

[1] "The Dartmouth Experiment," pages 146–151.

the B or B-plus student placed in an educational system with the A or A-plus student tends in four years to slip back rather than to go ahead. He doesn't come up into the A group. The sad fact is that he declines into the C group, and if for no other reason than the perhaps outmoded one of significance for national health, prosperity, and welfare this decline is regrettable. Those B-plus students are potential members of management echelons in this country. They will own or manage nearly all our institutions except those requiring the topmost leadership.

All this is the background to our view of a proposal. And so far it is merely a proposal. We are negotiating for property off the campus where we would like to start our project in the fall of 1959, if possible.

We would like to start with a group of 100 to 120 students of this good-average type. They will be commuting students, both men and women. They will come from middle-income families and from the class below. They will be drawn from the suburbia of Long Island in an area served by admirable public schools. (Some of the public schools on Long Island have salary scales among the highest in the nation. If you list the top ten, six or seven of them are right there in Long Island.) This will be the area where we will start our branch, if only to draw upon the cooperation of those school systems and the excellence of the training they will provide.

We would like to have our 100 to 120 students form an intimate association with six teaching fellows. Incidentally, these teaching fellows are going to have to be youthful instructors, for we propose to differ with almost anything colleges and faculties have been doing.

We would like to put these students and fellows together in the most varied cycle of educational processes that we can devise. The emphasis will be on self-learning. I cannot tell you specifically what the curriculum will be because our planning group finally decided that we do not much care about the exact composition of the curriculum. The curriculum will be the point at which the student, the teacher, and the materials meet.

Let me touch on another problem. The commuting student — in fact, the American student — apparently lives for the automobile. Many of us have seen those discouraging figures of what the ownership of a car does to the grades of a youngster in high school. They run something like this, I believe. Of students getting an A average, only 2 per cent have access to a car which they may use fairly regularly as their own, whereas about 40 per cent of the C student group have cars. Put it the other way round. Some 60 per cent of the youngsters having cars are destined to have a C or D average in their high-school experience.

Hofstra is also faced with the car as an academic problem. I suppose that Hofstra, with its 2,200 parking spaces, is built on the premise that the youngster has his own car — or commandeers the family car after driving father to the station — and has the use of it through most of the day. This, in itself, might not be so bad except that the wrong values are established. The car becomes his way of life. It is his horse, his club, his dream, his motive for working — and his need to work. It is his peer culture, and this experimental program of ours is designed to fight that.

We shall have a lecture early in the day beginning, shall we say, at 8:30. The lecture may go on for an hour and a half to two hours. It will be a general course, and everybody will be there, including all six teaching fellows. It will be an introduction to learning. In the course of the year it will attempt to combine the humanities, the social sciences, and the natural sciences.

The morning's work will then go on, under control. Students cannot leave the place. We are going to lock them in, so to speak — into discussion groups led by the six members of the teaching staff; into individual conferences and small group discussions with student leaders. Let the team of instructors drop in — "Any questions? Okay. I will be back in half an hour," or, "Come and see me, if you are really puzzled."

A short period for lunch and an hour's breather for loafing, for informal sports, or other light things of that kind. Then, right back to work with library tasks followed by a choice of six midafternoon classes, taught by each teacher in the field of his own specialization.

The youngster will have to go to the morning lecture. He may elect, under advisement, whichever of the specialized courses he wants in the afternoon. Presumably, that will supplement some field he is not covering in his reading program. General lectures, group discussions, seminars, conferences, tutorials, self-learning processes, hours in the library (and much of the written work done while there), and a recitation class — and the day is over.

Our statisticians worked out two or three other things. If you have a forty-two-week year with this eight- or nine-hour intensive day and then link these to a summer institute of twelve weeks of language or math instruction, (the eight-hour-a-day grind with every type of machine available), you will come close to matching the work of a two-year two-semester system.

If we can make this program work and if we can get the College Entrance Examination Board and the Educational Testing Service to devise a really reliable sophomore examination for us, we cannot see why a good hard-working youngster, with a rush and a roar, should not enter the junior year after his first full calendar year of such instruction. I, for one, am rather bored with the fact that we take as many years as we do to get a man ready to teach, or to practice medicine or law.

Even with a four-day week, you can still accomplish this accelerated program, using the fifth day for anything needed in the way of special tutorial or remedial services for our type of student body. Perhaps this youngster is deficient in mathematical skills or that one is deficient in verbal and reading skills. Despite its good secondary schools, the Long Island area is lower on the national reading norms than it should be.

Now, these economies that I next touch upon are only for purposes of illustration. I do not see why we need to build a football stadium for this program, nor a swimming pool nor a polo field. We intend to have tennis courts and modest track facilities. But any youngster who wants to play in our Hofstra orchestra (which is pretty good, partly because we have about a dozen of the New York Philharmonic performers playing alongside the students), can come over and play on Friday, Saturday, and Sunday. If he has to play football for his father's sake, he can join the football squad for scrimmage on the main campus late in the day.

In general, major sports and student activities will be supported only on the main campus; hence there is a physical reason for keeping this experimental program within twenty minutes' run. On Long Island's parkway systems, one can go about seven miles in that time quite easily, except in the peak traffic hours.

We hope to start our teaching staff with something like a $10,000–12,000 salary range. The fellows will really commit themselves to the whole program, including its tutorial and counseling aspects. We want to have each of these hundred youngsters know one fellow very well; we want to have every fellow know twenty students pretty well.

The program will eliminate most of the written examinations because the students are to be under a continuous survey of their progress. We want, then, our terminal examinations to be conducted by outsiders to get verifiable results that we do not then need to argue about.

There are one or two other problems which we think bear strongly on this matter. You have heard that the chief untapped resource in American education today is the American student. The chief barrier to his latent development appears to be his parent. The problem may not exist in Ivy League institutions, but I can assure you that, in the commuting college serving such a group as I speak of, it is all too often Mama's intent that Billy is going to become a doctor when, by heaven, he couldn't become a doctor until hell freezes over. This constitutes one of our problems.

To counteract this, we are going to begin every year with a preliminary institute. For the student, "Here is the commitment you are going to have to make. This is exactly what you must undertake. Moreover, here is the commitment that this faculty is going to make with all its resources. And lastly, here is the commitment that your parents are going to make. No ifs, ands, or buts about any one of the three." I think, in addition, we may have to have our parents in for a talk from time to time when trouble develops.

Most colleges develop a certain feeder system of schools from which they draw the majority of their students. By the nature of a community such as ours, most of our students continue to come from a specific list of high schools. We are already thinking that we could work out a liaison with these schools which narrows the gap between the one place and the other. We hope to be able, therefore, in the second or third year of this program, to reach back into the high school and get some of these commitments established at that point. But that is very speculative now.

We shall have no classes in formal composition, because we are hoping to make the written work of every class essentially a class in composition. I have struggled for many years to remind the professor of history, "Why don't you fail this youngster's paper because it is badly written?" He says, "Mine is not a class in English." But to my mind, it should be a class in English, and that goes for the whole curriculum.

We believe that listening skills, reading skills, writing skills, and speaking skills are the concern of every fellow every day in every teaching situation. Moreover, if we do have student clubs and activities because of the American collegiate fashion, let them be educationally related to the program's objectives.

Now, we cannot avoid the compulsion which these youngsters all have to take on a paying job, but we shall try to keep it in bounds and, if possible, make the job also relate to the student's academic objectives. Our scholarship committees offering assistance grants to supposedly impecunious students recoil in cynical dismay when the youngster buys a new Buick in the place of the jalopy with which he started his term. It is that peer culture which grips them, and they insist on holding down the outside job. It can be argued, of course, that work has its educational values, up to a point.

I cannot "Antioch" this scheme yet, but in an area such as Nassau — 1,200,000 people, the third largest airplane and second largest electronic manufacturing district in the nation, together with shopping centers, banks, and so forth, within fifteen minutes' ride of any one of these campuses — there will be job opportunities which, with some overseeing, could be educationally related. We are going to make a real point of this.

The average youngster will have the week ends free for that job. Let him get the job urge out of his system at that time, but devote all of Monday, Tuesday, Wednesday, and Thursday to his educational program (and Friday, if he can profit from either remedial or further tutorial experiences).

What about the economics of this plan? Hofstra has operated for many years within its tuition income. Our salary scale is modest compared with those of such institutions as Harvard. We start at about $4,600 and go to $12,000, supplemented by fringe benefits that match any college I can think of. We have managed this out of tuition which, to date, has been modest. It was $750 the last three years and it will go to $900 next year.

I think we can operate the experimental program for a year or two on the tuition charge supplemented by a modest subvention, and we have put out an appeal for such a subvention in one or two influential quarters.

I would like to be able to offer a three-to-five-thousand dollar salary differential for our six teaching fellows because I want the best teachers I can get. I also must be able to reimburse them for the dislocation involved in bringing them from a distance. At the same time, if I put one of my best Hofstra young people opposite him, I don't want him to feel penalized.

The capital cost we probably will have to underwrite through a trustee grant, but we believe that it will not be ruinously expensive to buy a nearby property of some forty acres and a house which is now too large for a single family to staff and maintain.

I would like to shoot at a final enrollment of 400. But we will start with one 100–120 student unit and will multiply units, as experience gives the green light. We think it best not to put more than four or five units on any one campus.

THE NEW COLLEGE PLAN

I. The Planning Process

Shannon McCune

A MAJOR part of the impetus for the New College plan came from the cooperation we have among the four colleges of the Connecticut Valley in western Massachusetts — four very different colleges: Amherst, Mt. Holyoke, Smith, and the University of Massachusetts. Our committee of four was set up by the presidents of the four institutions, with its members acting as individuals rather than as representatives of their colleges. We were a historian, Donald Sheehan from Smith, a psychologist, Stuart Stoke from Mt. Holyoke, an English professor, C. L. Barber from Amherst, and myself, a geographer doubling as Provost at the University of Massachusetts. We had a grant from the Fund for the Advancement of Education which gave us a full summer, with resources for consultants and so forth. So the four of us sat down to try to plan a fifth college or, as we came to call it, New College.

We consulted a number of specialists. We spent a lot of time working together as a group. None of us had really met the others before, and it was satisfying that, with our differences in background, we were able to work together and arrive at a common idea at the end of a summer.

We were given a commission to plan a new college located in close proximity to our own places, a four-year college, residential in character, with an initial enrollment of a thousand students. Given those conditions, we were to plan an institution which would give education of the highest quality and yet be as economical as possible, especially of staff.

This, of course, was a very great difficulty: we called it an assignment to dream big and dream cheap. In Charles Cole's words, it had to be "an honest-to-God education." We couldn't take less than that, and yet we needed to economize on staff so as to create a model or example for meeting the teacher shortage without depreciating our currency.

We did not, in our printed version of *The New College Plan*, present any financial data. We did, however, have financial studies made, including a complete staffing pattern for four years, what it would take to begin, how much it would cost annually, and estimated building costs.

We have these figures, but we have purposely not published them for a number of reasons. First, we did not want to start everybody arguing about whether it should cost this many dollars or that many dollars and so detract from the educational ideas which we felt were paramount.

Second, we were not certain of the figures. We do feel quite sure, however, that, once built and started, New College could pay its own way except for scholarship aid. We think we have designed a pay-as-you-go college that would also be an absolutely first-rate college.

We are now operating under another Ford Foundation grant to do the preliminary financial and architectural planning and to try out some of the ideas on our existing campuses.

This study has made certain convictions very strong to me. One is that savings can and should be made in the economics of higher education. I feel that these savings, for the most part, must be implemented with faculty initiative and through faculty desires. The very fact that we were a committee of faculty members was important, for it meant that we could see how we could achieve savings while having regard for the ideals and attitudes of faculty members and students.

Major departures, however, are necessary to achieve real results. Many people want to slice the same old bologna in different ways and so solve the problems of higher education. It just cannot be done that way. You have to change the recipe for your bologna. I happen to be a member of a committee that is called the Committee on the Twelve Month Year. We have been discussing this for fifteen months and the only thing we have agreed to thus far is that the year does indeed have twelve months.

I am also convinced of the benefits of model building. I wish every faculty could have a committee that would make a model of what they would like to do. Just this very process of model building is a tremendous stimulus. It certainly has been a stimulus to the four institutions that have been associated with the project. We have already been led to make innovations on our own individual campuses. Take the idea of a student's planning his own program and writing out a rationale for it. We are [1958–59] having forty-four freshmen at the University of Massachusetts do this in two classes to see how it goes. If it goes successfully, we will put this plan into effect for all 5,000 students.

I must stress the fact that these ideas did not come full-blown from four minds. We are indebted to a number of consultants, including some forty colleagues from our own colleges, who made suggestions and reviewed our proposals at various stages. We read quite widely, and we have been particularly interested in some of the experimental colleges that had been created or proposed.

I must confess that I have been troubled by what the enthusiastic reception of *The New College Plan* suggests about the state of current thinking about higher education. We get letters from college presidents and other people who should know about this type of idea saying that the New College plan is a major advance in higher education, one of the most interesting things they have read in ten years. We have distributed several thousand copies of our booklet by request.[1] What has happened to writing about higher education if a fifty-six-page booklet can have this effect on people? I am worried about the dearth of new ideas and new plans which this response suggests.

II. The Plan and its Rationale

C. L. Barber

I think probably the best thing to do is to make a thumbnail sketch of what we propose and then give some of the reasons why we came up with this particular structure. We are proposing a four-year coeducational college, with a faculty of fifty, and one thousand students, at which the student takes only three courses. Each faculty member gives only one upper-class course — one man, one course. The rest of the faculty's time goes to working with smaller groups. By cutting down drastically the number of upper-class courses, we make possible the sort of close-up teaching that normally requires a luxurious teacher-student ratio, even though our ratio is one to twenty. We plan at the same time to train the students, from the outset, to work on their own and in small study groups, so that they will be able to cover a great deal independently, and thus will not need as many upper-class courses. The two things, training in independence and reduction in the number and importance of courses, are interdependent. We also have the advantage that our limited course offering will be supplemented in the more specialized areas by courses available at the neighboring colleges.

The freshmen will *start* their programs with seminars, small groups working intensively with small areas, learning how to work as scholars and how to work as members of a group exploring a subject together. After such initiation into the three main divisions, they will go on to upper-level courses where lectures will always go with related projects studied independently by student groups. So the habit of such "committee work" will be constantly reinforced.

As they move into their programs of concentration, students will be responsible for acquiring, in part on their own, a disciplined mastery of three recognized fields of knowledge covered by three "field examinations." These examinations, one in the junior year and two in the senior year, will not be departmental comprehensives (we shall have no departments). The fields covered will instead be recognized areas of knowledge *within* disciplines.

Examples of such fields would be nineteenth-century political theory, Renaissance English literature, governmental systems in the twentieth century — the fields would be areas recognized by the profession as a standard division

---

[1] Copies of *The New College Plan* can be obtained free of charge from The Secretary of the College, Amherst College, Amherst, Massachusetts.

of the discipline — the sort of groupings that turns up in the programs of the annual meetings of the learned societies, the American Historical Association, the Modern Language Association, and so on. Of course, the particular field examinations offered at New College would depend on the interests and capacities of students and staff, but we want the areas to be professionally recognized, not idiosyncratic, and we hope that frequently the examinations will be set by outside examiners. By limiting the examinations to areas smaller than those which departmental comprehensives usually cover, we hope for examinations which are more cogent than most general examinations today, in order to test the student's independent preparation as well as his experience in formal lectures. Departmental comprehensives today usually fall back on multiple-choice questions which really refer to the courses offered by the department, or, on the other extreme, the questions are so vague that all a bright student needs is a little knowledge and a lot of facility.

The system of field examinations will permit students to make up their own programs of concentration *ad hoc*, while at the same time assuring disciplined mastery of substantive content. A student may undertake any combination of field examinations that he can "sell" to a faculty committee — a committee drawn from all three disciplines. A student who chooses may take all three exams within one discipline — all in history, say — or he can make a combination that falls across disciplines. So programs of concentration can develop and change in response to the developing intellectual life of the college and the times. They will not be the expression of departmental politics, and yet — without our having to have departments — the professional standards of the disciplines will be maintained.

In trying to avoid the development of vested interests and preserve an open market for ideas all along the line, we found that we were leaving out one highly desirable thing — a common intellectual experience shared by the whole student body. Our solution is to have the whole college take a month out after Christmas to study the same two courses, one an exploration of a subject important in Western culture, the other in non-Western culture. This "Midwinter Term" would put freshmen shoulder to shoulder with seniors, and indeed with some of the faculty, all of them together tackling something new and bringing to it their several kinds of resource. The subjects, chosen in response to the interests of the faculty leaders, would change over a four-year span, so that each class would have what would amount to a "core" experience of Western culture, and also an illuminating common experience of civilizations other than our own.

I think I have mentioned all the main features of our curriculum. We have no language requirement, because we think that too much "made work" results; but we do intend that the study of ancient and modern literatures and linguistics shall be encouraged actively, and we plan to make elementary languages available in every way we can think of, even including scholarships for interested students to study at summer institutes.

We are not going to have fraternities. We hope not to have intercollegiate athletics. We do intend to have a very widespread program of student initiative in athletics and other extracurricular areas. We want nothing in the extracurricular field to have tenure, so that there will not be any of those organizations that people have to be dragooned into by appeals to keep the science club going or to keep old Delta Phi afloat.

Now let me try to say something about what we hope to accomplish by the specific proposals sketched above. Our underlying idea is to achieve economy by arranging an open system, where vitality in students and faculty can have full play because arbitrary requirements and vested interests are at a minimum. We have tried to minimize the mixing of intellectual considerations with faculty politics by eliminating two great opportunities for empire-building — the department and the big required course. We keep a requirement of distribution by divisions and a requirement of concentration. We provide a system of field examinations to maintain standards. But within this structure we want as free a flow as possible, so that time, energy, and money will not be wasted on a priori arrangements expressing the imperialisms of disciplines or individuals.

One way to judge what we are proposing is

to ask what actually happens when a good student — or better, an informed, enterprising student of whatever ability — goes through a great university. In practice he makes his own program as best he can on the basis of what is alive rather than what is required. The departments tell him that he must take a departmental program; the notion behind this is that he has to cover his subject. The fact is that, in practice, he cannot take all the courses that are offered in his department, and he cannot cover his subject. He knows this, so as an enterprising student, what does he do? He elects the courses given by the best professors. Students say to each other, "Be sure to get a course with Mack; it doesn't matter so much whether you have him in constitutional history or legal history, but don't miss him." The student elects a combination of the good professors, trying so far as possible to fit subjects to his own actual developing structure of interests, rather than the official structures represented by departmental programs.

From the student's standpoint, therefore, it does not matter whether the professor offers everything that the professor knows. It matters that the professor offers whatever is most vital in his intellectual life at the time. Therefore at New College we propose a program in which each professor offers only one upper-class course. He can change the course from semester to semester, and from year to year, as he chooses. You sometimes hear unusually informed students say, "Don't take him in such-and-such. He isn't really interested in that. Take him in the Eighteenth Century on Pope. You wouldn't think that Pope was interesting, but that is where this guy really lives. So get him on Pope."

New College's course offering will be small — no more than fifty upper-class courses at any one time. But with each course will go collateral projects, for which the three-course student program will allow time. And our faculty will be able to offer scores of seminars for initiating freshmen to their academic endeavors and for helping seniors toward the consummation of their programs of concentration. The fifty courses will be full of life, since they will consist of what the faculty are at the moment most concerned to share with the students.

To propose such a small course offering is certainly to give up the notion of an offering that "covers" the liberal arts. Of course we plan to have the main disciplines all represented. But we feel that colleges should face the fact that they cannot possibly cover everything anyway — that they do not have a great university's responsibilities to learning as a whole. We also feel that colleges, where their locations permit it, should recognize that they can depend on one another. New College is designed *not* to be an autarchy; instead, it is to mesh with the unused marginal resources of the four neighboring institutions. At the diplomatic level, this will make it possible for us not to offer subjects like astronomy or geology at all on our own campus and still not be regarded as incomplete or second-rate — since these and other subjects not offered at New College will be available nearby. We can well afford to pay our way, so much per student, in such cases. The Connecticut Valley colleges already practice such cooperation among themselves, but the scope of it is limited by the fact that each existing college has a nearly full quota of courses and departments, and the faculties are loath to give up any of them. (A common astronomy department and an area studies program do exist already, however.)

New College, if it is actually created, will greatly increase the amount of such intercollegiate interchange, for New College would be built with gaps for the purpose. Its students' experience will be enriched accordingly. For example: we have among the four Connecticut Valley colleges probably as good a group of professors in the departments of the Classics or of French as any one university can boast. We cannot, of course, propose that New College simply launch its students on this complicated sea. New College students will normally do most of their work at home, according to their own patterns (though all will be required to take at least one course away). We cannot be a beggar, a second-class citizen. But in the case of fields like French or the Classics, the New College professor can say to his colleagues at neighboring places: "Look, you fellows in your advanced courses are teaching half-empty rooms now. Isn't it nice that we are able to feed some students to you — and sweeten your relations with your administration by paying it something for the privilege?" So, too, when a physics major at New College wants a course in astronomy, or a particular specialized course in physics. We calculate that, on the average, students will take two courses at other colleges. We have no maximum. We hope, for example, that in the language fields, which are shockingly undersubscribed in the neighboring colleges, the New College major might take more than half his program at neighboring colleges. We would, of course, pay for this on a piece-work basis.

Many press reports of our plan said that a committee in western Massachusetts has had a brilliant idea — independent work — and that this idea is so brilliant that it makes it possible for the New College to do with only one professor for every twenty students. Of course, independent work is not a new idea at all; and as Mr. Blair Stewart has pointed out, it should frequently better be described as dependent work. Dependent or independent, such work demands a great deal of faculty time — even in the variant which we hope to develop so largely, where a student group works together. To counter the newspaper reports, we are taking every opportunity we can to point out that it is not independent work that will make a small faculty possible; it is the small course offering which makes it possible for a small faculty to handle independent work. Together with the *training* in independence and the use of collateral student seminars throughout the four years, this approach makes independent work part of a whole style of life.

Beardsley Ruml certainly influenced my thinking, and I suspect, that of my colleagues, in his insistence that our many small classes are keeping us all poor. But our plan starts from intellectual and educational interests, not economic considerations. Because we put first what faculty members regard as first things, we have hopes that economic advantages can actually be achieved, instead of being baulked by idealism and other considerations. One cannot obtain the pattern of large and small courses that Mr. Ruml wants by forcing the faculty to lie on Procrustean beds, some of them stretched out to teach groups of two hundred students and others chopped off or compressed to work with groups of only ten. We agree that the efficient thing is to have for the most part large lecture audiences and small discussion classes. But we achieve this result not by dictating enrollments, but simply by the rule: only one lecture course per teacher. This gives us fifty upper-class courses for a college of a thousand, and this peg of one course-one man will control the proliferation of courses and keep the *average* class size large.

The size of particular courses can swing all the way up and down from 200 for the man who is that kind of teacher to 10 for the man who is another kind of teacher. Each of them will be reaching his appropriate public, but the average course size will be 42, and this is very economical indeed as compared to the usual average size of upper-class courses.

We would have student assistants for those people who have the larger courses. One other thing that we do not want to be misunderstood is the full scope of the faculty member's duties. His lecture course is not his whole job. He will also run two seminars, either for freshmen or seniors, with the exception of those who have a very large lecture course, who will handle only one seminar in addition.

We feel that if we give promising undergraduates collateral teaching responsibilities, they will rise to the occasion, especially after a program in which student initiative has been developed from the outset by seminars and study groups. Our Smith colleague, Donald Sheehan, has emphasized from the outset that we should get rid of the usual pyramid which starts with surveys and ends with seminars; at the same time, he has insisted that we must require, by field examinations, mastery of substantial, professionally recognized subject matter. The importance of our using the contemporary American tendency to work in peer groups has been a particular concern of our Mt. Holyoke colleague, Stuart Stoke, who is a psychologist: he has convinced us that a great deal can be expected from a program which keeps reinforcing in subsequent years patterns of independent behavior and group responsibility introduced at the outset. We hope, for example, that students will learn when to stop talking — a difficult art!

Let me place what we are doing in relation to certain major problems and tendencies in American education. You will notice that we turn from much that is now standard practice in general education, notably the usual large required (or semirequired) general education courses for freshmen or sophomores. One reason is that we want to avoid the situation where one faculty member is in charge of several others and uses them as a conveyor belt to reach the students. Such arrangements *can* be very fruitful, all around, especially in a university situation. But it also seems to me that such a pattern can be pernicious — perhaps is more often pernicious than we in the profession recognize — in that it promotes the vertical structuring of personality which is the curse of academic life, the combination of a propitiatory attitude toward individual masters with truculence and childish intransigence toward the world at large.

At New College individual faculty members will be free to offer cooperative courses when they choose, but each will have his own lecture course, regardless of rank. And the core program avoids the problem of monopolies and political subordinations by being organized crosswise as a period of the year rather than as a requirement running lengthwise through the year.

We think of leaving half the faculty free each year during this midwinter term to pursue their own work (or go to Florida), while the other half pitch in on the common program. It seems reasonable to expect that living common interests would be developed in the process of working up the common, college-wide midwinter courses, with, naturally, particular leaders from year to year, who would be given time off for the purpose. One man might develop a course in Western culture on, say, polytheism in the ancient world, enlisting help from an anthropologist, a psychologist, a historian of religion, literary scholars, and so on. Such a course would make polytheism in the ancient world a subject not for information alone, but for the college's encounter with crucial issues in the modern world, such as the question, "What is the status of a symbol?" I ask that question about polytheism because I happen to be that kind of scholar, but other people would see other issues, and we would only pick out polytheism if it were something that made a focus for the living issues of the emergent intellectual life of the college.

We would have the additional advantage that such midwinter college-wide courses bring in visiting scholars from elsewhere. Most of the college's outside lectures would come at this time, in connection with an organized need for them, instead of coming as an intrusion in an already full schedule. The opening of the midwinter term could consist of lectures and readings presenting materials, while the latter part could be an exciting series of discussions on the live issues of the subject, with leading representatives of important points of view brought in from outside. For the non-Western midwinter topic each year, visiting teachers would be particularly important. Papers and examinations at the end of the midwinter term would grow out of experiences with a variety of people actively engaged with the subject.

THE DARTMOUTH EXPERIMENT

Donald H. Morrison [1]

I AM very happy to attack a topic which I would not have chosen myself — that is, "The Dartmouth Program." There are a number of reasons why I would not choose that particular title.

The first is that we in Hanover are not as monolithic as is sometimes thought and I could not describe to you in fifteen minutes what could be called The Dartmouth Program.

There is nothing new about what most people call The Dartmouth Program either. As a matter of fact, Dartmouth was on a three course–three term calendar and program about fifty years ago, as one of our historians pointed out when a member of the committee, in advancing these ideas at a faculty meeting, referred to them as the "new" program.

The ideas or notions or principles that we have tried to work into this program are not new either. They are exactly the same ideas that are being talked about in New College, at Oberlin, and at many other institutions.

The academic year consists of three terms rather than two semesters. The terms are about ten weeks in length. The spring term is just a few days shorter than the other two terms. The examination period of about three and a half days is in addition to the ten-week term.

Second, the weekly calendar is so arranged that the number of class hours is the equivalent of those under the semester system. Thus, a term course with us is the equivalent of a semester course in terms of the time available, number of classes per course, and hours spent on the course. These are not quarter courses in the sense in which that term is used in some institutions.

Third, the normal program of the student is three courses each term. We require thirty-seven courses for graduation. One of these is a "Great Issues" course, which continues through all three terms of the senior year and is counted as one course. This makes, in the senior year, three and one-third courses per term. This is the only course which is extended in time beyond one term.

In addition to the three courses per term, a program of independent reading is required of all students. In the first two years, the books are essentially divisional in character. The student is required to read representative works in all three divisions. In the last two years, reading is related to the field of concentration of the student.

Other important characteristics of the independent reading are: first, it is not done in connection with any course which the student takes; second, there is considerable freedom in choice of books; third, the student reads according to his own time schedule within the limits set by the examination schedule.

The other degree requirements are traditional. They are pretty much those which we had under the semester system. They are, for most students, two terms of English, which is, roughly, two-thirds literature and one-third composition, two or three terms of foreign language, depending upon the proficiency which the student demonstrates when he arrives, four terms of social science, four terms of science, and eight term courses in the major field.

The number of hours spent by a student in the classroom each week has been reduced from fifteen to twelve. Under the semester system, our students took five courses, each with three hours of class time, for a total of fifteen. In our deliberations we at first gave serious thought to a four-course scheme on a fifteen-week semester basis. One of our great discoveries was that four times three and three times four are equal. At this point, we began to shift to a three-course scheme on a ten-week-term basis. The total class hours per week remain the same. The normal teaching load for the faculty is two courses per term.

A word about the background of this program. A revision of the curriculum began to be talked about in the late fall of 1947 and the spring of 1948. In 1954, the trustees established a Trustees' Planning Committee, with the assignment of reviewing almost all aspects of

---

[1] Provost Morrison died a few days after making this presentation. His extemporaneous remarks have been edited by a colleague at Dartmouth College.

the college. One of the first committees that was appointed was a committee on size, which was given the assignment of recommending to the trustees the target figure for the future enrollment of the college. As the charge was put, it suggested that Dartmouth might have to be bigger in order to be a better educational institution.

The committee thought about this suggestion. It concluded that Dartmouth does not necessarily have to be bigger in order to be better. However, it considered how a possible increase in enrollment could be exploited as a means of strengthening the educational program of the college. We talked about students, teachers, and facilities and very quickly came to the obvious conclusion that the ultimate quality of a college or university depends upon the quality of the faculty. We knew that salary levels had a great deal to do with recruitment in the profession. Thus we explored the possibility of increasing enrollment in order to raise additional funds for raising salaries.

The primary objective, however, was not economic, but to improve the educational program of the college by means of a higher-quality, higher-paid faculty.

At that time, we had about 2600 undergraduates, each taking a normal load of five courses each semester. We had about 200 faculty members, with a student-teacher ratio of 13 to 1. The subcommittee on size proposed that enrollment be increased gradually, beginning in the early 1960's, when we felt that we could get somewhat larger entering classes of quality equal or superior to that of the classes we were getting at the time, and that the eventual target of the undergraduate enrollment be established at 3,000 students. This represented an increase of about 15 per cent.

We hedged. We said, among other things, that this should not be done unless we could get the additional physical facilities that we needed without using the present resources of the college or the increased tuition income to finance them. We also said that enrollment should be raised only if the great bulk of the increased income (I think that our tuition was then $800 and we calculated the increase at $320,000) could be applied to faculty salaries, and we stipulated that ways should be found for handling the proposed 15 per cent additional enrollment without a commensurate increase in the size of the faculty.

We were overcrowded in dormitories at the time, and we already needed more plant. We were not, however, so concerned about necessary increases in plant because our assumption was that funds could be found — for instance, through federal housing loans for dormitories. Some facilities did not have to be expanded. For instance, the library was deemed adequate for the larger student body.

Our recommendation in this particular committee was essentially the Harvard program of four courses a semester, a reduction of the degree requirement from forty courses, which we then required, to thirty-two courses. This would increase our student-teacher ratio from 13 to 1 to about 15 to 1, and, on the basis of course registration, we felt that we could handle the increased registration without additional faculty and have perhaps somewhat fewer registrations per course.

We also made some recommendations in such areas as teaching methods, and dormitory life. The most important one from the standpoint of economics, probably, was our belief that we should concentrate more of our work in a combination of large lectures and small seminars and move in on the classes of from 25 to 75 to see whether we could squeeze some of them up into larger lecture groups and cut the others down into the tutorial or seminar type of work. The calculations which we made at that time indicated that this could be done.

The committee felt that the talk about class size, of which there has been a great deal for many years, really had something to it. Most of us — I think, all of us — felt that there needed to be a great increase in intimate forms of instruction such as that provided by seminars. At the same time, we were convinced that there had been an unfortunate disregard and neglect of large lectures at Dartmouth College. The lecture method of instruction, excellent in its place, was being misused. As a result, we were getting lectures before twenty-five or twenty students with the professor doing 90 or 95 per cent of the talking. It was conceded that this was not only poor educational technique but also very uneconomical from the standpoint of the number of students handled in the lecture. We were not getting either the audience for good lecturing or enough good discussion in smaller groups.

We concluded that we had too small a proportion of instruction being done in fairly large lecture groups and too much in these awkwardly sized sections. We did not propose to eliminate all of these larger sections by any means, but at least we suggested writing a large question mark over each one and asking that it be justified educationally. We hoped that we could push a sufficient number of the awkward sections down into the more intimate type of instruction, the proportion of which we were very much interested in increasing substantially.

We then began discussions with another committee which included administrative officers, one or two trustees, and several members of the faculty. Their assignment was to review the report of the size committee with respect to the effect of our recommendations on educational programs.

This new committee very quickly came to the conclusion that the recommendations were sound. It then began to develop some ideas about courses to fit into the broad curricular framework that we had outlined.

At this point, the faculty standing Committee on Educational Policy was brought into the discussions. Here, we ran into very stiff opposition on one point: namely, the reduction in the number of courses required for graduation from forty to thirty-two. Men who otherwise subscribed wholeheartedly to the principles of the main recommendations felt that they could not support the program because this reduction would too greatly restrict the elective opportunities of the student.

We talked about the difficulty for a long time, and finally one member of the faculty Committee on Educational Policy said that he could subscribe to 98 per cent of our recommendations, but he could not favor a four-course program. He thought that all that we wanted could be achieved if we went to a quarter system with students taking four courses per term.

This, in my judgment and the judgment of the other members of the joint committee, missed one of the most important of our objections: to reduce the fragmentation of study during the year and over the four years of a student's time.

Out of this committee discussion came the suggestion that perhaps we could do what everyone wanted with a three term–three course arrangement. Almost everyone said immediately that he did not think such a plan was possible. We have many premedical students, pre-engineering students, and others with very stiff prerequisite requirements which simply could not be fitted into that kind of plan, according to some faculty members. A mathematician who was a member of the faculty committee went home that night at about eleven and came back the next morning with a plan showing that all of these requirements could be fitted into a three term–three course plan. The new scheme was scrutinized from every angle. It seemed to work. From that point on, all of these committees were unanimously in support of what we came to call "three three."

We next discussed new general education courses which might give both strength and richness to the curriculum. One of these was an attempt to combine with history some of the work done in English composition and literature. It was based on the concept that there are periods of explosive creativity in history, and that a course could easily be built around these periods, focusing on both time and place, for example, on Athens, on Rome, or Florence.

We ran into great difficulty because some members of the English and the foreign-literature departments felt that one should not study literature as a manifestation of a period, but as a work of art, irrespective of anything that surrounded it. With them, our ideas found some support, but not enough to overcome the unanimous opposition of the historians, who said that the proposed approach was not chronological, therefore it was not history. (I am oversimplifying the historians' point of view, but not very much.) As a result of these two onslaughts, that particular course went by the board.

We also had some simple notions in social sciences. We have at Dartmouth a social science distribution requirement that the student elect certain introductory courses in four separate departments. We held that the departments could possibly upgrade their work if one of these courses could be taken by all of the students before they took any other courses. This would enable the professors in economics, political science, history, sociology, or psychology to assume that their students had had a certain body of material on which they could build. We got nowhere with this scheme. The social science division was not really interested in this approach. More than that, it appeared impossible for the division to agree upon what the content of such a course should be.

At faculty meetings, the opposition to these two curricular proposals emerged very sharply, and the committee finally withdrew its recommendation for these two courses. The withdrawal of these courses was the only major compromise made by the committee in presenting the overall plan.

We came out of faculty meetings with approval of the general program that I outlined earlier, the three term–three course arrangement, with reduction in semester requirements for English and languages. In fact, we achieved a large majority in support of the plan.

This program went into effect in September, 1958. It is much too early to appraise the results. As a matter of fact, our general tactic was to get it started, to get going. This required a tremendous amount of faculty time. Committees were meeting even more often than usual, and a whole year was spent revising courses, revising majors, reviewing requirements, and trying to meet catalog deadlines. There was a period when it looked as though we simply would have to postpone for a year. We said, "Well, we won't postpone. We won't do some things now. We will do them later in order to get the thing started."

So, even though some details are hanging loose, the plan is now in effect for the entire college. We are in a transition period, of course. But one of the important features of this plan which made the transition easy was that the term course is the equivalent of a semester course, so we do not have a system of quarter courses and degree requirements based on quarter courses, and a system of semester courses and degree requirements based on semester courses. We could have worked our way through any transition, but any other pattern would have been tremendously complicated. We think the present transition is complicated enough.

The first observation is that the introduction of this calendar schedule is only the first step of what we consider to be an evolutionary process that will go on for several years before we begin to get the results economically and educationally that, in our minds, justify all the work that has gone into it. So it would be a mistake — indeed downright dishonest — for me to say that this is as far as we are going. This is just the beginning.

The objectives that we are seeking are those which all college administrators also seek. One is more emphasis on developing a student's study hunger for independent learning. Another is the increased use of the library and other primary sources of information. Still another is more rigorous studies in the areas of concentration with, for example, unmistakable differences in the rigor between elementary and intermediate and advanced courses. We have — perhaps all of us have — major subjects in which there is no structuring. In the social sciences and humanities, particularly, there is no structuring, and it is often difficult to tell the difference between an advanced course and an intermediate course except that one may have a higher catalog number than another and, in some departments, it is not always the advanced course which has the higher number.

Another purpose of the new curriculum is to try to make independent projects, in the senior year, the climax of the college experience. We have some departments that require a thesis. We have others that do not. These theses vary in quality and in the quality and expenditure of time expected by the faculty. Some of these theses are excellent. They are occasionally published in professional journals. And some of them are really nothing more than term papers, both in quality and in time spent on them. We would like to strengthen the thesis requirements and make them much more uniform than they are now.

We would like also to see the introduction of reading courses for credit. By a reading course, I mean a program in which a student would be provided with a syllabus and would be given an examination on the reading. He would not be expected to attend class. We would, in fact, not offer any lectures except perhaps, if the professor was interested, some three or four scattered through the term. We would like to see the introduction of such courses.

We want to achieve a better management of our teaching resources with an overall increase in the student-teacher ratio and an increase, at the same time, in the seminar-tutorial methods of instruction. One of the members of our Committee on Educational Policy made an analysis of what would be possible with a 17 to 1 student-teacher ratio. This was at a time when we had a 13 to 1 ratio.

According to his calculations, about 6 per cent of the class meetings could be lectures, assuming effective management and controls which we do not now have. About 94 per cent of class meetings would be of seminar size, somewhere from ten to twenty students. I think he assumed an average of twelve.

This is what would be possible with a 17 to 1 student-teacher ratio. About 63 per cent of the work of the students could be in seminars, about 37 per cent in large lecture sections. The faculty would have an average of fifty-one students per term, and 9 per cent of the teaching load of the faculty would be in lectures.

These statistics aroused a great deal of concern among the faculty, for a number of reasons. Many people simply did not believe them. They considered the computer guilty of mathematical sleight of hand, and one of our more poetic faculty members coined the phrase, "mathematical rhetoric," a slogan which may have won the opposition a lot of votes.

A second observation I would like to make is that we have had really a tremendous by-product out of this change simply because of the fact of change itself. When you make a change that upsets things as much as this does, then it has a catalytic effect, and many people have been saying, "Wouldn't it be a good idea to review the work in our major and get rid of some of these courses and put in some fresh courses?" They have been talking this way for several years and, under the impetus of a change of this magnitude, they actually do make the revisions. We have had some very useful by-products of this kind. There is a zest and excitement that goes with change in its initial phases that is very, very important, in my judgment.

Having said that much, one has to go on and say the obvious, and that is that pedagogic habits become deeply ingrained. There are professors who can run their courses on the three term–three course system just as they did before. The very fact that these term courses are equivalent to semester courses makes it very easy to do.

So we have, for example, many more courses meeting four times a week than I personally had hoped we would have. The system is sufficiently flexible so that it is perfectly possible for a professor to say, "I will meet my course two times a week and double or triple the reading." There has been almost none of this thus far, and this has been very disappointing. But we are in the first year. We are lucky to get through it whole, and these other improvements that we are hoping to see we shall have to work on in the years ahead.

Another observation is that (so far as our rough statistics to date indicate) there has not been a significant saving in faculty time. One of the reasons is that most members of the faculty have simply gone to the normal schedule of four classes per week, and they find ways of using all the time available. Parkinson's Law operates in teaching as well as in administration.

The work load of the Dean's and Registrar's offices has increased. We now have three sessions a year in which we formally review cases of academic deficiency. We are suspending and separating and placing on probation students three times instead of twice a year.

This means letters going out to parents three times a year, letters coming in from parents three times a year, telephone calls, and so on. From the standpoint of the Dean, the Christmas vacation formerly was a pleasant period in which he could relax a little. At the present time, we have our Committee on Administration meeting just before Christmas. The Dean gets some of his letters written the next day. He may even take the twenty-fourth and twenty-fifth off. He gets the rest of the letters out in the next few days and then letters and telephone calls begin to come in. By the time the students come back after New Year's, the Dean feels as though he has done a year's work already.

Actually, the number of suspensions and separations — these are the cases that cause most of the trouble — we had was about the same after the first term as we had last year after the first semester. I am not too upset about this because we wanted to increase standards and make the students work harder. I think we may be having some success.

You may be interested to know that the faculty Committee on Educational Policy is now working on a fourth term which it feels ought to be introduced in 1961 or 1962. I have no idea myself whether this will prove feasible. Some of the reasons for introducing a fourth term are these. One, we think that we could use it as an experimental period, trying out new courses, reading courses for credit, innovations that the Committee on Educational Policy for the last five years has been very interested in pushing, but which it has difficulty in working into the more complicated regular program.

Some of us have wondered, for example, whether some of the ideas which the New College program proposes and which we proposed in our first report in 1956 might not be tried out in a summer fourth quarter and, if proved effective, subsequently absorbed into the regular program. We think we might be able to overcome some resistance which appears when the program of the department or the professor in the regular year is upset by suggested changes of this sort.

We also feel that there is a possibility of a substantial new source of revenue from the plant, and we ought to take advantage of it. There is also, of course, the belief that it is questionable public policy for a privately endowed tax-exempt institution to close its doors three months of the year when public institutions are operating year round, especially when we are turning down many students who would like to be admitted.

Student reaction has been a concern, but not a major one. By and large, however, the reaction has been good. The charge-out by students of books over the main library desk — I am excluding now the reserve books and the books read in the library — is running about 32 or 33 per cent ahead of last year. This figure probably will have to be adjusted down because we do not expect to have so many books charged out during spring vacation as we did last year, so that we may end with about a 25 per cent increase over last year.

We have, from time to time, letters of complaint to the editor of *The Dartmouth*. One appeared recently by a member of the Class of 1962. His complaints are a source of considerable encouragement. He objects to the fact that he can't postpone his work until the end of the term. He has to keep at it all through the term. He has more work to do — term papers, independent reading, and so on — and many of the changes he is bitterly opposing are exactly the objectives we had for the Dartmouth Plan. This is a matter of some encouragement.

THEORIES OF HIGHER EDUCATION AND THE EXPERIMENTAL COLLEGE

Nevitt Sanford

I WANT to present a plan for an experimental college and then support this plan with considerations of theory and some considerations of fact.

In speaking of the values of education, I shall limit myself to the values of liberal education as ordinarily understood. I mean values that have to do with the development of the individual rather than with the types of performance that are valued by society and that are furthered by technical, professional, and dogmatic education.

My general view is that we must have some conception of the values and attitudes in the individual which are desirable and then some ideas of the college environment, the college processes, which are correlated with the achievement of these aims.

The type of theory that we need has still to be developed. We need theory about the whole personality and about the conditions and processes of its development, and we need theory concerning social institutions such as colleges, particularly theory which will enable us to get from a broad "social structure" type of analysis to the actual stimuli which impinge upon the student in a way that is truly relevant to his development.

According to my theoretical bias, personality is all of a piece. We should not go along with those teachers who would like to make some kind of categorical separation of the intellectual aspect and the rest of the person. Surely, the intellectual and the "characterological" and emotional are mutually related. If a teacher succeeds in giving the individual student knowledge and skills and intellectual powers, the rest of the personality is influenced, just as more generalized changes in the personality affect the intellectual functioning of the individual.

The virtues which are so frequently spoken of in connection with the aims of liberal education can be understood as patterns of intellectual variables and variables in character or personality. Broadmindedness, independence of thinking, openness to the world, capability for further growth — these things are matters both of the intellect and the character, it seems to me.

The great need is for the concepts which will permit us to describe, in the individual, different degrees of development of these kinds of virtues. This conceptualization must precede successful measurement, and I can understand why Dr. Bowles in his paper was somewhat reluctant to speak about the college product in terms of this kind. We today are really quite stuck, I think, on this problem.

Of great importance from the theoretical point of view is the general principle that growth in the person is a matter of challenge and response. People don't just naturally grow after they get to college. They have to be stimulated to grow. We should not conceive of a college as a culture in which everybody automatically grows comfortably and happily. It is as natural for college students to stay as they are as it is for them to grow. At this stage, forces from outside are necessary in order to cause a change of direction in the development of the student.

An example of the developmental processes which I think we should consider would be expanding the bounds of consciousness. This, essentially, is the process that psychoanalysts talk about almost exclusively when they speak of changing or developing the personality. Such expansion occurs in college, for example, through courses in English literature, or through courses which give the individual a real knowledge of the world and, therefore, knowledge of himself.

The personality also develops through the circumstance of having to make new responses because of being placed in new kinds of situations. This is the kind of growth that the behavioristic psychologists stress. The fundamental notion is that individuals learn when they are required to make new responses. Ac-

[152]

cordingly, in college, what we frequently try to do is arrange situations in which individuals are not permitted to go on behaving as they did before. They have to make some new responses and, in that way, expand their personalities.

We further assume that values come to be assimilated through a restructuring of the individual's cognitive world, and that a new structure, in order to be maintained, must be integrated with the underlying and persistent forces in the personality.

In considering an experimental college, we should, I think, pay particular attention to arrangements or social organizations which will permit developmental processes to occur.

Several observations are relevant here. One, with which I am sure you are all familiar, is the potency for good or ill of the student culture and the student society. Dr. Riesman has already pointed this out.

The second point would be that, in a college such as Vassar, it is quite clear that some students develop in the directions which we desire — increased independence, broadmindedness, et cetera — and some students do not.

At Vassar, several of us have studied total classes since 1952. We have results from total classes of freshmen and of seniors, all classes since 1952, and samples from sophomores and juniors and from freshmen examined in the spring of the freshman year. Ordinarily, the testing of freshmen occurs on the day they arrive on the campus.

We can document the point that where one observes notable developmental changes in college students, relations of these students with the faculty are the most important determining factors. The developmental processes that I have indicated typically involve faculty-student relationships.

I would point to the phenomenon of diminishing returns in college. For example, at Vassar, authoritarianism decreases markedly over the four-year period, as it does, I think, in most liberal colleges. The greatest changes in respect to variables of this kind occur in the early years rather than in the later years. Authoritarianism falls rapidly in the freshman and sophomore years and then levels off, with little difference between the junior and the senior years. The reverse of this curve is to be found in the case of increases in desirable traits, such as freedom in self-expression or self-confidence or signs of independence of thinking. Juniors have acquired about all the independence of thinking that Vassar students ever acquire in college.

A further and related point that we have stressed in some of our reports is the special situation of the senior, who shows more psychopathology in mild forms than do any other students, something which we associate with the senior's situation of being about to change her environment in an important way.

So, in thinking about a new college, I should say that we want a kind of social organization which will counteract the anti-intellectual or unintellectual trends of student culture, but will put the natural social needs of students in the service of intellectual objectives, that will create situations in which the faculty can really be effective, that can capitalize on the higher educational returns of the first two years, and, finally, that will take advantage of the special stimulation which students receive when they move from one type of structure to another.

The college that we develop if we proceed from these considerations turns out to be very similar to what has often been proposed by others. I will offer the plan that is being presented to faculty groups at Berkeley.

It is proposed that the University establish, within its own body, a two-year experimental liberal-arts program. An educational program would be set up and administered in accordance with stated hypotheses concerning the conditions of intellectual growth, and controls would be introduced and maintained in such a way as to test the hypotheses. The experimental design and the necessary measurements and evaluations would be in the hands of a research group or team organized for that purpose.

When we say "experimental," we mean experimental in the scientific sense of the word. We do not mean merely trying something new. Admittedly, however, trying something new that has been rationalized on scientific grounds might be one of the most beneficial things that we can do, even though its effects are not measured. We would at least have all the latent values of the Hawthorne situation, which demonstrated the stimulating effect of participating in programs known to be different and designed to secure optimal results, no matter what their specific content might be.

The effectiveness of the proposed college would be compared with the effectiveness of liberal arts programs already existing in the University. Comparisons would be in terms of performance during the remainder of the students' undergraduate years, number of students admitted to graduate school, performance in graduate school, and even performance in life after four years of college. In addition, there would be comparisons in terms of tests, developed at the University of California and at Vassar, for measuring certain features of personal maturity.

The experimental college would accommodate approximately 150 students and would be housed in one of the University's dormitory units. As many as possible of the activities of the college would be carried on in that building.

The faculty-student ratio would be the same in the experimental college as in the existing liberal-arts programs of the University. An effort would be made to insure that the new program demanded no more formal teaching time than did the others. It is hypothesized that the amount of time faculty members spend with the students is not as important in influencing the latter as are the conditions under which that time is spent and the way in which it is distributed.

It would be of crucial importance that the student body of the experimental program be representative of freshmen and sophomore liberal-arts students in the University at large. In order to insure that the new program started with no more than its share of the very able, or the relatively unpromising, students, a rigorous selection procedure would be followed.

The experimental college should have as much autonomy as possible in its relations with its mother institution; its separate and independent existence should be emphasized. The college would be a community in and of itself. It would take further steps to define its uniqueness, its separateness, and thus to further its solidarity. In time, it would develop its own mores, its own idiom, its own jokes. Far from seeking to suppress or to ignore the social needs of students, the new program would mobilize these needs in the interests of an intellectual community. This would be a faculty-student or student-faculty community. It would be designed to overcome the separateness of faculty and student cultures so common on American campuses today, and directly to counteract the unintellectual or anti-intellectual trends in student culture.

The most distinctive feature of the proposed college would be the integration of its intellectual life. All the students would study the same things at the same time — a curriculum in general education. Within limits, the same would be true of all the teachers. At least, all would collaborate in one general reading course, being sometimes expositors or interpreters for the whole group of students and teachers, sometimes leaders of discussion groups, and sometimes listeners and learners. Thus there would be a situation in which students saw faculty members in the roles of learner, discussant, disputant, leader, or follower of their peers, rather than merely in the roles of authority and dispenser of information. In the complex and flexible social situations that would be created, students would not only see what it means to take a variety of adult roles, but they would be virtually forced sometimes to take such roles themselves, thus encouraging their own maturity.

Should the proposed college prove successful, we should expect to see continued experimentation with curricula by different groups of teachers, under conditions of social organization similar to those that have been described here. Indeed, the present proposal is calculated to maximize diversity, both within a given institution and among institutions generally. If ten or a dozen teachers have some new ideas about how to educate college freshmen and sophomores, we should expect other groups of teachers to have other ideas. All such groups should have the opportunity to try their ideas in practice.

It is interesting that when this proposal was presented to humanities faculties at Berkeley, the most common criticism was "Yes, but this cannot be a real experiment because you cannot have the proper experimental controls, inasmuch as the good effects of such a program would be determined largely by its newness rather than by its nature." The humanities professors have learned their social science rather well, but perhaps not well enough. In any case, the answer we gave on this point was that, if experimental colleges succeed because of their novelty, the University's task, where undergraduate education is concerned, becomes relatively simple: it has to keep on setting up experimental colleges and thereby creating a permanent "newness."

EXPERIMENTATION AND THE LIBERAL ARTS COLLEGE

Blair Stewart

FINANCIAL problems and the impending increase in applications for admission to college are the main themes of many current discussions of the state of the nation's institutions of higher education. More fundamental than these is the question whether the quality of the educational opportunities provided to American young people is sufficient for their needs and deserts.

The American liberal arts college is largely indigenous to the North American continent. In most countries the student goes directly from secondary school into a program of specialized study in the university or some other institution for advanced study. Viewed from the perspective of such a system, the American post-high-school institutions appear to be secondary schools, or hybrid institutions exhibiting some of the characteristics of both the secondary school and the university.

Evidence of the existence of the secondary school component is readily seen in many aspects of the American college. Illustrations are the system of credit-hour accumulation, required class attendance, surprise quizzes, daily (or weekly) assignments, and the prevalent assumption that a major responsibility of the instructor is to see to it that the students in his courses are reasonably industrious.

The prevalence of procedures and attitudes more appropriate to the secondary school is undoubtedly one of the reasons for the gap that is so frequently found between the actual performance of students and the level of achievement of which many of them are capable. Too few of our students, even in the best colleges, find an intellectual environment that continuously challenges them to the limit of their abilities. Our curricula and many of our procedures create situations in which students are too frequently content to meet specified assignments and formal requirements without developing the questioning, critical mind and the thirst for knowledge and understanding that are the putative objectives of liberal education. A few students do perhaps approach this ideal, possibly because of innate qualities of mind, or because of especially stimulating teaching or educational procedures. Even these students frequently have capacities for intellectual growth that are only partially utilized.

If the colleges are to realize their educational objectives more fully they must somehow provide their students with more intellectual stimulation and with wider intellectual horizons. They must develop in the individual student not only the desire to pursue knowledge further, but also the ability to do so (in many fields at least) without further formal educational guidance.

Some teaching techniques undoubtedly contribute to these ends. Courses made be so taught as to fire the enthusiasm of the student for more learning, and to reveal significant areas not covered or worthy of more intensive study. Book lists too full for adequate reading during term time, research papers, and seminar reports contribute to both the desire and the ability to pursue subjects beyond the confines of the course. Senior theses, comprehensive examinations, and so-called independent studies programs clearly have desirable educational effects. But in many cases the students subject to these devices become more, rather than less, dependent on the teacher. Thus many an "Independent Studies Program" might better be called a "Dependent Studies Program." Students pursuing it are independent in the sense that they are traveling a road different from that followed by other students, but it may be a road carefully mapped out by one or more faculty members, and in some cases the student may be led by the hand almost every step of the way. He is seldom required to spy out the ground, map the route to follow, and then clamber over the terrain without assistance. But surely the best way to learn to travel on your own, intellectually as well as physically, is to do it.

A proposal that has been the subject of considerable discussion at Oberlin College is that the requirement of independent work on the part of all students should be the central core of the curriculum of a college with a highly selected student body.

From the very beginning, the student's experience should be designed to prepare him for independent work, and he should be required to try his hand at it at an early stage. His successes and failures should then be reviewed, and further independent work required. Only by providing the student with a progressive experience of this kind can we hope for a large measure of success in achieving our educational goals; and only by testing the results of attempts at independent study can we make sure that our students have acquired the traits that we covet for them.

Some instructors in some courses may have the knack of requiring independent work of their students. But surely comprehensive and progressive experience in such work is found in few, if any, American colleges at the present time. It is doubtful if such experience can be generally assured without a program explicitly designed to provide it.

The suggestion that independent study become the central aspect of a college education may, at first glance, appear to compound the problems that colleges are facing because of the great increase in the number of persons who will be seeking a college education in the next two decades. Independent colleges with selected student bodies have for many years limited their enrollments, and it might be argued that they need only to continue to limit enrollments to avoid any untoward effects from the increased demand for a college education. Indeed, it may seem to some of these colleges that the only significant effect of greater demand may be to make it possible for them to be more selective, and thus to improve the quality without increasing the size of their student bodies. A number of colleges may be able to do this, although the pressures on them to admit more students are bound to become extreme. But these colleges will be faced with enormous difficulties in recruiting and holding suitable faculties. There will not be nearly enough competent teachers to staff our colleges in accordance with present standards. Colleges and universities that do expand enrollments will be desperately seeking faculty members, and they will somehow obtain the funds to pay them. Two important results are inevitable: less competent persons will find teaching posts, and faculty salaries will increase substantially. Every college will have to face the question of the extent to which one or the other of these two results is to become predominant in its affairs. The college that does not expand enrollments will face the prospect of declining faculty competence unless it can find extraordinary sources of financial support for higher faculty salaries.

Another problem of real consequence is the inefficient use of physical facilities under our present methods. The expensive buildings of many of our colleges stand idle at least one-third of the year and are almost always only partially utilized when college is in session. These capital improvements have been acquired over decades, but unless they are utilized more effectively the increase in the demand for college education will make it necessary to duplicate them completely in a few years. Heroic efforts to increase the use of present facilities must be made, and the push to put available funds into brick and mortar rather than more effective teaching must be continuously resisted.

The plan proposed at Oberlin to contribute to the solution of these problems called for the organization of the college year on the quarter system.[1] The second quarter of each academic year, however, would not be spent in residence but would be devoted to full-time study off the campus. The emphasis in this nonresident experience would be on independent work on the part of the student. The degree of independence would naturally increase with the student's growing experience and maturity. In the freshman year, for example, the students might, in the nonresident quarter, concentrate on obtaining language skills in a second or third language. They might do this in a foreign environment and they might be accompanied by an instructor, but in the instructional process the student would be given much more responsibility than is commonly the case. Consequently the student-to-teacher ratio should be quite high, at least 30 to 1.

In the upper-class years the students would

[1] The writer modestly is silent on the central part he played in evolving the Oberlin plan (Ed.).

also, for the most part, travel in groups to areas most suitable for the pursuit of the subjects being studied. They would be given progressively more independence in study procedures. If students were accompanied by faculty members, the student-faculty ratio would be high. An important feature of the first quarter of each academic year would be preparation for the nonresident activities, and one aspect of the final quarter would be the assessment and supplementation, if necessary, of the students' nonresident experiences. The assumptions are that the colleges aspire to develop intellectually self-motivating and self-directing graduates, and that an effective way to achieve these aspirations is through repeated experience with progressively more independent study, for which the student has prepared in the college environment and which is evaluated by the college on his return. Patterns of work similar to this have long been successfully followed at Oxford, Cambridge, and other British and European universities.

Such an organization of the college year would call for radical departures from present practices in American colleges and universities. Many difficulties would arise; some of these can be foreseen in part, but many quite unexpected problems would undoubtedly be encountered. We cannot be certain in advance that all these difficulties can be overcome, but the favorable, even startling achievements of many students who have worked independently supply the basis for faith in the success of this proposal in the hands of an able and resourceful faculty working with intelligent and eager students.

If this procedure can be followed effectively, it would provide additional funds for faculty salaries and utilize faculty and other facilities more efficiently. It should not be necessary to double the faculty, and existing physical facilities could accommodate two colleges instead of one. The two colleges would alternate in their use of facilities according to the following scheme:

	July–Sept.	Oct.–Dec.	Jan.–March	April–June
College A	1st Quar.	Nonresident	3rd Quar.	Vacation
College B	Vacation	1st Quar.	Nonresident	3rd Quar.

The extent of the possible saving in faculty time cannot, of course, be predicted with accuracy. There is reason to believe, however, that such savings might be substantial. Much would depend on the extent to which the student's work during the nonresident quarter is truly independent, and on the efficiency with which the residential instructional program could be organized. The best way to obtain preliminary estimates of the possibility of these proposals and of their possible effects and costs would be through a series of preliminary experiments.

One outcome at Oberlin that was stimulated by the discussion of the nonresident quarter idea was the development of the Oberlin-in-Salzburg program. This is a program which was instituted by the faculty of the Oberlin Conservatory of Music under the leadership of the director of the conservatory, David Robertson. Under it all members of the junior class in the conservatory spend the entire academic year at the Mozarteum in Salzburg, Austria. This procedure was first put into effect during the academic year 1958–59. It differs from the nonresident quarter in a number of respects, but it has made it possible for the Conservatory to increase by approximately one-fourth the number of students served. It has also given the students the experience of study in an academic environment which calls for greater maturity and independence than is expected in the typical American liberal arts college.

A proposal for a preliminary set of experiments involving groups of freshmen students carrying on foreign study during a nonresident period was not accepted by the Oberlin faculty. Several members of the faculty, however, who had become sufficiently interested in testing the hypothesis that students at the elementary level could study effectively on their own, proposed a series of on-campus experiments in independent study. These experiments were carried out during the 1957–58 academic year with the aid of a grant from the Committee on Faculty Teaching Resources of the Fund for the Advancement of Education. Somewhat similar experiments were being carried on at Antioch and Carleton Colleges, and the three colleges held a series of conferences for joint planning and for the consideration of experimental results.

The three courses in which experimentation took place at Oberlin were elementary mathematics, psychology, and zoology. In mathematics and zoology all members of the experimental and control groups were freshmen. Psychology is not open to freshmen, so the participants were sophomores, juniors, and seniors.

The design involved two experimental and two control sections in mathematics and psychology and one of each type in zoology. The students were assigned to sections in a random fashion in mathematics and zoology, but chose their own sections (without knowledge of the experiment) in psychology. Pretesting revealed no evidence of differences between the experimental and control sections in ability or previous knowledge of the subject. In all three courses the experimental group engaged in a period of eight weeks of independent study, during which there were no classes and practically no contact with the instructor.

The progress made by the students was determined by the differences in scores on tests at the beginning and end of the course. No significant differences were found between experimental and control groups in any of the three courses. In mathematics an effort was made to measure the development in the student of ability to work independently on new mathematical concepts through what was called a "learning-resourcefulness" examination.[2] On this test the gain of the experimental group was greater than that of the control group by an amount that might be expected by chance 13 per cent of the time. This difference, while not statistically significant, is suggestive. It suggests that the experience of autonomous study may have made some contribution to the ability to study mathematics without the assistance of an instructor.

These experiments in independent study at the elementary level indicate that it is possible to place responsibility for learning on the student at an earlier stage than has usually been assumed. They suggest that if we in fact desire to develop intellectual independence in students we should start with independent study in the freshman year, and offer it in continually increasing amounts throughout the undergraduate program. They suggest, further, that the idea of a nonresident academic period equal to one-third of each academic year may be entirely feasible, and might result in more challenging and rewarding intellectual experiences for students and at the same time contribute to substantially greater efficiency in college operations.

[2] For a fuller description of this examination see John D. Baum, "Mathematics, Self-Taught," *American Mathematical Monthly*, LXV (November, 1958), 701–705.

SOME PROBLEMS AT AMHERST

Willard L. Thorp

I DO not see why I should write about the Amherst report in the midst of these more provocative reports from inventors and revolutionists, except perhaps that the mountains look higher if there is a mouse standing nearby. Our report dealt simply with the question of whether Amherst should plan to become larger or not. We were not asked to plan a new college or to work out any major changes. We were asked merely how to make the college consistent, since for ten years the enrollment had actually been around 1050 but the approved official maximum size was 965. We also were asked if and how we were going to contribute to the absorption of the presumed flood of future students, of which we might be able to take .0001 per cent as our share.

A committee of the faculty looked into this problem for hours and hours and hours and had a very pleasant time together. It was the first committee which ever looked at the problem of size of Amherst without coming to the conclusion that the college should become smaller. Instead we decided that the college could become somewhat larger.

I might say that previous reports were always clear in their conclusion, but I examined them all and never was able to find out the basis on which this conclusion for contraction had been reached by any previous committee, except that intimacy among the students and close relations with the faculty were alleged to be an important feature of a very small college. We were not impressed with the notion that everybody knows everybody else in a small college and that this relationship has some special value. As we examined it, we felt that perhaps a college of more than twenty souls lost what one might call intimacy and that there was no particular advantage in being able to call people by their first names when the number got up into double figures. There are other advantages of the small college, but none which we felt would be threatened by an increase in the size of the Amherst student body even if it meant a jump from 1,000 to 1,500 students.

We did, however, go a little further to look at various possible ways in which Amherst might accommodate more students, thinking of different methods of utilizing our resources. In connection with this we considered the problem of greater utilization of our physical resources. The business advisors suggested that we had a campus which was not fully used and that we ought to figure out ways of using it more of the time.

So we began examining various possible alternative schedules. We were also interested in the possibility of our educating students in three years.

I must say that we came to the conclusion that there was very little economic advantage in using the Amherst campus for students through the summer in the normal way with normal charges because we would probably lose money, even though we didn't have to pay anything for buildings and grounds. Assuming that we would have to expand our faculty proportionately and that we would not raise our tuition rate except proportionately to a longer school year, then the direct costs of extending the period would probably be more than we would collect as tuition. We already were giving scholarships to a third of our boys, and we would probably have to give even more scholarships for this added part of the summer, at least under present financing procedures. This conclusion is drawn from the fact that Amherst boys as a rule seem to earn substantial sums during the summer period.

We are supported very largely by returns on endowments and by gifts, and these we receive for twelve months and spend over nine. These sources of income presumably would not expand if we had a larger student body except after a long period of time.[1] Some day this larger alumni body might give more to the college, but we were not impressed with this as a sufficient gain to justify running the college on a twelve-month basis.

---

[1] Increased enrollments may be costly to colleges with large enrollments. Income per student from this source is then reduced (Ed.).

We looked at the problems of a staggered plan and of a three-year plan. We found that such plans are much harder to work out in a small college than in a larger institution. It may well be that there is some size that makes this rather easy to do, but, for instance, a four-quarter plan in a place like Amherst, with the students having a choice of coming either three or four of the four quarters, just wouldn't work because the students would get out of phase. We would not be giving courses for many of them at the right time in terms of prerequisites. We could not work it without having to repeat courses. An added problem is that we probably would operate at low capacity in the fourth quarter in the summer, and in a small college this means getting down to a very inefficient size.

We tried schemes of breaking up entering classes so that not all the freshmen would start at the same time and they would be away at different times, and again we ran into this same basic problem. We finally came to the conclusion that the only workable arrangement would be for entire classes to be staggered at intervals, so that if you were working on a trimester scheme — there are many different formulas for this — one whole class would be away at any given operating time during the year. This would not help the students to graduate in three years, but it would use the campus for a longer period of time each year.

This, however, again looked to us like a program which had no great advantage for the student. He would have his vacation at a different time each year. We might use some of this vacation time for a reading period. We left this consideration open for the curriculum committee. But such a plan has the difficulty of entailing a proportional expansion of faculty.

The more we looked at our problem at Amherst, the more it seemed to us that we should not be preoccupied with more efficient use of campus. The problem really turned around the use and adaptability of faculty. We felt that any procedure for expanding Amherst which involved a proportional expansion of the faculty was questionable. We already had a low faculty-student ratio, one of about seven and one-half to one. If we should have an expansion, the goal that we might set would be to see how much we could expand the college while maintaining our present faculty size.

This immediately brought us to the curriculum problem, which we were lucky to be able to say had not been assigned to us. We returned the report to the President saying that we thought some studies needed to be made, as follows.

First, we thought that someone ought to look at Amherst and say, if we add another 100 to 500 students, how much will be required for added buildings and equipment?

We suspected that expansion may prove to be a lumpy thing — that you may be able to add 400 — say — at half the expenditure at which you could add 500. We need to know what this schedule is. In a small college, some facilities are bound to be more than adequate and others not. At some point you would have to rebuild the entire college. So this is a study which we are eager to make, and it is being done.

We also suggested that the curriculum be reviewed with some thought as to what changes might permit a larger student body to be handled with the same size faculty without loss of quality. We were surprised to discover that our faculty at Amherst, which already was larger in relation to student population, had expanded considerably in the last decade with no growth in the student body. We were also surprised to discover that a very large fraction, about a quarter of the teaching time, was used in about 2 per cent of the student time, because we have so many classes of five or less. On the other hand, this may be part of the value, and cost, of a small college, although the number of courses seems to increase in the larger universities, with many small classes in more specialized subjects.

We also suggested that some way be found in which we might increase our efficiency with respect to the upper classes. We are quite efficient, we think, with freshmen and sophomores, at least in terms of class size. Our costly operation is in the junior and senior years. Probably from the point of view of use of resources, if it were conceivable to add students for the junior and senior year, perhaps a selected group coming out of junior colleges, this would be something that might be very beneficial to the college. On the other hand, the notion of transfers runs head-on into the notion that we have an integrated four-year plan of liberal-arts education at Amherst whereby the first two years prepare the students for the last two.

We did develop one basic principle as to what should be the college limit on size. This was that the college could be no larger than would permit the students to have the feeling of a common experience and a sense of community experience. They don't have to know one another, but they have to know that they have all had somewhat the same experience in the college. This implies that we do not want to take steps which would tend to fragment or to break up the community into varying groups.

We reached the conclusion that the shape and pattern of the curriculum was a key problem. The use of the faculty and the number of small courses which were to be tolerated are important determinants here.

Some of the problems that I have raised would be aided by the new college which is now under study. We suggested in our report that if there were a new college nearby which provided graduate work, this would be very helpful. We would then have some graduate students to exploit, both as sub-faculty and as advanced students. This is an area in which we are unfortunate compared with the universities. The new college might help in more efficiently filling up the classrooms for the advanced courses and, at that point, there is a very real possibility of economic benefit for Amherst and the new college.

The curriculum study on which we expect to have a report is likely to be quite fruitful of changes in Amherst. Two years ago we had a meeting in which four members of the faculty talked to a visiting group about Amherst's "New Curriculum." They discovered that the "New Curriculum" was ten years old. It becomes somewhat embarrassing to keep talking about the "New Curriculum," so now we are again hoping that since we cannot abandon the words we can get a new curriculum again. In turn, the curriculum will determine how many students can be handled with a faculty approximately our present in size, and that will probably be the major factor in deciding the future size of the college.

THE COLLEGE PLAN AT WESLEYAN
Donald D. O'Dowd

THE Wesleyan College Plan is a proposal now under discussion by trustees, faculty, students, and alumni of the college. Fully five years have been spent in evolving the proposal that is now before the Wesleyan community. The plan was submitted for general consideration and evaluation in January, 1959, by the faculty's Educational Policy Committee. Plans were made to initiate exploratory programs in 1959–60. Two groups of faculty indicated a concrete desire to establish colleges in September, 1959.

A general purpose of the Wesleyan plan is to allow the college to recover the benefits of the small and rather intimate group of students and teachers which many small colleges enjoyed in an earlier era. At the same time, the college hopes that this reorganization will enable it to serve a larger public by increasing the size of the student body. One of our objectives is to double the present enrollment. Perhaps the final goal will be a little lower. At present, Wesleyan has 750 students.

There are two basic educational aims of the program. First, it is an attempt to organize the academic situation in such a way that students will have maximum opportunity to acquire the basic modes of thought and techniques of analysis which are the heart of general scholarly fields such as literary studies or social science. If we are successful the student will come to perceive the world in a way which is both appropriate and unique for his area of study. He will be equipped to achieve insights and realize intellectual rewards which are traditionally reserved for the professionally trained scholar. In a way, the program attempts to adjust to the reality that the half-life of a fact is now about two months. We believe that it is the mental set and the trained sensitivity of the scholar which have great general utility outside the academic world as well as within.

The second basic aim of the Wesleyan College Plan is to prepare students to make a personal commitment to purposes and institutions. In other words, there is a moral drive behind this plan. It is designed to alert students to the public issues which demand their attention and devotion if society is to progress. This requires that students come to understand that a rich, full life is not to be gained solely by acquiring a family complete with two cars and a split-level house. This program is dedicated to reversing in a small way the trend toward "privatism" so forcefully described by Gillespie and Allport as well as by Jacob.[1] It is aimed at producing responsible men to enrich the ranks of professional, business, and public life.

Basically the College Plan seeks to guide students to emotional engagement with the academic aim and outlook of their teachers and through this to involvement in political, social, and moral issues of public import.

The attainment of these ends at Wesleyan, according to the College Plan, may be realized by freeing the academic situation from many of its characteristic features. For example, traditional departments will either be dissolved, divided, or combined into new units. The traditional props of courses, hours of credit, generalization requirements, examinations, and grades which most colleges feature will be altered or eliminated, depending on the needs of a particular college within the University. It is hoped that by re-examining and perhaps remaking many of our pedagogical implements a more dynamic educational environment can be created.

Now, let me describe some of the details of the proposal. The College Plan includes suggestions for the physical and administrative reorganization of the college. The design envisages the establishment of five or six colleges of between 100 and 250 students each, with from twelve to twenty-five faculty members in a college. Each college would be an administrative unit with a director, perhaps an assistant director with extensive responsibility for administrative details, and its own faculty.

[1] Gillespie, J. M. and G. W. Allport, *Youth's Outlook on the Future* (Doubleday: 1955), and Jacob, P. E., *Changing Values in College* (Harper: 1957).

The two colleges to be inaugurated in September, 1959, would have their own offices, seminar rooms, libraries, social rooms, and so on. If the over-all proposal is accepted, it is hoped that each college will be residential, with facilities for housing and feeding the majority of its student members and some of its faculty.

As they are presently conceived, the colleges would combine several separate disciplines within one course of study. One of the colleges currently under discussion would combine literature, philosophy, and history. A college of performing arts has been proposed which would include students and teachers of theater, music, and fine arts. A particular discipline might be represented in two or more colleges. Philosophy, particularly, seems to be in demand in a variety of potential curricula.

Students would be admitted to a college at the beginning of their sophomore year. A tutorial committee of three or four faculty members would accept responsibility for directing the education of a group of approximately twenty entering students. The tutorial committee would ordinarily direct their group throughout the full three-year course.

The program of study consists of three parts — a major program, a supplementary program, and general education. Let me describe briefly the form this curriculum will take in each of the three years. In the sophomore year, the major program is intended to introduce a student to the basic concepts, analytic devices, problems, and concerns of his field. As much as 40 per cent of a student's time, in bookkeeping terms, will be devoted to the major seminar, which will meet one or two times a week for the entire year. Regular essays will be required of the student in this seminar. He will be expected to submit an essay for critical evaluation at least every other week throughout the year. The supplementary program, accounting for perhaps 20 per cent of a student's time, is designed to present highly relevant materials in related disciplines in order to broaden the student's understanding of his major field. If he were working in literary studies, a few months of work on psychoanalytic theory of personality might be a suitable supplementary program. The remaining 40 per cent of our hypothetical student's life should be devoted to general education. In this phase of his work the student will be encouraged to explore interests and develop talents outside his major area. The student of literature might study mathematics, economics, or music, for example. General education can be pursued by individual reading, attending seminars in another college, or following a series of lectures provided for the general community. The student will be given every encouragement to organize a program of particular meaning to him.

The major seminar will continue in the junior year with increased stress on rigorous thought and analysis. The junior supplementary program will investigate new areas. Formal meetings will be less frequent in both seminars, with increasing responsibility for his educational growth being placed on the student. In general education the student might elect to develop his talents as an actor or he might choose to work in a laboratory. Here he is free to continue exploring possibilities of potential value outside his major field.

The senior program will consist of preparing a thesis with the guidance of an individual teacher, continuing general education, and employing the fruits of the previous two years of study in a socially meaningful way. As examples of the latter expectation, seniors will be encouraged to teach freshmen and sophomores, or to work as research and laboratory associates of the faculty. Some students might wish to direct a play, organize an art exhibit, or become involved in community activities. All of these socially valuable and responsible activities will be encouraged as part of a man's academic development.

The student will be provided with periodic multidimensional qualitative evaluations of his work. Grades will not be recorded. Written and oral examinations conducted in part by outside examiners will be given only at the end of the junior and senior years. They will cover the major and supplementary program, and also general education. At this time grades of honors, creditable, or failure will be used. In the curriculum itself there will be no distinction between candidates for honors and other students.

There is as yet little agreement on the

content of the freshman year. It has been suggested that it might begin with an intensive full-time six-week language course, followed by two twelve-week semesters in which a very comprehensive humanities course would be central. At the end of the year five weeks would be devoted to intensive full-time training in writing and speaking.

Let me conclude this rather condensed outline of the College Plan with a few general remarks. This plan may make it possible for faculty to come to know and understand a number of students in a manner which will stimulate within the students an appreciation for and occasionally a commitment to the goals of the scholar-teacher. Too often the teacher becomes interested only in the students who prove themselves by demonstrating proficiency in his field. When this occurs, only the rare student gets deeply involved in a course of study. On the other hand, it is often evident that students tend to be attracted to subject matter because a teacher treats them with warmth and respect for their integrity. While the teacher is oriented to his field, the students are teacher-oriented. The College Plan accepts the reality of the scholar's concern with his discipline while increasing the personal contact between the teacher and student in a way that will foster mutual understanding and, ideally, the intellectual growth of the student.

Another feature of the plan is the freedom of the tutorial committee to tailor requirements to the needs and interest of each student. This is a handcraft education in the sense that it is fitted to the individual. Because of the close association of students and faculty it is hoped that in some important respects the faculty will come to be models for many students. It would seem particularly desirable for students to learn from the faculty a mode of approaching private and public issues especially susceptible to intellectual analysis. In the most extreme case, the faculty may come to control a segment of the culture which students share. If this should come about they would be in a position to exert a powerful influence on student beliefs and attitudes. Because of this, I doubt that any appreciable savings can be achieved through increasing the student-faculty ratio. When faculty members start working with students on a more individual basis, it becomes more and more obvious that educational quality would be sacrificed were the number of faculty members for any given student body to decline, even though the administration still hopes that both quality and a higher student-faculty ratio can be obtained.

VI. ECONOMICS AND EDUCATIONAL VALUES

Summary of the Discussion on "Economics and Educational Values," of April 21, 1959, meeting of the Seminar on the Economics of Higher Education. Papers were given by Messrs. Riesman, Wolfle, Bridgman, Sanford, Eurich, Bowles, Deitch, and Skinner.

Higher Education and Economic Status

In the free flow of ideas following presentation of the papers, many matters were touched upon briefly but not always conclusively. After a short discussion on the economic value of college to graduates, and of college graduates to society, the group's attention focused on the nebulous but important question of the relationship between college and student — the extent to which educational policy today may actually harm rather than help students, and the extent to which socially imposed and self-imposed goals hinder the scope of the college in directing the education of its students. Finally, this discussion led to the consideration of two special cases, the work-study program of Northeastern University, and the unique character of the intimate college community at Haverford.

The papers of Messrs. Wolfle and Bridgman, taken together, left some question about the degree to which a college education really does increase the economic well-being of a person. Several objections were voiced against the use of 1949 as a year from which general conclusions are to be drawn. In the first place, the recent spectacular rises in the salaries of teachers, one of the largest groups of college-educated people, have taken place since 1949. Secondly, 1949 was still in the postwar readjustment period, and it is probably true that college graduates adjust to their permanent occupations less quickly than those in non-professional careers. Moreover, there is perhaps more wage flexibility in the nonprofessional occupations, so that in a period of strong demand, such as the postwar period, nonprofessional incomes are less sluggish in rising. Both of these factors suggest that use of 1949 figures underestimates the differential between incomes of college graduates and noncollege persons in a more normal year.

One factor suggested to explain the apparent decline in the income differential received by college graduates was the large increase in supply of graduates and the consequential upgrading of educational requirements for jobs. As a corporation executive rises in the industrial hierarchy, he feels constrained to indulge in "conspicuous production" — by having a college graduate as a receptionist, for example. The Department of Commerce is under strong continuous pressure by numerous vocational groups to redefine its category of "professional" to include them. A job which twenty years ago required a competent girl from a good secretarial school now demands a Wellesley graduate.

Because of this upgrading of educational requirements, it would be a mistake (for this reason among others) to use income differentials between college and noncollege people as an index of the contribution of college education to the productivity of the country. In the first place, the figures usually cited are average, not marginal, differences, so that one additional college graduate may contribute much less to the country's output than the average graduate now does. Secondly, the income differential may reflect, not differences in productivity, but merely the marketing advantage of the college graduate. In other words, his education may serve to land him a job, although a nongraduate might be able to perform this job just as well. In that case, the addition of a college man does not result in an increase in output, so one should take care in interpreting figures on higher earnings of college graduates as proving an economic benefit to society from an increase in the supply of highly educated men. The benefit is undoubtedly real, but perhaps not so large as the figures seem to indicate.

On the other hand, not all educational upgrading is due to an oversupply of college graduates. In a real sense, many vocations are becoming more complicated. The recent success of accountants in moving into the "professional" category perhaps reflects the vastly increased complexity of accounting problems, and is belated recognition of the extensive training now required for becoming a qualified accountant.

Changes in educational requirements, moreover, are downward as well as upward. With the increasing shortage of engineers relative to the demand for them, many industries have discovered that trained technicians will do quite as well in jobs formerly reserved for engineers. A similar movement is seen in the use of "informants" — persons who are expert linguists but have had no training in teaching — instead of teachers for language instruction.

All this suggests the desirability of having a continuum of educational attainment in the society, so that men will have enough education to perform their tasks, but not so much that they regard their tasks as "beneath" them. This minimizes waste of educational resources and friction in the competition for occupational status. Such a continuum does not exist, for example, in several of the underdeveloped countries, where frequently there exist no intermediate strata between the university-trained and the unlearned, with the result that while the educated are unwilling to fill middle-range positions, the uneducated are unable to do so.

One participant objected that the use of large aggregates often obscures important differences within categories. While it may be true that, on the average, college graduates earn more than nongraduates, there is many a steel-worker who earns more than the average minister. Graduates of two-year technical institutes often can look forward to higher average incomes than those of a four-year college granting the A.B. In short, many people choose certain colleges at a considerable financial sacrifice. Others added that there were serious risks in emphasizing the economic advantage of a college degree. The percentage of A.B. degrees given in the liberal arts has dropped noticeably in recent years, and there are wide regional variations within the country — around 50 per cent of the bachelor's degrees granted in the Northeast are in the liberal arts, but the percentage is as low as 25 in the Mountain States. These differences may reflect differences in emphasis placed upon the economic aspects of a college education; many are attracted into the more lucrative fields such as business administration. There is some evidence that students from wealthier families are more likely to pursue courses of study which do not promise high economic return.

Educational Policy — What Should Students Study?

In this connection, one member of the seminar questioned Professor Riesman's suggestion that students are now encouraged to "play from strength" rather than to diversify their educational interests. He thought that many students in fact are attracted by economic considerations into areas other than those in which their greatest strengths lie. Students inclined towards literature will take courses in business administration; musicians will go into music education; and so on. Market forces as well as "strength" contribute to the choice of field. Mr. Riesman replied that this was certainly true for many students, but he had been concerned especially with those top few with enough talent to succeed in not just one but in many fields. It is this group which is encouraged to develop the first area of talent that appears, rather than to "shop around" among several fields of interest, sampling them and learning from them.

This observation evoked a lengthy discussion on the role of the college in educating youth. Should girls be encouraged to go into such "nonfeminine" subjects as mathematics and physics? Or boys into the "nonmasculine" subject of music? There are cultural barriers to study which are artificial and which may inhibit people from entering fields from which they might profit a great deal. It was pointed out that about 50 per cent of the incoming freshmen at Harvard College anticipate concentration in science or mathematics (although many of them switch later), partly because these were subjects in which they were outstanding in high school. One participant pointed out that at his university a large amount of counseling is required for juniors and seniors who have made mistaken vocational choices early in their education and have not discovered it until much "investment" had been made in the required subjects. Premature specialization results in the costly and occasionally agonizing process of "dis-investing" and starting afresh in a new field.

In a way the problem is more serious for young men than for young women, since the latter need not be so concerned with the choice of an occupation. Yet early marriages are for women very much what early career decisions are for men: turning points which cut short the process of exploration and discovery. Interestingly enough, the rate of attrition for those beginning a college education is about the same for men as it is for women, although most men drop out in the first two years, while women tend to drop out of college in the last two.

The reasons for early specialization are easily enough understood. In an era in which vocations are becoming increasingly technical in nature, in which on-the-job training is becoming less common and more reliance is being put on formal education or training, and in which the training which is received in the high schools cannot be relied on to provide an adequate introduction to the subject, the departments within colleges feel that they must carry the student from beginning to end in the subject: in a babe and out an accomplished professional. And while it is true that a person ten years out of college will remember few of the details which he was taught and upon which he was so meticulously examined, a close study of the details of a subject is often necessary for a complete grasp of the concepts and generalizations. Once these are mastered, the technicalities will come back to mind with just a little review of the subject. This claim is made especially for subjects like chemistry and premedical training, where a very large part of the undergraduate curriculum must be devoted to the major subject.

Others doubted that this degree of specialization was at all necessary; the basic ideas can be taught in far less time than is now taken. If the bright student is introduced to the subject in his freshman year at a level which he is capable of absorbing and understanding, and is carried further in his sophomore year, and so on, what will be left to teach this student in his senior year or in graduate school? This is perhaps less true of the sciences than of some other subjects, but one candid physics professor had told a participant that taking a physics course in high school, or the freshman year of college, or even in the sophomore year, is not necessary to become a distinguished graduate from that department. Much the same material is taught over and over again at increasing levels of difficulty. But there is probably an optimum time to teach this essential introductory material, and other courses covering the same notions are often a waste of the student's time.

"Coverage" and the credit system are principal villains in this tendency to specialize. The credit system of American education equates what a student knows with what he has "had." Formal courses must be offered and taken in all areas; otherwise the student cannot be expected to know anything in these subjects, or so our conventions now say. Few students are really aware that they can learn about something without taking a course in it, even though there is evidence to support the view that the most productive educational process is the organized "bull session," the mutual stimulation of intelligent young people of similar interests. For instance, at the College of William and Mary, in the eighteenth century, there was a "flowering of statesmen" — Thomas Jefferson was among them — from the student body, yet records suggest that the quality of teaching at that time was conspicuously poor.

The compulsion for coverage is epitomized by the Ph.D. program; too often this degree is taken as an end in itself, a symbol of mastery of the discipline, and requires so much coverage that an early start in the subject is difficult to avoid. One participant suggested that this may be the partial cause for so much emphasis on coverage for undergraduates — not because most students consider going on for the Ph.D. degree, but because the younger men in the departments have been through this program themselves, and their ideas on education are influenced by that experience. One member observed a notable difference between the older men of a department, who would encourage the students to branch out in their studies over the whole universe of knowledge, and the younger men, who urged stiffer and stiffer departmental requirements for majors in their field. While the older men on the faculty are reluctant to accept undergraduates into the inner sancta of their disciplines, the younger men are very much concerned with competence and reputation within their disciplines, and so unwittingly influence their students to place too much concern on the symbols of competence: grades.

Another reason for drawing students into a particular discipline early in their undergraduate careers, one not due to the absorption of younger men in their own fields, is the competition among departments for students. The earlier they get them, the more likely they are to keep them. Hence it is important for the physics department, say, to offer a freshman course in physics, not because it is necessary to teach freshmen physics, but because it seems necessary to catch freshmen for physics before they are lured away by classics, for instance.

All this suggested to one participant the necessity to consider more carefully what a college education was really all about. Educators should examine the aims of higher education more explicitly than they have in the past, and should scrutinize the present methods being used to achieve those aims. Unfortunately there will be much resistance from self-satisfied faculties, and even more because of understandable human inertia, but it is clear that not enough attention is paid to what an "education" is — what the students, ten years after graduation, should have derived from a college education. More consideration should be given to the "level of maturity" at which a subject is taught, and to the level of maturity which the college feels that a student should have reached in his own subject, in related subjects, and in more peripheral fields. On being told by a friend that "college professors work at their profession much less than any other major professional group I know," another participant was at first irritated, but on reflection had to agree: very little time is devoted to the problems of *teaching* the discipline, as opposed to the problems of the discipline.

Another line of thought, however, placed the major responsibility for early specialization on the students rather than the faculty members. "I do not see this picture of the student eager to browse around and to acquire a broad culture and have plenty of time for choosing, and this unremitting faculty and administration trying to pressure him into specializing and forgetting about the rest," one member observed. Whatever the reasons for the behavior of the students in this respect, this member felt that merely providing the student with more choice would not work; more positive pressures would have to be exerted in order to induce the student to diversify his program.

A spreading of requirements compelling reluctant compliance by the students is not enough. The college must create the appropriate milieu for imaginative searching and creative thinking. At most colleges, especially the larger ones, the prevalence of a peer culture impedes any movement in this direction. Unless the student can find something at the college with which he can identify himself, unless he somehow feels that he "fits in" with the college community, he will continue in the culture to which he is accustomed, which too often is a culture alien from the faculty and from academic life in general.

For this reason, several participants felt that the college must provide the leadership in bringing their students to view higher education as a great exploration and a continuing debate, and not a mere continuation of high-school book-learning. Furthermore, it must create a culture into which the students can be drawn, and it must provide the "caution" signals which will guide students away from overspecialization, encouraging them to branch out into other areas.

Others felt that more emphasis should be put on the informal aspects of learning, the "bull session" and other ways in which students learn from one another. "I think that it is not necessarily true, in American life, that the only way to get a buzz out of a student is to put the battery of a professor on him. They buzz one another." In both cases, however, there is less emphasis on formal course work, which too often does not convey to the student the excitement of learning, and results only in the ingestion of already predigested material.

In this connection, several members raised questions about the interpretation of Professor Sanford's study of Vassar undergraduates. One cannot determine definitively the impact of the college on these girls, since it is natural that a freshman, proud of being admitted and looking forward to four years of pleasant and stimulating experience, should on the average be a contented, well-balanced, secure individual. The seniors, in contrast, face considerable uncertainty. They do not know whether marriage or career is expected of them, and they are older, more mature, and better apprised of the problems of the world. It is not surprising that they should be much less self-confident than the freshmen, and yet the upsetting experience of leaving a secure world has educational value in terms of developing the personality. Several participants agreed that the discontent engendered during four years at college is not a bad thing at all. One suggested that more unsettling experiences, such as changing colleges after two years, would be a very desirable innovation. An interesting result of the study is that juniors are perfectly secure; the malcontents have probably left after the sophomore year, so that for those remaining the period of insecurity comes only in the senior year. To the extent that forced adjustment to a new environment is educationally desirable, the junior year is not a fruitful one for the personality development of the student.

Another proposal would permit students to enter graduate school after three years of undergraduate work. This would produce the desired change in environment, would save the parents one year of college expenses, and would "overcome the sacred cows of the four years and the A.B. and graduation and the alumnae association." Others felt, however, that encouraging such transfers would only increase the "vocationalism" which was already so troublesome in higher education today. However specialized the typical college senior may be, he is far less so than the typical first-year graduate student. Encouraging students to skip their senior year might result in a great educational loss by shunting them into more narrowly confined interests.

The Cooperative College

A type of institution which does provide its students with varied experiences and frequent opportunities to "readjust" to a new environment is the "cooperative" college, one with a combined study-work program. Northeastern University, for example, offers a five-year program leading to the bachelor's degree. The first academic year is spent entirely at the university, and thereafter the student alternates for ten-week periods between studying at the university and working at a job related to his academic program. This sort of program, which is used in over ninety colleges and universities in the country, both aids the student financially and contributes toward expanding the educational capacity of the schools which use it. In their last two years of college the students are often earning between $100 and $150 a week. Moreover, the graduates of these institutions usually adjust more rapidly to their occupations, and command a higher starting salary than the average graduate, because of the practical knowledge and experience they have acquired before graduation. That this intermingling of study and work contributes to the financial wellbeing of the students is attested by the 40 per cent of attrition between matriculation and graduation, considerably lower than the national average. Additional problems are created, however, if the student decides that *because* he is so well off, he can afford to marry.

The "cooperative" program also increases educational capacity by using the plant and faculty more efficiently. The school needs hardly more than half as much dormitory and classroom space as an ordinary institution teaching the same number of students, since almost half the student body is away on jobs at any given time. At Northeastern the students are paired, so that the firms for which they work have, in effect, a full-time employee. Even so, a serious recession creates many difficulties in placing the students in jobs, since they tend to be regarded as marginal workers.

In this connection, one participant pointed out that it was misleading to speak of higher education exclusively in terms of a four-year program. The cooperative programs are designed to take longer, but for many students of conventional urban institutions undergraduate work involves not four but five or six or seven years of study. In one such school the average length of time taken for the bachelor's degree was five and a half years. Many of the students at these institutions carry only a partial study load, and also have part-time or full-time jobs, so that their educational experience is considerably different from that of a student at a four-year residential college.

Size in Relation to Costs and Educational Value

Haverford is an example of a college caught between the horns of education and economics. Many people concerned with the college feel strongly that there are several important though intangible benefits in retaining its present small size, just over 450 students. Being small prevents the college from offering the wide range of courses to its students which a larger institution could. Moreover, it could achieve significant economies by increasing its enrollment (since costs per student tend to decline as enrollment rises, up to a point), but by doing so it would run the risk of sacrificing its atmosphere of a small, close-knit intellectual community and perhaps of any possibility of student responsibility in the affairs of the college. At some rate of increase in size, a "tipping point" is reached in the minds of the faculty and the students, at which each group becomes an undifferentiated "They" to the other. In increasing enrollment, the school would be moving into an unknown area regarding its effect on the community, and many are not willing to take the risk. At the same time, remaining small entails a certain cost, and these costs must be balanced against the alleged advantages of the present size and structure.

One participant suggested that the rate at which a school grows is perhaps more important than the absolute size. He cited a college which doubled the size of its incoming freshman class in one year. The college community was not able to absorb such a proportionate increase at one time, so the new students developed a culture of their own instead of being assimilated into the academic community already there, and the whole atmosphere of the school changed.

Haverford has attempted to contribute to the national need for more educational capacity by increasing its enrollment 52 per cent since 1930. At present, however, the bottleneck to further expansion, symbolic of the type of community which Haverford wishes to maintain, is the size of the meeting house. Growing further would eliminate the opportunity to bring together under one roof the greater part of the student body.

At the same time, as the demand for higher education grows rapidly Haverford and other colleges in a similar position cannot remain the same merely by resisting proposed changes. Increasing admissions standards will perhaps alter the college faster than increasing enrollment, and as the list of applicants grows in the near future such colleges are faced with a formidable admissions problem: shall they take only the most talented and most promising up to the limits of their capacity, or should they reach further down into the list in order to ensure a more diversified student body, knowing that this would involve accepting some persons less qualified than those that were rejected? In a changing environment an institution must change in order to appear the same. One member suggested that schools like Haverford should accept the consequences of this new admissions situation, and become in effect honors colleges. This is already happening to some extent; some colleges are admitting students with considerably higher average aptitude scores than they were ten years ago.

The discussion turned to the role of small, church-affiliated colleges in the American system of higher education. Some felt that these schools have a unique character and render a distinctive service to the country. As Dr. Conant has said, the only thing common to all the A.B. degrees awarded in this country is the length of exposure and the charges made. To allow enrollment in the small, residential, church-related colleges to fall to an insignificant proportion of total student enrollment would be a great loss to the quality and diversity of higher education. These colleges ought to increase their capacity so as to continue to provide their unique quality to larger numbers.

Others felt that the importance of these

small colleges could be exaggerated. As one member put it, "Too often they take refuge in what they call their unique character in order to escape the responsibilities of quality education. Many are little more than extended junior colleges with a substandard bachelor's degree." Unless they raise their quality to the level of many public universities, their future is likely to be very bleak indeed. There are some important exceptions to this, of course; some of the schools in this category are among the finest in the country.

Yet it may be an error to judge institutions of higher education by a single educational standard. Frequently the quality of output reflects little more than a very effective recruitment program, so that the entering freshmen are exceptionally promising. Moreover, not all colleges have the same goals: some emphasize academic training and graduate work, others a religious outlook on life, still others some technical proficiency. One participant suggested that the most appropriate measure of the accomplishments of a college is the amount of *change* which has been generated in the students between entering and leaving, rather than the absolute level of attainment of the graduating seniors. Indeed, the reputations of some institutions are founded more on the aptitudes of the incoming freshmen than on what they impart to their students during the four years, while there are probably other colleges with negligible reputations which are doing a great deal of shaping and polishing of some very rough stones. More recognition ought to be given to this group of institutions.

SOME PROBLEMS OF ASSESSING (AND IMPROVING) THE QUALITY OF A COLLEGE

David Riesman

I WANT to look at the problem of assessing quality and its problems as it appears at two very different ends of the academic spectrum, near the floor and near the ceiling.

Mr. Thackrey and I have corresponded, as have Mr. John Holland and I, about the problem of the Wesleyan studies, which tried to assess the "value added" by college and to see how many students went on to win graduate fellowships, and so on; and in the study that the Fund for the Republic commissioned, published as *The Academic Mind*, Paul Lazarsfeld developed a quality index on the basis of standard weighted measures of professorial "productivity": books in the library, et cetera.

All these studies assume that the kind of "product" which is wanted can be determined by some form of national selective service, biased on the professional side, as in the Wesleyan studies, by assuming that people who are given stars in *American Men of Science* are a tribute to the college, whereas, as I suggest in some of my books, this may be a tribute only to the parochialism of the college which puts the student in a position where the best thing he can think of is taking his professor's job. The work of the National Merit Scholarship group has carried this a step further by asking what were the students' Scholastic Aptitude Test scores — that is, what did the colleges have to start with? — but here the problem is one that goes further, the problem of what might be called the "short-run trajectory."

The feeling is growing among people who teach graduate students from the relatively high-powered colleges that somehow there is a kind of decompression effect in a "high-octane" situation, to mix my metaphors, and that the students who are admitted to these graduate schools and who have obviously high scores in the standard aptitude tests turn out not to be very creative or very exciting, if one tries to measure them by more wide-ranging tests. The short-run sprinter and the miler are not differentiated.

One way of trying to get at this issue is to move in the direction of studies which look at different psychological or personality variables among students and see what kind of setting is best for them, given these students as they are. Thus, studies done by Allport and Wispé at Harvard, similar to studies Nevitt Sanford has done at Vassar, ask whether authoritarian-minded students may not flourish best in a strict environment and flounder in a permissive one; and, as the study done by Bloom, Stein, and Stern at Chicago shows, if the whole environment is "permissive," "liberal," "emancipated," and so on, what happens to the bigot — the bright bigot — who feels at sea when the local academic culture, the residential culture, tells him that he is the wrong kind of a bird? This kind of work leads to efforts to match student and college, assuming that each of them is invariant — that the bigot will remain a bigot, but get brighter, and that the unbigoted will remain unbigoted and get brighter. I want, later, to say something about that assumption and also about the assumption that each student himself counts as one: that is, all these studies, I think, exhibit the psychologist's typical bias (there are biases in all fields) of assuming that all students count equally — it is a very democratic assumption — and that the movement of each student is like the movement of every other student, and that each student's movement has the same impact on the college climate itself, whereas, in fact, we know that in any group, some people have more impact than others, and some people move more than others. This is one difficulty in the measures which so often do not work out (which Seymour Harris quotes in his own paper) — that is, the measures of, say, large class against small class — where the problem of whether one student can be weighted more than another in terms of his trajectory, his development, cannot be dealt with.

Now, the standard measures of college

quality not only assume that each student counts as one, but assume a unilinear path of excellence — that is, they assume that if, let us say, academic attainments are raised, this means that sights are raised in every dimension. That is what I want to question, because I think it makes sense at the floor, but not at the ceiling.

The floor is what we might call the accreditation floor: how to lift the more benighted places? I have recently read a report written by a faculty committee at a midwestern university, which visited one of the junior colleges in the state; the faculty report evinced academic ethnocentrism, because it assumed how dreadful it was for these people to be teaching eighteen or twenty hours a week, whereas, since they were upgraded high-school teachers, they thought no doubt that they were in the gravy. The problem of raising the levels here occurs in terms of the model set in the accrediting institutions and the provision of some leverage for the occasional marooned teacher in such a place. The report that I read has, I think, the beneficent assumption built into it that if these teachers were freed from such a heavy class load, they would do research in their extra time. The chances are that they would take second jobs. And yet, as I say, this may be a way of raising sights and raising expectations at the bottom of the academic procession.

The real problem which we have discussed more or less parenthetically is: should these low-level institutions be closed down because they may be a trap for an occasional good student, or are they a transfer station for a good student? Involved here are a number of things. In the first place, I am not sure that the "good" student is benefited by going to the "good" institution. I want to turn to that more fully in a moment, but I think that what is happening now in our very top-quality institutions is that many students never attain the very fortunate ability to think that their teachers are stupid, a perception that may be part of their developing competence; hence, some students might be better off in a poorer institution. The institutions, however, that I am now talking about are so poor that this is not yet an issue for them. The real issue is, how should a red flag be set up by some Federal Trade Commission for higher education to announce: "Substandard Merchandise" — not a college, although it calls itself a college or even a university? I have been reading the weekly paper put out at an upgraded normal school, now a university, in order to try to discover: is this a man-trap, as it appears? Can a man get an education here, as he can in many of the lesser-league places? And I doubt it. I have talked to faculty members there who say that, at the risk of their lives — not their real lives, their academic lives — they sometimes see a good student and say, "Get out of here. Go to Chicago. Go somewhere else, so that you will not become like us."

And then the problem is: where can these students transfer? Harvard, for example, won't take them. Most of the elite institutions have no room for transfers, and I don't believe that one can morally attack the low-level or junior-college institutions unless one is prepared to take many more transfers and unless prestige institutions are prepared to stand up against the attack that will be launched against them for taking transfers, like the attack that Hutchins came in for when he began taking eleventh-graders. Taking such transfers may, in fact, be the quickest way to upgrade a place — that is, the students' own verdict on the place may be the quickest way.

The study that Coleman and Rossi have been doing at Chicago shows the extraordinary thing, to me and to many people, perhaps: how narrow are the limits students set on what colleges are available to them. There are many students within a hundred miles of the University of Chicago who have never heard of it — bright students, who have heard only of the University of Illinois or Carbondale or one or two other nearby places. At St. Paul's School there is at the moment an exciting experiment with New Hampshire high-school seniors, taking them in for a challenging summer course of advanced work. It turns out that most of these students know only Durham, the University of New Hampshire. Into their orbit, perhaps even into their semantic consciousness, other institutions have not entered.

Now let me turn to one more word about this level of institution and the problem of at once assessing quality, as an accreditation team does, and upgrading it, and that is the problem of what we might call the "star and wagon" theme. How can the standards of high-powered institutions be applied to low-powered institutions without leading the latter into despair and the rejection of the high-powered model and of all idealism? One response to this is to realize that the high-powered institutions are not so excellent themselves; if these institutions were more modest about their own limitations, faculty members could come to so-called third-rate places and try to work with the given situation. I believe, along similar lines, that our high schools would give better courses in English, if our high-school teachers were not cut off from popular culture, teaching Milton to uncomprehending teenagers, but could teach Milton and Shakespeare in the same rhetoric and with the same passion with which the students discuss Jack Benny or a Western. So I think that, for example, social science departments in many of these local institutions could take advantage of the regional nature of the institutions, if they were not engaged in giving courses which are a pale and watered-down version of what is taught in the graduate school of some eminent university. This could be an excuse for mediocrity, but I think it could also be an excuse for improving the eminent university.

And now, I want to turn to the latter and the ceiling to which I have referred. A study (as yet unpublished) by Roy Heath done at Princeton, an extraordinarily interesting study, to which we referred at our last meeting here, describes a quasi-experiment in which Heath, a Princeton graduate and a psychologist, became an advisor to a group of thirty-nine students, whom he matched in a rough way for the four-year college term with a control group who were not his advisees. That is, he took a preparatory-school boy from the East and matched him with another preparatory school boy from the East of relatively similar grades and background, and so on, and a high school boy from the Midwest, et cetera.

"His" boys, in a kind of Hawthorne Plant phenomenon, did extraordinarily well in Princeton. They became leaders in everything. More of them than of the boys in the control groups graduated after writing distinction theses. The fact of being interviewed sympathetically and alertly in itself was sufficiently crucial to move these boys ahead.

If one looks at the individual case studies of these boys, one sees a group who are very characteristic of some of the ablest (in grade terms) of the youngest generation of college students today. They are boys who live on a very short tether of impulse life: they are noncommittal, cautious, unenthusiastic, sophisticated, and, like some drug in too indigestible a capsule, the enzymatic processes of college can do little for them because they are already "collegiate" before they come.

In thinking about what could be done for the best students at the best places to prevent this result, I have become convinced that what is happening now to the most gifted young is that they are pushed and encouraged from a very early age to play from strength rather than weakness. If they exhibit a mathematical or scientific aptitude in the eighth grade, they are moved ahead very fast in this field. They go into college, and their teachers look upon them as potential recruits for the graduate school. Our best colleges are becoming preprofessional and protograduate, even if they are liberal arts colleges. And the students never get a chance to explore their full selves.

The old humanistic tradition which would lead them to do so is suffering tremendous attrition. A thesis done by a Harvard senior tends to show that the preparatory-school boys in their first year at Harvard, coming from a place like Exeter, become more like the high-school boys than vice versa — that is, they become as work-minded, as preprofessional, as much in search of a vocational and occupational identity as the high-school boys who have to make good. This is a great change.

A group of Sarah Lawrence girls recently visited Harvard and Radcliffe, and they put sharply what I am getting at, in talking with their Radcliffe hostesses. They said, "The difference between a Sarah Lawrence education and a Radcliffe education lies precisely in this — that you get through Sarah Lawrence still believing that you can make a contribution to knowledge." And the Radcliffe girls said, "Do you really suppose that you can?" I am for Sarah Lawrence in this respect, and I think that to destroy the feeling that one can make a contribution, is no contribution.

This is in part the result of being awed by a distinguished faculty, some of whom still believe that the problem in a high-powered institution is to make it still more high-powered, who still act as if a place like Harvard were a place like Carbondale and that the problem is to mop up whatever free time and independent resources and looseness there is in the curriculum. And the students fall in all too readily with this, because they are in search of an identity. They are going on to graduate school while, as one of my colleagues likes to put it, "Each member of the Harvard faculty is looking for his fair share of the meat" — that is, his fair share of people to go on to graduate school in his domain.

So that, while, at the low-prestige institutions, the student culture, the peer culture, has all the power, and the faculty virtually none, in the high-prestige institutions the student power is fragmented and reinforces the faculty power. This is the wave of the future.

Now, one might ask in conclusion whether the humane ideal implicit in what I have said is merely snobbish. Am I speaking for an outdated gentleman-Oxford-prestige image of education, the "whole man"? Is there something to be said for playing from weakness rather than strength? I think so, although it would take us far afield to go fully into it. My own belief is that the mixture within the individual student which is best for him is not necessarily to develop his best talent exclusively. I see a great many students who, because they are good at something, feel that they must do it as a career, although idiosyncratic elements in their makeup would make something else at which they are less good, but still very good, more hospitable for them.

At a recent career conference at Harvard, a group of students were saying, "We have had this expensive education. We cannot let it down. We would like to be A, but we are going to be B, because B is what the country needs." Now, Lord knows what the country needs. The only people who can find out are these same students. They are the only people who can redefine it, and the only way they can do it is by an image of themselves which is larger than any which a college now tries to pin on them or which they are eager to accept in order to narrow the range of alternatives, because the best students are also good at many things, and their problem of choice is among several "goods."

Let us apply that problem to the colleges themselves. For a number of years, I have asked admissions officers and faculty members and others, "What can be said about the best product mix for an institution?" Maybe the best product mix, as I have already implied, includes some dreadfully stupid faculty members at a high-powered institution, to whom the student can feel superior, in whose classes he can engage in overlearning. To illustrate what I am talking about, at colleges like Harvard or the University of Chicago, a teacher in the humanities may put before a student a poem which the teacher privately considers oversentimental, to get the student to realize this, and then destroy the poem and, with it, the student. Maybe one of the advantages of Skinner's machine is that the machine is not sadistic. It is not going to try to make the student feel weak or cheap or unsophisticated or naive.

To turn from the faculty to students, is the optimal product mix among the latter, what one now finds in the better colleges, a roomful of high-school valedictorians? Are there catalytic agents that one could throw into such a setting to give it greater range? Most of the things done in this direction include using regional distribution as a questionable source of heterogeneity of standards; we don't know much, it seems to me, about the "critical mass" problem, as the chemists would say: the catalytic problems involved in these very demanding settings. We must also ask about the fate of the student who is put into the "mix" because of what his presence may contribute to it: he himself may not benefit commensurately, as the boy from a poor high school in a small town may not always benefit from the democratic impulse at a select university that encourages him to enter a freshman class where he may feel too outclassed ever to catch up.

Seymour Harris deals with the problem of size of class and size of college, and this is crucial in dealing with critical mass because, if the institution is too small, as the Haverford people point out, there will not be enough different types within the student body to bring out the different sides of an individual which could develop through varied contact with others. You don't get a delinquent culture in a high school of fifty, because the delinquency within each young person doesn't find mates, but neither do you get the most differentiated and cosmopolitan urban culture, either. (My understanding of these matters has been greatly enlarged by conversations with James Coleman concerning his studies of the climate of a group of Northern Illinois high schools.)

But there is another problem, and this involves the ideology of the student as he looks at his peers and as he looks at the faculty. One of the problems in a big institution and in an institution that appears big by the way it organizes its classes and curricula is the We/They problem: the students look at the faculty and say, "They"; the faculty look at the students and say "They." There is a mass identification involved in size per se. This comes about because, if the group is too large, the differentiations which the students might make, were they in a place where they knew everybody else, are not made. All Chinese look alike to the American. All faculty members look alike in an institution the size of Berkeley.

The optimum size, then, of various settings must be thought of in terms of the students' ideology about size, about how big is a mass. Students today feel, rightly or wrongly, that there is a certain breaking point beyond which they can only say "They." What the breaking point is, we don't know. Part of it must turn on what we might metaphorically call the sociometric energy of faculty and students to have a wider range. For instance, I was fascinated to think that at Harvard a fairly energetic student could know by name two hundred people, not one hundred, and that the most energetic faculty member could go into a room with a class this size and know the names of everybody at the end of the first day. These are qualities about which we know very little.

But, if we are going to improve higher education and even understand it at the very ceiling, at the very top, these are the types of issues to which I think we must turn.

ECONOMIES AND EDUCATIONAL VALUES

Dael Wolfle

STATEMENTS are frequently made about the dollar value of going to college. The evidence for these statements is that college graduates, on the average, earn larger salaries than do persons who stopped their education at some earlier point. In 1953 the Commission on Human Resources and Advanced Training decided to examine this problem more carefully by comparing the earnings of college graduates with the earnings of nongraduates who appeared at the time of high-school graduation to be comparable on three variables — the grades they had made in high school, the scores made on intelligence tests, and the family background from which they came. We were able to get records of high-school graduates of fifteen to twenty years earlier from the city of Rochester, New York, and from most of the high schools of the two states of Minnesota and Illinois. The high schools supplied names, addresses, school grades, intelligence-test scores, and fathers' occupations for as many as possible of their graduates (within designated years) whose grades or intelligence-test scores indicated a reasonable probability of being able to do satisfactory college work. By mail questionnaires we then sought information on current positions and salaries from each.

There were, of course, the usual difficulties of questionnaire studies — of wrong addresses and of incomplete returns. A comparison of the characteristics of persons who returned the questionnaires with characteristics of the total group suggested that a number of conclusions could be drawn with reasonable confidence.

Technical details on the questionnaire, the representativeness of the sample of the respondents, and the results in greater detail can be found in the original article by Dael Wolfle and Joseph G. Smith, "The Occupational Value of Education for Superior High School Graduates" (*Journal of Higher Education*, Vol. 27, 1956, pp. 201–213).

In general, the results confirmed common sense. Male high-school graduates who stood high in their classes tended to earn more than those who stood low in their high-school classes. Those who made high scores on intelligence tests later earned higher salaries than did those who made low scores on intelligence tests. The ones who came from more favorable family backgrounds had higher incomes than those who came from less favored portions of the socio-economic scale. (Not enough of the women were employed to justify statistical analysis.)

Superimposed on these three trends, and in a sense overriding all three, was clear evidence of substantial salary differences associated with differences in the amount of education beyond high school. For the men within any given level of high-school class rank (for example those in the top ten per cent) or for the men within any given range of intelligence test scores (for example from the sixtieth to the eightieth percentile) the median salary rose steadily with larger amounts of post-high-school education.

Similar results were found for the high-school graduates whose fathers were in similar occupations (for example, the sons of professional men, or the sons of farmers): the greater the amount of education beyond high school, the higher was the average salary.

High-school grades, intelligence-test scores, and father's occupation were all correlated with the salaries being earned fifteen to twenty years after graduation from high school, but the amount of education beyond high school was more clearly, more distinctly related to the salaries being earned.

There is another conclusion from the data, one of perhaps greater importance. It is this: the differences in income were greatest for those of highest ability. It is of some financial advantage for a mediocre student to attend college, but it is of greater financial advantage for a highly superior student to do so. For the whole group, at this period in their careers, the college graduates earned approximately $1,400 a year more than the men of apparently equal ability who did not go beyond high school. But for the top 20 per cent of the men, the difference was about $2,400 a year.

There are several cautions to be observed

in interpreting these results. In the first place, there were important but unmeasured differences between those who went to college and those who did not. They may have made similar high-school records, earned similar intelligence-test scores, and had fathers in the same occupation, but some went to college and others did not. Presumably there were differences in interest and motivation, and presumably these differences should also be considered in interpreting their later salary differences.

The second caution pertains to the time period. The men studied finished high school in the years 1933–1938. If earnings in different fields of work become more similar in the future than they have been in the past, differences in earnings associated with differences in education will also decrease. If the percentage of the population graduating from college continues to increase, the financial advantages of a college degree are likely to decrease. Certainly the absolute magnitude of the differences found in this study cannot be promised to students now deciding whether or not to enter college.

The third caution is that this study paid no attention to qualitative differences among colleges. We treated together the graduates of good, average, and weak colleges. It would require a larger body of data than we had to justify any analysis of differential effects of different kinds of colleges.

Nevertheless, the basic trends seem clear. The moderately capable high-school graduate who goes to college earns more than the one who does not. The very capable graduate earns considerably more than the one who does not. Moreover, since the college graduates had spent fewer years in their fields of work than had those who went to work immediately after graduating from high school, it is probable that at the time of the study they were farther from their peak earnings and that the differential would be greater some years later.

Finally it should be pointed out that although there is some correlation between the value of a man's contributions to society and the monetary reward society gives him, this relationship is far from a perfect one. The bright student is rewarded for going to college. The benefit to society of sending him to college may be even greater.

PROBLEMS IN ESTIMATING THE MONETARY VALUE OF COLLEGE EDUCATION

D. S. Bridgman

DISCUSSION of the value of college education to the individual graduate in monetary terms should not imply failure to recognize its great potential contribution to a richer personal and family life, to constructive citizenship, and to a career of greater inherent interest and challenge, as well as larger financial rewards. Emphasis on monetary returns is largely due to the possibility of measuring them in quantitative terms, but it also realizes that for many individuals such returns and accompanying social advantages are a major incentive for going to college. In any case, it is important that the data concerning this value be as accurate and representative as possible and that the influence upon it of factors other than additional education be made clear. The following discussion presents points of this kind for consideration.

In recent years, the figure most frequently mentioned as the monetary value of a college education has been $100,000. This amount represents the approximate difference between the lifetime incomes of college graduates and of high-school graduates with little or no college education, calculated from the mean or average 1949 incomes of white males in each age group, as reported by the 1950 Census, with actuarial survival rates applied to each age group. The original computation by Glick and Miller of the U. S. Bureau of the Census put the lifetime income of college graduates at $268,000 and that of the high school graduates at $165,000, a difference of $103,000.[1] More current data, as yet unpublished, from which Miller has made similar computations, are available from the 1956 Current Population Survey. Although based on relatively small but very carefully drawn samples of between 2,000 and 2,500 male college graduates and about 6,000 male high-school graduates, these income data are internally consistent and also consistent with the corresponding preliminary findings from the 1958 survey. They may be accepted as reasonable approximations of the figures for the populations represented.

Table 1 presents data pertinent to this discussion from the 1950 Census for 1949 and the 1956 Current Population Survey.

TABLE 1. — [a] LIFETIME INCOMES OF UNITED STATES MALES (FROM AGE 25 TO DEATH)

Length of Schooling	Means 1949	Means 1956
High School 4 years	175,000	238,000
College 4 years or more	287,000	392,000
Difference	112,000	154,000

	Medians 1949	Medians 1956
High School 4 years	140,000	199,000
College 4 years or more	200,000	291,000
	60,000	92,000

	Percentiles (1956) 25th	75th
High School 4 years	149,000	270,000
College 4 years or more	195,000	417,000
	46,000	147,000

[a] Means and medians from unpublished data of H. P. Miller, U.S. Bureau of the Census. 1949 means higher than those previously published due to elimination of cases with no income for the year. Twenty-fifth and seventy-fifth percentile figures for 1956 obtained by D S. Bridgman by computing those points in each age-group distribution and multiplying the sum for the two points by the ratio between the corresponding sum of the medians and the median lifetime incomes.

Several points seem worth consideration in interpreting the significance of the data in Table 1. First, it should be recognized that the cost of a college education, either its direct cost or its cost in foregone earnings, has not been deducted from the differences in lifetime incomes for the two educational levels. Second, these data represent incomes rather than earnings, and this fact seems likely to increase significantly the advantage of the college graduates. Substantially more of those graduates than of the high-school graduates have appreciable incomes from investments, as the result of inheritance or family gifts as well as personal savings. No earnings figures were secured for these years, but both income and earnings data will be obtained in the 1960 Census.

[1] P. C. Glick and H. P. Miller, "Educational Level and Potential Income," *American Sociological Review* (June, 1956).

Table 1 itself brings out the extent to which the lifetime income differences between the college and high-school graduates are larger when calculated from the means, or averages, of the age-group distributions than when calculated from the medians, representing, for example, the fiftieth man in a group of 100. The latter method eliminates the greater than proportional weight given in calculating means to a relatively limited number of quite large incomes (likely to be more frequent among college graduates), due, in some cases, to investment income or earnings resulting from family business connections. If comparisons of this sort are designed to bring out the effect of additional education, the median appears to be the more appropriate measure.

The data for the twenty-fifth percentile, the upper limit of the lowest quarter of the two groups, and the seventy-fifth percentile, the lower limit of their top quarter, have been included to focus attention on the fact that the college graduate at the first of these points has only a small income advantage over the corresponding high-school graduate, while at the latter point the advantage of the college graduate is very substantial.

The significance of this disparity, particularly with relation to differences in mental ability, as well as extent of education between the two levels, may be considered by examining data for one of the several age groups included in the total samples from which lifetime incomes were computed. An appropriate group for that purpose is the one thirty-five to forty-four years of age in 1956, since in that age group the college graduates are approaching — even if they have not quite attained — the maximum income differential over the corresponding high-school graduates, and no measures of ability differences can be found for older groups. In fact there are no such measures for a true cross-section even of that group, but the educational and ability patterns of World War II veterans contained in it may be considered reasonably representative of the group as a whole.

Table 2 shows the income data for this age group. Table 3 presents data concerning the mental ability levels, as measured by the Army General Classification Test (AGCT), of a large random sample of army enlisted men selected in 1944 and 1946.

TABLE 2. — [a] 1956 INCOMES OF UNITED STATES MALES (AGED 35 TO 44) BY PERCENTILES

	Percentiles		
Length of Schooling	25th	50th	75th
High School 4 years	3992	5128	7028
College 4 years plus	5170	7537	10110
Difference	1178	2409	3082

[a] Data from 1956 *Current Population Survey*, not published by age groups.

TABLE 3. — [a] ARMY GENERAL CLASSIFICATION TEST SCORES (110,000 ENLISTED MEN, OF WHOM 82% WERE TESTED IN 1944, 18% IN 1946) (AGCT SCORE DISTRIBUTION)

	Percentiles		
Length of Schooling	25th	50th	75th
Scores			
High School 4 years	103	113	122
College 4 years or more	117	126	139
Percentiles of Total Population			
High School 4 years	55	74	86
College 4 years or more	79	90	97

[a] Data from Personnel Research Branch, Adjutant General's Office, Department of the Army — July 14, 1947 (unpublished). Scores related to percentiles of total age group (Appendix Table G2-*America's Resources of Specialized Talent*).

It should be recognized at once that these two tables present completely independent data and that the extent to which individuals, for example, falling below the twenty-fifth percentile points on the income scales correspond with those falling below that point on the mental-ability scales is quite indeterminate. Motivation, personality traits, choice of occupation, and pure good luck are some of the other factors affecting an individual's income. In some cases, influential family or social connections, likely to occur far more frequently in the college-graduate group, are an important factor. Yet the belief is generally accepted that mental capacity does play a significant part in the opportunity to enter the better-paid fields and in the earning ability that accompanies a successful career. Table 3 indicates that the differences in such capacity for the corresponding segments of the two educational levels are large enough to have important influence in this respect. At or below the twenty-fifth percentile, that difference would appear far more important than the difference in education; at or above the seventy-fifth percentile, the latter seems likely to be the major determinant.

It is true that there is only limited evidence available concerning the extent of the relationship between mental ability and earnings or income. Very few studies in this field include an adequate number of cases, particularly of cases more than a few years out of college. Two large-scale studies carried on by the writer a number of years ago within groups of college graduates may be cited. In neither of these studies was there direct evidence of the differences in mental ability within the groups, but the indices used may be regarded as closely related to it. One was undertaken because earnings data were available for a very large number of cases, although the only measure of ability secured in the original survey was age on entry to college. Since other factors undoubtedly delayed the college entrance of many able high-school graduates, this factor is admittedly imperfect, but within a large group it presumably differentiated broadly between college entrants whose earlier scholastic achievements had been above, close to, or below the average of such entrants.

Table 4 presents earnings data selected by this criterion. In view of its limitations, the resulting pattern is surprisingly regular and indicates a significant relationship, despite large overlaps between the age at entry groups.

TABLE 4. — MEDIAN EARNINGS BY AGE ON ENTERING COLLEGE: 19,568 GRADUATES OF LAND GRANT COLLEGES.

(Data as of 1928)

Age on Entry	Years after Graduation			
	1	10	20	30
17½ or less	1600	4050	6100	7200
17½–18½	1600	4050	5900	6800
18½–19½	1600	4050	5600	6500
19½–20½	1600	3800	5200	5700
20½ or more	1600	3700	4500	5000
Total Group	1600	4000	5400	6300

SOURCE: Special study by D. S. Bridgman from U.S. Office of Education data, published in part in Bulletin No. 9, 1930 report on Land Grant College Survey. Bridgman's report, not including this table, published in *Journal of Engineering Education*, XXII (November 1931), 175.

The data for Table 5 also have been taken from a study made about 1928, but the preliminary findings, with regard to college scholarship, of a similar study now under way in the Bell Telephone System seem to parallel very closely those presented here. In order to sharpen the scholarship criterion, institutions which are included in the new study have been classified into four groups on the basis of their scholastic standards, and preliminary findings indicate higher correlations between salary and combinations of scholarship and institutional groups. The earlier findings with respect to extracurricular achievement have been included in the chart to bring out the fact that, for college graduates employed in the Bell System, scholarship seemed to be more highly related to salary progress than such achievement. The new study also confirms that finding. In both studies, salary progress was determined by the relation of actual salary to years since bachelor's degree.

TABLE 5. — DISTRIBUTION OF COLLEGE GRADUATES BY SALARY GROUPS: 1310 GRADUATES 4 OR MORE YEARS OUT OF COLLEGE IN BELL TELEPHONE SYSTEM.

Scholarship Rank	Number of Cases	Salary Thirds		
		First	Second	Last
First Tenth	185	53%	29%	18%
First Third	552	45	29	26
Middle Third	511	27	38	35
Last Third	247	22	33	45
Campus Achievement				
Substantial	247	43	33	24
Some	442	35	34	31
None	621	28	34	38

Salaries weighted to eliminate geographical differences.
Data from D. S. Bridgman, "Success in College and Business," American Telephone and Telegraph Company — *Personnel Journal* (June 1930).

The material thus far presented has dealt mainly with the current differences in income of high-school and college graduates and the influence of factors other than level of education which seem likely to affect the magnitude of such differences. It also would seem useful to examine the trend of the incomes or earnings of these two groups over a period of years. Unfortunately no comparable data for both groups for years prior to World War II seem to be available, but the Land Grant College study already mentioned does provide median earnings by age for a highly representative sample of college graduates in 1928, which can be compared with the 1956 incomes of such graduates.

Actually, that study also collected information concerning the earlier earnings of the responding graduates which indicated that between 1914 and 1928, beginning earnings had increased about 60 per cent and earnings of men with five or more years of experience about 40 per cent. During this interval, industrial earnings generally had increased 120 per cent and the cost of living 70 per cent.[2]

Table 6 presents similar information for the 1928–1956 and 1949–1956 intervals. Although there is no valid reason to doubt the representative character of the Land Grant College sample, the earnings secured from it stated in round figures have been reduced arbitrarily by 10 per cent and the adjusted figure has been designated as total income. This results in the minimum base from which to calculate the percentage increases to make certain they are not understated.

levels and, during the war and immediate postwar period, the policy of salary increases equated to cents-per-hour wage increases resulted in relatively small increments on a percentage basis. In addition the 1949 incomes of the large number of college graduates who were veterans of World War II had been adversely affected by delayed graduations for the younger men and interruptions in promotions and related salary increases for the prewar graduates. As a consequence, the incomes of college graduates suffered a severe lag in the adjustment to postwar economic levels, and their rapid rise since 1949 is in part the recovery of lost ground.

Another factor of possible major importance is the fact that in 1910, the usual year of college graduation for men forty years old in 1928, the ratio of males receiving bachelors' degrees to all males twenty-two years old was

TABLE 6. — [a] TRENDS IN MEDIAN INCOMES OF MALE COLLEGE GRADUATES COMPARED WITH GENERAL ECONOMIC INDICES

Year		College Graduates Median Incomes by Age			Average Weekly Earnings — Production Workers	Consumers Price Index
		25–34	35–44	45–54		
1928	Land-grant College Graduates (Earnings)	3000	5000	6000	..	..
1928	All Graduates (Incomes)	2700	4500	5400	24.97	73.3
1949	All Graduates (Incomes)	3500	5100	5500	54.92	101.8
1956	All Graduates (Incomes)	5400	7500	8800	79.99	116.2
					Percentage Increase	
1928 to 1956	Percentage Increase	100%	67%	62%	220%	59%
1949 to 1956	Percentage Increase	54%	47%	58%	46%	9%

[a] 1928 Earnings from D. S. Bridgman "Earnings of Land Grant College Alumni and Former Students," *Journal of Engineering Education*, XXII (November 1931).
1949 incomes of college graduates from *Special Report on Education* — 1950 Census. 1956 incomes from unpublished data of H. P. Miller — U.S. Bureau of the Census, based on Current Population Survey.
Average weekly earnings for production workers and Consumers' Price Index figures (Base 1947–49) from publications of U.S. Bureau of Labor Statistics.

In interpreting the fact that a large proportion of the total 1928–1956 increase in college-graduate incomes occurred after 1949, as contrasted with the small proportion of the increases in wages and prices, it will be recognized that most of the years between 1928 and 1949 were those of depression and of war. During the Depression, salary levels, when related to age, suffered far more loss than wage

[2] Paul H. Douglas, *Real Wages in the United States, 1890–1926* (Boston, Houghton Mifflin, 1930).

about 3 per cent. In 1940, when those approaching forty in 1956 had graduated, this ratio was about 9 per cent. In 1956 itself, the corresponding ratio had become about 18 per cent. With continued high levels of business activity and the mounting demand for highly trained and competent men in management and many of the professions, the opportunities and commensurate rewards for such men seem certain to continue, but the income figures shown in Table 1 for the lowest quartile of college graduates raise doubts about the effect of continued increases in the rate of college graduation for those less qualified for such fields.

The material presented in this paper may be summarized as follows.

1. The differences between the lifetime incomes of high school and college graduates, as well as the amounts of such incomes, were substantially greater in 1956 than in 1949.

2. These differences, however, are increased by the fact that college costs have not been deducted from them and by the larger unearned incomes of college graduates.

3. Differences derived from mean or average lifetime incomes are greatly affected by a limited number of high incomes, in some cases resulting from earnings influenced by family connections or unearned income and far more common among college graduates. The difference in income for the two educational levels derived from median lifetime incomes for each, computed from 1956 data, was only 60 per cent of that derived from the means. The difference for the upper limit of the lowest quarters of the two groups was half that for the medians and one-third that for the lower limit of their top quarters.

4. Evidence of marked differences in the ability levels of high school and college graduates was presented for a large sample of World War II veterans, likely to be reasonably representative of one of the age groups included in the 1956 data. Such ability differences, as reflected in scholastic achievement, were shown to have some influence on the salary progress of two groups of college graduates. They are one major factor in the higher incomes of college graduates as compared with high-school graduates.

5. Although from 1928 to 1956, the incomes of college graduates increased only one-third to one-half as rapidly as those of production workers and, except for those under thirty-five years old, only slightly more rapidly than the Consumers' Price Index, much of this lag was due to the Depression and World War II. Recent increases have paralleled those of other groups but the future effect on them of larger proportions of college graduates in oncoming youth is uncertain.

It seems clear that there is serious danger of exaggeration of the monetary values in a college education and that the influence of other factors, such as higher ability levels, in the larger incomes of college graduates have not been adequately recognized. It will be most useful to have information concerning earnings as well as incomes secured in the 1960 Census, but other studies concerning the earnings and position levels of graduates from different curricula and of the relations between achievement in college and in later life are needed. Much greater understanding by the public of the elements in this problem is required. In particular, individuals whose abilities and interests indicate that their success as college graduates is likely to be well below average may recognize the very small monetary return to be expected from a college degree and seek other more appropriate training or occupations. This may well spare them frustration and sense of failure and lead to greater satisfaction in their work and a happier life. Realistic decisions of this kind on a substantial scale also may relieve four-year institutions of students not capable of meeting high standards of scholastic work and contributing to a stimulating intellectual atmosphere. Without such standards and stimulation in not only a few but a large number of our colleges and universities, we may fail to provide the challenge essential for the full development of able students whom our society must count on as its leaders in an increasingly complex world.

INCREASING PRODUCTIVITY IN HIGHER EDUCATION

Alvin C. Eurich

IN education we seem to dread the word "efficiency." It is a word from business, and educational institutions must not be businesses. At the same time we know, however reluctantly, that competition was the principal factor that forced business to develop efficient procedures. Colleges and universities, now faced with the prospect of demands and expenditures rising faster than income, are just starting to learn what business had to find out long ago: that resources — financial, physical, and human — can and must go further in the future than they have in the past.

The urgency of finding new ways to stretch dollars for the educational program is clearly indicated by the following projections on the financial outlook for institutions of higher education in the years ahead. Assuming 1952–1958 trends continue, Table 1 shows what changes may be expected.

TABLE 1. — PROJECTED CHANGES IN HIGHER EDUCATION

Item	1958–59	1969–70	Change (percentage)
Students enrolled at colleges and universities	3,500,000	6,500,000	plus 85
Teaching staff (Full-time and part-time)	330,000	600,000	plus 82
Operating expenditures	$ 4.2 billion	$ 9.3 billion	plus 120
Capital expenditures	$ .7 billion	$ 1.4 billion	plus 100
Taxes for higher education	$ 2.3 billion	$ 4.6 billion	plus 100
Gross national product	$450 billion	$700 billion	plus 55

In 1959 total expenditures for higher education — capital and current items together — amounted to 1.1 per cent of the gross national product. By 1970, assuming unemployment of not more than 4 per cent and using 1958–59 price levels, the gross national product can be expected to be not less than $700 billion, with approximately 1.5 per cent allotted to higher education.

On the basis of these projections the country's ability to meet the growing needs of higher education in the coming decade is certainly unquestionable. The problem will be how to make the necessary proportion of national income available to education as enrollments rise and the expenditure needs for education increase.

The outlook for the future of our colleges and universities makes it imperative that they utilize every new idea and technique which might improve the quality of education and at the same time put into practice the most efficient and economically intelligent methods. Staff organization and function, proper budgeting, cost control, more accurate accounting, and close attention to investments are all promising areas for improving the business management of educational institutions.

In recent years a number of educational institutions across the country have explored procedures for achieving economies while maintaining or raising the caliber of their instruction. Management surveys supported by the Fund for the Advancement of Education in about forty colleges and universities reveal that in most cases the operation and maintenance of plant can be more efficient. In one case, for example, a large university was able to save approximately a million dollars on campus maintenance alone during an eighteen-month period following a survey, a sum roughly equivalent to the income on a $20 million endowment.

Institutions will have to analyze their business practices more critically. At the very minimum, they should charge the full cost of operation for dormitories, dining halls, and auxiliary enterprises of all kinds, including ski tows, golf courses, tennis courts, and book stores. Full costs should be determined on a cost-accounting basis and should include such charges as those for utilities, overhead, depreciation of building, and management services.

There are many who believe that, in addition, certain high-prestige colleges which feature very costly educational programs should charge the full cost of their academic programs, and provide scholarships and loans to those students who cannot afford to pay their full share.

Thus through greater efficiency in business management, the educational dollar can be stretched much farther under the direction of imaginative individuals in colleges and universities who are dissatisfied with old procedures, as the managers of modern business firms would be with the methods of earlier centuries.

Even greater possibilities for economies than in business management exist in the reorganization of the educational aspects of college and university programs.

A first step is the *greater utilization of educational plant*. At most institutions this is a sensitive subject dealt with almost wholly by the academic administration. An official of one midwestern college put it this way: "We run our college from 9:00 to 12:00 and 1:00 to 4:00, five days a week, eight and a half months a year, and we like it that way."

At Stanford University, when we made a study of the utilization of space in 1941–42 in order to plan for the postwar rise in enrollments, we found that our classrooms were used primarily in the morning up to noon, our laboratories were used in the afternoons but never in the mornings. We concluded from this study that we could double the enrollment, and do all the teaching in existing space. In the postwar years we actually found that with more than twice our prewar number of students, practically no new classrooms or laboratories had to be built for teaching purposes. More careful scheduling, so that both laboratories and classrooms were used throughout the entire day, solved the problem.

A space-utilization study made in 1956 by John Dale Russell for the American Association of Collegiate Registrars and Admissions Officers showed that, taking only forty-four hours a week as a base for maximum utilization, classrooms in 101 institutions were used 46 per cent of the time and teaching laboratories only 38 per cent of the time. When Russell analyzed the use of space in terms of student stations — that is, on how much a student chair, desk or laboratory space was filled during the forty-four-hour week — he found that these were occupied only 25 per cent of the time.

According to a management firm which specializes in space utilization studies:

For existing facilities it is possible, with rescheduling, to achieve a 60 per cent station-utilization rate in classrooms and 80 per cent in laboratories. . . In new facilities, rescheduling will permit attainment of a 70 per cent rate for classrooms and 80 per cent for laboratories.

How greatly space utilization can affect college and university financing is suggested by this same firm's estimates of institutional needs between 1957 and 1970: (a) $4.3 billion for new plant, if better space programing is carried out in both existing and new facilities; (b) $7.2 billion, if such space programing is implemented in new structures only; (c) $12.7 billion, if no improvement occurs in space utilization practices between 1957 and 1970.

Already some colleges and universities are uneasy about their idle plant and its poor utilization when classes are in session. However, with billions of dollars of plant idle for almost one-third of the year and one-half of the working day, they can hardly expect a generous response from business and industry in new drives for capital funds, if they do not attempt to put their houses in order.

A second area for improved efficiency is *better utilization of human resources*, particularly faculty. I mention only a few possibilities.

(a) Establish a student-faculty ratio of about 20:1, which would be considerably above the 13:1 ratio now existing at colleges and universities. This could be gradually achieved as the student body expands, by grouping students according to what they do to learn, rather than what the teacher does. At different times students listen, read, look, think, write, discuss, or do research. If we focused attention on creating the best conditions for student learning, we would make major adjustments in the ways we arrange students and teachers on the campus. This would lead to large economies and, in many cases, better education.

(b) Reduce the number of hours the student spends in class, from fifteen hours a week to perhaps twelve, to be accompanied by more independent work.

Some other steps that could be taken for better utilization would be to reduce the number of courses available, and to increase the use of new teaching devices, such as television, language laboratories, films, tape recordings, and teaching machines.

With roughly similar assumptions, as Beardsley Ruml has pointed out, a college of 3,000 students meeting on a three-term year basis could operate with no more than 150 faculty members to teach 1,050 courses or sections a year. At least 50 of these courses could be in the form of lectures, with an average attendance of 180 students. All students would take one large lecture course each term. In addition, there could be 100 lecture-discussion courses averaging 90 students each, and 900 more classes averaging 10 students each. These arrangements would result in faculty members teaching an average of 9⅓ hours per week. If a tuition of $800 per student was allocated to faculty salaries, the average compensation could be $12,000 plus fringe benefits, with a top of $30,000 a year. Such a program, carefully designed and competently staffed, could offer a first-class liberal education and a broad introduction to learning. In view of what seems the universal human tendency to resist change, it would undoubtedly be resisted by many faculty members.

Cooperation in sharing educational resources among several institutions within a limited geographical radius is another promising approach just beginning to be developed. This emerging pattern puts into effect many of the points already mentioned. In practice it has already proved valuable to some groups of institutions in reducing course duplication, extending the services of faculty to more students, and pooling library materials and graduate facilities in various imaginative ways.

Although we need better utilization of faculty members to help solve financial problems of colleges and universities, we also need it to solve the general shortage of highly-educated manpower. In 1953–54, 31 per cent of new full-time college teachers had the Ph.D. degree, and the percentage since then has dropped steadily. It has been estimated that if present trends continue, by 1970 the percentage may be only 15 per cent, and that weaker institutions may be without a single Ph.D. on their staffs.[1]

No crash program can possibly provide us with the well-trained college faculty members who should have been educated in the past decade to provide for the growing enrollments in colleges and universities. Moreover, the shortage is aggravated by current educational practices, for it takes eight to ten years and great incentive to acquire a doctoral degree. Nothing points this up more sharply than a report which summarizes the time spent by Columbia University graduate students earning their doctoral degrees between 1940 and 1956. Although we ordinarily assume that it takes three years to acquire a Ph.D. degree from the time a student registers until he completes all his work, it was found that the shortest average number of years spent in acquiring the doctorate was in the Department of Chemistry, where the 345 persons who were granted the degree between 1940 and 1956 averaged 5.3 years. The longest average was in the Department of Germanic Languages, where 34 students averaged 12.5 years to get their Ph.D.'s. And of these new doctorates, relatively few will now enter college teaching, for lack of reasonable monetary rewards. Financial incentives, however, can only come with greater productivity, and with them a new status for faculty members, but as yet the incentives do not exist, and time is running out.

The profession of teaching is the only profession in American society that has been untouched by the revolution that has transformed agriculture, industry, and all the other professions during the past fifty years. Only in teaching do we continue to place arbitrary limits on the extent to which an individual can serve mankind. In all other professions, the practitioner is rewarded both in prestige and in economic returns on the basis of the number of people he can serve. New possibilities can and must be developed in the teaching profession to extend the utilization of the best teachers on college and university campuses more widely, and to reward them accordingly.

There is no doubt that the educational dollar can go much further, through a realistic analysis of income and a more efficient spending of funds. Colleges and universities will be supported, parents will pay for the cost of educating their sons and daughters, for we in America

[1] Cf. President Wilson's essay, pages 115–117.

have great faith in education. We have experience, too, in other fields, in the better utilization of our resources. This is the task of college and university administration in the years immediately ahead. It involves making each available dollar mean most for the education of our youth. It involves salaries for faculty members comparable to those for equal competence and experience outside of universities. It involves making our educational institutions most effective in the development of the capacities of youth so that they may make their maximum contribution to our free society. In short, it involves the greatest possible use of the most important resources we have available — our human resources.

TEACHING MACHINES

B. F. Skinner

[At the Seminar on the Economics of Higher Education, Professor Skinner demonstrated two types of teaching machine. In one, incomplete arithmetic problems or incomplete spellings of words are presented to the grade-school student. The student completes the material by moving sliders bearing printed figures or letters. The student then turns a crank and, if his setting was correct, the machine presents a new set of materials. If his response was incorrect, it is cleared, and the same material must be completed again. In a second machine, designed for high-school and college students and used during the past two years in Professor Skinner's classes, the student writes a word or two which completes material presented by the machine. The student then operates a lever which puts his answer under a transparent cover and uncovers the correct answer. The student compares, records the correctness of his answer, and moves on to the next frame. He goes through the same material a second time, when the machine presents only those items previously missed. (Ed.)]

ONE thing which this machine does is to inspire the student; it gives him a high degree of competence and confidence. The long-term goals in education, like wanting to be a doctor, have little effect upon the student at the moment. He may tell you that he really wants an education, but he cannot write that term paper or read that text, and for a very good reason: nothing happens when he does. Something may happen a year or five years later, but that is too late.

In studying by machine something is happening all the time. The student continues to participate, in contrast with watching television, for example, where he may just sit and stare. He is active, and he gets something positive out of it which keeps him going.

Students will tell you this. They are learning, and they know it. Many of them say that it is a weird experience; they know something at the end of the hour which they cannot remember having learned.

The question of the programs to be used in the machines is important. It is difficult to construct such a program. It has many items — possibly eight or ten thousand for a one-term college course. To construct these items the teacher must be clear about what he wants to teach. He must analyze his end product. What does he want a student to do by the end of the term?

Once the teacher has decided that, he has his end points — complete ignorance and complete competence. He must now bridge them with a series of eight or ten thousand steps — not an easy task. But though he may not strike out a good program all at once, the teacher will have the benefit of a remarkable corrective feedback. By analyzing the responses of perhaps fifty students to a set of, say, thirty items, one can spot every bad item. Nothing like this is possible in a textbook or instructional film. The teacher cannot say, "Students do not understand the third sentence on page 57." But here he does know what the students understand, item by item. And an instructor can improve a program to the point at which practically no mistakes are made. Although we do not yet know how best to make up a program, we have every reason to believe that we can find out very soon.

There is no reason why most beginning courses cannot be taught this way in their entirety. A machine and a proper program should teach beginning French, for example. The teacher can then discuss French literature and culture, converse in French, and so on. The student moves up to a more advanced level quickly, and the teacher has a chance to do the kind of things which interest him as a human being.

Experiments on programming offer an opportunity to analyze verbal knowledge and the process of instruction of verbal knowledge. For example, in a technique which is now being studied, the right answer is at first out of focus. The student slowly brings it into focus, stopping as soon as he is able to get the right answer. We can study how much help is needed for the right answer at various stages in learning. The student profits from finding the answer with as little help as possible because he learns more efficiently under such circumstances.

Another possible feature in a machine would require the student to estimate his level of confidence. He puts down an answer and then pushes one of three buttons meaning "Guessing," "Maybe," and "Sure." If he says, "I am sure," and is wrong, his score suffers. If he says, "I am guessing," there is no penalty, and so on. The student learns to evaluate his confidence and adopt a useful strategy. However, if such techniques introduce significant anxiety factors, they can be discarded.

Students average about fifteen hours on the material we have. The novelty doesn't wear off. It is the material which is novel, not the machine. It isn't a very good pinball machine. We have thought of having the grade-school machine pay off occasionally with tokens which could be exchanged for privileges. But it appears that a student doesn't need extrinsic reinforcement when he is being successful. It is not the amount of reinforcement but the schedule of successes which counts.

I am afraid that programs must be centrally devised rather than set up by individual faculty members, at least in the initial period. It is difficult to make programs. However, we try to use material in such a physical form that anyone can prepare his own if he wants to do so. The danger is that people are going to start using machines without knowing what programming is all about. Teachers try to make quizzing machines of them, which is the worst possible misuse.

The programs are designed to begin with very easy material. The instructor builds on what the student already knows. At each stage the student's subject is practically completely covered. Each step is a very easy step, but it is always in the direction in which the instructor wants his student to go. It is surprising how quickly the student progresses.

Some critics have called the sample program in the reference "a very slow program in physics." But what does "slow" mean? In terms of time, it is actually fast, since the average student can master it more quickly than a comparable portion of text.

Some students have a sense of responsibility which would make a booklet with questions and answers almost equally satisfactory, but many will not use the same material in book form properly. We need not bother about those who will anyway, for they are going to be educated in spite of us. It isn't that the student actually cheats; it is simply so much easier to cut corners. Moreover, the college needs some control over the student's learning if the student is to receive grades.

Some people feel that some anxiety and unpleasant discipline are necessary features of learning. All I want is the final product of an educated man. I don't care how he reaches that condition, whether he works or takes it easy. I can get him there much more readily if he takes it easy.

It is sometimes suggested that television and the machines be used jointly for courses involving extensive verbal presentations, with the machines requiring responses. The only trouble is that television is incompatible with the machines in principle because it presupposes a class with all members moving at the same rate. This is the greatest source of inefficiency in education. This is what is wrong with efforts to "mechanize" classrooms with wire recorders and so on.

The psychology questions in the machine now are relatively simple materials, for it is a beginning course. But there is no reason why machine self-instruction cannot go as far as knowledge can be satisfactorily formulated. I should not expect more advanced courses in our educational institutions to be taught this way. The human teacher still has his place.

As to age level, machine instruction is as good for graduate students as for high school. Many corporations are interested in it for industrial training. We have not found any appreciable differences by sex, either. I have a rather selected group of Radcliffe students, but they stand up very well on the machine material and are among those, I think, who are most enthusiastic about it.

I do not see any differences in types of mind which might require different kinds of material.

I do see great differences in speed and possibly in retention. We have had two or three failures in some three-hundred-odd students. They go through material many times with little to show for having done so. I have sent them back to go through the whole set again, hoping that something would click. In one or two cases, it has, and they have suddenly got the point of the whole course.

If there proves to be anything more than speed differences in the problems of these students, different kinds of programs will have to be set up. But I do not see the need at the moment.

SOME OBSERVATIONS ON THE ALLOCATION OF RESOURCES IN HIGHER EDUCATION

Kenneth Deitch

THERE exists some sentiment to the effect that economic analysis is an inappropriate discipline to apply to the study of higher education. This sentiment exists, I believe, because of a misunderstanding on the part of those who share it of what the economist takes his objectives to be. Let me try to state briefly what these objectives are and what they are not: the economist does not want to channel resources away from higher education by "cutting costs" per se. Rather, he is simply interested in achieving what at a high level of generality may be called the "best use" of available resources within the framework of values that the administrators have established.

Thus the problem to be considered is an allocation of resources problem. Having recognized this fact we would do well to remind ourselves first of the purpose and then of the general principles of investment theory. From the viewpoint of an administrator the purpose of investment theory is to present criteria which will enable him to determine how to allocate his institution's resources. Ideally, the proper use of these criteria shows the decision-maker how to allocate his resources in such a way that the gap between his ideal objectives and his real achievements is as small as it can be under the existing conditions.

What then are the criteria which have been established in traditional investment theory? The two most widely considered concepts are the present value criterion and the marginal returns criterion. The present value method is applicable to a situation in which the decision-maker must choose between two alternative investment outlets because he has enough capital to undertake only one of them. The present value criterion thus answers the question, "Which one?" The decision is made on the basis of a present value calculation; the project whose discounted present value is greater is pursued. The marginal returns criterion is applicable in a different type of situation. It is used where the alternative investments do not require any one specific quantity of capital but rather where it is possible to make use of varying amounts of the output from each investment. The situation no longer involves an all-or-nothing decision; rather it is a substitution problem. Thus, whereas the present value criterion answers the question, "Which one?" the marginal returns criterion answers the question, "How much of each one?" It tells the decision-maker to allocate his capital between any two investment outlets in such a way that the returns on the last unit of capital placed in each outlet are equal. For, if the returns on the last unit placed in the first outlet exceed the returns on the last unit placed in the second outlet, the total returns can be increased by transferring units of capital from the second to the first investment. It is clear then that the total returns will be maximized only when the returns on the marginal or incremental unit are the same in both outlets.

From the viewpoint of a college administrator the interesting question is this: to what extent can the present value and the marginal returns calculations help to achieve the proper allocation of resources within an educational institution? I would suggest that these criteria are useful conceptually, but that in their present form they cannot give definitive and quantitative answers to the questions, "Which one?" and "How much of each one?" This conclusion is, in itself, hardly surprising. It is, however, useful, for by explicitly spelling out the reasoning which leads me to it I hope to accomplish two aims: first, I hope to point out some of the fundamental issues involved in the allocation of resources in education, and second, I hope to lead up to the subsequent development of the specific allocation criteria for education which I advocate below.

Why then are these two criteria of limited usefulness? The answer to this question can best be understood if we compare the educational institution to the theoretical business unit in a competitive world. For the business unit there is only one objective which is consistent with survival, and this is a monetary objective — namely, profit maximization. It is therefore possible to measure in dollar terms both costs and returns, the two major variables which enter into the present value and marginal returns calculations, when we are considering the business unit. Quite the contrary is true for an educational institution. It has not one but many objectives, all of which are consistent with survival, and none of which is monetary in any meaningful sense. Thus, although the costs, exclusive of opportunity costs, of investment in education are calculable in dollar terms, the returns are not, and this is the crux of the matter. In general, in order for the present value and the marginal returns criterion to be applicable, two conditions must be satisfied. First, returns and costs must both be measurable in cardinal terms, and second, both must be defined in the same units. It is clear from the above discussion that at present these conditions are satisfied in the case of the theoretical business unit but not in the case of the educational institution. And it is this fact which leads me to conclude that the present value and the marginal returns criterion, in their current form, are of limited usefulness for determining the proper allocation of resources within education. But it is not sufficient merely to recognize this fact; the next task — and the really important one from the point of view of an administrator — is to develop some general systematic framework, some useful criteria, which can help the administrator to make the proper allocation decisions. I turn now to that task.

There are two general lines of approach open to us. Either we can completely abandon the traditional criteria and develop some new methods of analysis, or else we can stick with these traditional criteria and try to overcome the impediments which render them, at present, nonoperational. I feel strongly that we ought to adopt the latter policy and work within the general framework of the traditional criteria, because these criteria are demonstrably correct. The only reason we find them difficult to use is that we have not yet devised good methods for obtaining the necessary data, but this is not sufficient justification for abandoning the methods; it is only an argument in favor of developing ways of defining and measuring that data.

The administrative problem which I wish to consider is the short-run problem of allocating a fixed amount of dollar resources among a number of competing activities whose magnitudes can be both increased and decreased in the short run; for simplicity and clarity, this can be called the allocation problem.

There are some preliminary rules of thumb which the administrator must follow before he can make his allocation decisions. These can be discussed under three headings: (1) knowing the objectives of the institution and determining the relative importance of each objective, (2) knowing those variables over which the administrator has control and those variables which he must regard as externally determined, and (3) determining where relations exist between changes in the relevant variables and achievement of the desired objectives. Each of these rules deserves brief comment.

That a clear statement of objectives and of the relative importance of each is a necessary prerequisite to an intelligent allocation decision may in fact be an obvious point, but it is also a crucially important one and, for that reason, deserves special emphasis. One can not determine to what extent any particular investment or allocation is useful until some desired ends have been clearly specified and evaluated relatively. Again, we can profit by comparing the educational institution to the theoretical business unit. The business unit's objective is clearly defined, and its investment policy is rationally determined with this objective in mind. To be sure, an administrator of an educational institution does not have as easy a task in defining his objectives as does the business manager. Nevertheless, there is one fact which ought to impress the educational administrator as he observes his business counterpart, and it is this: the relative facility with which a business manager can make the proper investment and allocation decisions is a direct result of the fact that he has a clear concept of his objectives and of their relative importance.

It is another obvious fact that it is desirable for an administrator to know the variables which affect his institution and to distinguish between those which he can control and those which are beyond his control. The only point I would make here is that the allocation problems which confront administrators will be more easily and more nearly correctly solved in direct proportion to the specificity with which the relevant variables are determined. In short, an intuitive approach to this problem is a poor substitute for empirical knowledge.

The third rule-of-thumb proposition — namely, determining where relations exist between changes in the relevant variables and achievement of the desired objectives — must be carefully differentiated from the more ambitious project of determining precisely what those relations may be. To determine where these relations exist we simply want to answer this type of question: if I change variable A, will this influence the achievement of objective P? Once we have determined where relationships exist, we shall then want to describe exactly what these relationships are; we shall want to answer this type of question: if I change variable A in the following way, how will this influence the achievement of objective P? I shall deal with this latter problem shortly. For now there are two comments which ought to be made about the former problem of determining where these relations exist: first, this is an exercise in imaginative as well as in methodical thinking, for the problem can become quite complex, and the answers are not always immediately apparent. Second, it is important to have a clear idea of all the relations that do exist, because the flexibility of operation which administrators permit themselves and the potential for maximizing their achievement are both directly proportional to their knowledge about the existence of these relationships.

Having considered these three general propositions, we can turn now to the allocation problem. I have devised a schematic framework for dealing with this problem. I shall describe this system in general terms and then proceed to present a concrete example of the way in which these tools might be used by an administrator to solve a specific allocation problem. Consider Figure 1. This square matrix is the central tool of the system; when the proper data have been entered into it, it will be what I have called a resource substitution chart.

How is this matrix to be dealt with and what does it represent? Across the top of the matrix, from left to right, and down the left side, from top to bottom, where "1st, 2nd, 3rd," and so forth now appear, the variables over which the administrator has control are to be listed in descending order on the basis

RESOURCE SUBSTITUTION CHART

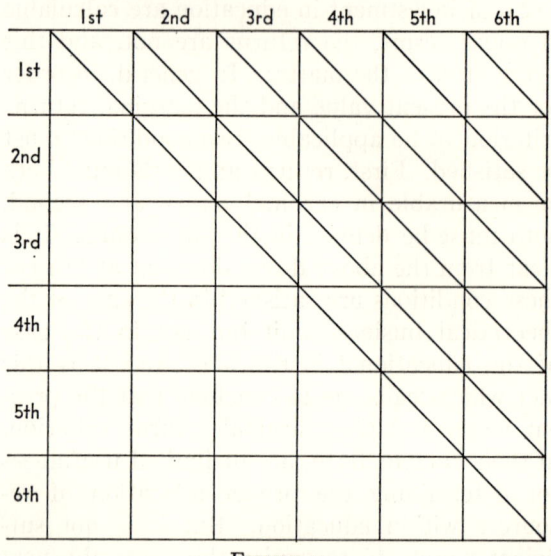

FIGURE 1

of the benefits that the institution would reap from a one-unit change in each. This requirement presupposes two things: first, that we can measure the contribution that a one-unit change in any variable makes towards the objective that it influences, and second, that we can weigh all the objectives and thus say something to the effect that a change which decreases the gap between our actual achievement and the ideal achievement of objective R by 1 per cent is three times as valuable as a change which decreases the gap between our actual achievement and the ideal achievement of objective Q by 1 per cent. Assume, for the moment, that these requirements can be fulfilled. Note also that all the squares to the left of the large diagonal can be ignored, since the data are repetitive.

What numbers are to be put in the matrix? Each square represents a connection between two activities; in each one there is a place for two numbers, one above and one below the diagonal line. Above the line we are going to enter a ratio which is the rate at which the two activities may be substituted for each other while the total costs are being held constant. For example, if the square which is the intersection of the third row and the fifth column has the ratio 1:6 above the diagonal line, this means that the cost of a one-unit change in the third variable is equal to the cost of a six-unit change in the fifth variable. Below the line we are going to enter a ratio which is the rate at which the two variables may be substituted for each other while the total benefits, defined in terms of the institution's objectives, are being held constant. For example, if the square which is the intersection of the third row and the fifth column has the ratio 1:4 below the diagonal line, this means that the benefits from a one-unit change in the third variable are equal to the benefits from a four-unit change in the fifth variable. Thus, when it has been completely filled in, the resource substitution chart might look something like this:

RESOURCE SUBSTITUTION CHART

	1st	2nd	3rd	4th	5th
1st	1:1 / 1:1	1:10 / 1:3	1:7 / 1:7	1:5 / 1:9	20:1 / 1:20
2nd		1:1 / 1:1	1:18 / 1:4	1:1 / 1:5	4:1 / 1:17
3rd			1:1 / 1:1	1:5 / 1:3	1:6 / 1:4
4th				1:1 / 1:1	1:8 / 1:6
5th					1:1 / 1:1

FIGURE 2

A word about calculating these ratios is in order. The necessary cost data are available, and the answer to the question, what will it cost to increase variable A by one unit, can easily be determined. Once all of these numbers are known, calculating the required cost ratios is routine. I want to postpone discussing the measurement of the benefits ratios; let us simply assume for the moment that they can be calculated.

Assuming now that the matrix has been completely filled in, we must determine the criteria that will lead to the optimum allocation of resources. There are two points to keep in mind: first, the cost ratios are constant, but the benefits ratios will change as the allocation of resources changes. Second, we should remind ourselves that the ideal solution is that allocation of resources which yields the maximum benefits for given cost. The general rule is that the optimum occurs when the cost ratio and the returns ratio are equal in each square. Where they are not equal, substitutions can be made to bring about the required equilibrium. The rule for making these substitutions is this: if one variable's cost advantage is less than its returns advantage over another variable, the first variable should be increased and the second decreased, and vice versa. Specifically, if the cost ratio is 1:6 and the returns ratio is 1:7 between two variables, we should increase the first and decrease the second; if the cost ratio is 1:6 and the returns ratio is 1:5, we should increase the second and decrease the first.

This system will become more easily comprehensible if we consider a simple numerical example. This example is presented in tabular form in Tables 1 and 2 and Figure 3. Consider Table 1. In Column 1 I have listed one possible objective that an institution might have, a certain geographical distribution of students within the United States. In Column 2 the unit by which the achievement of this objective is to be measured is defined as the number of states which have three or more students enrolled in the institution. In Column 3 I have listed the two variables which influence the achievement of this activity as, first, the amount of scholarship money made available to students in states with less than three students presently enrolled and, second, the admissions-office activities devoted to attracting students from these states to the institution. This choice of variables is arbitrary; however, these are probably the two most important ones, though the issue is really an empirical one.

In Column 4 the units in which these two variables are to be measured are defined. One unit of the scholarship variable is defined as the average dollar value of the scholarships that are now held, and one unit of the admissions-office variable is defined as one-tenth of a secretary's time plus one trip by a member of the admissions staff to the state in question.

pirical question, but, in order to facilitate the remainder of this discussion, I have supplied what seem to me to be some reasonable numbers. Thus I have said that every time $2800 is spent on scholarships, the institution moves one unit toward the achievement of this particular objective: that is, it increases the number of states with three students enrolled by one.

TABLE 1. — TABULAR SOLUTION FOR THE ALLOCATION PROBLEM

Objectives	Units in which achievement of objective is measured	Variables that influence achievement of objectives	Units in which the variable is measured	Dollar cost of one unit change in variable	Number of units change in objective induced by one unit change in the variable
Geographical distribution of students within the United States	Number of states with three or more students enrolled in institution	(a) scholarship money made available to states with less than three students	1 unit = average dollar value of scholarships presently held	$1400	1/2
		(b) admissions-office activities	1 unit = one-tenth of a secretary's time plus a trip to the state for a man in the admissions office	$700	1/3

TABLE 2. — BENEFITS CALCULATION

Returns from increasing scholarship variable	Returns from increasing admissions variable
Returns from a one-unit increase of the scholarship variable equal the returns from a one-unit increase of the scholarship variable which equal, by observation, the returns from a one and one-half unit increase of the admissions variable.	Returns from a two-unit increase of the admissions variable equal the returns from a two-unit increase of the admissions variable which equal, by simple calculation (when $1/1.5 = \dfrac{x}{2}$, $x = 4/3$), the returns from a 4/3 unit increase of the scholarship variable.

Conclusion: Units of the admissions activity should be substituted for units of the scholarship variable in ratio of 2:1 since, for given cost, the returns from the admissions activity are greater than those from the scholarship variable by a factor of 4/3.

Column 5 contains the dollar cost of a one-unit change in each variable. Thus, the cost of a one-unit change in the scholarship variable might be $1400, and the cost of a one-unit change in the admissions-office variable might be $700.

In Column 6, opposite each variable I have placed the number of units' change in the objective that would occur if we make a one-unit change in that variable. This is an em-

When it spends $1400 it moves one-half a unit towards the objective, and therefore "one-half" is entered in Column 6 opposite the scholarship variable. By similar reasoning I conclude that "one-third" is the proper entry in Column 6 opposite the admissions-office variable. In other words, for every three trips financed, the institution will move one unit towards its objective.

Having discussed Table 1, we can now look

at Figure 3, which is one square of the resource substitution chart. Let this square be the intersection of the scholarship and the admissions-office variables, and consider what ratios to place above and below the diagonal. We recall that the ratio above the line is the rate at which units of the two activities can be substituted for each other without the total cost being changed. The cost of a one-unit change in the scholarship variable is $1400; the cost

stitute in this ratio, the total returns will remain constant. A ratio of 2:3 is the same as a ratio of 1:1.5, and thus this is the figure which appears below the line in the proper square of the resource substitution chart (Figure 3).

Now we have a square of our resource substitution chart with two ratios, one above, the other below the line. These ratios are not equal, and so the proper direction of substitution must be determined. The problem is this:

ONE SQUARE FROM THE RESOURCE SUBSTITUTION CHART

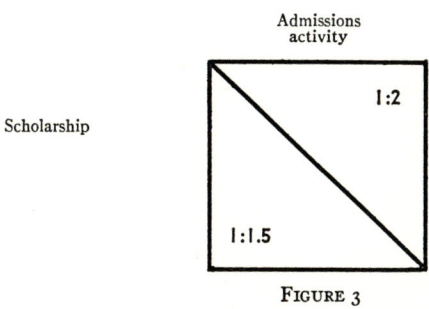

FIGURE 3

of a one-unit change in the admissions-office variable is $700. The proper ratio is thus 1:2. That is, two additional units of the admissions variable cost the same as one additional unit of the scholarship variable.

We recall that the ratio below the line is that rate at which the two variables may be substituted for each other while the total returns remain constant. Column 6 of Table 1 indicates that a one-unit change in the scholarship variable will induce a one-half unit change in the achievement of our objective. Or, what is the same thing, a two-unit change in the scholarship variable will induce a one-unit change in the achievement of our objective. Column 6 also tells us that a one-unit change in the admissions variable will induce a one-third unit change in the achievement of our objective. Or, what is the same thing, a three-unit change in this variable will induce a one-unit change in the achievement of our objective.

Thus, a two-unit change in the scholarship variable and a three-unit change in the admissions variable both induce a one-unit change toward the objective. The proper ratio of substitution is, therefore, 2:3, for if we sub-

the ratio above the line indicates that the administrator may have one unit of the scholarship variable or two units of the admissions variable for the same cost. He must decide which he wants, and he will do this by calculating the benefits from each alternative and choosing the one which gives greater benefits.

Consider Table 2. From the left column we conclude that the returns from one unit of the scholarship variable equal, according to Figure 3, the returns from one and one-half units of the admission variable. From the right column of Table 2 we conclude that the returns from two units of the admissions variable equal, according to Figure 3, the returns from four-thirds units of the scholarship variable. Thus, by substituting two units of the admission variable for one unit of the scholarship variable, an administrator can get, for the same cost, returns which are greater by a factor of four-thirds. Substitutions should thus be made in this direction until the two ratios are equal. When that occurs, the optimum allocation of resources between these two variables will have been achieved.

I apologize for the fact that these calculations have been so laborious, but my major purpose in presenting this example has been to suggest that this scheme does lend itself to potentially useful empirical work.

It seems appropriate at this point to come to grips with the most complex issue in all of this analysis, the measurement of returns. We must examine the validity of our assumption to the effect that the necessary returns data can be calculated. There are several observations to be made. First, this is an empirical question; the only satisfactory way to answer it is to calculate some numbers and then to decide whether or not the results are meaningful. Second, in the event that no results can be derived through empirical methods, the data will have to be supplied by intuitive estimation. Thus the results will, to a certain extent, represent arbitrary value judgments. But this is hardly sufficient justification for rejecting these results, for, as I have tried to emphasize throughout this paper, the primacy of value judgments is a fact which we are better off in accepting than in ignoring. Furthermore, to the extent that these arbitrary judgments are necessary, the fact that the resource substitution chart requires ordinal rather than cardinal data is a good thing. On an intuitive basis it is easier to assign relative rather than absolute merits to many varied activities. Finally, let me note that the ordering of the variables along the top and down the side of the matrix in descending order on the basis of returns is useful. In the likely event that some of the returns ratios can be explicitly calculated and others can not, this ordering device will help us to estimate the ratios which we can not calculate, for, by definition, we have determined limits within which all the ratios must lie. If, for example, in any column the top returns ratio is 1:20 and the bottom one is 1:1, we know, first, that all the other returns ratios in the column must lie between 1:20 and 1:1 and, second, that they must be ordered.

There are a few general comments which ought to be made about the resource substitution chart and about the criterion which I suggested. First, the method is general and may be applied by all institutions; only the data will change between them. Second, the method is, I hope, both easy and explicit. In presenting all the data in simple pictorial form, it reminds the administrator of substitution possibilities that he might never have considered otherwise. Finally, the notion of allocating costs deserves comment. There exists some sentiment to the effect that it is wrong to attempt to allocate the total costs of an educational institution among its subsidiary activities. I would argue, however, that these costs can and ought to be allocated because there is an investment decision to be made. This cost analysis is necessary if the criterion which I suggested is to be used. Furthermore, in the event that the returns ratios can not be calculated, it will become imperative to know the costs if we are to make any rational allocation decisions at all, for in that case we will be forced to make our decisions by observing what each activity costs and then answering the question, "Is it worth it?"

It should be eminently apparent by now that the measurement of benefits is the most problematical issue in this entire analysis. My own general impression is that research will yield meaningful results which, if they are less than perfect, will still be a better solution than the alternative of making no effort to measure benefits systematically whatsoever. It seems to me then that educational institutions could profit from pursuing this line of inquiry in a systematic fashion.

Finally, I would re-emphasize four general propositions: that education is worthy of careful analysis; that administrators have a moral responsibility to try to achieve the "best" utilization of their resources; that the economist can devise systematic tools to rationalize the allocation process and to facilitate the achievement of the proper allocation decisions; that educational institutions ought to undertake research projects to collect the necessary data so that practical significance can be accorded to the theoretical tools we have been considering.

THE HIGH COST OF LOW-COST EDUCATION

Frank H. Bowles

THE thesis of this paper is that what may appear to be — and may so appear even after fairly close inspection by the casual observer — a plan of higher education which is easy of access, which operates without the usual standard controls at a very low cost so far as the individual is concerned, and at a respectable standard of accreditation, may, in fact, be a relatively high-cost institution which is under such limitations as far as expansion is concerned as to be relatively restricted in its access, is actually overcontrolled by rules and regulations, and is severely limited in its academic horizons and standards. The institution so described is the University of Puerto Rico, a complex and diverse institution enrolling some 15,000 students on three campuses and including among its programs undergraduate liberal arts, business, education, engineering, pharmacy, and agriculture, and among its professional programs law, medicine, public administration, social work, and dentistry. Let it be noted that no graduate program is included in the above listing, and that no junior college or extension program is included.

The University, in existence since 1903, is the absolutely indispensable educational pivot of the island. It provides most of the teacher education that is available; it provides most of the professional education that can be acquired; it supplies the education for government officials, for the entire core of management of Puerto Rican industry and agriculture; it gives basic training and generous assistance to the vast majority of all teachers in colleges and universities in Puerto Rico. In keeping with these many and diverse activities, the University is firmly based upon a concept of freedom of access at all academic levels, of low tuition, and of further amelioration of the existing low cost by subsidy in the form of scholarships at need, and by general lack of restriction and supervision insofar as programs and activities are concerned. Interestingly enough, within this very permissive pattern so far as behavior is concerned, the programs of study offered by the University are notable for their lack of elective courses. Virtually all programs and courses are required.

Within this general pattern, then, which controls the University, five points may be picked out as products of this particular concept of administration.

1. The undergraduate curriculum is sharply split into two different segments. One segment represents a reasonably contemporary general-education approach which holds true for the entire freshman year and part of the sophomore year, for a majority of the undergraduate students. This is followed by an abrupt return to a conventional or departmentalized curriculum operated by the several schools of the University in which, to all intents and purposes, a student, having completed his freshman and part of his sophomore year in the General Studies Program, begins over again in the general subject matter offered in a special area. As a consequence of this, almost no student ever has a chance to get to any of the advanced courses in any field and, in fact, is really debarred from so doing by the program requirements which must be surmounted before he can get to an advanced course. There are, in fact, very few advanced courses listed in the catalog.

2. As a result of the lack of instructional supervision, or as a result of the fact that over three-fourths of the faculty has never progressed beyond the master's degree, all or virtually all of the courses are given by the textbook-and-lecture method. This has several interesting results. (a) Student programs are heavy. They run to eighteen hours or more, and this means that a student who is following a textbook and collating it with instructors' lectures has less studying and in a sense less thinking to do about his courses than a student who is being taught by the reading-list class-discussion method. (b) Students are notably studious and may be found deeply engrossed in their textbooks all over the campus, as well

[199]

as in the University library. However, in the library it is noticeable that they do not read library books.

3. Except in the General Studies (Freshman) Program, there is almost no student advisement. Hence, the students have developed a do-it-yourself advisement program in which they register for overload programs of twenty to twenty-four credit hours per semester. Then, taking advantage of one of the regulations (or a lack of regulations), which permits the dropping of a course up to the night before final examination, they drop courses as it becomes apparent that they will fail them if they continue in them. This method of registration and self-advisement goes on until the student has finally completed his graduation requirements. It must be noted that a surprisingly large number of the University's students do complete their requirements within four years, but it is also to be noted that the percentage staying on beyond four years appears to be quite large, even when the elementary-education students, who form a noticeably separate category, are not considered in this figure. Here it may be well to interpolate that the Registrar's Office is unable to supply accurate statistical information on any such problems as the number of students who enter who subsequently complete their programs, the number of courses not completed by students, the number of students who drop out of the University each year, and the number of students who, having previously attended the University, reregister in a given year after a lapse of time.

It is to be estimated that the cost to the University of Puerto Rico of operating this advisement system in terms of the cost of courses which have to be taught but within which students do not complete their work, classrooms which must be provided for students who complete no courses, space in the library occupied by these students, and various and assorted other costs, tangible and intangible, must certainly amount to approximately $200,000 annually, inasmuch as it is a fair estimate that one-fourth of all courses registered for under such programs are not completed. This may be a conservative figure, for, as noted, there are simply not enough statistics.

4. One of the most striking consequences of the method of instruction in the required courses is the use of the library as a reading room but not for the purpose for which it was intended: namely, as a place to come to draw out books. This may be due in part to the extraordinary precautions taken by the library to keep books from being withdrawn or used. This is the only library in the writer's acquaintance where the reference books are behind a counter and must be drawn on a call slip. Other books are even more tightly controlled, in that they are not even to be seen in the reading room but must in effect be drawn from the stacks. The collections are spotty; some of them are fairly good, but the rate of spending for the library is so slow that it is estimated that the library does not spend the minimum $200,000 a year on books that it should. As a consequence, its book holdings in general fall notably short of the requirements for supporting graduate and advanced professional instruction.

5. As might be expected from a program operating on a textbook-lecture method and supported by a meager library, the faculty is relatively undertrained and is really only safe, in a teaching sense, in textbook-lecture courses. It must be noted that there are no graduate courses in the University, hence no place in Puerto Rico where resident faculty can obtain additional graduate training. Accordingly, the American universities are the graduate schools for the University's faculty, and they, of course, offer no in-service training. As a consequence, any faculty member who wishes to go more deeply into his subject must take a year off from teaching and go to an American graduate school. It is in one sense of the word highly fortunate that the University makes generous provision for fellowships for its faculty. It pays a generous subsistence stipend plus the costs of transportation, books, and supplies. But, although this is fortunate for faculty members seeking training, an interesting result of this generosity in faculty fellowships is that the University faculty have held remarkably few of the fellowships and scholarships granted directly by American graduate schools. In other words, one result appears to be to remove the University's graduates from the need to compete for fellow-

ships and scholarships in the American market. This may or may not be a good idea, but it does tend to throw the entire burden of financing graduate training on the University of Puerto Rico, and in a less tangible sense it has the perhaps damaging effect of removing University faculty from competition with young continental faculty members. The amount of money that is paid out by the Commonwealth of Puerto Rico because the University does not have a graduate school in which it can train its own graduates for its own faculty, plus others of its graduates for civil service and for industrial administration and management and other forms of employment, is approximately $4 million a year. At any rate this is an estimate of the amount spent by the Commonwealth on all forms of graduate instruction, fellowships, and scholarships in continental institutions.

A dispassionate survey of the performance of the University's graduates in American and other institutions is extremely hard to produce since, again, the University's fatal defect in keeping statistics which indicate its actual progress and development has inhibited the keeping of statistics on the performance of its graduate students. There is no follow-up on the students by the University nor is any accounting required, and apparently no penalty or sanction in the event the students fail to get their advanced degrees. These circumstances tend to push up the cost of the graduate degrees that are earned to a point that would probably seem a little short of fantastic if the proper figures could actually be had.

One of the over-all results of these various factors is, curiously, to inhibit further development and expansion of the University in any direction. Some of the inhibitions come from the fact that there is simply not enough new faculty to support an expanded university, and this in turn seems to trace back to the apparent fact that the University's own standards and methods of instruction do not stimulate students to want to stay on and become faculty members. Hence, the University — and this appears to apply particularly to the undergraduate School of Education — appears to be somewhat in a downward spiral of excellence. This is particularly tragic insofar as the School of Education is concerned, since this is the principal supplier of teachers for the Puerto Rican schools. If excellence is not maintained in the School of Education, this deficiency is reflected on the schools themselves, and the University then feels a serious decline in the quality of preparation of its entering students. This decline has already been noticeable, in the view of many of the University faculty. A particularly serious problem of this nature is noted in the science areas, where the number of qualified secondary-school science teachers turned out by the University each year is almost negligible, and the University courses are suffering accordingly.

There is no effective yardstick for measuring the cost of low-cost education as produced at the University of Puerto Rico. The University turns out fewer graduates than it should, and this means that the cost of university education per graduate is high. It appears also that the difficulties in expansion are now definitely limiting the possibilities of obtaining higher education in Puerto Rico, at least under government auspices. High-school enrollment and the number of high-school graduates have expanded in Puerto Rico much more rapidly in a percentage sense than the University enrollments, and the demand for a university-level education is now so great that a number of relatively ineffective and certainly unaccredited institutions have sprung up to meet the demand. The University, in the meantime, does not really make any effective use of its plant after four o'clock in the afternoon and does not have any University centers giving regular classes more than one day a week at any distance from the University. In other words, a substantial educational opportunity is apparently being missed.

The factors having to do with the restriction of University enrollments and with holding down the costs of operating the University by the various expedients already described all have to do with the economy essential in the Island of Puerto Rico, if the complex governmental operations are to be managed within the budgetary restrictions. Perhaps the greatest casualty of all these restrictions has been the whole field of education, which is even more handicapped with respect to primary and secondary education than it is with respect to university education. The irony is that the money available for the support of education has been adequate up until recently, and its adequacy now ceases just as the previous work in the field of education can be adjudged successful and is now showing every sign of expanding very rapidly to meet an entirely new order of public demand.

It is suggested that a careful study of the costs of operating the University, including the cost of expansion, might well reveal to the government of Puerto Rico that expanding the University is one of the cheapest of all ways of creating additional capital resources and that with such resources the wherewithal to pay for University expansion, even retroactively, can soon be discovered. Certainly, it is clear that the University has been an asset in the rapid development of the Island under the present administration. Under these circumstances, it is at least predictable — although the prediction must be made with the possibility that there is a large margin of error lying within it — that the lack of a supply of expansion money for the University means a forced slowing down of the level of industrial development and economic expansion.

It is also predictable that unless the University is permitted by its own administration to maintain a fuller measure of internal freedom, its standards will be driven down and its costs driven up. It is already an institution in which many varieties of high costs are concealed under a policy of low costs, and in these there are no present prospects for change.

VII. INVESTMENT AND ENDOWMENT POLICIES

Summary of the Discussion on "Financial Problems of Higher Education," two meetings of the Seminar on the Economics of Higher Education, May 7 and June 4, 1959. Papers were given by Messrs. Bump, Houston, Kirkpatrick, Hall, Hollis, and Bates (May 7), and by Messrs. Tripp, Bennett, Meck, Cain, Underhill, and Cabot (June 4).

APART from questions of clarification and of information to the various speakers, discussion of the financial problems of higher education revolved around four major topics relating to the valuation of endowment and composition of investments. The first question to arise was whether it is legitimate to manage the investment fund of colleges with the aim of acquiring capital gains, and then to use these capital gains for current expenditures. Second, if one admits the desirability of growth in capital values, what portion of the investment portfolio should be put into growth stocks and what part into high-income stocks? Indeed, should colleges rely heavily on common stocks at all, or should they concentrate their portfolios on bonds, mortgages, and other investments? Third, should the restricted endowment funds in an investment pool be valued at book or at market value? And how should the income from such a pool be allocated among the claims on it? Finally, starting from Mr. Cabot's paper: is it really inappropriate for a college to borrow, or are there some circumstances in which it is desirable for a college to borrow?

Each of these questions provided adequate grounds for debate, in the course of which many positions were fully aired, if not always resolved. The grounds for disagreement were partly instrumental — whether the proposed policy would further agreed ends — and partly moral — whether the proposal could properly be considered at all within the moral obligations of college financial officers.

Capital Gains — Income or Principal?

One member of the seminar pointed out that if we persist in drawing a sharp distinction between capital and income, then production of income, the criterion by which Mr. Bump had suggested that the success of college financial officers in using endowment funds should be judged, excluded the important alternative of investing for capital appreciation. Rather than try to maximize the income on a given endowment, the investor might choose to settle for a lower income if the prospects for capital gains and possibly higher income in the future were attractive. Should such an investor be judged less successful than one who earns a higher current income but fails to increase the market value of the endowment through capital gains?

This observation precipitated a prolonged debate over the merits of investing for income or for growth, and whether it was appropriate to spend any capital gains resulting from investment in growth stocks as current income. Several members suggested cautiously that it was — that investment for capital appreciation was an important alternative to investment for income, and that the former might actually result in a higher yield than the latter, even if current gains were spent concurrently. In other words, investors might find themselves faced with a choice between securities paying interest or dividends of 4 per cent a year, but with no prospects of a rise in value, and securities paying only 1½ per cent a year but with some promise of appreciating in value at a rate, say, of 3½ per cent or better. In such a case the "income" available for annual expenses would be higher in the second instance *if* the investor allowed himself to sell some portion (3½ per cent) of the securities each year and spend the proceeds from these sales as well as the current earnings.

In fact, for many companies, capital appreciation of the stock is a direct substitute for dividends. Earnings are withheld from the stockholders and are plowed back into the firm. Over time the market value of the stock reflects the growth in assets and earnings of the firm. The management may judge that this will benefit the stockholders more than payment of earnings in dividends.

Others protested that this choice was not even open to the investors of college endowments, so that it was not fruitful to discuss the issue in the context of college finance. As one participant put it, "I understood that 'endowment fund' by definition was one under which the principal was inviolate and the income only could be spent. I believe that it is neither legally nor morally possible to make capital gains and then spend them." An endowment fund is a fund held in trust, and as such the fund itself cannot be used, but only the income from it.

But the "endowment fund" held in trust is subject to several interpretations. Is it a fixed sum of money, the original donation to the college or university? Or is it the securities purchased as a result of the donation, however they may change in value? Many donations actually involve the transfer of titles of securities to the college, rather than a contribution in cash. Is the addition to endowment, then, the market value of the securities at the time of giving, or the market value as it changes in time, including sales and purchases of new securities with the proceeds? Most would agree that the permanent endowment is closer to the second interpretation than to the fixed sum of money in each case, and legal opinion has supported trustees in the case of a *loss* of value since the original donation. Any trustee must be given discretion in management of his trust. If no negligence is involved, he cannot be held responsible for a decline in value of endowment due to bad investment judgment made in good faith or to general economic conditions quite beyond his control.

When the only purchases are securities fixed in money value, such as bonds and mortgages, the issue of spending capital gains does not arise. It is true that these fluctuate in value on the market, but the fluctuations are relatively small and cannot be expected to tend, over a period of time, in one direction. This relative stability in principal value is not true of investments in real estate or common stocks, however; in a growing and/or inflationary economy the value of such investments can be expected to rise over time, perhaps indefinitely. In such a situation investment for capital gains becomes a conscious alternative to investment for interest or dividends, and there is no complete parallel between capital gains and capital losses. One participant suggested that a more inclusive criterion for judging investment success than the one proposed by Mr. Bump would be the return on the original value of the gift. This would include both current earnings and capital appreciation. The college investment officers would then have to choose which they would rather emphasize. A trustee is obligated to the donor to preserve the principal of the contribution, but he is also obligated to use the principal in the most effective manner for the benefit of the institution. And in a growing economy the most effective use of a given sum may be investment for capital appreciation.

This is especially true in an inflationary economy. Several participants emphasized the steady decline in the purchasing power of fixed income from endowment. Any measure for preserving the *real* value — the purchasing power — of both principal and income is highly desirable, indeed necessary, for colleges and universities. The only way to prevent the erosion of principal is to make investments which show some promise for capital appreciation (but then not to spend the gains), and erosion in the real value of income from endowment can often be reduced by investing for capital appreciation and then using some of the appreciation as income.

This relates to a second reason for investing for capital gains: provision for future generations of students out of present endowment. For endowment to keep ahead of the decline in the value of the dollar, institutions must make investments with rising dollar values and continually reinvest the gains. Otherwise endowment will provide income to fewer and fewer teachers and funds for fewer and fewer blackboards. Of course, to the extent that capital gains are reinvested, they cannot be used for present purposes. This question was discussed further in connection with the composition of college investment portfolios.

A third reason for investing for capital gains is a tactical one. Not being burdened by income or capital-gains taxes, colleges are in a better position than other investment groups to take advantage of the possibilities for capital gains. They can be more flexible in purchases and sales of investments, need not worry about the six months' time limit which transforms capital gains into income (thus taxed at a higher rate), and can enjoy the full benefit of any capital appreciation which does occur. They can realize their gains when the need arises, without suffering the tax consequences which plague other investors. Capital gains as a regular source of income at least becomes possible.

In spite of these apparent advantages, some members of the seminar objected to the use of capital gains on moral grounds, as a violation of trust. Furthermore, one participant pointed out that capital gains were likely to be an especially unstable source of income, high in some years and very low in others, so that it would be a great mistake for institutions to rely on income from this source for recurring expenditures. A college should "try to avoid getting frozen into its budget a fixed expense which has to be met from a source such as capital gains." If capital gains are to be used for current expenditures at all, they should be used only for extraordinary expenditures.

Another objection to treating capital gains as income was raised. If capital gains are withdrawn for current expenditures, that means correspondingly less endowment to provide income for future generations of students. As one member insisted, "We are the trustees for the benefit of students who are now here and for students who are to come, as yet unborn. Between the two, those who are here now are more vocal than those who are not yet born." The trustees hold a proxy for the future students, and must not yield excessively to the exigencies of the present. "It is very easy to look at today's emergency and make a decision in the light of that emergency, gaily ignoring the emergencies which are to come." Of course, this reinforces the argument for seeking capital gains, especially in an inflationary economy, but these gains should be reinvested for future use rather than withdrawn and spent currently.

On the last point, however, one member observed that often expenditure in the present was the best way of providing for the future, particularly in an inflationary period. This is obviously true of buildings, but can also be true of other expenditures which affect the stature and the quality of the institution.

In summary, several members of the seminar drew a sharp distinction between principal and income, holding that the latter only could be used for current expenditures, while the former is inviolable, whether or not it grows in value. Others held that with many investments the distinction is not at all clear, that discretion has to be used, but that at present seeking capital gains is one of the most effective uses of endowment funds, and that this source of revenue should not be excluded dogmatically. We may be in a period in which the mores regarding these matters are gradually shifting. Fifty years ago most trustees would have argued that it was immoral to purchase common stocks with endowment funds. At present nearly half of college endowment funds are in common stocks, and a similar shift with respect to capital gains may be occurring.

Finally, a sharp distinction was made by several members between endowment proper and free funds functioning as endowment. Often colleges will choose to pool some of their unrestricted gifts with endowment income, and use only the income from these funds. In such a case most members held it was perfectly proper to invest such funds for capital appreciation and to use the resulting gains as income. Since these were unrestricted funds initially, the principal is not inviolable, and could be used entirely for current expenditures if the college chose to do so. While only a few colleges have large amounts of unrestricted funds functioning as endowment, most colleges have some funds in this category; and until the conversion of capital gains into income becomes much more attractive than it now is, the question is more one of theoretical than of practical interest. For a few schools, however, it is of immediate interest.

The view that unrestricted funds, once added to endowment, can be withdrawn at any time is not universally held. Mr. Blackwell has suggested that funds added to endowment by a past decision of trustees should be treated as part of the endowment itself, and its principal not violated. Even without going that far, serious difficulties do attend withdrawing from the endowment proper free funds functioning as endowment. After the funds have been mingled for some years, what portion of the total present value can be claimed by the unrestricted funds? This depends upon how the investment pool is valued, at book or at market, an issue fully discussed.

A technical aspect of the capital-gains problem is provided by depreciation allowances on investments in real estate. The officers of one university stated that they estimated the useful life of a piece of property and depreciated it on a straight-line basis. The decisions of the treasurer and his staff are subject to the review of the trustees. By overdepreciating its property a college can add to the income-producing funds at the expense of current expenditures. It is analogous to purchasing low-yield growth stocks and continually reinvesting any realized capital gains.

Composition of Investment Portfolios

The lively discussion on the role which capital gains should play in the financial life of colleges and universities served to introduce the more fundamental problem of general investment policy. What should the investment portfolio of a college contain, and how should it be managed? Conceptually two questions can be asked: (1) how can a college get the most income from a given endowment, and (2) how should the yield on the endowment be allocated between present and future uses? In practice, of course, the two issues cannot be so easily separated, since a policy yielding the highest return may require skimping on present expenditure for the benefit of future students.

Both questions arise most immediately over the emphasis which college investors should place on growth stocks. The papers by Messrs. Bates, Tripp, and Bennett considered this problem specifically. Several members emphasized that investment in growth stocks usually means a lower income in the present, unless the capital gains are realized and spent, and that in a period in which colleges are under financial strain this would be undesirable even if there were quite a rapid growth of principal. The experience of one investment trust suggested that 70 to 80 per cent of realized capital gains were taken in new stock; if colleges did the same, and simultaneously shifted a higher proportion of their portfolios into growth stocks, their present financial difficulties would be aggravated.

Most college financial officers admitted that they were uneasy about holding growth stocks now. One never knows when a growth stock ceases to be a growth stock, or whether it is merely on a temporary plateau and will continue to rise spectacularly in the future. On the basis of conventional price–earnings ratios, most stocks are now greatly overvalued, and holding them hurts the current income of the colleges. One criterion for holding stock is to ask if you would be willing to purchase more at the current price. If not, it is time to sell. But under the circumstances the decision to sell a stock which has grown rapidly in the recent past is a difficult one to make.

The problems attending investment in growth stocks are only those of common stocks generally, writ large. There has been a marked tendency for college financial officers in the past two decades to shift their portfolios into common stocks, but few are sure how far it is wise to go. One member suggested that colleges would be in a sounder financial position in the long run if about three-fourths of their portfolios were in common stocks, instead of the 55 per cent at present. Others were not nearly so sure. It is true that common stocks have done very well in the recent past, in terms of capital appreciation, but today the yield on stocks is only about two-thirds that on bonds. Furthermore, as more and more investors become conscious of the necessity to "hedge against inflation," the prices of common stocks will be bid up sufficiently to include the discounted capital appreciation which is expected. There are signs that this is already occurring. The very high price–earnings ratios on many stocks certainly reflect an increased awareness of the potential appreciation of stock values, whether it be due to inflation or merely to the long-run growth of the economy.

But not all members of the seminar agreed with the suggestion of some that a moderate inflation is here to stay. The great advantage of stocks over bonds — that the value of a bond, in terms of purchasing power, steadily declines during an inflation, whereas stock prices rise with other prices — disappears if one is not certain that inflation is likely in the long run.

In addition to the higher yields on bonds and

the lower risk involved in holding them when prices are not rising, the low prices at which bonds can now be purchased make them an attractive investment. Several participants felt that interest rates, while they might rise somewhat from their present levels, cannot rise indefinitely and indeed are likely to fall considerably within the next five years. If so, a tidy capital gain can be had by purchasing bonds now, or better, when bond prices reach their nadir. College investment officers would like to know just when that point would come, but several of them added that they were beginning then (spring, 1959) to buy bonds on a small scale.

On the other hand, the advocates of common stocks felt that this was likely to be a temporary advantage, and urged a long-run shift into common stocks. In answer to some of the objections to stocks raised by Mr. Bates, they pointed out that the income from stocks has been remarkably stable in recent years. Corporations now maintain sufficient reserves to continue dividend payments at former levels even in years when profits are exceptionally low. In most years they need not even draw on these reserves, since dividend payments have been running at about 40 per cent of profits in recent years, and regard for public esteem makes it advisable for corporations to reduce retained earnings before reducing dividends.

Furthermore, these members felt that the risk attending common stocks can be exaggerated. A college investor must choose among alternatives, and in an inflationary period the risk in holding bonds, in terms of purchasing power, is considerable, so that common stocks are relatively less risky than some of the principal alternative investments. In addition, colleges and universities have a great advantage in being perpetual bodies, so that a temporary decline in market value need not concern them if the long-run tendency is upward. Institutions of higher learning, because of their perpetuity, can afford to take a longer view than many investors, although it is an admittedly difficult task to persuade some trustees that a temporary decline in market value does not spell disaster for the institution.

Several members pointed out that a college can insure itself against an unforeseen fall in revenue by establishing an income stabilization fund. One year's endowment income was deemed quite adequate for such a fund. Many colleges maintain them, so in effect they are always spending last year's income.

Finally, even in the absence of inflation common stocks are likely to appreciate considerably. The managers of corporations are more likely to work for the interests of the stockholders than for those of the bond-holders. As corporations grow with the economy, the value of stock is likely to rise. And corporations (due partly to tax advantages) will rely for additional financing more on bonds than on new stocks in the interests of preserving stock prices for existing stockholders. For all these reasons, several members felt that colleges and universities had done themselves a considerable disservice by not moving even more than they had into common stocks.

Despite several papers on interesting adventures in real estate, a form of investment which was once much more important to colleges than it is today, there was little discussion of real estate as an alternative to stocks and bonds. Some universities have a policy against holding real estate for any length of time. One member pointed out that among the broad categories of investments, real estate showed the highest rate of return these days, although this may be only apparent, due to underestimation of the market value of the real estate. Actual ownership of real estate, as distinguished from holding mortgages, may involve occasional direct management which most colleges are not prepared to undertake.

One member asked why colleges and universities shun investment in their own expansion in contrast to business firms, which continually reinvest in themselves. If one is confident about the future prospects of the college, this would seem to be one of the most fruitful uses of endowment funds, and one consonant with the broad trusteeship obligations of the college. Several members quickly pointed out that many schools do use unrestricted funds in this way — often a use close to the interests of the donor, such as a music building bought with the gift of a person much interested in opera and symphony. Another member added that use of endowment proper in expansion might in the end compromise the independence of a university if it found itself in financial straits and had to be bailed out by the government. Investment in buildings not only involves a loss of income; it involves an annual maintenance expense. As this member put it, "I would rather be financially sound with the basis of expanding through increased endowment and private gifts than take the risk of becoming one of Mother Cary's chickens, with Mother Cary in Washington."

Leaving aside the composition of investments, there is still the problem of who should manage the investment funds. Only schools with large endowments can afford to hire full-time, highly competent investment officers; colleges with small funds cannot obtain such high skill, unless one of their trustees is such a man and is willing to put in the time required for managing the fund. On the average, colleges with small endowments do not do so well either on earnings or on capital gains as those with large investment funds. One member suggested that small endowment funds might be pooled for investment purposes. Several of the better endowed universities could start such a pool by merging some of their own funds, and schools with endowments between, say, $100,000 and $3 million should be encouraged to join. The Teachers Insurance Annuity Association did succeed in setting up a common trust fund for colleges in the state of New York.

On the other hand, trustees of the smaller schools may feel that they are abdicating their responsibility in turning the endowment over to a common trust to be administered by others. An alternative proposal would be the establishment of a common investment advisory group, nonprofit, for the explicit purpose of counseling investment of college endowments. Wise counsel would do much to increase the yield of small funds.

Even the larger funds can be managed by few or many men. The University of Chicago, for example, has a team of ten to manage its rather unusual investments, compared with two at Yale University. Much more management is required for investments in lease-backs and in real estate than in stocks and bonds, for instance. Chicago feels that its relatively large investment in personnel is more than returned to the University in the form of higher yields — ½ per cent greater than the average yield at Harvard, for example, a difference which runs into the millions.

An issue related to who should manage the funds is how they should be managed. As mentioned earlier, the longevity of colleges and universities places them in a position to take a very long-range view of their investments. They need not be concerned with the day-to-day or even year-to-year market fluctuations in the values of securities. Nonetheless, trustees are sensitive to changes in the value of endowment, and college treasurers, being human, find it very difficult to appear before a corporation meeting to say, "That X dollars profit that we had last time is now minus four or five million dollars on paper, and I was just stupid enough not to have done anything about it."

For this reason, and because it is very profitable if done well, investment officers admitted that they "play the swings" to some extent. The practice seems to be more common with bonds than with stocks, taking the form of small shifts in the composition of the total portfolio. Anticipating a change in interest rates, investment officers will often adjust the proportion of short- and long-term bonds correspondingly.

Valuation of Endowment Funds — Book or Market?

The third major issue which came up for discussion was how endowment funds should be carried on the books. This is partly a matter of convention and convenience and there is considerable variety among institutions. Some schools carry endowment at a book value which is the original contribution. Others carry it at a book value which changes as the institution changes its holdings. Still others rely on market value. For example, a college may have received a gift of $1 million (original value) which is invested in securities. Later these are sold for $1.2 million, which becomes the new book value, and the securities replacing them may now have a market value of $1.8 million.

As was suggested earlier, the original value

probably gives the best basis from which to judge the over-all success of the investment officers, including both earnings and capital gains. The market values are required for making comparisons of yields among alternative investments at any given time; for example, an investment officer wants to know the income which he can earn from various stocks and bonds and other forms of investment at current prices.

Occasionally a university which keeps its books on the basis of original value may mark up (or down) its entire portfolio if the gains in the gain-and-loss account become large. Boston University has done this recently. Harvard revalued its endowment in the early 1930's and again recently.

Since new contributions are continually being made to the endowment funds, however, their valuation is considerably more than a matter of mere convenience. How the funds are valued determines to a large extent the allocation of income on the endowment to various uses. To take a simple illustration, a chair in paleontology may have been endowed with $100,000 in the 1920's, and the investments of those funds might now have a market value of $300,000. In 1960, $100,000 may be given for a chair in nuclear engineering. If the endowment funds are pooled and are valued at original value, the income going to the two chairs from endowment will be the same. If endowment is valued at market, income going to the professorship in paleontology will be three times that going to the chair in nuclear engineering. Of course, reallocations appropriate because of new fields can be made from the general revenues of the university, but for income from restricted endowment the method of valuation makes a considerable difference. In a market in which security values are rising, use of book value gives preference to the most recent donations; market valuation gives past contributions the preference.

The proper method of valuation was the subject of strenuous debate in the seminar. Several members insisted that it was a violation of trust to keep contributions on the books at their original value, and this position is supported by rulings by the Federal Reserve Board and the Securities and Exchange Commission on common trust funds. "Fair shares" requires a distribution of income on the basis of the current market value of additions to the fund. As one member stated, "It is troublesome to find how many donors are not willing to give for unrestricted purposes, and you must decide whether to accept the donor's trust. But, once you do accept his trust, you have a legal and a moral responsibility to administer it the most faithful way you can find. The common trust fund has a ruling from the Federal Reserve as to what is fair and equitable, and the courts have upheld it."

Others felt that the rulings on common trust funds were not relevant for colleges and universities, and legal counsel has made it clear that valuation on the basis of original value is consistent with the duties of a trustee. Furthermore, one participant suggested that donors would actually prefer the addition of their donations to the pooled endowment fund at original value. Everyone has some time preference, and many would wish the money to be used most effectively in the near future rather than in the distant future. The donor might look at it in this way: "Well, for the next twenty years this is going to favor my money. I will get more out of it for the particular purposes for which I am giving the money than if it had been entered at market value. And I also realize that, after that, I will be hit as the past donors have been hit by this process."

In a falling market, the opposite will be true. Entry at market value would favor the current donors, while entry at book value would favor past contributions. Donors in the early 1930's often complained that they were not getting the full benefit of their 1932 dollars, so special funds were set up in which entries were made at market value. This experience tends to confirm the time-preference view of donors.

Others felt that these were merely methods to cheat past donors in order to seduce a new donor. The reason it was successful is that early contributors could not come around to plague the trustees: "Dead donors don't kick." On the other hand, actual experience with both methods of accounting has resulted in very few complaints about either. Most donors do not understand the system anyway, and small donors often think of their contribution as a gift of money to the university, not of the income which it will earn. Harvard and Yale both keep their books at original value, with occasional mark-ups from the gain and loss account. Harvard has only an occasional complaint from potential donors. Dartmouth, Brown, the University of Chicago, and the University of California all use market values, and Princeton has just switched to this system, as other colleges seem to be doing. They, too, have had only a few complaints. Thus there is not much evidence on the effect of one method or the other in stimulating or repelling donations. If any contributor does object strenuously, a separate fund can be set up. Most schools have some of these.

Apart from the possible effects on potential contributors, the participants brought out other grounds for preferring one method or another. Those favoring the use of original value argued that this would aid further the current needs of the university. Recent donations are more likely to reflect the current needs of society and of the institutions than are donations of twenty-five or fifty or even a hundred years ago. A system of valuation which results in a higher proportion of the income on endowment allotted to these current needs is therefore more in the interests of the universities and of society. Many of the older schools are heavily endowed in the field of the classics, for example, and to value these endowments at market value would be to give classics a larger place in the budgets of these institutions than is appropriate to current demands for that field.

Another argument mentioned in favor of the book value is that less endowment is required for a new professorship than under market valuation, because under book value a higher proportion of the pooled income goes to the new chair. For a $15,000 chair the required funds might be $300,000 under book value as compared with $500,000 under market value, and the smaller figure might encourage a larger number of new endowments for professorships.

As others pointed out, however, there are also important disadvantages to using original value. In the first place, where endowment gifts stipulate that the donor is entitled to the income for the rest of his life, whereupon it all reverts to the institution, use of book value increases the annuity claim on the income from the pooled investment funds, and thus is a loss to the school during the lifetime of the donor. On the other hand, Pomona College apparently uses this feature to attract gifts to the school.

Secondly, grants in the past may have been less restricted than recent ones, so the use of book value actually reduces the freedom of the university or college in allocating its funds. Use of market value would, in effect, increase the proportion of unrestricted funds available to the institution.

Finally, if unrestricted funds are added to the investment pool to function as endowment, and are later withdrawn, capital gains can be taken if market valuation is used, whereas under book valuation any capital gains actually due to those unrestricted funds must become a part of the permanent endowment fund, since only the original amount can be withdrawn.

As an illustration of the impact of changes over time, one member produced some figures from the University of Chicago, where the investment pool has been operating for twenty-three years. Chicago uses a system of market valuation. Of four $100,000 funds, the one which was merged when the pooled fund was started in 1936 was credited in 1959 with $7,500 in income, or a return of 7.5 per cent on original value. (This fund had suffered some capital losses in the late 1930's.) A $100,000 fund added to the pool in 1947–48 was credited with $7,064 in income, a yield of 7.06 per cent on original value. A fund added in 1952–53 received $5,454 in income, and one added in 1957 received $3,383, a return of 3.38 per cent. The market value of the 1936 fund is now close to $200,000, and that of the other funds correspondingly less. If the allocation of income had been made on the basis of book value, all four funds would have received the same amount. Hence the difference can be substantial.

The problem of allocating income from pooled funds has come up in other ways. Columbia University, for example, puts all tuition income into a central pool, and expenditures for the various programs are made from this. This pooling enables some programs to be subsidized by others; at Columbia the "general studies" program takes in considerably more revenue than it costs, so it provides a net financial contribution to the university. It is the extension program of the university, composed largely of night classes and part-time students.

Several members of the seminar felt that this sort of pooling was undesirable, since there would be no incentive for the various schools to economize or to appeal extensively for alumni aid. If, say, the law school reduces its costs, the savings will go into the general pool and the law school will not reap the direct benefit. Furthermore, alumni might be considerably more reluctant to give to the school if they felt that the only result would be a larger part of tuition income returned to the university pool. To the observation that some parts of a university cost a great deal to operate and need to be subsidized by general funds — the medical schools provide an example — these members argued that the high-cost branches should seek larger endowment to cover the deficit.

Some schools cannot easily get more endowment; the alumni of a school of education are not usually in a position to afford large grants to their alma mater. To appeal to the Ford Foundation or some other philanthropic organization for aid in such a case means that the university has passed on an educational decision to another organization. Some suggested that a university should be regarded as a unit. As such, it must make decisions about which programs are educationally worthwhile and which are not, and must have funds to implement its decisions. Any program which cannot cover costs internally, through tuition or its own endowment, needs some sort of subsidy. Those opposing the use of pooled funds did not suggest where the line should be drawn beyond which pooling is undesirable. For financial purposes, should arts and sciences be separated from law? Chemistry from classics? International economics from labor economics? Few would suggest that classics should be dropped from the curriculum because it cannot cover its costs.

One member asked whether there was any difference in principle between pooling tuition income and entering endowment at book value. With the second policy those schools in a university which received endowment gifts most recently benefit disproportionately from the pooled investments. It is analogous, he felt, to one school's subsidizing another through a tuition pool. Another member put it this way: "What it boils down to is that, because you run a pool, you do things you could not possibly do if you invested every fund separately. If you had no pool, you could not possibly steal from somebody else; each would have only what he earned."

A few schools go even further in the redistribution of income from pooled funds, and co-opt part of the income for the general purposes of the university. An investment fund may pay out 4 per cent to all its claimants, and turn the difference between this and the actual earnings into unrestricted income at the disposal of the university. This is justified on the grounds that some of the university's overhead should be paid out of the endowment income, since the overhead is incurred partly to maintain endowed programs.

Still, pooling funds, at least for investment purposes, remains the most effective way to handle them for all parties.

Borrowing versus Internal Financing

The final issue which raised some controversy among the members of the seminar was Mr. Cabot's suggestion that it was inappropriate for a college, at least for Harvard, to borrow. For a variety of reasons several participants felt that the case against borrowing, either by colleges in general or by Harvard in particular, was not so strong as he had suggested.

In the first place, borrowing in an inflationary economy is one way to get the necessary share of national output into higher education. At present the community is not prepared to pay the bill voluntarily, although it wants the services, and exploiting the inflationary process through borrowing is one way of shifting the burden to the community. If a college borrows $5 million for a building now, the real burden when it is paid off will be considerably less, both because of inflation and the decline in the purchasing power of the dollar, and because of the gradual rise in incomes associated with increasing productivity. Nor is this behavior immoral in any sense. It is perfectly appropriate in a capitalistic society, and in fact it is used by many other sectors of the economy.

Second, several members doubted whether Mr. Cabot's fears regarding alumni gifts to a college in debt are justified. They felt that a college could borrow in clear conscience without a decline in alumni gifts, much less a complete stoppage. On the contrary, borrowing by the University of Chicago in order to build a dormitory was thought to have helped their fund drive of several years ago. By borrowing for many of their new units, the officers of the university could convince others that these units — dormitories, residences for married students, a conference center — were going to operate on a self-sustaining basis, paying for capital as well as operating costs. The fund drive was thus for $33 million instead of the much larger figure which would have been required if funds for the new income-producing buildings had had to be raised from contributions as well.

Dartmouth authorities also felt that to add the capital costs of new dormitories to their fund-drive goal would have been to place it outside the realm of possibility. By borrowing for these income-producing units, the goal was reduced to a manageable $17 million. Alumni opinion seems so far to be in favor of borrowing for these items, and devoting the gift money to more pressing educational needs. Thus borrowing, fortunately, does not seem seriously to reduce gifts.

Even if the institution has enough free internal funds to lend for building purposes, it may be more economical to borrow outside. Often the lending rates to colleges are less than the yield on college endowment funds, and the wider this difference, the more profitable it is to borrow outside the institution. If the university charges its components 5.3 per cent for borrowed funds, as Harvard does, and many outside lenders are willing to lend at 4 per cent, there is certainly a strong economic argument for borrowing outside, especially for buildings where the financing charges will continue for a long time. Against this economic gain, of course, must be set the possible loss of complete freedom involved when there is an outside creditor.

This spread of interest rates was a second reason advanced by the University of Chicago for borrowing for its dormitories. Two and seven-eighths per cent for thirty-eight years is a much lower rate than that earned by the university investment pool. And by spreading the cost of the new dormitories over the entire residence-hall system, they could be financed at very little increase in charges to students.

Finally, several members could not see the difference in principle between a loan from the university to one of its components, on the terms on which such loans are made at Harvard, and borrowing outside the university entirely. If the Graduate School of Arts and Sciences, for example, borrows from the university, it must amortize completely both principal and interest on the loan. If it fails to do so, the university will appropriate some of the free funds of that school, so it will either have to find some other source of income or curtail its activities. The university is a harsh creditor. For this reason, the Graduate School will be very confident about its investment before borrowing. But if a school is certain about income sufficient to amortize the debt, why not borrow from outside, and at a lower interest rate?

Part of the difference in opinion reduces to a difference in ideology. Some people think that borrowing per se is undesirable, while others have no strong a priori feelings about it, or actually feel that borrowing is stimulating to the economy and therefore desirable. Another factor governing one's views on borrowing is one's estimation of the movement of the economy. Several members conceded that some of Mr. Cabot's objections to borrowing would become very forceful in the event of a major depression. But this was not thought to be a likely possibility.

Summary

Management of a college's financial affairs is not the simple matter it might at first sight appear. Many "policy decisions" which will affect the freedom of action in the future must be made by those in charge of financial management. Four of these decisions were discussed at length in the seminar: (1) Should a college invest for income or for capital gains, and if the latter is chosen, may it use the capital gains for current expenditures? (2) Related to the first question, how should a college divide its investment portfolio among stocks and other securities yielding high income, on the one hand, and growth stocks on the other? (3) Should the income from pooled investment funds be allocated by the current market value or the original value of additions to the fund? (4) Finally, should a college rely entirely on gifts and self-financing, or should it allow itself the luxury of borrowing for self-liquidating and other investments in its own plant?

In each case acceptance of the second alternative may allow the college authorities more freedom and flexibility in planning its programs and allocating funds. Adjusting to a growing and inflationary economy may require policies which were frowned on in the past if colleges and universities are not to be left behind in the competition for national output. But, as the discussion well demonstrated, each move in this direction also carries its costs, often in the form of higher risks. Financial authorities must decide whether the possible gains are sufficiently attractive to outweigh them.

DIFFICULTIES IN DETERMINING INVESTMENT POLICIES

George E. Bates

HAVING been asked, after reading Professor Harris' notes on the management of productive funds, to discuss some general issues concerning the investment of college endowments, I can do no better than to quote at the outset Professor Dunbar's purported definition of the One Rule of Finance, which was "to do the best thing possible under the circumstances." His rule seems especially appropriate to the subject under discussion, and I am confident that college treasurers and others responsible for institutional investing are trying to do just what the rule implies — to avoid the limitations of generalization and to do what is right in the particular circumstances.

It appears to me that with respect to investment the major trend of Professor Harris' argument is toward increasing the proportion of common stocks in the average college endowment portfolio. Given a certain image of the average portfolio containing very few stocks, and with due reservations respecting matters of timing and relative values, I do not disagree with his thesis. As I shall try to point out later, however, a college treasurer or board of investment is not managing an "average" portfolio. The balance between bonds, or equivalent, and stocks, or equivalent, in any specific portfolio should, among other things, be determined in light of the total financial situation of the particular college concerned.

Before directly pursuing that point, though, it will be pertinent to review a bit of common stock investment history. To begin with, I cite a case from our files dated nearly thirty years ago. The issue in this case stemmed from a report of investment counsel to a college board of trustees advising a change from the college's traditional policy of confining investment primarily to bonds. The report recommended a major shift from bonds to common stocks with a view to providing a hedge against inflation. In this, the report ran somewhat parallel to the thesis in Professor Harris' paper. Perhaps the parallel ends there, for that report was made in February, 1930, on the eve of the greatest deflation in our memories and of further drastic declines in stock prices. Analysis of the report indicates that counsel was giving what I shall call textbook advice, based on a text developed from the financial experience of colleges during and after the inflation associated with World War I. It is an understatement to say that the timing of this advice was unfortunate.

For several years after the date of that report, experience with common stocks was such as to dampen enthusiasm for stocks as college investment media. Lower-grade bonds having equity characteristics fell in the same category. As an instance of the consequences, I vividly recall the faculty's unhappiness in a sister institution with what happened to instructional budgets as a result of investment policy not geared to deflationary possibilities. Despite the experiences of those years, however, a noticeably more liberal attitude toward common stocks came to be adopted in a number of institutional portfolios in the mid-thirties. Again there was the threat of inflation. And there was an easy money policy which led to the wholesale refunding of high-grade bonds, with consequent lowering of investment income, even though investment principal may have been increased slightly through the receipt of call premiums. In addition to the attrition in bond income, institutions were having trouble with their mortgages. These and possibly other factors, coupled with a rising stock market, tended to bring common stocks back into favor. War and further threats of inflation accelerated the trend. Another factor tending to increase the proportion of common stocks in the "average" institutional portfolio was the gradual disappearance of geographical differences in investment policy, differences which had tended to confine institutional interest in common stocks to the northeastern part of the United States. Elsewhere investment tended to be restricted to bonds, mortgages, and real estate, with the latter (usually minor) category representing the only equities. Liberalization of legal restrictions on fiduciary investment outside New England has been a very recent development in this trend.

Reverting to the bond investment policy followed until 1930 in the case cited above, we should remember that until quite recent times there was a strong school of thought which held that the only true investment was an obligation, a debt instrument, with a presumably enforceable maturity value and series of interest payments. And such investments were considered better investments if they were "secured"; that is, if specific security were given which might be availed of, in one way or another, in the event of default. A fundamental issue consequently was whether common stocks could qualify as investments, particularly for fiduciaries, in view of the oft-stated virtues of bonds, mortgages, and other evidences of debt. Except for relative marketability, which need not be considered here, only two grounds could be advanced for putting common stocks into the investment category: (1) higher income, and (2) capital gains. Both seemed to imply a speculative element.

Of those two grounds, capital gains (and a corollary of greater future income) has proved the stronger. Temptingly greater current income has only been available intermittently and usually at times when a continuance of corporate profit levels has appeared in doubt, so that there was always a question of whether substantially greater current income might not be more than offset by risks of capital losses and lower future income. On the other hand, at least two factors have moved strongly in favor of common stocks as sources of capital gains. One has been the introduction in bond indentures of the call feature, forcing investors to conclude that with bonds, unless bought at substantial discounts, they can experience losses but not gains, and to offset inevitable losses in the bond portfolio the chance for gains in a balancing stock portfolio has naturally proved attractive. The other and more powerful factor has been the threat and actuality of inflation eroding the purchasing power of fixed dollar obligations.

I recall five principal ways of achieving such gains through common stocks which have been stressed at various times: (1) buying stocks in depressions and selling them in booms, (2) buying "undervalued" stocks and selling them when they become fully priced relative to their "intrinsic values," (3) buying stocks of companies expected to "grow" and selling them at the end of the growth phase or when the growth has been overdiscounted, (4) buying stocks generally to grow with a growing economy, and (5) buying such stocks as might be expected to show increasing dollar earnings over periods in which the purchasing power of the dollar is expected to decline. It will be noted that the first three clearly, and the last two possibly, are but variants of the time-honored principle of buying low and selling high, and that timing is the key to most of them, whether short-term market movements, cycles, or secular trends (which may be reversed) are involved.

Reviewing the search for capital gains during the past half-century, I recollect that in the first part of the period the many studies and considerable literature on the business cycle led to the advocacy of a policy of shifting between bonds and stocks at various points in the cycles of interest rates and stock prices, and to confidence that those points could be recognized and would precipitate appropriate and timely action by the intelligent investor. The failure of most cycle students to profit by the 1929 and 1932 turning points did not appear to shake belief in the practicability of the general cycle theory but rather led to increased determination that "next time" (if only they were granted such an opportunity), with the benefit of both theory and hard practical experience, they would assuredly take advantage of a relatively high market to move out of stocks. The "next time" came in 1937, and was followed by one of the sharpest drops in stock-exchange history. Again too many supposedly intelligent investors were caught with long positions in stocks. What was wrong? The principle of buying low and selling high seemed unassailable, but investors had not behaved as they should. Reflecting the very sentiments which made markets low, they were pessimistic when they should have been buying, and conversely were optimistic when markets were high and when they should have been selling.

Thus it is significant that we first began to

hear of so-called formula plans about 1938, just after this second discouragement for the would-be cycle operators. (Formula plans may have a special interest for educators inasmuch as two of the prominently mentioned early plans bore the names of institutions of higher learning.) In essence the formula planners were saying that the cycles were there for all to see, that they were of a magnitude to provide attractive capital gains, but that men could not be trusted to take advantage of them because human judgment and forecasting were unreliable and too greatly influenced by contemporary emotions of optimism and pessimism. Judgment and forecasting consequently should be replaced by a predetermined mechanical system.

Unfortunately, the advocates of the formula plan did not seem to realize that their plans called for much initial judgment and relatively long forecasts — and that the greater the capital gains potentially realizable from their plans, the more initial judgment and forecasting were required. And again, the plans provided no final protection against the human element because the plans might be altered or abandoned at the wrong times. While some of the more skillfully devised plans possessed merit in facilitating group decisions on investment and in providing some benchmarks in the areas of valuation and timing, the great rise in stock prices during the past decade has led to the abandonment or substantial modification of many of them.

The next fad to supersede formula planning was the cult of growth stocks. By hindsight such stocks may be readily recognized — the trick, of course, is to be able to recognize and buy them before their growth has been fully discounted. An underpriced true growth stock is what we should all like to buy, and even fully priced ones could have attractions for high-bracket taxpayers but not for tax-exempt institutions. I say "true" growth stocks because I am under the impression that, with the spread of the cult, many stocks showing merely cyclically advancing earnings have been added to the list.

Professor Harris showed some concern lest investment in growth stocks would favor future, at the expense of current, income. This result would be true with respect to some but by no means all such stocks. He was evidently thinking either of those stocks which the market already fully recognized as growth stocks or of new ventures of a speculative quality which would probably preclude them for fiduciary investment. There is historical evidence that numerous stocks in the growth category could have been purchased to yield as much as bonds in the year of purchase, and by the second or third year would have produced a much higher percentage return on cost. It is simply a matter of choosing those stocks which will quickly increase their dividends! Seriously, that would be only a minor analytical complication to the difficult task of recognizing, valuing, and timing the purchase of any growth stock. There are obviously more perplexing problems related to investment in growth stocks than the one of current versus future income. I gathered from Mr. Tripp's paper, for example, that Rochester University has not bought any in the last few years. Apparently he feels that those which he can recognize and which are of a type deemed suitable for endowment fund investment are now overpriced. If all the growth in growth stocks has been discounted or overdiscounted, it is obviously not profitable to buy them.

The popularity and consequent high price of supposed growth stocks is probably responsible for the opinion frequently expressed in the last two or three years that investors now have to seek something else. The "something else" often turns out to be what are called special situations. The idea of getting into special situations is not new, but seems to receive only intermittent emphasis. The special situations which my friends have found, or at least the ones they like to talk about, have been very good — and very special. Not many of us would have the courage, nor think that we had the authority, to buy them in any substantial amount for a college endowment fund. Most of them, as I recall, would scarcely have been considered securities suitable for trust investment. But some of them have been exceedingly profitable.

Difficulties inherent in recognizing and properly valuing growth stocks and special situations may, along with generally rising stock prices, have been responsible for many investors' returning to the philosophy of thirty years ago that common stocks should be bought and more or less permanently held for long-term growth. The studies made by Smith and others in the middle twenties led many investors to believe that all they had to do was buy stocks, at any time and at any price, and sit back to wait for their inevitable growth with a growing America. The nineteen-thirties brought a rude awakening. It was found that America might not always grow, and that such growth as there was could be overdiscounted in the prices of stocks. Furthermore, stocks of mature or declining companies would not grow even in a growing economy. The result of these discoveries was a healthy reaction in which selectivity, valuation, and timing received overdue attention.

Believing that today in a long-continued bull market we should again be stressing these factors of selectivity, valuation, and timing, I am not particularly impressed, for practical investment purposes, with extrapolations of historical stock indices. For example, Professor Harris' paper refers to the growth of stock prices shown by the Cowles Commission study. He mentioned an average growth rate of 8.4 per cent a year from 1871 to 1937, and quotes a recent article suggesting a 12 per cent rate as being appropriate for the present day. The Cowles Commission study merits more careful examination. In the first place, that 8.4 per cent figure was not based on all stocks, but only on the so-called "industrial" stocks. The years 1871–1898, nearly half the span of the study, covered a generally deflationary period when it is surprising to see the industrial index rising — surprising, that is, until it is appreciated that the so-called industrials comprised but a small segment of the total list of stocks, and that in this small segment most of the stocks moved more or less horizontally or downward while the average was pulled up by the buoyant action of a few stocks. Those few were the stocks of express companies, and it seems to me extremely doubtful that anyone contemporaneously would have classified them as industrial rather than transportation stocks.

The use of the 8.4 per cent figure, furthermore, is questionable for our present purposes since it combines capital gains and cash dividends. Even more important, it is based on a program of investment which is absolutely impractical — one which, even were it practical, none of us would dream of following. Not only would one have to invest a limited fund in all listed stocks and reapportion the investment monthly (I shudder to think of the expenses involved, which, of course, are not taken into account in an "index" prepared for other purposes), but one would have to jettison all normal concepts of diversification in order to make each investment proportionate to the market value of the total number of shares of each corporation represented. However well such an index may portray "average" experience, the probability is slight that it will accurately predict the future experience of any single investment fund.

In this paper I have touched briefly on some of the theories of common stock investing in order to give perspective to our discussion and with the aim of emphasizing the word "management" in the profession known as investment management. Management should not be bound to general theories. Such theories have too often been based on the experience of an immediate past which has not been duplicated in an immediate future. It is small solace for a college treasurer to be told that a given investment program may average out successfully in thirty or forty years if, in fact, his term of office extends for only ten or fifteen years and in those years the program works badly. He had better stick to Dunbar's "one rule."

Does that leave him completely at sea? I don't think so. In the first place, the good judgment implied by the rule will dictate that he look at the total financial situation of his institution and not merely at the bonds and stocks in his endowment portfolio. How significant is the endowment income relative to the college's other sources of revenue, such as tuition, current gifts, grants, appropriations, and prospects of additional endowment? How controllable are the expenses? How much investment management overhead will the size of the fund permit? How will policies of investment affect the ability of the college administration to obtain additional gifts of endowment? And so on.

What I am suggesting is that the college treasurer analyze all sources of revenue, not just those from endowment, and that he also analyze all fixed and variable expenses of his institution, to determine the risks in each category relative to various conditions which it can be assumed might arise. Various combinations of fixed and controllable expenses and of stable and volatile revenues will dictate the proportion of risk or aggressiveness which may be acceptable in the endowment portfolio. My thought is that the proportion of the fund invested in common stocks will be expected to vary from college to college according to the total financial circumstances of each, and will not be fixed by any single rule. Another thought, developed from the experience of investors in trying to outguess the cycles of stock prices, is that some reasonable balance between bonds and stocks should be determined according to the circumstances of each college and that only a minor portion of the endowment funds — say 10 to 20 per cent — should be considered available for shifting between the two classes of securities. This should give adequate scope for the irresistible inclination to try to buy low and sell high, while protecting the portfolio against major errors of timing. Such a limitation will also make it practically easier to reach investment decisions.

To introduce one further thought, I think that a broad view of our subject will suggest that the investment manager cannot be expected to meet the major financial problems of our colleges. Acutely aware of the ever-present needs, he may take undue risks or he may devote much time and energy to working on a few special situations in order to raise the total portfolio yield fractionally. It may be wondered whether the same effort directed to securing additional gifts or new sources of revenue might not prove more productive. The money raisers still have their work to do, and they have excellent talking points with alumni and others if costs of operation have risen or demands on the college have increased, or even if investment yields in general have declined. Personally, I should much prefer to solicit funds or to impose economies for such reasons than to beg for money or to cut salaries or staff in order to replace investment losses or to meet income lost through dividend cuts on an overlarge stock portfolio. In this vein, I believe that donors of endowment funds are inclined to look to the sanctity of the trusts they create and to expect them to continue in perpetuity. Most would not be disturbed by a moderately conservative investment policy for the funds they have given. They would naturally anticipate that we would be alert to try to increase income, but at the same time would not expect us to incur losses of principal or income. The demonstration of a sound investment policy over a period of years should be of inestimable value in securing additional gifts of endowment funds. This may prove a better long-run source of increased endowment income than greatly increasing the risks in the endowment portfolio.

Lest I be misunderstood in these latter remarks, however, I now repeat what I said at the beginning: given a picture of the average college endowment fund containing only a small proportion of common stocks, I would expect and subscribe to an increase in this proportion at appropriate times. But I would also hope that the proportion in individual instances would be geared to the carefully studied circumstances of the individual college. Regarding the need for a well-balanced portfolio in the average situation I visualize, as does Professor Harris, a long-run inflationary trend, but I do not doubt that there will be occasional reversals. Moreover, not all common stocks will fare equally under varying types of inflation and the accompanying wage, tax, and other pressures, nor will the timing of their response to inflation be even approximately immediate. The fact that we are investing in the face of an ever unknown figure leads me to suggest the balanced portfolio as a matter of insurance.

OBJECTIVES OF INVESTMENT POLICIES

Boardman Bump

I WOULD like to proceed immediately to an examination of the IHL (institution of higher learning) investors' dilemma: that is, more income, now or later?

First, let us focus our thoughts on the traditional purposes for which college endowment funds exist. There can be no argument over the fact that capital entrusted to our custody for investment was intended to produce annual income in support of some academic pursuit, be it specific or general. It has always seemed to me that the giving process which creates endowments is concerned with the spiritual as well as the material. So later, when we try to decide on the propriety or wisdom of making certain investment shifts or policy changes, a recollection of how these funds of ours originated can perhaps be a helpful guide to us in action.

Now, to identify and mention briefly two important fundamentals which distinguish IHL portfolio management from other investment operations. First, *tax exemption*: there are no capital gains tax, no income tax, no taxes because of death in our IHL families.

Second, *perpetuity*. The fact that an institution is a perpetual income beneficiary of its invested funds means that it can afford to watch a slower time clock than others and to feel a minimum concern for market fluctuations taking place over short time spans. Furthermore, institutional immortality favors policy thinking and group action which discourage adoption of extremes in the managing of portfolios.

In combination, tax exemption and perpetuity confer on IHL investors a unique and precious investment mobility which often bears upon the choice to be made between so-called income and growth securities.

As we look back over the years, we observe how far popular sentiment at times causes certain securities to sell on an extreme basis compared to the current income they produce. These conditions have obtained for both bonds and stocks at different points in their cyclical movements. To identify extremes in the market where present or future income can be purchased or exchanged most advantageously would seem to be our major investment objective. And, of course, no one here today can safely predict what stocks or bonds will work out best as purchases in today's market. But it refreshes the soul to talk around the subject, even though the conclusions reached in this seminar will not be reflected in any particular portfolio action.

If we could agree on *why* we invest endowments, I suspect our answer would have to be this: "To obtain over a period of years the highest possible continuous income return measured in terms of productive spending power."

Taking this sentence apart, we come up with three ideas.

1. The words, "over a period of years," suggest that our scale of measurement of income return is not today's market yield. This should give some comfort to those who cherish the highest hopes for the lowest yielding growth stocks.

2. The words, "highest possible continuous income return," add the quantitative (maximum, that is) and qualitative (continuity) elements of income which are most desirable.

3. The words, "in terms of productive spending power," compensate for changes in the value of the dollar, that somewhat elastic unit of money. And, lest you conclude that the institutional stretch lies in one direction only, bear in mind that in 1932 the commodity purchasing power of endowments was over 50 per cent above the 1926 level.

Having thus attempted to define why we invest, I shall explain why I have not mentioned the work "principal," either in respect to its protection or growth. On the premise that the principal value of any capital is derived from its capacity to produce income, potentially or in fact, we need only to relate prices of securities to the income characteristics about which we have spoken. Still this leaves room for wide disagreement among us as individuals for selecting stocks on the basis of our appraisals of anticipated price-earnings ratios and yields or for selecting bonds on the basis of yield differentials from stocks, for example. Mr. Harris's notes amply document with statistics the pattern of IHL behavior in this respect in various institutions in various eras.

As the most carefully prepared statistics — such as the 1958 Comprehensive Study of College and University Endowment Funds prepared by the Boston Fund, Inc. — show, about 52 per cent of IHL funds are now in stocks,

unquestionably the highest, a wide yield spread of less than ½ per cent for I.B.M. to 4 per cent for Jersey and General Motors gives us food for thought when, in comparison, we observe that nearly every Treasury security today yields 4 per cent or better.

I should like to conclude by putting before you several general comments.

1. IHL should maintain fully invested positions except for short periods or when new funds await investment.

2. The investment structure should provide

TABLE 1. — COMPARISON OF TEN LEADING STOCKS

Stock	Price (as of May 4, 1959)	Estimated Dividend (dollars)	Yield (per cent)	Value as of June 30, 1958 (millions of dollars)	Proportion of Total (per cent)
Standard Oil (N.J.)	53	2.20	4.15	95.0	3.1
Eastman Kodak	88	1.48	1.68	32.5	1.1
Texas Co.	85	2.40	2.83	30.9	1.0
General Electric Co.	82	2.00	2.44	28.5	1.0
Standard Oil (Calif.)	55	2.00	3.64	25.3	.9
Gulf Oil Corp.	114	2.50	2.19	24.4	.8
General Motors Corp.	50	2.00	4.00	23.6	.8
Christiana Securities	16,000	450.00	2.81	20.4	.7
duPont	243	6.00	2.47	20.2	.7
International Business Machines	581	2.60	.45	17.3	.6
TOTAL		(weighted)	3.00	318.1	10.7

maybe a little more. Examination of each institutional portfolio confirms Mr. Harris's conclusion that investment policies are more nearly alike than a generation or two ago — at least in so far as security classifications are concerned. But we may share some doubts when it comes to comparing the make-up of the common stock diversification figures compiled for IHL in the Boston Fund Study and further doubts upon examining the particular securities composing the group percentages.

One very interesting table, Schedule 6 on page 24 of that study, lists the ten most widely held common stocks, based on market value of sixty endowment portfolios, valued June 30, 1958, at over $3 billion. Here is what we find as we look at the list on May 4, 1959.

1. The following ten stocks comprise about 10 per cent of the sixty portfolios and yield today 3 per cent on the average.

2. Table 1 shows how these ten run in order of size.

3. While the quality of these holdings is

reasonably wide diversification among companies and industries and should not result in an unreasonable balance between (a) present and future income, or (b) equity and fixed income investments.

3. Formula approaches to investment can never substitute for good judgment and hence are not deserving of extended attention or debate.

4. As economic conditions and markets change, our doubts concerning the usefulness of individual security holdings can best be resolved by reappraisal of their income productivity or potential and by action taken in accordance with such appraisal. In short, our investment objective should be to invest and reinvest our endowments in those intrinsic values which produce continuous maximum income, irrespective of any labels we may elect to put upon them.

Colleges with only moderate endowments must often seek new forms of investment to raise incomes while holding down managing costs. An item appeared in the New York Times a few weeks ago, March 9, in the Monday column on investment trusts, advancing seriously the argument that institutions, because they are income-hungry, may wish to buy investment trust shares whose income frequently includes capital gains distributions.

It is pointed out that a $10,000 investment made in various investment trusts — five of them — on January 2, 1949, would, by the spring of 1959, have produced $6,786 in dividends, and $4,272 in capital gains, whereas the same investment in bonds or savings banks at 3 per cent would have earned only $3,500.

Then, the investment trust figures are translated back into a 10 year return of $8,317 thus making it appear that you have legitimately got over 8 per cent on your investment of endowment by counting in capital gains. I am sure that this doesn't have too wide an application, but the fact that the suggestion is directed specifically to our colleges and universities, churches, and so forth, made it very interesting to me.

SOME EXAMPLES OF EXPERIENCE WITH GROWTH STOCKS

George F. Bennett

I LOOK at growth stocks as one of the tools which portfolio managers can use to meet the inflationary problem that raises costs, expenses, and salaries, which all colleges have to pay.

We do not have the same tools at our disposal to meet inflationary trends that industry generally has, and yet we are subject to those same trends. We cannot freely raise tuition the way many industries can raise prices, because such a rise causes many problems. Maybe the steel companies would say that they cannot freely raise prices either, but they seem to do it successfully. We know it creates problems when tuition goes up.

I know that we all realize what the effect of inflation has been in university and college budgets. I have taken a look at some of Harvard's figures to get a background. Our expenses have risen in the last fifteen years from, roughly, $15 million to just under $60 million. That starts at the period just prior to the postwar inflation of 1943 through 1958.

Salaries, wages and pension benefits went up about the same amount, about four-fold, from $9 million to $36 million. Costs of materials we bought and maintenance of equipment went up about the same. During that period, investment income as a percentage of our total expenses declined — in other words, investment income covered about 45 per cent of our expenses at that time, about fifteen years ago, and now it covers about 35 per cent. So, there is the nature of the problem. How are you going to lick this inflation problem if you don't have freedom to raise your prices? (Incidentally, Harvard deals with ten unions and about eighteen bargaining units, so that we really have a wage agreement problem.)

Now, getting back to what tools we have for use in meeting the problem, it seems to me that growth stocks are one of them. Other tools that we have used are conservative accounting (which results in a plow-back of some of our cash income) such as amortizing our bond premiums fully and depreciating investment real estate on a liberal basis, and reinvesting a part of our investment income. All that tends to help us on the inflationary problem by building capital on which we can earn.

But as far as growth stocks are concerned, we all know and Mr. Tripp's figures show that, when you buy a growth stock, assuming that you can identify it as such when you start, normally, you forego immediate income for growth of principal and later realize an increase in income. So I thought it might be interesting to take a couple of specific examples out of our portfolio to see how the growth stocks have worked out.

I picked three stocks. One is Florida Power and Light, a growth utility; second, I.B.M., because it is a well-known growth stock; and the third, Polaroid, which has recently come into its own and has had short-term but rather phenomenal growth.

In Florida Power and Light, we made an investment in 1951, eight years ago, of about $600,000, and it is now $4.5 million; so that, as a growth stock, it has paid off. The capital appreciation is about 8 for 1, whereas during the same period, income has approximately tripled. I think that therein lies one of the problems, namely capital appreciation in growth stocks has run far ahead of the increase in income, which means that, as of the moment, something may be out of line — either prices have gone ahead too fast or the income is not ahead enough to support the price. I would say, therefore, that the risk or exposure is much higher at the moment than it was when we bought the stock.

In purchasing growth stocks, one expects to pay a rather high price-earnings ratio, hoping that earnings will come up fast enough so that that ratio will be a reasonable one at some later date. In the case of Florida Power and Light, when we bought the stock in 1951, it was priced at nine times earnings. Now, the original purchase price is only three times current earnings, and, on our estimate of 1962 earnings, our purchase price will be two times earnings; so that the earnings have grown up fast enough to make the price of the stock very attractive at the original price, which is what was hoped when it was purchased.

Let's take our I.B.M. investment from the same 1951 date, because that is when we bought Florida Power and Light, so that we have some comparable figures. In Florida Power and Light we had an eight-fold appreciation, whereas in I.B.M. there has been about a twelve-fold appreciation; so that an investment at that time of about three-quarters of a million dollars is now about $9 million, using actual figures.

The price-earnings ratio at the time we bought I.B.M. was, roughly, twenty times. In other words, we paid twenty times earnings for it in 1951. Using the 1951 price and this year's earnings, it is four times earnings. So, again, having paid a very high price-earnings ratio, we find current earnings very reasonable related to the cost price.

Then, let's take the third one, Polaroid, which was purchased about a year and a half ago. At the time we bought it, we paid about twenty-five to thirty times current earnings. The purchase price in November 1957 was $30 a share, and we think that this year they will earn around $2.75 per share; so that while we paid twenty-five or thirty times earnings for it two years ago, again, that purchase price is only ten times current earnings and, looking into our crystal ball, we think that the $30 price may be no more than three times earnings a few years ahead.

So the figures bear out that these have been growth stocks, that earnings have grown up to the prices paid for them, and, to the extent that income has grown and capital has appreciated the purpose has been accomplished of trying to keep pace with or get ahead of inflationary pressures.

I think the sixty-four-dollar question from here out is, if we in principle agree that growth stocks are good, as they have been in the past, where do we go from here?

We hear much talk now about a kind of growth stocks that seems to be one echelon higher than what we are accustomed to; they are called imagination stocks. I think, when we get in that area, it behooves us to be rather careful and, while the growth stocks have been a tool in the past, I personally feel that we should be very cautious in our selection and in the timing of new purchases because of the extent to which present prices discount the future.

GROWTH AND INCOME

Hulbert W. Tripp

ON several occasions in the past I have presented to the Trustees of the University of Rochester the performance record of individual stocks, particularly those held by the University, over a period of time. Since the portfolio of the University includes a very large proportion of so-called "growth stocks," the performance of these stocks has been compared with the performance of a few income stocks held in the account at one time or another, and it has been quite clear that the growth stocks in this account have been better holdings than the income stocks.

In a theoretical sense, *at any given time* it would seem difficult to defend the indiscriminate purchase of growth stocks because, while definitions of growth vary, the growth companies selected usually possess a strong increase in unit demand for the company's products, a high cash flow, a low current return, and the investor in growth usually adopts a *long-term view*. Since many of the stocks purchased for the University of Rochester's endowment fund have been held for only a few years, it is difficult to prove anything by citing the performance of these particular stocks in the short time they have been held. We have, therefore, selected ten stocks which can be termed "growth" stocks (all of which, incidentally, are held in the University account) and ten stocks which can be termed as "income" stocks (all held by the University at one time; only one of them is now held). The two groups selected are as follows:

Growth
American Cyanamid Company
Corning Glass Works
E. I. duPont de Nemours & Company
Eastman Kodak Company
Florida Power Corporation
General Electric Company
International Business Machines
Merck & Company
Standard Oil Company, New Jersey
Texas Company

Income
American Can Company
American Telephone and Telegraph
American Tobacco Company
Bankers Trust Company
Borden Company
Boston Edison Company
Coca Cola Company
General Mills, Inc.
International Harvester Company
National Dairy Products Corporation

It is felt that this selection is a fair one. For example, in the income group we have not included many stocks which at one time were very highly regarded in the postwar period. Omitted are such issues as New Jersey Zinc, Texas Gulf Sulphur, Loew's, and United Shoe Machinery. The growth list does include IBM, but it must because this is one of the more important growth stocks. However, this list excludes many dynamic examples of growth such as Polaroid, Haloid, Dow Chemical, and Minnesota Mining & Manufacturing.

In making this study we have included only the postwar period. The study is not entirely "pure" in a statistical sense, as we have used only the year-end figures and we have dropped fractions in our computation. A check using twice as many dates and retaining fractions reveals a variable of only 2 per cent in the final figures.

From the end of World War II to the present, the current yield (annual cash dividend divided by the last sale price of that year) on a portfolio equally divided dollar-wise among these several companies is as shown in Table 1.

TABLE 1.— RETURN ON GROWTH AND INCOME STOCKS, 1946–57, ROCHESTER SAMPLE

Year	Growth (per cent)	Income (per cent)
1946	3.43	4.15
1947	4.27	5.02
1948	4.44	5.57
1949	4.61	5.12
1950	5.64	5.60
1951	4.12	5.45
1952	3.86	5.04
1953	4.06	5.15
1954	3.26	4.59
1955	2.97	4.45
1956	3.03	5.07
1957	3.09	5.25

It should occasion no surprise to realize that the record of appreciation for the growth stocks far outweighs the price performance of the income stocks. Assigning the price on December 31, 1946, as 100, this performance is shown in tabular form.

TABLE 2. — PRINCIPAL APPRECIATION INDEX, GROWTH AND INCOME STOCKS, ROCHESTER SAMPLE, 1946–58

Year	Growth	Income
1946	100	100
1947	120	93
1948	130	89
1949	162	103
1950	187	101
1951	241	106
1952	275	116
1953	290	118
1954	420	135
1955	508	142
1956	632	131
1957	698	130
1958	880	167

The growth list also has reported a very superior performance in continuing to increase dividends on a fairly steady basis. The result of this steady increase is shown in Table 3, again assigning the yield on December 31, 1946, at 100.

TABLE 3. — DIVIDEND INDEX, GROWTH AND INCOME STOCKS, 1946–58

Year	Growth	Income
1946	100	100
1947	119	112
1948	134	123
1949	168	129
1950	234	139
1951	236	142
1952	241	140
1953	260	145
1954	315	147
1955	355	152
1956	387	166
1957	411	167
1958	412	169

One may say "This is all fine, but in order to purchase the growth stock in the first place, one has to sacrifice current yield. Is it worth it?" The study of the record of these two groups would certainly indicate that not much sacrifice has been necessary, at least up until the last few years. The following tabulation shows the number of years necessary for growth stocks to equal the yield on cost for income stocks.

TABLE 4. — YEARS NEEDED FOR GROWTH STOCK YIELD TO EQUAL AND SURPASS INCOME STOCK YIELD

Year (investment made December 31)	Years needed
1946	3
1947	2
1948	2
1949	1
1950	0
1951	4
1952	3
1953	3
1954	6 (estimated)

In Table 5 there is presented a division of the postwar period into groupings of four years' duration. Again we have assigned the December 31 price as 100, and we have calculated the yield at that date based upon the cash dividends received during the year just ended. The yields given in parentheses represent the yields available at the start of the four-year period, and there is also recorded the yield based on cost at the end of the four-year period. It will be seen that the record of the growth stocks is exceptionally dynamic both as to price performance and income performance. In an income sense, not until the year 1954 do we start running into trouble, and even here, of course, the price performance far outweighs the lower income. The yield on growth stocks purchased in 1946, for example, rose from 3.4 per cent to 7.8 per cent in four years; on income stocks the rise was only from 4.2 per cent to 5.7 per cent.

It is misleading for people to talk about growth stocks, and then immediately to give I.B.M. as the example. While I.B.M. is perhaps the most famous growth stock, it is not the only one, and if the market for the stock sometimes runs ahead of the growth of sales or earnings, it does not mean that this is true for all growth stocks at that particular time. It also seems to indicate that an investor goes 100 per cent into growth at any given time. Well, that never happens.

At this point it is perhaps well to cite one simple, practical fact. In practice, investment

TABLE 5. — GROWTH AND INCOME STOCKS, INCOME INDEX, YIELD ON COST AFTER FOUR YEARS, AND PRINCIPAL INDEX, 1946–1958

Year	INCOME INDEX Growth	INCOME INDEX Income	Growth [a] (percentage)	Income [a] (percentage)	PRINCIPAL INDEX Growth	PRINCIPAL INDEX Income
1946	100	100	(3.4)	(4.2)	100	100
1947	112	109			120	93
1948	117	109			130	89
1949	154	133			162	103
1950	228	138	7.8	5.7	187	101
1947	100	100	(4.3)	(5.0)	100	100
1948	106	108			108	96
1949	138	115			135	111
1950	203	124			155	109
1951	199	127	8.5	6.4	201	114
1948	100	100	(4.4)	(5.6)	100	100
1949	132	107			125	116
1950	206	115			144	113
1951	202	113			185	119
1952	208	115	9.3	6.4	212	130
1949	100	100	(4.6)	(5.1)	100	100
1950	151	109			115	98
1951	149	110			149	103
1952	151	108			170	113
1953	164	111	5.8	5.7	179	116
1950	100	100	(5.6)	(5.6)	100	100
1951	99	96			129	105
1952	101	99			147	115
1953	105	101			155	117
1954	125	102	7.1	5.7	224	134
1951	100	100	(4.1)	(5.5)	100	100
1952	102	99			114	109
1953	113	101			120	112
1954	129	103			174	129
1955	147	105	6.0	5.7	211	136
1952	100	100	(3.9)	(5.0)	100	100
1953	110	103			105	103
1954	127	103			153	118
1955	143	106			185	124
1956	165	114	6.4	5.8	230	115
1953	100	100	(4.1)	(5.2)	100	100
1954	113	102			144	118
1955	129	105			175	121
1956	145	111			218	111
1957	154	112	6.3	5.8	241	137
1954	100	100	(3.3)	(4.6)	100	100
1955	114	103			121	105
1956	123	109			150	97
1957	138	110			166	96
1958	141	110	4.5	5.1	228	120

[a] Basic yield in parenthesis.

advisors usually do not have the foresight or the courage to place entire funds in one type of stock at any given time. Most of us, then, if we believe in growth stocks, add two or three growth stocks per year after careful study. This procedure permits a leveling out of any income disadvantage even under conditions prevailing during the last two or three years.

Facts and statistics are necessary tools in arriving at an investment decision. It is my personal opinion that exercise of fundamental judgment using these tools is the most important ingredient in arriving at a correct decision. There is also always present the human factor. Despite some rumors to the contrary, security analysts and even investment committees are human. We have already mentioned the fact that the list of income stocks does not include some securities which were very highly regarded in the past but have had an unfortunate record in recent years. Take, for example, the case of New Jersey Zinc. This stock, in the period under review, sold as high as 83, and in 1947 it paid a dividend of $4.50 per share. Since that time it has sold down below 19, is now selling at around 27, and is paying no dividend. The reduction of dividends has been rather gradual, and for a period of better than three years in the early fifties the stock paid $3.00 a share regularly. Just prior to the time of dividend reductions the stock usually sold at a price to yield above 6 per cent. This is where the human factor comes into the picture. It takes great courage and judgment to submit an investment recommendation involving sale of a stock which is yielding a very high current rate of return. More often than not this decision is delayed and delayed. The same sort of problem would confront one in dealing with a holding of Texas Gulf Sulphur which paid over $2.00 per share in the early fifties, sold as high as 44, and is now paying $1.00 and has sold down as low as 15. If one selects a growth stock that encounters difficulties, the decision to switch into another security is not nearly so difficult. U.S. Borax, as an example, sold as high as 76 and as low as 33⅜ in the last two years. Yet its dividend, until omitted recently, was only 60 cents per share. The University of Rochester held this stock and sold it at a profit. We may again hold the stock, but the price of stepping aside, at least for a temporary period, was not a great one.

The figures which we have submitted covering the two groups of stocks would seem to indicate that we have been well repaid for holding growth stocks. Even in recent years the appreciation record has been comparatively satisfactory. In view of the longer time required to catch up with improving dividend payments in the growth group, one is certainly entitled to question the recent sharp rise in prices for some of these stocks. In the process we must not overlook some of the fundamentals involved. Over the longer term it would still seem desirable to own stocks which have

a low labor factor, high-grade and effective research, a strong continuing product demand, new product development, and, above all, an intelligent personnel system and a high-grade, aggressive management. Again the human factor comes into play, not only in judging these points, particularly the management, but in evaluating the price of the stock itself. Any decision to withdraw from such a security as I.B.M. involves automatically another decision on the repurchase side. This assumes, of course, that one continues to regard I.B.M.'s management favorably, and that the I.B.M. Company continues to possess the other qualities which are necessary and desirable for the long term. If, for example, the stock were to be sold at the high of 552 and then declined to the 300 level, would we have the courage and judgment to repurchase it before it resumes another growth cycle? All I can say is that it looked extremely high statistically when we purchased it for the University account considerably below the 300 level. In arriving at this or any other investment decision we must continue to weigh many, many factors and try

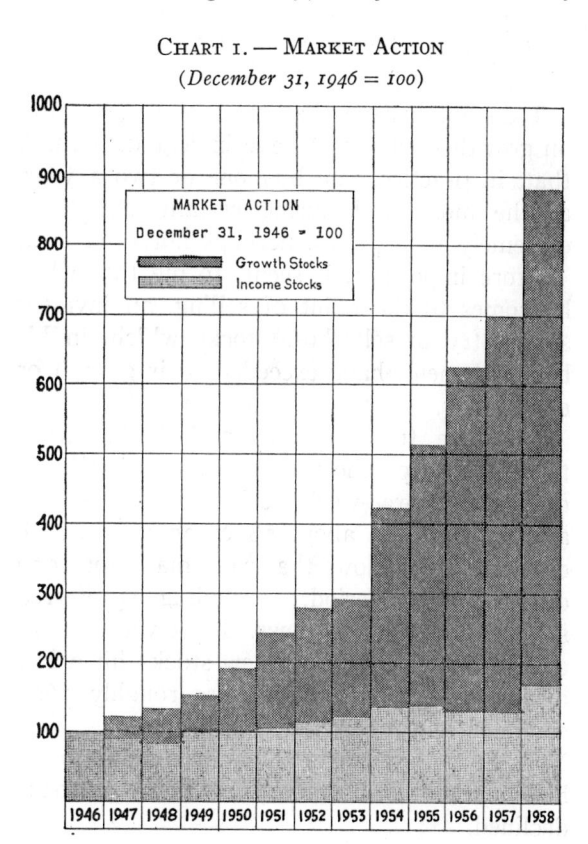

CHART 1. — MARKET ACTION
(*December 31, 1946 = 100*)

CHART 2. — DIVIDEND ACTION

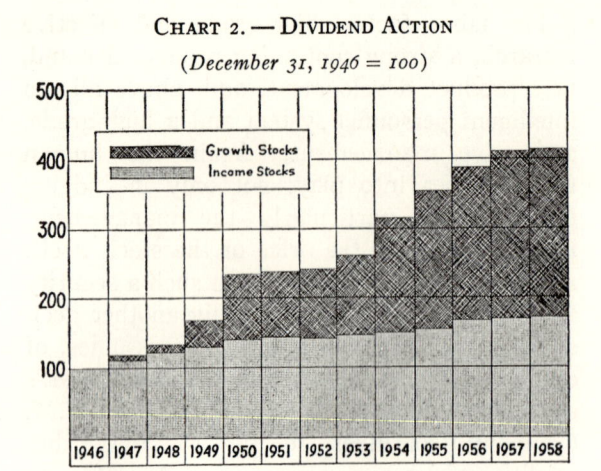

(December 31, 1946 = 100)

to balance our decisions without being extreme. We always need next year's newspaper.

Now I will give you my conclusions. One, it is hard to define "growth," but we still believe that companies having aggressive management, good research and technological skill resulting in new products, low labor costs, and a need to plow back earnings will continue to fare better than others. I think that this is fundamental, that the companies that require money for growth cannot pay out too much initially and will have a need for that money. In other words, invest the funds in the business.

I do not believe that we should generalize on growth stocks, as I have indicated. I think that, in practice, you buy one or two a year, at the most, and during certain periods of extremely high prices, perhaps not even that.

More important, it seems to me that when he comes to the point of selling, an investor should try to sell those stocks which, in his best judgment, have exceeded their growth or expectancy.

I believe, furthermore, that it is dangerous to generalize on the "stock market" itself. In one recent three-week period the Dow-Jones average went up about 18 or 20 points and, counting up the lows that were made for 1959 during that period, excluding preferred stocks, there were 423 lows. There was a duplication, but 140 absolute new stocks hit a low during that period. There are roughly 1600 common and preferred stocks on the New York Stock Exchange. Thus even in a violent bull market a substantial number of stocks declined.

There is one other point that I feel quite strongly about. It was brought up before in these pages. I call it "putting your mitten into the tambourine," but it is simply the invasion of principal. Strangely enough, with all the trouble and all the shooting at advocates of growth-stocks, today we have a new problem: some University trustees are saying, "Since you have made so much money on this, why don't you skim off some of the profit and use that to put into buildings."

I think this is part of the growth-stock problem. Unfortunately, we have become targets of that sort of reasoning. Maybe it shows that Parker Hall's method of having special investments is less vulnerable to this kind of argument. It is a vicious sort of argument, purely from an investment point of view. Right now, in our account we are taking some profits and putting the money aside for future use, for a purchase back. Although I believe the timing is wrong, I am doing it just because one cannot ride good fortune too hard; and one takes the gain on the basis of selectivity.

The purchase back may be any special situation — it may be a bond; it may be a number of things — but my contention is that one should always be flexible and have money available for purchasing bargain assets. Using principal because you have extraordinary appreciation is likely to lead to trouble. You may not even recognize a good growth stock, for example, if you do not have the money available, and it seems to me that it may be rather costly to force a use of part of the capital gains.

This matter of use of principal is highly debatable. You don't have to agree entirely with Beardsley Ruml, but I feel that use of principal discourages a search for increased efficiency in education. Using principal favors the articulate of today at the expense of the inarticulate of tomorrow.

But I am supposed to be talking about investments. I argue simply that one should not use the argument of growth to consume principal. If a college wishes to do it, I think it should just go ahead and do it and admit doing it, without using gains on growth stock to bolster the argument.

INVESTMENT POSSIBILITIES

John F. Meck

OTHER papers have covered most of the substantive topics on college investment policies; there are just three questions which I feel have been given insufficient attention, and I will merely mention the first two. The third I will discuss more thoroughly, since I think it is rather interesting, and it pertains more directly to investments.

The first point concerns the management of investments of small institutions — those which have portfolios in the $1 million to $5 million range. I am frankly surprised that recent figures show an improvement in their earnings record. I have had some doubt about whether these investments are managed from the standpoint of the best interests of the institution *as an educational institution* and its need for special emphasis on income, compared to the typical trust fund beneficiary.

My second point concerns the use of income reserves for stabilizing investment income. That is another question which deserves more attention. Professor Harris mentions the rule of thumb of having one year's investment income in the reserve. I think that evolved because Harvard set that as a rule of thumb, and it has now become generally accepted.

I wonder whether one year's income is too little or too much. I believe Henry Wood, who used to be in the Harvard investment office, has a reserve larger than one year's income at Wellesley. Thus Wellesley is spending last year's income; they earn income before they pay it out. I believe that Harvard and Princeton are the only other institutions that are fortunate enough to be able to do this. It would be helpful to have a careful analysis of the problem.

My third point arises from the discussion of the declining role of endowment in the financial picture at institutions of higher learning. I have always been reminded of a story that John Mason Brown told about five years ago which put endowment in perspective for me. At that time the Navy was building its first "super" aircraft carrier. Brown pointed out that Harvard's total endowment at market value was just equal to the cost of this new aircraft carrier. This gives you some idea of the place of endowment in relation to national-defense expenditures.

I compared our own endowment at Dartmouth, and ours was then equal to the cost of one of the new United States Lines ships.

What I want to say here, however, is this: it is true that endowment funds are declining in relative importance, but I think we ought to spend a little more time on a subject that we touched on in the last section: what is in endowment funds, and what is not.

Most of us have what we call "funds functioning as endowment," and in that category are usually some funds which are wholly unrestricted funds — principal can be spent as well as income. I do not know how the income of these funds is treated at other institutions, but at Dartmouth we use some of it for current operations.

I think that these funds functioning as endowment — the ones that are wholly unrestricted — can have a high strategic value, and I think it will be worth getting some figures on what percentage of total endowment funds consists of unrestricted funds functioning as endowment.

In Dartmouth's case, looking at market values, 15.3 per cent of some $70 million is in that category. That is a substantial amount. We are spending the income of about half this 15.3 per cent for current expenses.

I looked at the reports for several other institutions, and it is hard to tell what they are doing. Some of them have expendable funds, including building funds. There are *no* building funds included in Dartmouth's 15.3 per cent.

I estimated that only 4.1 per cent of Princeton's funds are in the wholly-unrestricted category, but I am sure that is too low: Yale, 7.2 per cent; Wellesley, 19.5 per cent; Amherst,

4.5 per cent; and Wesleyan, 23.2 per cent.

It is often difficult to distinguish from the reports which funds are endowment, which are funds functioning as endowment, and what, if any, restrictions there are on funds merely functioning as endowment. In Dartmouth's case, the 15.3 per cent are funds that are wholly expendable for any purpose and are not earmarked for buildings. They appear on the liability side of the balance sheet along with endowment and similar funds, but we mark these funds with an asterisk to distinguish them.

I will give just one illustration of how such funds might be used. The purpose of the illustration is not to prove anything about Dartmouth's investment policy, because I am sure that other treasurers can bring in even better examples. The interesting part of this example is not how this fund increased, but how it was used.

In 1938–39 we received a bequest of about $500,000 from one of our former trustees. It was wholly unrestricted; the principal could be expended. The administration of the estate had been delayed. The donor died in 1934 or 1935, when the estate was worth almost $1 million, with the residue coming to Dartmouth. The executors did not convert the common stocks in the portfolio to short-term investments, and by the time we received it in 1938–39, its value was down to $500,000.

This man's friends on the Board of Trustees knew that the donor's lifelong ambition had been to leave Dartmouth $1 million. So they decided, for entirely noninvestment reasons, to put the whole $500,000 into equities as a separately invested fund. This was in late 1939 and early 1940. They put it into such then "speculative" items as Aluminium, Ltd., Continental Oil, International Paper, Newmont Mining, and other things of that kind.

At the present time, the market value of this fund's investment is roughly $3,700,000, or about 7.4 times the amount received. However, we began using part of it around 1954, and the fund did not get the full benefit of the rise in the market after that time. Today $2,800,000 out of the $3,700,000 which had been entirely separately invested (this is the important point here) was transferred to our investment pool, which is a balanced fund. The object in part was to set up a maintenance fund for a $7,500,000 building which we will complete in 1960–61. The $2,800,000 will yield over $100,000 in income. Without that fund, I am not sure that we would have dared to go ahead with the building.

The remaining $900,000 has been kept separately invested. For the most part, it has been shifted from equities into local real estate investments which we simply had to make to house college personnel. We now have as investments nine faculty single residences, two faculty apartment houses (housing ten families), and a thirty-unit housing project using Tech-Built homes. All this housing earns virtually no return, but we are depreciating it so that twenty or thirty years from now we will have most of the $900,000 to put back into other houses or to put back in the stock market or other investments.

The moral of this is that there is something to be said for using growth stocks and having certain funds, not needed for current income, invested separately, so that the college can take advantage of appreciation. It gives an elasticity to our financial strategy without which we would not have been able to carry forward important phases of our program.

I think a subject worthy of some attention would be to find out just what are the relative percentages of funds functioning as endowment which are wholly unrestricted as to principal, how they have been used, and whether it is a wise policy to defer use of funds in order to undertake investments as in the case I described.

Of course, you can argue that Dartmouth would be much better off if we had built in 1939 with the $500,000. I do not know whether this would have been possible or not, but we were not ready to build then.

Dartmouth could have put this fund in the endowment pool, and, as Dick Mestres has pointed out, one advantage of the market-value method or unit method is that we would take it out now at a higher value. Say we put $500,000 in. We would have now perhaps, $1,000,000 or $1,200,000. But the argument here is that the separate investment gave us a chance to use growth stocks 100 per cent, while appreciation in the pool, which is a balanced fund, would have been relatively less.

I think there may be too much stress on the desirability of merging all investments into one pool. I certainly think you ought to merge all endowment funds, especially small funds, but there still is a role for separate investment in special situations by choice.

61 BROADWAY

Livingston W. Houston

WE have felt — I am going to have to write more or less personally on the subject that I have been given — we at Rensselaer have felt that we were sort of country cousins to all of the rich people in the United States — to the big corporations, the big foundations, the big givers — and we knew that our own friends, our own alumni, had not been properly indoctrinated over the years in their responsibility to their alma mater. Early in my career as president, I became very discouraged, but decided that there was only one thing to do: to try to inaugurate a development program that, in one or two generations, might begin to approach the results that most of the larger institutions have. We would also have to try to put a little of our own ingenuity toward solving our own problems. That, of course, meant watching the costs, trying to put a little more business management in some of the things that we do to see if we could curtail expenses wherever possible — not necessarily in regard to people but in regard to things — seek more intensive use of our facilities, and other savings of that nature.

We also came to the conclusion that we must try to make our small endowment do a better job for us in the way of producing income. You have seen samples of what some of our larger institutions are doing, such as Chicago, with their lease-back of equipment, parking lots, 100 per cent mortgages on certain types of property, the *Encyclopaedia Britannica*. You know, also, about some of the real estate deals that other institutions have gone into. The most recent one, publicized since the first of the year, concerned the St. Louis Car Company arrangement that benefited Lafayette University, and, a few years ago, the spaghetti factory bought by N. Y. U., and things of that type.

Some ten or twelve years ago, we began to wonder why we were not in on some of these schemes that were helpful to the income, necessary, and perfectly legitimate. About the time we started thinking in those terms, we found that our neighbor, Union, had acquired all the real estate of one or two department stores in New York and were publicizing the $40 million of real estate that they held, what it was going to mean to Union twenty-five or thirty years hence and how they did it all with $100,000.

So, I spread the word around among our trustees and close friends that we should find some of these imaginative ways to make money that were legitimate for the Institute, and, as a result, over a period of several years, we studied a great many of the types that have been discussed here today. We even looked into oil payments and water flood of oil fields, equipment leases, and a few things like that; we even had one offer of a pipeline.

I shied away from anything that required a great deal of management. I felt that we were not management engineers or experts. We didn't want tankers. But we did go into several deals, as you might call them, with respect to leasing equipment. These were very profitable. You buy the equipment, lease it back. Over the period of five years, we earned a modest income and amortized the original cost of the equipment; in the next five years, we received a more than adequate income. Then, on top of that, we often have had an opportunity to loan some of our stock to stock exchange firms for covering short sales. In this way, we could pick up a thousand dollars or so that we felt was legitimate, without very much risk.

We finally had an opportunity to investigate a building at 61 Broadway. Before I go into any detail about this building, I want to say that, in 1950, we were not able to foresee the high stock prices of today any more than today we can foresee what the stock prices will be another nine or ten years hence. So, our judgment in going into 61 Broadway in 1950 was based on what we could see at that time in the way of security values and income that could be obtained on those securities. The way we worked out the plan, it seemed to be so advantageous that, after I had persuaded myself, there was very little difficulty in getting the trustees to go into what they thought was a rather elaborate, extensive, and large plan for the Institute given our modest funds.

We started out by buying the 61 Broadway Building from the fabulous Mr. Fox of New York and Boston fame. He was willing to sell it to us for $100,000 subject to a second mortgage and a first mortgage which was already on the building, plus $1,035,000 that we borrowed from the banks, with the understanding that he would rent the building back from us and pay us a rent of $540,000 a year. From this payment we would pay the first mortgage and we would quickly retire our own bank loans, and there would be no obligation on the second mortgage until our bank loans were paid off. At the end of six years, Mr. Fox had an option to renew the lease for six more years, and, after that, he would have no opportunity to re-lease the building. The first mortgage was to expire in 1971 and the lease of the main tenant (the Schroeder Bank) would expire in 1972. It looked as though we were in pretty good hands to have the building produce the revenue that was budgeted.

That went along very nicely for the first three years and three months, until our friends in Washington decided that lease-backs were not desirable, and the Supplement U section of the Internal Revenue Code became law for the next January. The plan we had worked out was now going to be subject to normal income taxes, and we could not, as a result, follow out our plan as projected.

Fortunately, the day before we entered into this agreement, we told Mr. Fox over the telephone that we had to have some way out of this or we couldn't sell it to the finance committee. He finally agreed to a fee to permit us to buy his lease-back at the end of six years. After Supplement U went in, we negotiated a reduction of the fee from a million and a half to a million dollars, which we paid him in 1953, and took over the building and the management of it ourselves.

We also, at that time, had had three years' experience in real estate that we had not had before, and we decided that we would put in some of our own money, which we did: $2,225,000. We again borrowed from the banks and, as of today, we have paid off all the bank loans. We have reduced the first mortgage considerably. This June, we will have reduced the first mortgage by $1,800,000, and will have paid off all the bank loans of $2,190,000. We now have a capital reserve that came from buying the second mortgage back from Mr. Fox at a discount of $250,000.

In the meantime, the college, up to June, will have taken $1,195,000 out for current purposes. This averages $129,000 a year, or 5.8 per cent on our $2,225,000.

Now, in the next twelve years, we will pay off the first mortgage and, having the building free of bank loans, we will take $2,700,000 more, an average of $225,000 a year, or 10 per cent on our investment. We will also take $2,500,000 for what I call a depreciation reserve — and that is set up in cash. We will use the reserve, if we wish, for special appropriations by the trustees. We feel that is sure aid when sorely needed. We are getting our 10 per cent during this period, from our invested funds, and we will still have an asset at the end that we hope is going to be worth $10 million. This depreciation reserve is going to represent 8.9 per cent a year. Thus, for the next twelve years, we are going to take about 19 per cent, based on our original investment, out of that building.

Now, when you look at the entire twenty-one-year period, the Institute will have taken out of the building $3,895,000 of ordinary income, and the special reserve income will be $2,500,000, or a total of $6,395,000 on our $2,225,000 investment. That is an average of 13½ per cent a year. In addition to that, we have paid off the first mortgage of $5,365,000 and bank notes of $2,190,000, or a total of $7,555,000, which is 15.9 per cent a year, so we have increased our equity in the building and taken out cash to a total of 29.5 per cent.

Beginning in 1971, based on our hopes and expectations — of course, we cannot tell, as I say, exactly what is going to happen — it looks as though we would be geared to take $855,000 a year out of that building, which will be about 39 per cent on our original investment. Now, today, our equity in the building has built up to a little over $6,500,000. The mortgage today is only $3,400,000.

Based on figures of M. I. T. (Massachusetts Investors Trust), if that $2,225,000 had been placed there and reinvested, it would have been worth just about that same amount of capital, but the income from 61 Broadway to the college has been more. I suspect if we could have foreseen how security prices were going to inflate in these last two years, we might not have gone into all of this.

Now, our problem today is what should we do? Should we play the horses right to the finish in 1971, or should we sell the building for $10 million cash? We are considering the latter at the present time. If those who are negotiating with us offer $10 million cash and assume the first mortgage, I shall urge our trustees to sell in a hurry. But, if they don't, I think the way we have planned it will work out best for the college.

One reason we were interested in real estate of this type — and there are many more buildings down there than can be purchased, although not always on such favorable terms — the thing that appealed to us is that the management problem in real estate in New York City is not so difficult as it sounds. There are half a dozen top-grade management firms, and if one of them doesn't want to handle your building or do a good job, there will be no problem in finding another. If we were to own a factory or a pipeline, and the management changed for any reason, we might have a management problem, and we, in a medium-sized college, are not in a position to handle industrial management problems.

Now, our reason for going into real estate was very simple. We had to do something to try to increase the income to help out our institution in supplementing the modest support we were receiving from other sources. In that connection, if I may, I would just like to comment on endowments. Endowments have been the backbone of most of the private colleges for a great many years, and it is very distressing that they have not kept pace with our growth, because, to some of us, endowments are just as important today as current giving. If a report deprecating endowments goes to the general public, it might hurt the attempts of colleges to get more endowment. I am not against current giving. I appreciate that, in many cases, it is the easiest way to get new money. But let us not play down in any way the importance of endowments.

I know, in our particular case, the endowment funds produce about $350 a student, which is 17 per cent of the cost of educating a boy at Rensselaer. We would like to have the proportion higher; but we certainly want to hold it at that present point, so I interject this thought on endowments in addition to my few remarks on special methods that some people use to get some extra income.

I think that one of Professor Harris' tables really does prove that endowments have been helpful, and I think that it is up to the colleges as managers of funds to try to see that they keep the value of their funds and the income from those funds just as high as possible, so as to continue to help the projects and the educational programs in the various institutions.

UNORTHODOX INVESTING

J. Parker Hall

MY paper is concerned with unconventional investments, of which the University of Chicago, along with Yale and one or two other institutions, has made quite a few. What I am about to describe is something I do not think can be done by the small college because it takes a great deal of investment effort and time.

The University of Chicago started these unconventional investments in 1948, when we became interested in the shipping business. At that time we bought an oil tanker. We borrowed some money from the Chase Bank and, knowing nothing ourselves about the tanker business, we used their knowledge to write a very good charter with an oil company. For our equity ownership to make any money, we knew that the debt would have to be paid off first, so that the bank and the University had a common interest as far as the charter was concerned.

The University has owned the tanker now for ten or eleven years. It has been under continuous bareboat charter (net lease) to a big oil company, and we have received a large sum of money in charter hire. We have paid off Chase Bank with interest, amortized our entire investment with 6 per cent interest, and, in the last five years, have received $100,000 annually, clear, with no further investment.

Now we have rechartered the ship for another fifteen years and have "jumbo-ized" it at a cost of $3 million. This means that the bow and the stern were cut off, a new, bigger midship section was installed, then the bow and stern were reattached. We will receive 4.9 per cent on this additional investment. We also capitalized a million dollars of profit, meaning that the tanker was worth a million dollars at the time we put it in to be jumbo-ized; so that, with the cost of jumbo-izing at $3 million and the vessel valued at $1 million, we are receiving in charter hire over fifteen years the $4 million plus interest.

This led us into other kinds of transactions. We have made, probably, half a dozen different shipping deals. One of them is the above; a new enterprise is building three 40,000-ton tankers in Swedish yards. Insurance companies are putting up most of the cost of these tankers ($6 million apiece) on a first mortgage. The promoters needed working capital, so we put up $1 million junior to the first mortgage, and they put up $500,000 junior to us. In return for our loan, we received 25 per cent of the stock.

Now the charter to a large oil enterprise will pay off both the insurance companies and ourselves over the fifteen years, with interest, and then we will have 25 per cent ownership in three tankers free and clear. In fact, our ownership will probably be limited to two tankers, because one of them is optioned to the oil company for a nominal sum at that time.

I do not know what a 40,000-ton tanker will be worth fifteen years from now, but we hope it will be worth perhaps $2 million, so we will have a 25 per cent interest in something worth, say, $4 million, which would give us $1 million profit. We paid nothing for this equity except the willingness to put up the money behind the first mortgage.

The question of our liability in the case of collisions and other maritime disasters may occur to you. Under maritime law, the owner is never liable for more than the value of his ship. In general, this applies to death and injury as well as to property claims. In any case, it is possible to insure fully against this contingency, so that it is not a deterrent to investment in ships.

Another way the University of Chicago invests its funds is in various lease-backs. These are common these days, but ten years ago they were not. We must have about $6 or $7 million of lease-backs, which involve our purchasing a property and "leasing it back" to a user for a period of ten to twenty years. The investor recovers his principal plus interest during the term of the lease and then owns residual property, free and clear of a lease, for whatever it may be worth at the end of the term.

The kind of people we have leased properties to are Harvester, Bausch and Lomb, Burroughs, Walgreen — all firms with good credit.

We like these better than mortagages because we hope for a residual value.

We have as yet made no profit out of these lease-backs, and we shall not know whether they are really good until my successor comes along. He will have an investment either worth something or worth nothing; if it is worth nothing, at least we shall have recovered our money with interest. If the residual has value — and many of these properties are well located in downtown areas — it could be substantial.

Competition is becoming much more severe now, but interesting lease-backs are still available. Many of the big oil companies do theirs with gasoline stations and are delighted to transact business with pension funds and colleges. You can get stations in Canada and in this country. I do not know what these corner properties, located all over the country, are going to be worth, but at some point, some of them will be worth something after our money has been recovered. That is the hope.

We have leased equipment to concerns with high-grade credit standing. We pioneered, I think, in leasing cars and trucks to Phillips Petroleum, which sold and leased back the thousands of cars and trucks used by salesmen and others. A group of investors, including the University, put up the money on a roll-over basis. Title is held in a trustee, and the trust is not subject to income tax. The lessee pays rent each month, and, at the end of four years, we have written off a car and a new one is purchased. All purchasing and servicing is done by a professional car-leasing concern for a fee which the lessee pays. We are repaid some principal each month, but we put up more money when they buy new cars, so the fund is revolving.

This kind of investment yields 1 to 1.5 per cent more than do Phillips' debentures. We were given Phillips' credit, but we received another 1.5 per cent.

More recently, we have broadened our unusual investments. We financed the purchase of some Neoprene containers that are eight feet in diameter — big, hollow, rubber holders which Union Carbide uses to ship liquids and flowable solids from one of its plants to another. Title to these is taken by a trustee. We put up the money and, with Union Carbide agreeing to pay the rent each month, we have a very high-grade investment.

We have done the same thing with duPont, and return is, again, 1 to 1.5 per cent more than whatever a normal debenture interest rate would have been at the time we did it. We have also purchased a number of oil and gas payments and royalties.

We have done a couple of seemingly crazy things. For example, once we earned the equivalent of about 8 per cent on our money from making a bank deposit in a large West Coast bank. It came about this way. A company was in desperate need of funds to use as a compensating balance. A "compensating balance" is a method by which a banker gets a larger interest rate than he acknowledges he charges. You borrow $100 from him but withdraw only $80 because you must keep $20 on deposit with him. He charges you interest on the $100, but you get the use of only the $80.

In this case, a company was in the business of purchasing equipment which it leased to corporations for five-year periods. The company went to a bank and said, "Look, we will assign these leases to you, if you will lend us the money to buy the equipment so that we can lease it to these big companies. The big companies will then pay rent. It will come to you, the bank, to pay off your loan."

Well, the bank said, "Fine, but we want a compensating balance left here."

This company, with only $2 million of net worth, didn't have enough money for a compensating balance, so it asked the University of Chicago to deposit a million dollars with this bank. We were reluctant to place our funds at risk in this enterprise. The company pointed out that this was to be just a plain, ordinary bank deposit by the University. We would agree to keep the money there for one year. The company would get credit for it with the bank, but if the company went broke, this would not affect our deposit, which we could still withdraw from the bank after one year. Hence no risk was involved.

The bank confirmed all this, and interest was paid to us, not by the bank, but by the company, at the rate of 5 per cent, and then, in addition, we received some warrants to buy the company's stock. The stock went up, and, when we finally sold it, the net effect to us was interest of between 8 and 9 per cent for one year by making a bank deposit of $1 million.

The deposit was in the University's name. Of course, it was not subject to withdrawal; we had to keep it in the bank. It was a time deposit for one year, in effect.

Probably the best known of our unconventional investments is *Encyclopaedia Britannica*. There is this great distinction between the *Britannica* and the other types of investment I have been mentioning. The others were purchased by the University with its endowment funds; *Britannica* was a gift to us in 1943 from Sears, Roebuck. Interestingly, the University at that time nearly did not accept the gift because we were unwilling to put up working capital. An imaginative man, William Benton, then a Vice-President of the University, put up $100,000 of working capital as a loan, which was later turned into stock. We had an option, which we did not exercise, to buy him out; today, he owns two-thirds and we own one-third.

Britannica is a tax-paying enterprise. We receive royalties for consultation with our faculty about the books. It has been very profitable indeed. The Company's sales have grown from $7 million to $60 million, and profits have gone from nothing up to around $4 million after taxes.

Thus, you can see that ownership of our one-third has been valuable. We have received dividends, royalties, and other things out of it that have brought us close to $10 million over this period.

If one values the stock and royalty, the *Britannica* donation to the University of Chicago has been second only to that of John D. Rockefeller. We have not realized on the royalty, and we have not realized by selling the stock. If we did, I feel sure that this would be true.

The companies, including *Britannica*, are all tax-paying concerns. Some of the shipping companies are incorporated abroad, in Panama for instance, but I would point out that this is normal in the shipping business. For example, Standard Oil of New Jersey has Panamanian subsidiaries. I do not think we are dodging taxes by doing this, because it is normal in the shipping business.

Well, these are some of the things the University of Chicago does. In summary, I would say that one reason we do them is to gain more than average income. In the last twelve years or so, our income on these types of investment has averaged 30 per cent more than we could have had from comparable marketable securities at the time we made the investments.

We also like to make capital gains when possible, and, up to the present time, our realized capital gains on these unorthodox investments have been $2.5 million and our unrealized gains about $5 million, a total gain of about $7 million. This does not include any of the residual we might get out of these lease-backs that we have, and, of course, it excludes the *Britannica*, which we do not consider in this group at all. Although the unrealized gain is still an estimate, we believe that we could realize such a figure now.

One difficulty with making such investments is the amount of time it takes to analyze and supervise them. This raises a question which Yale has publicly stated: if they had spent the same amount of time on their common stocks as they had spent on unorthodox investments, would they not have done just as well or better?

Also, there is risk in these investments, in that they are, for the most part, nonmarketable. So, if you are once in them and they go bad, you are out of luck. But, to date, we think that they have worked out pretty well.

Now, the question has been asked, how much money do we have in these things? At this moment, we have about $18 million so invested, out of a total pooled fund of $180-odd million, or about 10 per cent. This is all at market value.

Up to this point, we have realized no loss. We have one transaction, in which Harvard and Dartmouth are involved with us, which began with the construction of a new oil refinery in Puerto Rico. Here we put up junior money in the form of debentures and got some common stock as a bonus. The hope was that the refinery would be profitable, that we would get our debenture money back with interest, and then have the stock, which would in effect double our money.

At one time, our investment was worth exactly double its cost. We could have sold out about three years ago for double what we put in. Since then, the refinery has not worked well. Everything under the sun went wrong with it. Inasmuch as it was not working, it was decided to double its size, on the theory, no doubt, that this would improve the situation. Now, it is beginning to work more satisfactorily. We may wind up coming a cropper here, in which case we would lose six or seven hundred thousand dollars, or we may clear a substantial profit.

So far, we have not lost any money, but I think we should point out that we are at a peak of the cycle here, and who knows? If we get into bad times — nobody thinks we are going to have any bad times any more, but if we get into a first-class depression (which, I am sure, will hit us at some point when we think we are through with them) — we may well end up by losing some money, and we will have to offset some of our realized gains against possible losses at that time.

We cannot be sure that these investments have been attractive or profitable. At the moment they look as though they have been. But it does take a great deal of time for them to pay off, and they are nonmarketable and do entail risk.

In making comparisons with the yield on more conventional investment programs, it must be kept in mind that we do not charge the extra time and personnel involved against these special investments. They do require more attention.

Notwithstanding the extra time involved, and the appreciation in recent years of the market value of securities which normally fill the investment portfolio of a university, I feel that these unorthodox investments have been worthwhile. Whether the answer will be the same when my successor takes over and realizes (or fails to realize) the gains we anticipate, is problematical. And, of course, a serious decline in business activity might have blunted our optimism if we had taken heavy losses.

It is a difficult thing to equate the degree of risk in these investments with that in common stock. In some cases, there is less risk. For example, in tanker transactions, where there is a net lease to a large oil company, the risk is no greater than leasing property to A & P, for instance, and with tankers one would hope to get some stock free. We have part ownership, and that is where our profit comes.

I think that in some of the others, such as the promotion to build a refinery in Puerto Rico (where there were no taxes for ten years, which may enable the company to pay off the debt during the period when, normally, they would have been paying taxes), there is real risk.

I would find it very difficult to say whether there is more or less risk in this sort of scheme than, let us say, in General Motors or Texas Instruments.

Relatively speaking, we have done more in the way of unusual investments than almost any other university. Wesleyan, with its publishing firm, and Yale, with a program similar to ours, are about the only universities with comparable emphasis in such ventures. Most large universities — as well as the smaller institutions — do little or nothing similar. Harvard, for example, has made several special investments in the oil field, including the refinery in Puerto Rico, but nothing else of any significance. The University of Chicago has dealt in these investments primarily because of the greater return which they offer, as compared with more conventional investments owned by most universities.

SHOULD HARVARD BORROW?

Paul C. Cabot

I AM particularly interested in the question of a university's — Harvard's, in particular, because I cannot speak for anybody else — borrowing money. That is one reason that I picked the subject.

I think that borrowing is a subject that we have had very much in our mind, and I have had a great many people suggest that Harvard ought to borrow money. I will not give all the arguments for borrowing money. We will let Professor Harris do that, if he will. The most obvious purpose for borrowing money is to acquire some sort of facilities, be they physical or faculty, that the institution doesn't now have and that it needs badly. It perhaps becomes particularly acute in this era when the colleges are all having a frightful time with the rush of students who want to get in, and growing pressure on all of us to increase the size of our institutions.

I think that those are the obvious reasons why administrators or institutions are tempted to borrow money.

I have listed here nine reasons why I am opposed.

One of the notable pressures to borrow money is for the erection of dormitories. There are others, but taking that as an example — from Harvard's point of view, at least — I would like to point out to you one of the arguments used.

Harvard has a great many dormitories, in which we house a great many students, and none of those dormitories is carried as an asset on our books. As soon as a dormitory becomes an academic property, we write it down to zero. We try to run our dormitories on a break-even basis. We do not always succeed — one year we will make a little surplus, and the next year we will make a little deficit. But over the years I think it is fair to say that we run them on a break-even basis.

Harvard does make a maintenance charge in all of these buildings. We don't do it very well yet. We are hoping to improve that.

We have for a great many years, under the administrative vice-president, asked the relevant officials to set aside funds to take care of the normal maintenance that would keep the buildings in top condition, on the theory that for a few years, we will have no expenditure, but in the third year, say, we may have a rather large one, and there ought to be a reserve for that.

Beginning on July 1, 1959, in order to encourage the officials to accumulate such a reserve, we have decided to give the University paying rate on that reserve. Heretofore that was a dead reserve and earned no interest — no return — and therefore all the administrators were naturally very reluctant to convert balances which were drawing interest into no-return balances. We have changed that, as of July 1, 1959. I hope that we shall be able to go over the deferred-maintenance problem building by building in a much more scientific way, and that we can encourage the collection of a maintenance reserve that is more adequate.

Now it is perfectly obvious that if you were going to put up a dormitory, using borrowed money as against our present scheme, you are adding an immediate cost that is not there if you mark the thing off to zero, with neither interest nor amortization of the debt. Therefore, if we were to put up Dormitory X on borrowed money, other things being the same, we would have to charge the students in that dormitory somewhat more than we would the students in each of the other dormitories, because in that last dormitory, they would have to pay for interest on the debt and amortization of that debt.

I do not think it is fair to charge 90 per cent of our students no interest or amortization and charge 10 per cent of them, say, interest and amortization.

When a suggestion was made that we borrow money to build a dormitory, I brought up this argument and said, "What I think we ought to do in fairness is to make a charge on all the other dormitories, to be borne by the students in those buildings, equivalent to the interest and amortization factor that the students would have to pay in Building X. If we did that, we would very quickly accumulate enough money out of that type of earning to build a new building."

But none of the deans reacted favorably to the notion of suddenly charging for interest and amortization on a building that had no debt and had no amortization. So I think it would create an element of unfairness to start to charge on one given building out of a great many buildings and not on the others.

The second reason I would like to give you for not starting down this primrose path of borrowing money is that it appears to be never-ending. Most of the pressure that has been applied to me has been to borrow for buildings, particularly at the very low rate the federal government offers for such constructions.

To continue on the subject of how this borrowing can multiply, let us say that you rationalize borrowing to build a dormitory. I think the next biggest pressure we have had (and there isn't any question in my mind about the goodness of these loans) has been to borrow money for loans to students and, in some cases, to faculty. There isn't a bank in the United States that wouldn't love to take over and lend money to a very sizable percentage of students and faculty at prime rates. If one went down those two alleys, then soon the deans would come up and say, "Look, our tuition fees are very stable. We have twice as many students who want to enroll in our schools as we can take and tuition is pretty sound money. We are sure to get it. What about mortgaging some of that revenue and hiring a new professor?"

I therefore am opposed to starting to borrow because I see no end to it.

Then I would like to point out that borrowing on a given asset is limited and cannot be endlessly repeated. It is robbing the future to take care of the present. Once you have everything mortgaged — let us say that you will not do it to the extent that you will be bankrupted but that you will borrow all you can — why, then you have used up that source and you cannot possibly do any more borrowing.

Now there may be a time for borrowing (although I cannot see it and am utterly opposed to it), but certainly I think borrowing ought to be kept for the greatest possible emergency. I am opposed to anybody's borrowing so much money that he has no assets left for future mortgaging.

Then there is the obvious advantage to not borrowing money: a debtor has to repay the debt, and he has to pay the interest on it. If you don't have a debt, you don't and can't go bankrupt from that cause.

My fifth argument is that most alumni are opposed to borrowing. We have been conducting a very large drive for additional funds at Harvard College, and, judging from talks with a great many of the alumni, I, at least, am convinced that the very, very great majority of alumni are opposed to seeing their college get into debt. There are some outstanding exceptions to that, and they are apt to be very vocal, but I think that the great majority are absolutely opposed.

Now, I am not one of those who say that you must always do what the alumni want, but I do suggest that it is largely from the alumni that colleges are going to get additional funds, and, if the administrators can with reason agree with them, I think it is wise to do so. I happen to agree with what I think is the great majority of our alumni.

My sixth reason, which may not be a very good one, is that I cannot think of an instance where we have ever done it. Maybe there are a few isolated cases in which Harvard has borrowed money, but they don't amount to anything. Again, I don't say that precedent is everything, but to break a precedent like that, I think you have to have very excellent reasons and be very sure you are right.

My seventh argument is that if you start borrowing you hinder fund raising. For example, at Harvard, I think it would kill our Program for Harvard College dead as a clam. I think that every alumnus would immediately say, "Well, if you borrowed this money for these buildings and for the student loans and for this and that, why, you can keep on borrowing, and I don't know why I should give to you when you have a large borrowing capacity that you can use and are using."

Another factor at Harvard — and I think this would apply to any institution that has large endowment funds — is that, on the whole, we are lenders of money. Practically all institutions are lenders of money. They lend to Uncle Sam, they buy corporate bonds, and I think it is an anomalous position to be a lender and a borrower of money at one and the same time.

Now, it may be said that perhaps you can borrow your money at a far lower rate than you lend it and make a spread in so doing. To my mind that is nothing more than running a margin account. If you run a margin account, and even if you run it carefully, you find that interest rates sometimes will go the other way and you lose. I think it is not proper for a university or, indeed, any other charitable organization, to run margin accounts.

My final argument against borrowing, which to me weighs very heavily, is the basic concept behind the fact that people say to me, "Well, industry borrows money, and you don't disapprove of that, do you?" And I say, "No, I certainly do not, as long as they do it in moderation and do not get so extended that they will get into trouble."

But there is an enormous difference between an industry borrowing money and a university borrowing money. An industry is a money-making institution, and every industry that borrows money borrows it for only one purpose, which is to make more money. Every now and then they miscalculate and lose, but the entire motive is to make money, and it is out of the increased earnings of the borrowing industry that they see their way clear to pay their interest and ultimately pay off the principal of their debt.

There are not many colleges that are money-making institutions. Maybe there are one or two. Certainly Harvard is a very heavy money-losing institution. As a rough figure I would say that for the whole of Harvard University, the student is probably paying less than 75 per cent — a good deal less than 75 per cent — of the cost of the education he gets. Therefore, on every student we have we lose at least 25 per cent. The more students we have, the more we lose. So if we borrow money to get more, we are just compounding the loss.

Those are my reasons for being opposed to the suggestion that Harvard borrow money. At times — we don't do it as a general practice — the University account will lend to another budgetary part of the University. I can cite a case in the Faculty of Arts and Sciences. They wanted to complete a building, as I remember, a married students' dormitory, so the University loaned them some money.

The University didn't borrow any money; this was the University lending to the Faculty of Arts and Sciences. The first thing I have to do in such cases is to make very sure that any debt that we buy or any loan that we make to any one part of the University is so good that, if we put it in our general investment account, which is for the good of the whole University and in which the whole University participates, there cannot be any criticism from Budgetary Unit A, say the Medical School, asking, "Well, you made a loan out of the general portfolio to help the Faculty of Arts and Sciences, but what good does it do me in the Medical School that you have made that loan to them? It is a bad loan, and we share in the bad part of it."

Therefore, in each instance where we have done this, if there has been any question about the goodness of the loan, about its fair market value at the time we make it, and the fair rate of interest on it, we insist that the Budgetary Unit — in the case I cited, the Faculty of Arts and Sciences — shall pledge to the general investment account any unrestricted funds that it has in order to make good on that loan.

We have done a little of that, and, I suspect, with all of the things that we are contemplating doing, we may have to do more of it. That, however, may I point out, is all in the family. That is one part of the University, or the University general account, lending to a specific part which pledges unrestricted funds. If they don't meet their interest charges and their amortization, we will move right in and take away that unrestricted fund and put it into the general account for the benefit of all.

RECENT TRENDS IN ENDOWMENT

J. Harvey Cain

ABOUT a year ago Dr. Ernest V. Hollis of the United States Office of Education asked me if I would make another study of the investment statistics of higher education similar to the ones prepared for the American Council on Education from 1941 to 1944. This was on the theory that not everything has been said on the subject of college investments.

Dr. Hollis said that we should go ahead and prepare a questionnaire. What came out was quite different from what we started to do. In the studies made for the American Council on Education about 130 institutions participated. In the current study there are 200. Of course that doubled all of the statistical work, but it did not significantly change the results.

I will give you a few of the figures. In the Office of Education *Biennial Statistics for 1955–56* there are 1858 institutions of higher education. Of these, over half, 1094, reported endowment funds. These included 909 private and 185 public institutions. Seven hundred sixty-four institutions reported no funds at all, no endowments. We obtained figures on both book and market values. The total funds ran to $3.7 billion, book value, in 1956, and the book value of those funds had doubled from 1940 to 1956, so you see endowment funds are growing substantially.

In this 1958 study 22 per cent of the funds at market value are concentrated in five institutions; 50 per cent are concentrated in 54 institutions and 92 per cent in 101 institutions. Thus on a national basis, 5.2 per cent of all institutions have 92 per cent of the total endowment.

Then again for 1920, I found that 76 per cent of private gifts were for endowment; in 1956, the proportion was down to 33.6 per cent. And again, in 1930 earnings on endowment represented 14.2 per cent of total education and general income, but they had fallen to 5 per cent in 1956.

My estimate is that at the end of June, 1958, the market value of all funds at the 200 institutions with the largest endowments was $5.5 billion. The earnings — of the 200 institutions — were 4.91 per cent of book and 3.84 per cent of market value. Eighty per cent of the institutions were in the range of 3.2 to 4.2, based on market values. The highest rate came from preferred stocks, which was 4.87 per cent. The lowest was 2.86 from government bonds. Over the period 1941–1958 the market value of the common stocks purchased by the 200 institutions included in the study had risen 89 per cent over the original or book-value cost.[1] For all other types of investment, with the exception of a small number of investment-company securities, the market value declined below original cost. It should be pointed out, however, that a different comparative situation would exist between institutions which sold large blocks of stocks, and took profits, with a resulting change in values, and those which retained their original investments. Everything else showed a depreciation — the bonds, 2.2, and the preferred stocks, 2.4.

From a study made by the Council for Financial Aid to Education in 1956–1957, I took some figures for 33 large private universities that had $20 million or more of endowment, and the same number of men's and women's colleges, 33 Catholic colleges, and 33 small private institutions. Here are the figures that I obtained showing market over book.

The university group had a 45 per cent appreciation; the men's and women's colleges had only 30 per cent, the Catholic colleges, 12 per cent, and the small private institutions, 11.5 per cent. I do not know what is the moral to be drawn from that; perhaps the universities had better advice on timing.

Then we asked the 200 institutions in the

---

[1] Treasurer Cabot of Harvard noted a weakness in this measure of appreciation. "I am not questioning your figures, but I think the procedure is a little bit meaningless because, if Institution A or Company A sees fit to turn its investment and sell General Electric to buy General Motors, they take a gain which is not shown there, but they mark up their cost so that you would get an apparent shrinkage of appreciation which is not real."

[242]

study what were their sources of investment advice. Nineteen reported that they employed their own institutional investment staff, 68 employed outside investment counsel, 49 employed a trust company, and 64 depended on a governing board's committee.

The next question we asked them was what method of accounting they used, whether they employed market value or book value, and 60 reported that they used market value and 140 still use book value. This is for putting new money into the fund.

Then we asked them about the establishment of income reserve accounts for the purpose of stabilizing the budget; 54 replied Yes, and 146 replied No. That is, about one-fourth have such an account. We also asked them if they had a reserve for losses on their securities. One hundred four replied Yes and 96 No.

We asked them if they had a policy on the amount to be invested in common stocks. Seventy-five said Yes, and 125 said No. This meant that they had no policy as to how much they invested in common stocks versus bonds and other securities, not that they did not hold stocks at all.

Those who answered Yes had an average of 56 per cent in common stocks as their goal. But the over-all study showed that the average achieved level was only 48 per cent.

We asked about the maturities of their government bond holdings: one to five years, five to ten years, and over ten. Forty-five per cent of the holdings were less than five years, 20 per cent five to ten years, and 34 per cent over ten years.

Then we asked how much had been received in addition to their funds during the year. They replied that they had a $217,000,000 increase in funds.

We also tried to get an approximate percentage invested in different kinds of common stocks. This is the percentage of total common stocks at market value: utilities, 19.7; petroleum, 19.4; chemicals, 12.8; banks, 5.2; natural gas, 4.9; insurance, 4.2.

The industrial stocks that were held by very few institutions were in airlines, agricultural equipment, beverages, distillers and brewers, motion pictures, railroads, rubber, soap, textiles, and tobacco. None of the colleges reported any aircraft manufacturing or transportation (other than airlines and railroads).

In 1941, in a study I made for the American Council, there was included a list of companies in which the composite funds of 130 institutions had made the heaviest dollar investments. We compared this list with the ones in the present study and found there are 37 companies still represented in the majority of the portfolios.

They were not in all 200, but the institutions still had the largest holdings in these 37 companies. In other words, the holdings in these companies remained fairly steady. In agricultural machinery, they had International Harvester; in automobiles, Chrysler and General Motors; and of the New York banks, Bankers Trust, Chase-Manhattan, First National City, and the Guaranty Trust; five chemical companies were included; Allied Chemical, duPont, Eastman, Monsanto, Union Carbide; two containers, American Can and Continental Can; General Electric and Westinghouse; Corn Products and United Fruit in the food group; Hartford in insurance; Penney and Sears, Roebuck and Co. in the merchandising group; International Nickel and Kennecott Copper in the metals group; IBM in the office equipment group; in the oil group, Continental, Socony, Standard of California, also Standard of Indiana and of New Jersey, and Texaco; in the railroads, the Santa Fe, the Chesapeake & Ohio, and the Union Pacific; Procter & Gamble among the soaps; U. S. Steel; and two utilities, American Telephone and Telegraph and Commonwealth Edison.

We received many letters and much comment when we did the study for the American Council. It seemed to me that the college treasurers and the investment officers were much more willing to write and tell the Council what they were doing than they were when the government asked the questions. Our correspondence in the latest survey was very small, whereas, in the American Council studies, I had two big volumes of letters and comments. I thought that was interesting.

I received one letter from a trustee. I do not think it would be fair to mention his name, but I would like to conclude with a few remarks that he made. He said:

We want to encourage you to go ahead in this important work because we think you are doing a real service for the cause of education. With the exception of those institutions who have their own fine professional staffs, and those who employ investment counsel, the portfolios are not given sufficient day to day attention. They are usually placed under the responsibility of a so-called Finance Committee consisting of a few prominent bankers, brokers, lawyers, or wealthy merchants and manufacturers, whose successful handling of their own affairs presupposes an ability to manage investments.

I am aware that in too many cases a man's election to the Board of Trustees, as perhaps to the Finance Committee as well, is prompted by the hope and expectation of a donation rather than by the value of the individual's attention to the management of the fund. This is a great mistake because in too many cases these gentlemen simply cannot devote the time necessarily required for careful supervision of the college funds. True, final judgment and responsibility may rest in the Board of Control, but it is false economy not to have continuous supervision, no matter how small the fund.

SPECIAL PROBLEMS IN PUBLIC INSTITUTIONS
Robert M. Underhill

PERHAPS one of the special investment problems of the state university is to become more like the successful endowed colleges in its attitude and operations. I shall not limit my remarks to this one statement, but I think it may be central. The problems of a state university in investment matters differ from those of the endowed colleges in several respects, which are intermingled in their effect. These may be briefly stated as the size of the fund, amount of legislative control, federal obligation, and obligations to a different ownership.

It is quite possible that the general form of legislative control or the activities of the university itself in its investment matters may stem from the first Morrill Act, sometimes called the Land Grant Act, of 1862. By that Act, each state, or through each state the university designated as a state university in each state, was given 30,000 acres of public land for each senator and representative, and the provisions of the sale of this land were set forth. Quite probably this was the first endowment of many of the state universities. Indeed, many of the state universities did not exist in 1862, and those which did exist were small in size. The endowment created by this grant was required to be invested in bonds of the United States or of the states, or in some other safe bonds. If the state had no bonds, the legislature could direct the investment in any manner which would yield a fair and reasonable return on investments, and the principal thereof was to be forever unimpaired. It is quite apparent that this set the general pattern for the investment of state university funds, and state governments which had legislative control over all the affairs of the university have been slow to release this restriction. And, in general, they have not released the restriction insofar as it affects the money received from this particular grant. As time goes along this ceases to be a significant matter with the larger state universities. For example, in the case of the University of California, the so-called "Federal Endowment Fund" of the proceeds of this land, together with the proceeds from two other smaller grants, now represents only a little over 1 per cent of the total book value of the permanent endowment fund. Whether or not these funds are kept invested in bonds does not have a significant effect on our university, but it does have a very significant effect for many of the other universities. The annual report by Vance, Sanders & Company entitled *Brevits*, which lists college endowment funds, lists only ten state universities. Provided Cornell University, which is the state university in agriculture and a few other departments, and the University of Pennsylvania, which receives some support from the state, are not regarded as state universities, the number falls to eight.

Another which should be eliminated is the University of Texas, which has benefited so much from its west Texas oil lands that it has a fund larger than any other state fund. The University of Illinois should be omitted, since it does not have a large fund compared to the funds represented here. Finally, Rutgers was mentioned, but it was formerly a private university and probably has not had the influences that have been brought to bear upon the investments of the other state universities.

With these eliminations, the information presently at hand would indicate that there are perhaps only six state institutions of higher education that have endowment funds exceeding $10 million. The pattern of state fund investments is therefore controlled in large measure by size. The small size of most funds is probably chiefly responsible for the control exercised by state authorities and the historical limitation to the investment in fixed income securities, and then largely in governmental securities of national and state origin. This in turn points back to the influence of the grant from the government in support of the Morrill Act. State control of investments is diminishing in institutions with $5 million or more of investment assets. It seems that the smaller funds are inclined to hold a smaller percentage of equity investments, and in these cases real estate investments seem to make up a higher percentage than the average.

The recent tendency for liberation in the form of investments can be indicated by the action of the State of California Pension Fund. It was not until after July 1, 1948, when the total investment fund amounted to $78 million, that public utility bonds were permissible for the Fund, and in the succeeding year $19 million of these securities were purchased, bringing the total of bonds other than federal, state, and municipal bonds to 18 per cent of the total. During the last fiscal year that Fund purchased $36 million of public utility bonds, bringing the total of that type of security to 42 per cent of the Fund, but other corporate issues are not permissible.

In sending out some small questionnaires to a few of my friends, I stated that it was not my intention to name their institutions, and while some of the conditions that I will mention are set forth in state constitutions and therefore would not seem to be a violation of my statement if I did mention names, I shall avoid this.

In one of the funds, the constitution authorized the university board to invest in corporate securities up to 50 per cent of the total, subject to certain broad limitations — in effect, the "prudent-man rule." But this institution still has almost 85 per cent of its investments, exclusive of land, in federal and state bonds, and its investment in common stocks would be regarded by all of us as, in effect, insignificant.

Another relatively large state university fund is divided, with two-thirds of the fund under investment which now includes one-half in equity items, therefore leaving the fund about five-sixths in fixed-income securities and most of that in government and state bonds.

These facts seem to indicate state influence upon accounts which have received some discretion, but where there seems to be hesitancy in exercising it. The accounts to which I have referred are not those of the institution which I represent, which fortunately has never been subject to any legislative direction and therefore has a much more diversified investment portfolio.

There would appear to be other influences on these accounts because of geography and economic background. Most of the state colleges with endowment funds of over $10 million are in states that have had a long background of economies based on agriculture. In these cases you will find a higher proportion of real estate investments than in many other funds. These seem to have met the approval of controlling bodies. It seems probable that the basis of the lower percentage of common stocks in the smaller funds is due to the fact that a common-stock account is much more expensive to operate than a fixed-income account. For the smaller funds the cost of adequate staff and information is disproportionate to the additional yield that has been available on common stocks. Again the smaller state funds often appear in areas where the economic background is largely agricultural, thus encouraging the investment in agricultural lands, which are familiar to all in the area and can be managed without undue expense.

I have spoken of the influence of legislative control, federal obligations, and the size of the fund. I think, also, that it is important to point out the influence of the different class of ownership and the different class of support in the state colleges.

In the private college there is not the direct responsibility to the public, and no one seems to claim to have a part ownership in the institution. Therefore management is left to the board of trustees and full investment authority is available to it without the amount of inquiry, control, and suggestion found in public institutions. In the state university, the investment account is more likely to become everyone's business, even down to the demand of brokerage houses which cannot serve the institution adequately for a proportion of the business, making claims on the ground of being taxpayers and rent payers in the area. Members of the alumni body also stake special claims for achieving contracts from the business office or for having an interest in what goes on. Perhaps because of these inquiries and interest by the supporting taxpayer, the state institution has historically been more conservative than the private college. I wish to make it clear, however, that I do not believe that in the last few years the investment in bonds was more conservative than investment in stocks. I think that our account at California will indicate that we have not so believed. The situation today, of course, seems to be quite different in this respect and the yield requirement to support continuing activities indicates a current advantage in the purchase of bonds over stocks.

Another problem affecting the state institution is its tax exemption and its consequent obligation to the public. Our institution — and I presume almost all the state institutions and, in fact, even some private institutions — has complete exemption from taxation on income and real estate. It had at one time been our policy to invest a very considerable amount of money in real property, but in doing so we rather naturally concentrated our investments in an area close by, where we could have some idea of value and keep a close touch on current values and activities.

This procedure resulted in a larger tax burden on the citizens of that particular area, since the cities and counties are supported by property taxes, while the state is supported by income taxes, sales taxes, franchise taxes, and other indirect sources. The complaint of the citizens of areas in which real estate purchases were concentrated that the city or county was asked to take an undue portion of the expense of the state university, which should be paid for by the state and not by the locality, seems quite valid. Since our support comes from the public, we do not go out of our way to offend the public. We are not large real estate investors. This is a problem that must be recognized by state institutions which have freedom from taxes. I know of one private institution that has this tax advantage and has concentrated its real estate investments in the city where it exists. There may well be a local objection to this, although since the city does not support the university through taxes or other contributions, I presume the institution can do as it sees fit. I do not advocate this for a state institution.

Mortgages on private homes, perhaps even on small, privately held business buildings, may cause other difficulties to state colleges should foreclosure become necessary. If tax-supported institutions forcibly take private property in settlement of a debt, there can be no doubt the effect will be felt in public sentiment and in public support.

One of the investment problems for a state institution seems to me to be to encourage the state to permit it to take advantage of the technical and financial information that is available to it from successful persons who conduct their own affairs with the restrictions of investment provided by many state laws. There are available to every institution financially successful people who can assist the university in its growth and support through investment proceedings, and this wealth of information and assistance should be encouraged.

The gradual but slow trend of liberalization in the form of investments has resulted in a great advantage to a number of institutions. The investment production of the university through the use of its endowment funds allows the university to have facilities and personnel that would not normally be supported by the public. Since these funds come from private sources, it would be greatly to the institution's advantage if the private sources that supplied them could have an opportunity in assisting in their more productive investment. To continue to require or even encourage the state institution to place any portion of its funds in state or municipal tax-exempt securities is a penalty that should not be imposed upon the educational institution.

The special problems of the state university should not continue to be special. The institution that is not forced to an investment pattern divergent from that of the private college does not deprive the state of the greater benefits that its institution can provide. With a free fund there are few special investment problems of a state university that are worthy of mention.

APPENDIX

List of Those Attending One or More Meetings of the Seminar

John Cranford Adams, *President*, Hofstra College
Vernon R. Alden, *Associate Dean*, Harvard Graduate School of Business Administration
Charles W. Allen, *Treasurer*, Bowdoin College
Richard G. Axt, *Associate Director*, Western Interstate Commission for Higher Education
Walter Baker, *Vice-President for Development*, Haverford College
Cesar L. Barber, *Professor of English*, Amherst College, Member of Committee on the New College Plan
George E. Bates, *Professor of Investment Management*, Harvard Graduate School of Business Administration
Wilbur J. Bender, *Dean of Admissions and Financial Aids to Students*, Harvard University
George F. Bennett, *Deputy Treasurer*, Harvard University
Dr. Carl A. L. Binger, *Consultant in Psychiatry to the University Health Services*, Harvard University
W. Robert Bokelman, *Chief*, Business Administration Section, Division of Higher Education, U. S. Office of Education
Frank H. Bowles, *President*, College Entrance Examination Board
Kingman Brewster, Jr., *Provost*, Yale University
Donald S. Bridgman, *Consultant*, National Science Foundation
John W. Bristol, John W. Bristol & Co.
Edward C. Budd, *Professor of Economics*, Yale University
Boardman Bump, *Treasurer*, Mt. Holyoke College
McGeorge Bundy, *Dean of the Faculty of Arts and Sciences*, Harvard University
Paul C. Cabot, *Treasurer*, Harvard University
Theodore Caplow, *Professor of Sociology*, University of Minnesota
J. Harvey Cain, *Educational Consultant*, U. S. Office of Education
Harold C. Case, *President*, Boston University
Margaret Clapp, *President*, Wellesley College
F. Morris Cochran, *Treasurer*, Brown University
Charles W. Cole, *President*, Amherst College
James S. Coles, *President*, Bowdoin College
Philip H. Coombs, *Program Director*, The Fund for the Advancement of Education
Edward K. Cratsley, *Vice-President*, Swarthmore College
André Daniere, *Assistant Professor of Economics*, Harvard University
Kenneth M. Deitch, *Student*, Harvard College
Evsey Domar, *Professor of Economics*, Massachusetts Institute of Technology
Robert F. Duncan, *Consultant*, Kersting, Brown & Co.
James Eacker, *Assistant to the Director of Student Aid*, Massachusetts Institute of Technology
Otto Eckstein, *Associate Professor of Economics*, Harvard University
Alvin C. Eurich, *Vice-President*, The Fund for the Advancement of Education
Irwin K. French, *Executive Director*, National Federation Consulting Service
Charles S. Gage, *Treasurer*, Yale University
John Gillespie, *Administrative Assistant to the President*, University of Massachusetts
Millard E. Gladfelter, *President*, Temple University
Minot Grose, *Business Manager and Assistant Treasurer*, Amherst College
J. Parker Hall, *Treasurer*, University of Chicago
Ralph W. Halsey, Jr., *Associate Treasurer and Investment Officer*, Yale University
Seymour E. Harris, *Littauer Professor of Political Economy*, Harvard University
Ernest V. Hollis, *Director*, College and University Administration, Division of Higher Education, U. S. Office of Education
Livingston W. Houston, *Chairman*, Board of Trustees, Rensselaer Polytechnic Institute
Everett C. Hughes, *Professor of Sociology*, University of Chicago
Robert E. Iffert, *Specialist for Faculty and Student Services*, Division of Higher Education, U. S. Office of Education
Eldon L. Johnson, *President*, University of New Hampshire
J. Samuel Jones, *Assistant to the Director of Student Aid*, Massachusetts Institute of Technology
Carl Kaysen, *Professor of Economics*, Harvard University

APPENDIX

Barnaby C. Keeney, *President*, Brown University
Francis Keppel, *Dean of the Faculty of Education*, Harvard University
Owen B. Kiernan, *Commissioner of Education*, The Commonwealth of Massachusetts
John I. Kirkpatrick, *Vice-Chancellor for Administration*, The University of Chicago
Malcolm G. Kispert, *Administrative Vice-Chancellor*, Massachusetts Institute of Technology
Asa S. Knowles, *President*, Northeastern University
Robert H. Kroepsch, *Executive Secretary*, New England Board of Higher Education
William H. Lane, Jr., *Comptroller*, Columbia University
John Lowell, *Vice-President*, Boston Safe Deposit and Trust Company
Fred Luddy, *Executive Secretary*, Scholarship Program, The Commonwealth of Massachusetts, Department of Education
D. Justin McCarthy, *Director*, Division of State Teachers Colleges, Massachusetts Department of Education
Shannon McCune, *Provost*, University of Massachusetts
Wallace McDonald, *Director*, Financial Aid Office, Harvard College
Michael Maccoby, *Teaching Fellow in Social Relations*, Harvard University
Donald Marburg, *former Assistant Treasurer*, University of Vermont
Wesley W. Marple, Jr., *Director of Financial Aid*, Harvard Graduate School of Business Administration
J. Paul Mather, *President*, The American College Testing Program
John F. Meck, *Treasurer*, Dartmouth College
Ricardo A. Mestres, *Treasurer*, Princeton University
Walter L. Milne, *Administrative Assistant to the President*, Massachusetts Institute of Technology
John U. Monro, *Dean of Harvard College*
Rexford G. Moon, Jr., *Director*, College Scholarship Service
Donald H. Morrison, *Provost*, Dartmouth College (deceased)
John F. Morse, *Vice-President*, Rensselaer Polytechnic Institute
Richard A. Musgrave, *Professor of Political Economy*, Johns Hopkins University
Donald D. O'Dowd, *Dean of Freshmen*, Wesleyan University
Gordon L. Parker, *Investment Officer*, Brown University
Charles F. Phillips, *President*, Bates College
Thomas P. Pitre, *Director of Student Aid*, Massachusetts Institute of Technology
Thomas B. Ragle, *President*, Marlboro College
David Riesman, *Henry Ford II Professor of Social Sciences*, Harvard University
Dwight P. Robinson, Jr., *Chairman of the Board*, Massachusetts Investors Trust
Hans Rosenhaupt, *National Director*, Woodrow Wilson National Fellowship Foundation
William J. Sanders, *Commissioner of Education*, State of Connecticut
Nevitt Sanford, *Professor of Psychology*, University of California (Berkeley)
Cyril G. Sargent, *Professor of Education*, Harvard University
Henry L. Shattuck, *former Treasurer*, Harvard College
B. F. Skinner, *Professor of Psychology*, Harvard University
Joseph Snyder, *Vice-President and Treasurer*, Massachusetts Institute of Technology Corp.
Blair Stewart, *Dean of the College of Arts and Sciences*, Oberlin College
Samuel A. Stouffer, *Professor of Sociology*, Harvard University
Harold Taylor, *President*, Sarah Lawrence College
Howard M. Teaf, Jr., *Professor of Economics*, Haverford College
Russell T. Thackrey, *Executive Secretary*, American Association of Land-Grant Colleges and State Universities
Willard L. Thorp, *Professor of Economics*, Amherst College
Hulbert W. Tripp, *Financial Vice-President*, University of Rochester
Sharvy G. Umbeck, *President*, Knox College
Robert Underhill, *Secretary and Treasurer of the Regents*, University of California (Berkeley)
John Vaizey, Oxford, England
D. B. Varner, *Chancellor*, Michigan State University, Oakland
Rev. Michael P. Walsh, S.J., *President*, Boston College
Eugene Wilson, *Dean of Admissions*, Amherst College
O. Meredith Wilson, *President*, University of Minnesota
Dael Wolfle, *Executive Officer*, American Association for the Advancement of Science

INDEX

Adams, John Cranford: paper by, 136–139; references to, 20, 129–130
Allport, Gordon W., 163, 173

Barber, C. L.: paper by, 141–145; references to, 18, 19, 140
Bates, George E.: paper by, 214–218; references to, 24, 25, 27, 206, 207
Bennett, George F.: paper by, 222–223; references to, 25, 27, 206
Benton, William, 28, 237
Blackwell, T. E., 205
Bloom, Benjamin, 173
Bokelman, W. Robert, paper by, 73–74
Bowles, Frank H.: paper by, 199–202; references to, 152
Bridgman, D. S.: paper by, 180–184; references to, 22, 166
Brown, John Mason, 229
Bryce, James, 46
Bump, Boardman: paper by, 219–221; references to, 27, 203, 204
Bundy, McGeorge, 113, 114, 116

Cabot, Paul C.: paper by, 239–241; references to, 27, 203, 211–212, 242n
Cain, Harvey J.: paper by, 242–244; references to, 25
Caplow, Theodore: paper by, 122–124; references to, 16–18, 102, 103, 107–108
Case, Harold C., 36–37
Cole, Charles W.: paper by, 111–114; references to, 15, 16, 17, 94, 140
Coleman, James, 174, 177
Conant, James B., 133, 171
Coombs, Philip H.: paper by, 83–87; references to, 14, 34–35
Coons, Arthur G., 25
Cooper, Richard N., summaries by, 29–39, 75–82, 102–110, 129–135, 166–172, 203–213

Deitch, Kenneth: paper by, 192–198; references to, 24

Eckstein, Otto: paper by, 61–72; references to, 12
Elder, J. Petersen, 128
Eurich, Alvin C.: paper by, 185–188; references to, 23–24

Gillespie, J. M., 163
Gladfelter, Millard E.: paper by, 91–92; references to, 14, 80
Glick, P. C., 180

Hall, J. Parker: paper by, 235–238; references to, 25, 27–28, 228
Harris, Seymour E.: Introduction by, 9–28; references to comments on endowment and investment, 214, 216, 217, 218, 220, 229, 234, 239, on faculty status, 108–109, 111, 113, 114, 117, 122, 123, on government aid, 94, 95, 97n, 98n, on size of classes and colleges, 173, 176, on tuition and costs, 45, 46, 64n, 66, 73
Heath, Roy, 175
Hollis, Ernest V., 242
Houston, Livingston W.: paper by, 232–234; references to, 27–28
Hughes, Everett C.: paper by, 118–121; references to, 17–18, 102
Hutchins, Robert, 18, 25, 174
Hutchinson, E., 117

Iffert, Robert E.: paper by, 125–128; references to, 16

Jacob, P. E., 163
Johnson, Eldon L.: paper by, 44–47; references to, 10, 29–30, 88, 89

Kaysen, Carl: paper by, 55–60; references to, 11, 63
Keeney, Barnaby C.: paper by, 40–43; references to, 10–11
Kirk, Grayson, 14

Lazarsfeld, Paul, 173

McConnell, Thomas, 23
McCune, Shannon, paper by, 140–141
Mather, J. Paul: paper by, 88–90; references to, 13
Maul, Ray, 116
Meck, John F.: papers by, 93–95, 229–231; references to, 15, 24–25, 76
Mestres, Richard, 230
Miller, H. P., 180
Moon, Rexford G., Jr.: paper by, 52–54; references to, 10
Morrill, James L., 45
Morrison, Donald H.: paper by, 146–151; references to, 21, 136
Morse, John F.: paper by, 48–51; references to, 11
Mort, Paul, 87
Musgrave, Richard A.: paper by, 96–101; references to, 15, 75, 80

Niebuhr, Elizabeth, summary by, 129–135

O'Dowd, Donald D., paper by, 163–165

Pusey, Nathan M., 50

Riesman, David: paper by, 173–177; references to, 23, 94–95, 153, 167
Robertson, David, 158
Rockefeller, John D., Jr., 27, 237
Rosenwald, Julius, 27
Rossi, Peter, 174

[251]

INDEX

Ruml, Beardsley, 21, 144, 187, 228
Russell, John Dale, 186

Sanford, Nevitt: paper by, 152–155; references to, 19–20, 170, 173
Sheehan, Donald, 140, 144
Skinner, B. F.: paper by, 189–191; references to, 23, 176
Sloan, Alfred, 27
Smith, Adam, 26
Smith, Joseph G., 178
Stein, Morris, 173
Stern, George C., 173
Stewart, Blair: paper by, 156–159; references to, 19, 144

Stoke, Stuart, 140, 144
Stouffer, Samuel, 31

Thorp, Willard L.: paper by, 160–162; references to, 21
Tripp, Hulbert W.: paper by, 224–228; references to, 25, 27, 206, 216, 222

Underhill, Robert M., paper by, 245–247

Wilson, O. Meredith: paper by, 115–117; references to, 17, 18, 126
Wispe, Lauren, 173
Wolfle, Dael: paper by, 178–179; references to, 22, 23, 166
Wood, Henry, 229

Index prepared by Edward Segel